From Hanoi to Hollywood

From Hanoi
to Hollywood

The Vietnam War
in American Film

EDITED BY
LINDA DITTMAR
AND
GENE MICHAUD

RUTGERS UNIVERSITY PRESS
NEW BRUNSWICK AND LONDON

Library of Congress Cataloging-in-Publication Data

From Hanoi to Hollywood : the Vietnam war in American film / [edited
  by] Linda Dittmar and Gene Michaud.
        p.   cm.
      Includes filmographical references.
      ISBN 0-8135-1586-6 (cloth)   ISBN 0-8135-1587-4 (pbk.)
      1. Vietnamese Conflict, 1961–1975—Motion pictures and the
  conflict.   2. War films—United States—History and criticism.
  I. Dittmar, Linda, 1938–   II. Michaud, Gene.
  DS557.73.F76   1990
  791.43′658—dc20   90-32548
                                                                     CIP

British Cataloging-in-Publication information available

Frontispiece: Supply trucks on the Ho Chi Minh Trail (from the collection of N. V. Long)

To our families, Jim and Jeremy Dittmar and Carol Malthaner,
whose love, understanding, and support inspire
us daily to work toward a better world

Contents

List of Illustrations

All illustrations are courtesy of the Museum of Modern Art/Film Stills Archive, unless otherwise noted.

Preface

Chronologically, the germination of this anthology began with a three-day conference entitled "The War Film: Contexts and Images," which was held at the University of Massachusetts at Boston in 1988. Sponsored by the William Joiner Center for the Study of War and Social Consequences, the conference brought together a diverse group of scholars, veterans, filmmakers, teachers, students, peace activists, and others to watch films, give presentations, and discuss works-in-progress. Though these screenings, presentations, and discussions ranged from World War II through the Korean War to current U.S. engagements in Central America, the Vietnam War turned out to be a major focus for this event. This is hardly surprising, considering the then recent release of the highly publicized and widely viewed *Platoon* (1986) and *Full Metal Jacket* (1987). But the broad interest generated by this war's filmic representations goes beyond the conference's chance timing. Rather, we found ourselves participating in an ongoing national effort to retrieve and assimilate this chapter in our recent history. In adding our voices to the debate over the lessons to be drawn from the Vietnam war, it is our hope to provide new ways of "seeing" the representations of that conflict, and that this process will in turn result in a fuller understanding of the past and positive action in the future.

In important ways, this anthology is a communal project informed by everyone who participated in the "War Film" conference. Though we cannot list every name, we owe a special debt to all those who presented papers and works-in-progress at the conference, and engaged in the discussions and debates that inevitably followed. In this sense, *From Hanoi to Hollywood* is truely a "multi-authored" text.

We also want to recognize many people who gave freely of their time, labor, and expertise to make both the "War Film" conference and this collection a reality. Joiner Center co-directors Kevin Bowen and David Hunt have demonstrated unwavering support, enthusiasm, and encouragement for these projects throughout their various stages. The dedication of all Joiner Center staff members was key to the conference's success, but the timely contributions of Special Events Coordinator Leslie Bowen, Office Manager Dorothy Deluze, and Media Assistant Marc Noel deserve particular mention. We are also grateful to Joiner Center staff members John McIntyre and Paul K. White, whose hard work, good will, and good humor sustained us over many months of conference planning, correspondence, writing, and editing.

Feroz Ahmad, Sumiko Higashi, David Hunt, Winston Langely, and Jack Spence brought their expert knowledge to bear on the chronology section, and Rick Berg, Philip Brookman, Barry Dornfeld, David James, and Karen McGovern did the same for the filmography, each adding significant information and protecting us from embarrassing gaps. We are also indebted to Lisa Schwartz and Roxanne Arbuckle for their assistance in the time-consuming and painstaking research these sections required.

We must also acknowledge the contribution of our editor at Rutgers University Press, Leslie Mitchner. She met with good spirits and a seemingly endless supply of patience the myriad difficulties that we, as first-time anthology editors, heaped upon her. Her dedication to us and to this work cannot be diminished.

Notes on the Contributors

RICK BERG was drafted into the United States Marines and served in Vietnam in 1968. He teaches film and literature at Scripps College in Claremont, California and is co-editor of the special issue of *Cultural Critique* entitled "American Representations of Vietnam," from which his essay here is drawn.

KEVIN BOWEN is co-director of the William Joiner Center for the Study of War and Social Consequences at the University of Massachusetts at Boston. A draftee, he served as a radio operator in Vietnam with the First Air Cavalry Division, 1968–1969. A former Danforth Fellow and Fulbright Fellow at Oxford University, he teaches courses on the literature of war in the twentieth century at the University of Massachusetts at Boston.

LEO CAWLEY served as an infantry squad leader in the First Battalion of the U.S. Marines during the Vietnam War. He has taught political economy at Vassar College and Columbia and Georgetown universities, and his essays have appeared in *The Nation, The Village Voice,* and *The Monthly Review.* He is a radio commentator for WBAI-FM in New York City.

DAVID DESSER teaches film in the Unit for Cinema Studies and the Department of Speech Communication at the University of Illinois at Urbana-Champaign. He is the author of *The Samurai Films of Akira Kurosawa* and *Eros plus Massacre: An Introduction to the Japanese New Wave Cinema,* as well as numerous articles on Japanese film. He has also published on science fiction in the cinema, and on the sociology of American Judaism and its impact on the movies.

BARRY DORNFELD is a documentary filmmaker and a Ph.D candidate at the Annenberg School of Communications in Philadelphia. He produced and co-directed *Dance Like a River,* about a traditional West African performing troupe touring America, and recently completed the collaboratively produced film *Powerhouse for God,* a documentary portrait of an Appalachian Baptist church. Dornfeld is presently conducting research on the representation of culture in Public Broadcasting System (PBS) documentaries.

DAVID GROSSER teaches courses on American history, politics, and culture in the 1950s and 1960s for the American Studies Department at the University of Massachusetts at Boston. He is the coordinator of the Sister City Project in Cambridge, Massachusetts, which provides material assistance to the people of San José Las Flores in El Salvador.

HARRY W. HAINES teaches communications at California State University at Sacramento. His work includes cultural analyses of the Vietnam Veterans Memorial and media representations of veterans. He was assigned to a medical unit in South Vietnam from 1970 to 1971, and was active in the G.I. antiwar movement.

SUMIKO HIGASHI teaches history, film, and women's studies at the State University of New York College at Brockport. She is the author of *Virgins, Vamps, and Flappers: The American Silent Movie Heroine,* and *Cecil B. DeMille: A Guide to References and Sources.* Currently, she is working on a project about DeMille as a director-general of the Lasky Company during the teens.

DAVID JAMES teaches at the University of Southern California. In addition to *Allegories of Cinema: American Film in the Sixties,* from which his essay here is taken, he has recently published several articles about the Vietnam War and music.

SUSAN JEFFORDS teaches feminist theory at the University of Washington. She is the author of *The Remasculinization of America: Gender and the Vietnam War* and is currently at work on a book about women and combat in the United States entitled *They Shoot Women, Don't They?*

MICHAEL KLEIN has taught film and American Studies at California State University, the University of Warwick, and Rutgers University, where he was the director of the film program at Livingston College. He is currently professor in Media and American Studies at the University of Ulster. His publications and works-in-progress include *The English Novel and the Movies, The Vietnam Era,* and a novel on the United States in the sixties.

MARTIN F. NORDEN teaches film as an associate professor of communication at the University of Massachusetts at Amherst. His writings have appeared in such publications as *The Journal of Film and Video, Film and History, The Journal of Popular Film and Television,* and *Wide Angle.* He is at work on a book-length study of movies that feature people with physical disabilities.

LEONARD QUART is an associate professor of cinema studies at the City University of New York's College of Staten Island and an editor of *Cineaste.* He is the co-author of *How the War Was Remembered: Hollywood and Vietnam* (Praeger) and has just completed a revised and expanded edition of his earlier co-authored work, *American Film and Society Since 1945* (Praeger).

MICHAEL RENOV is an associate professor in the School of Cinema-Television at the University of Southern California. He has written on documentary film in *Wide Angle, Film Quarterly,* and *Afterimage* and is currently editing a volume of essays on documentary theory to be published by the American Film Institute and Routledge.

MICHAEL SELIG is an assistant professor of mass communication at Emerson College in Boston. He is the editor of *The Journal of Film and Video* and has published essays in *Wide Angle, Jump Cut, The Journal of Popular Film and Television, Velvet Light Trap,* and *Post Script.*

GAYLYN STUDLAR teaches in the Film Studies Program at Emory University. She is the author of *In the Realm of Pleasure: Von Sternberg, Dietrich, and the Masochistic*

Aesthetic (University of Illinois, 1988) and numerous articles on psychoanalysis and feminist film theory. Her book on female spectatorship and the American cinema of the 1920s is forthcoming.

CLYDE TAYLOR is an associate professor teaching literature and cinema in the English Department at Tufts University. He is also an associate editor of *Black Film Review*. He edited *Vietnam and Black America: An Anthology of Protest and Resistance* (Doubleday, 1973). He is currently working on a study of the politics of representation.

FRANK P. TOMASULO is an associate professor in the Cinema and Photography Department at Ithaca College, where he teaches film history, theory, and production. His articles on film and television have appeared in numerous scholarly journals and books.

GREGORY WALLER teaches film and popular culture in the Department of English at the University of Kentucky. His articles on television, early film history, and popular film genres have been published in *Cinema Journal, Velvet Light Trap, The Journal of Popular Film and Television,* and other journals. His most recent book is *American Horrors: Essays on the Modern American Horror Film.*

TONY WILLIAMS is assistant professor of cinema studies at Southern Illinois University at Carbondale. Co-author of *Italian Western: Opera of Violence* (1975) and *Jack London: The Movies* (1980), he has also written articles on Vietnam and cinema for *Inventing Vietnam* (1990) and *America in Vietnam/Vietnam in America* (1990).

The contributors and co-editors are donating their proceeds from the sale of this book to the William Joiner Foundation, a nonprofit organization that provides material aid to assist in the processes of rehabilitation and recovery from the Vietnam War in both the United States and Vietnam. For more information about the Joiner Foundation, contact Kevin Bowen at (617) 287-5850.

From Hanoi to Hollywood

INTRODUCTION

LINDA DITTMAR
AND GENE MICHAUD

America's Vietnam War Films:
Marching toward Denial

This book is about power. Implicitly, it is about the power to make war and to destroy lives. Explicitly, it is about the power to make images that may displace, distort, and destroy knowledge of the history in which those lives (and many others) participated. Many of the essays here investigate the significant ways in which these two forms of power are related. In addition, each essay stands as a demonstration of yet another kind of power: the power of critical thinking to challenge dangerous myths and to confront prevailing ideologies. Such scholarship can hardly be impersonal. Carrying with it the burden of ethics and politics, it involves reassessments of personal as well as national history and politics.

If anything, the rapidly growing number of histories, biographies, novels, poems, journal special issues, and other publications about the Vietnam War and its aftermath attests to an urgent, current, and deeply felt public concern. Even as this volume goes to press, relevant new films enter distribution. The PBS documentary series *Vietnam: A Television History* (1983) drew a large audience and received a great deal of critical attention. A major multimedia art program, "War and Memory: In the Aftermath of Vietnam," was organized by the Washington Project for the Arts in Washington, D.C., in 1987, and has been followed by similar exhibits, lectures, and symposia elsewhere. CBS's *Tour of Duty* and ABC's *China Beach* returned the war to American television on a regular basis, and courses on the Vietnam War are now taught in colleges and universities across the country. As with the films discussed in this volume, different and not always compatible intentions underlie this activity. The wish to uncover, to know, and to critique is clearly at work, but so also is the wish to rationalize, to repress, and to exorcise. As indicated by the symbolic appropriation of the Vietnam War Memorial in Washington, D.C., including the controversy over its design, our cultural icons signal reengagement with that war and its veterans, though the terms of that reengagement are still being negotiated across a vast expanse of cultural and political activities.

These reengagements and negotiations are the context for the current production and reception of Vietnam War films. At issue is partly the nation's embattled assessment of the ideals of patriotism, heroism, and sacrifice (all invoked in the name of freedom and democracy) as against a material reality deeply implicated in racism, masculinism, imperialism, and class oppression. At issue is also the relation between military production and the cultural artifacts that sustain it. Filmmakers have always had to negotiate such contradictions. Like all cultural products, films have always been implicated in ideology. This became well-nigh explicit during the period between the end of World War II and the end of the Cold War. It started with State Department memoranda which alerted Hollywood to its role as a producer of ideology for domestic and foreign consumption, and it reached its apex with the HUAC hearings. During the Vietnam War years, it has been suggested that this complicity effectively meant silence, since the commercial film industry released only one film that dealt directly with the Vietnam conflict, John Wayne's *The Green Berets* (1968). However, in the same way that the commercial film industry fed America's Depression-era audiences images of opulence and prosperity, the Hollywood of the Vietnam era continued to provide a steady diet of representations of World War II, the war most often characterized as the finest example of America's political, moral, and military strength.[1] The growing criticism of this war both at home and abroad made it hard for Hollywood to produce a sequel to *The Green Berets* (1968), while policymakers' determination to escalate the fighting allowed for only covert, highly mediated, and murky expressions of concern (for example, *The Night of the Living Dead* and *The Wild Bunch* in 1969, *Patton*, *Soldier Blue*, *M*∗*A*∗*S*∗*H*, and *Little Big Man* in 1970).[2]

The title of this anthology, *From Hanoi to Hollywood*, is meant to draw attention to the process whereby aspects of that war have been appropriated into particular modes of representation by specific sectors of the American cultural industry. To understand this process clearly, we must also understand where this body of films stands in relation to the history of documentary and fiction film production. To begin with, films which deal with aspects of the Vietnam War do not, in themselves, constitute a genre; they borrow their narrative and cinematic codes freely from other media and other films. One significant pattern that has emerged within Vietnam War films has to do with the public's familiarity with televised representations of the war. While the debate over the political impact of television's coverage of the war continues,[3] its influence on filmic representations of the Vietnam War is unquestionable. For one thing, extensive television news reportage of the war generated countless yards of footage, which in turn have been made available for inclusion in documentary and compilation films such as *In the Year of the Pig* (1969), *Hearts and Minds* (1974), and *Dear America: Letters Home from Vietnam* (1988). More importantly, news reportage of the war has been providing narrative cinema with a storehouse of authentic iconography upon which to draw, and with a style of visual representation that enhances the sense of immediacy and realism in a number of films. The visual and acoustic treatment of such episodes as the evacuation of the U.S. embassy in Saigon in *The Deer Hunter* (1978), the burning of the Vietnamese village in *Platoon* (1986), the bombed-out urban landscape of Hue in *Full Metal Jacket* (1987), and troops in the field listening to U.S. Armed Forces broadcasts in *Good Morning, Vietnam* (1987) is derived directly from the content and signifying practices introduced to the American public by television in its coverage of the war.

Whatever other meanings the appropriation of this coverage may have

The bombed-out urban landscape of Hue in Full Metal Jacket.

within the specific texts, the sudden appearance of television film crews in the midst of battle in both *Apocalypse Now* (1979) and *Full Metal Jacket* articulates the filmmakers' awareness of the ubiquitous role reportage plays in the process of imaging the Vietnam War. At work here is the relation between reporting and imaging, between the claims to immediacy and accuracy that reportage always makes (i.e., Roland Barthes's "having-been-there" quality of the photographic image) and the evaluative mediation and dialogic reception inherent in the process of "telling," whatever its medium.[4] In this respect, the desire to know invoked by documentary cinema is not readily separable from the kinds of desire tapped by the narrative cinema.[5] Though films differ in the degree and ends to which they tap these desires, ultimately both documentary and fiction films involve interdependent modes of address. This interdependence, which was already emerging during World War II, has become pervasive with the shift to extensive television reportage. Television-inspired props, sets, and iconography are clearly at work documenting the Vietnam War in its fiction films, while emotion-tapping cinematography, organization, and commentary indebted to both narrative and avant-garde cinemas elicit identification and guide emotion within the ostensibly factual framework of its documentaries. As analyses of representations of the Vietnam War repeatedly suggest, the crossing over of reporting and imaging in both genres appropriates and recasts these desires.

That films about the Vietnam War are embedded in the American film industry's narrative and documentary representations of other wars further complicates their address and reception. Indeed, when one applies to current Vietnam War films the framework developed by Jeanine Basinger for the World War II combat film, this fact stands out clearly.[6] As a number of our contributors point out, similarities between films about the Vietnam War and those produced in response to World War II abound. If anything, Vietnam War films depend on this correspondence. Tapping formula expectations, they guide viewers by invoking time-honored narrative and cinematic conventions. Vietnam combat films such as *Platoon* and *Hamburger Hill* (1987) owe aspects of their narrative structure, character construction, and cinematography to their 1940s predecessors, such as *Bataan* (1943) and *Objective, Burma!* (1945). Likewise, it is easy to find echoes of 1944's *Purple Heart* and 1957's *The Bridge on the River Kwai* in Vietnam prisoner-of-war films like *Rambo: First Blood Part II* (1985), *Missing in Action 2: The Beginning* (1985), or *The Hanoi Hilton* (1987). These latter films are especially noteworthy because their reiteration of World War II's image of the sadistic Asian who brutally tortures captured American fighting men exploits the real concerns of the families of MIA servicemen, and because they employ racist stereotype to suppress the distinctions between the Japan of the 1940s and Vietnam in the 1960s. Again and again, the overall effect of such citation has been to mute or distort the historical specificity of the Vietnam conflict, collapsing the significant political differences between the fascist policies of the Axis powers and the anticolonialist movements in underdeveloped countries in the post–World War II era.

Still, despite this continuing tendency to present a formulaic version of history, in other ways significant differences between these films and their antecedents do emerge. One area where such difference are readily apparent is in the confused and contradictory treatment of returning Vietnam War veterans. During the period from the mid-1960s through the mid-1970s, when the commercial film industry largely avoided direct representations of the Vietnam War, the image of the veteran became the site where America's ambivalent feelings toward the conflict were made manifest. This ambivalence can be traced from the "Billy Jack" character who, in a series of four films beginning with *The Born Losers* (1967), simultaneously embodies countercultural spiritualism and disaffection and the martial skills of a well-trained ex-combat soldier; through the dangerous social misfits of *Angels from Hell* (1968), *Welcome Home, Soldier Boys* (1972), and *Taxi Driver* (1976); to the veteran-turned-vigilante of *Rolling Thunder* (1977), *Good Guys Wear Black* (1979), and *The Exterminator* (1980). By the end of the 1970s, when *The Deer Hunter* reaffirms for its returning soldier the values of family, community, and love of country, it does so with much less trust in those institutions than its World War II counterpart, *The Best Years of Our Lives* (1946). *Coming Home* (1978), *Cutter's Way* (1981), and *Ashes and Embers* (1982) use Vietnam veterans to unmask the racist, economic, and patriarchal institutions that sustained a war they clearly encode as unjustifiable; significantly, the latter two films are seldom included in the "canon" of Vietnam films. By the mid-1980s, Holly-

Ashes and Embers . . . unmasks the racist, economic, and patriarchal institutions that sustained a war it clearly encodes as unjustifiable.

wood films are promoting the Reagan era's reinterpretation of the Vietnam War through the characters of Sylvester Stallone's Rambo and Chuck Norris's Braddock. As of this writing, *Born on the Fourth of July* (1990)[7] has been the only film to win widespread recognition as a narrative that uses the veteran to question this war's patriarchal and racist agendas. In short, unlike the fairly stable filmic characterizations of veterans that followed World War II, the image of the soldier returning from Vietnam has swung back and forth as American film attempted to negotiate the ideological shifts of the times.

Another area in which fictional Vietnam War films diverge from their World War II predecessors is in the treatment of soldier communities. For example, while internal conflicts within a group of American fighting men under combat conditions were a constant element of World War II filmic narratives, these differences were employed to make the point that only by working together could Americans hope to defeat their common enemies. In Vietnam films such as *Platoon*, *Full Metal Jacket*, and *Missing in Action 2*, working together is not offered as a realistic proposition. That internal conflicts among American soldiers now lead to violence and death suggests the depths of societal division and the lack of a clear sense of purpose about the war.

In addition, certain types of narrative films that appeared in the post–World War II period are strikingly absent from the current pantheon of films produced in the post–Vietnam War era. These include the "command level" films that were especially popular in the late 1940s, such as *Command*

Decision (1948), *Twelve O'Clock High* (1949), and the "foreign espionage in wartime" thrillers such as *13 Rue Madeleine* (1946) and *Decision Before Dawn* (1951). Such films were intent on explaining "the Big Picture" to American audiences; their task was to help audiences understand and come to terms with the sacrifices of individual men and women within the larger context of defeating the global territorial and political aspirations of America's enemies. Yet precisely because these models would inevitably call into question America's own global aspirations during (and since) the period of the Vietnam War, "the Big Picture" remains off screen. Most Vietnam War films place themselves squarely at ground level, focusing on the situation of men in combat. Like many of the recent films about Vietnam veterans, they avoid historical specificity, repress politically sensitive issues, and, on top of that, blame G.I.'s for the ideology that led Americans into the war in the first place.[8]

In all these respects, the particularity of the Vietnam War must be stressed in that it plays a key role in setting the films discussed in this volume apart from the filmic discourses of World War II and other wars. What is important about this particular historic moment is that it deeply divided the country's population and brought about a profound crisis in the American imagination. This crisis concerns more than the costs of this war, and these were enormous in themselves—the massive destruction caused Vietnam and its people, and the tremendous price Americans had to pay for it. But beyond these costs are the unresolved conditions that this war brought to light. For Americans, the legacy of the Vietnam War is a legacy of lies, errors, and impotence. It is a legacy of futile sacrifice and glaring inequalities, of ideals coming up short against reality, and of defeat that is so unacceptable that it cannot be named. That the films under consideration invoke this crisis reflects both a retrospective need for healing and an anticipatory need to prepare for the next round. What such preparation might mean gets defined variously by *Coming Home*, *The Deer Hunter*, *Rambo: First Blood Part II*, *Full Metal Jacket*, and the rest. As the essays included in this collection suggest, neither the healing nor the anticipation work, finally. In film after film, the means to recovery is withheld. Audiences are offered neither insight as to why the United States took on this war in the first place nor an understanding of its long-term consequences or possible alternatives. The urgency of assimilating this war is evident, but the mere fact that so much effort and money have gone into making these recent films suggests that the crisis of that era has not yet been put to rest.

Beginning with the civil rights movement and continuing through the Watergate scandals and beyond, the credibility of the icons by which American nationalism and a mythical "American way of life" had traditionally been expressed was shattered. The civil rights movement revealed the racism that inhabited many spheres of American life. Likewise, feminists uncovered the decidedly inegalitarian workings of patriarchy in a number of sacred American institutions, including the American family. America's technologically superior military forces lost a war against an army from a small agrarian society. The very goals of American foreign policy were called into question. Leaders who in theory embodied the best expression of American ideals and values were revealed as fallible, inept, and dishonest. Vietnam War veterans, most of whom were drawn from the American working class, returned from battle not to the parades, speeches, and celebrations that had characterized World War II but to a society that for complex reasons often regarded them either contemptuously or indifferently. Being a veteran was not something to be proud of, as it had been historically. Rather, it was something to forget or hide. This was one significant product of the Vietnam era: many of the important symbols by which members of a society construct and communicate their national and personal identities were destroyed or damaged.

The loss of confidence in paternal authority figures, social institutions, and commonly held beliefs, coupled as it was with a sense of powerlessness in both the foreign and the domestic spheres, all had a costly and even traumatic effect on veterans and civilians. There was a broadly though diversely understood need for reempowerment at home and abroad, as well as a need to reconsider the United States' traditional commitment to democracy in light of emergent class, race, and gender agendas. On both the right and the left, this need found expression in a quest for moral rightness and in efforts to restructure American institutions and reassess the ways in which power had traditionally been exercised at all levels of society. For some, this need translated into an attempt to return to an uncomplicated patriotism; for others, it translated into oppositional politics. But as the essays gathered here suggest, our society has been glossing over or deflecting this need for reempowerment in ways that ultimately suppress its urgency. At issue here are the workings of ideology as a social practice that harnesses imaginative expression to political ends. Put simply, at issue are the ways culture in general and film in particular are complicit in social and political efforts to bring about acceptance of existing power relations. Applied to the specific case of Vietnam War films, the thrust of this volume is to suggest that most of the films under discussion work to reaffirm those same beliefs that the war threw into doubt, and that they do so by obscuring, not illuminating, the painfully unresolved feelings Americans still have about the war.

Of course, the mediating codes of cultural expression have often been used to suppress inquiry, calm unrest, and elicit conformity. The overdetermined signifiers, structured absences, formula procedures, and other means of sense-production that comprise culture are ideally suited to this end. Film in particular, with its penchant for spectacle and acoustic resonance and its highly developed and even systematized ability to encode artifice as realism and endow it with a compelling aura of actuality, has proven a powerful medium for this project of refurbishing symbols, obscuring contradictions, and shoring up wavering beliefs. Not surprisingly, almost all Vietnam War films made thus far use this potential ambivalently. They strive to find something redeeming to say about this war even as they echo the public's myriad and often contradictory misgivings about it.

The essays included in this volume approach this ambivalence variously. Some bring a psychoanalytic perspective to bear on filmic address; others focus on cultural heritage and historic contexts. Readings that highlight the hegemonic influence of racist and patriarchal beliefs as they operate in current depictions of this war get supplemented by discussions of the address made by spectacle and archetype. One way or another, they all resist the relief that these films proffer by way of catharsis, nostalgia, and eternal "truths." Most importantly, these essays resist the political and historical obfuscation that Vietnam War films' intensely emotional appeal and realist grittiness posit as somehow beyond scrutiny. Instead, they suggest that these films differ from films of other wars in the ways they put forth an essentialist notion of combat and, in doing so, preclude discussion of causes and goals, context and consequences, ideals and practices.

Inevitably, this discussion of filmic address raises questions of spectatorship—both inclusive questions that generalize "an audience" responding more or less uniformly to a given set of audiovisual operations and specific questions that distinguish among audiences. At issue here is the dialogic nature of reception and the role of this dialogism plays for spectators engaged in the process of ideological production. Thus, while it is important to note the ways in which most of the films under discussion strive to represent war as if outside the reach of debate, it is also important to examine the methods by which these films single out certain audiences for a particular address. For the most part, these films presuppose an empathetic, not analytic, model of reception, except that the uses of this empathy vary from film to film. *Coming Home*'s weaving of gender, sexuality, and lifestyle issues into its antiwar stance clearly addresses a number of political strains within the counterculture, using the widely known icon of the disabled veteran chaining himself to a symbolically overdetermined gate as a rallying point for its audience. On the other hand, *Apocalypse Now* and *The Deer Hunter* use literary allusion to address college-educated audiences that are less engaged politically. *Apocalypse Now* does so by imbuing Kurtz's atrocities, Willard's quest, and thus the audience's reception, too, with a sophisticated modernist *angst* signalled by its citing Conrad, Eliot, Weston, and Frazer, in ironic apposition to the Bible. *The Deer Hunter*'s implicit citing of James Fenimore Cooper broadens its address to include America's ethnic working classes in its romanticized nostalgia for an Edenic "frontier"—a strikingly deceptive nostalgia, considering western Pennsylvania's escalating shutdowns and unemployment notably in the steel industry. In this respect, the *Rambo* film series updates *The Deer Hunter* in its use of an alienated working-class hero and in its emphasis on violent action, designed to address the frustrations and desires of a white, male, blue-collar audience. On the other hand, *Born on the Fourth of July* updates *Coming Home* and *Platoon* in singling out Vietnam veterans and educated liberal and left-of-center viewers as special audiences within a broader (though nonetheless male and white) address clearly intended for a wide public. As several of the essays included here argue, the spectatorship and discourse posited by leftist documentaries are quite different. It is only here that attention shifts from individualized empathy to political analysis.[9]

But even as different films make their appeal to specific audiences, cinematic and narrative structures within each film work to minimize spectator difference. For example, Oliver Stone uses a series of close-ups and point-of-view shots at the beginning of *Platoon* to prompt audience identification with his narrator-protagonist, Chris Taylor. In contrast, Stanley Kubrick undermines audience empathy by purposefully leaving his narrator-protagonist, Private Joker, unidentified in the opening sequences of *Full Metal Jacket.* Like most filmmakers, Stone and Kubrick deploy varying technical and narrative means in an attempt to initiate all spectators into the emotive and evaluative modes of reception that each film constitutes as its norm. Most often, this process works to prevent critical viewing and analysis and to make viewers susceptible to a universalizing address that suppresses awareness of important differences among them. The relation between social class, race, gender, enlistment, and the draft may get raised occasionally in narrative films, but it quickly blends into the general murkiness that envelops the history and politics of the Vietnam War. Overall, these films give men of color stock treatment and show them in disproportionately small numbers in relation to their actual presence in combat, and they largely confine women to the domestic and erotic sphere, though ten thousand women served in Vietnam.[10]

There is nothing universal about this lack of specificity. Rather than be color or gender neutral, as one might be tempted to suppose, these films require that minority and female spectators respond to their own erasures in representation from positions of self-denial. At work here are more than short-time considerations of profit (although profit obviously grows when specific audiences get subsumed into a generalized "spectator"). At work are also the politic of erasure and their long-term ideological investment in maintaining existing social structures and practices. In this respect, the viewing positions inscribed in these films invoke the "double consciousness" discussed by W. E. B. DuBois.[11] Especially in combat films, where specificity of identification concerns nothing less than life and death, such erasures are striking.

Instead, authenticating props take over, coming across as a central concern. In film after film, careful attention to realism in the sound track, costuming, billboards, candy wrappers, peace symbols, slang, and myriad other visual and aural details specific to the Vietnam era provide validation. For veteran audiences in particular such props have been serving the important function of authenticating experience: their nightmares and memories have been made public and "proven" fact, not madness. For home-front audiences the authenticating role of the "war is hell" and "this is how it really was" formulas works differently. For them it is a vehicle for mourning, for empathy, for guilt, and perhaps for a measure of relief at having not been to 'Nam, after all. Either way, as memory shades into horror-driven nostalgia, the props of authenticity displace specificity. Either way, history has been at once recorded and denied.

As new films enter circulation, different audiences and new issues may emerge. *Casualties of War* (1989), for example, opens up the hitherto repressed question of war crimes, now bringing Willard's and Rambo's individualism to bear on ethical questions that recall the Nuremberg trials.[12] *Born on the Fourth of July*, the most acclaimed of these recent films, has been unique in combining combat and protest and in bringing taboo issues to public attention. Yet even these recent films have been suppressing the discourse of meaning and responsibility. In this respect *Born on the Fourth of July* is especially noteworthy precisely because, for all its disaffection, it lets its "art" cinematography, sustained "black-out" transitions, syncopated narrative discontinuities, and misogynistic focus on the family's role within populist ideology stand in for political analysis and silence it. Such refraining from elucidating the relation between history and action, choice and consequence, representation and judgment recurs in the narrative films of the Vietnam War. The overall effect is to "black out" understanding and create a spectatorship that does not readily forge new understanding. In this respect this body of films does not discriminate among audiences. Its address is inclusive, even democratic, precisely in the ways it structures discourse to allow ideology to do its work. Thematically, they do so largely by omission, in that their essentialist treatment of the Vietnam War as somehow destined precludes analysis and assessment. Formally, they do so through excess—through an overdetermined audiovisual track that foregrounds identification and spectacle and, thus, similarly precludes analysis and assessment. In sum, in these films, kinetic excitement, acoustical stress, and thematically structured intimations of overarching necessity inscribe a fairly homogeneous and uncritical spectatorship.

In this connection, it is important to remember that the narrative films under consideration are already historical films; they are costume dramas that allow us a retrospective glance at a bygone era. Minimally, they draw upon historically accurate language, music, and props in much the same way as do films about other historical periods. But in one respect history and nostalgia function similarly: both inscribe concern with the present under cover of the past. Moreover, the obsessive attention to accurate props, costumes, music, and idioms of speech suggests that the Vietnam War can be seen and heard, and that this seeing and hearing makes it comprehensible. Yet trust in the visible surface of the world and its visual and aural representations denies the importance of human subjectivity and negates the necessity of critical thought.

But the continuing appeal and popular consumption of images of the war attest to the power of America's belief in the simple correspondence between what can be seen and heard and what can be understood. Accordingly, the relationship between history and its depiction is a key problematic that shapes and informs the essays gathered here in that they all posit that representation is necessarily interpretive and responds to contemporary agendas. Thus, attention to authenticity is at best insufficient and at worst even misguided. Film, like any system of representation, cannot accurately reproduce historical events. Its simulation of the actual circumstances of the war is necessarily mediated by the cinematic apparatus as well as by the perspectives brought to bear on the depicted events by those engaged in a given film's production and reception.[13] In short, at issue in this volume is not simply the believability of these films as records of the past, but what these films tell us as artifacts about ourselves, our culture, and our political choices in the years since the war has ended.

Accordingly, this collection of essays focuses on ways the current body of Vietnam War films is bound in ideology, and on ways it recasts the past so as to orient viewers toward their future. In some measure, this recasting is bound by the commodity status of films produced under the conditions of capitalism. The openness, indeterminateness, and contradictions found in the films under consideration here can be traced to the economic necessities created by the need to sell the commodity to the largest number of possible consumers. Thus, each film's appropriation of time-honored narrative structures, symbols, images, and extracinematic allusions negotiates its particular relation to the economic imperatives set by the market place. In addition, the collaborative nature of most film production adds to the already complex considerations of commodity and apparatus the problem of dispersed intent. At issue here is not only the dialogism Bakhtin might find in single-authored texts or the refractions that emerge under deconstructive, semiotic, psychoanalytic, or Marxist methods of analysis. Also at issue are the material conditions specific to film production as they interact with the interpretation of history, the status of individual and collective memory, and the definition of personal and national identity that constitute the unspoken agenda for all Vietnam War films. In different ways, the point made repeatedly by contributors to this volume is that, rather than empower spectators to review this past critically and make informed choices about their future, many Vietnam combat films have their audiences emerge from screenings sharing the stunned ambiguity that Conrad, Coppola, Marlon Brando and others ascribe to Kurtz's enigmatic words, "the horror, the horror."

There is something profoundly anxious about the obsessive way in which current Vietnam War films keep reinscribing this ambiguity formally and thematically. Viewers may bring to bear on these films different theoretical frameworks and different priorities, but the overall fact their collective work highlights is that the Vietnam War continues to haunt both its veterans and the public at large. So far, the national imagination has failed to assimilate it. In addition, the selectivity of reiterations is itself significant—not only because repetition ascribes urgency to whatever it foregrounds, but because repeated silence on issues effectively erases them. To date, the complexity and diversity of the roles played by people of color and women both within the military and in response to it, the relation between social class and the conduct of this war, and the full ugliness and brutality of a war experienced differently by the Vietnamese and the American G.I.'s, are all largely exiled from the realm of representation. Clearly, then, attention to what is said and what has been left out uncovers these films' relation to contemporary arenas of ideological contradiction and conflict.

This relationship is most readily evident in narrative cinema's replacing of this war's historic specificity with the archetypal preoccupations of military training: that learning to be a good soldier is a natural phase in the process of reaching adulthood; that the enemy is everywhere but, through treachery and deceit, remains invisible; that technological superiority is crucial to success in combat; and that war is hell but God is on our side. But another way to understand these films' relation to contemporary arenas of ideological contradiction and conflict is to consider them in terms of their own historic specificity as artifacts produced at given points in time. Seen in relation to the chronological table at the end of this volume, this body of materials clearly has other functions beyond helping audiences assimilate their past. Its sights are set on Latin America, the Middle East, and other "trouble spots" in Asia and Africa. Like all retrospective accounts, Vietnam War films also interact with the history that is in formation at the time of their production and, thus, anticipate a history yet to come. In this respect, their looking backward serves contemporary political and ideological agendas. Like the Western or the extraterrestrial combat movie, these films weave together conventional iconography and modern messages about the nature of human beings and the world they inhabit in order to define our relationship to the present and future. Rambo, like the Wyatt Earp of the post–World War II *My Darling Clementine* (1946), participates in a national project of healing the war's wounds and prepares us for new ones.[14]

In light of the following essays as well as earlier works on Vietnam War films, it should not be surprising that in many cases narrative closure does not translate into something like full and final understanding.[15] Given the use-value of violence and the commodity status of representations, it is to be expected that in this body of films closure will come across as a closing out of those aspects of the Vietnam era which might threaten the current social order. In this sense, the Vietnam War is presented as something that happened, not as something that was done. As we suggest above, and as a number of essays gathered here spell out in greater detail, such representations of the war prevent any "healing" from taking place. Indeed, repression is often made to stand in for it.[16]

Thus, while the essays gathered here differ in critical methodology and perspective, they address certain concerns across the body of this anthology that bear directly on the matter of healing. These include: the failure of most films to raise the question of what got us into Vietnam in the first place; the failure of most films to address the consequences of the war for the people of Vietnam; and the ambivalent and sometimes contradictory ways Vietnam War films may function to realign the nation and its government for present and future action. The first two demand accuracy—not as a spurious yearning for authenticity, but as a need for full and informed disclosure. The latter concerns the workings of ideology. One way or another, these essays probe the nature, extent, and uses of such healing.

The organization of this volume aims to assist in this inquiry by moving from the general to the particular, from text to subtext, and from narrative to documentary. The essays in Part One, "Wide Angles: History in the Remaking," provide a panoramic overview of the filmic representations generated by the Vietnam War and the problems they raise, issues developed and applied to specific films in Part Two, "Close-ups: Representation in Detail." Part Three, "Other Frames: Subtext and Difference," highlights questions of the representation of minorities, women, the disabled, and veterans; Part Four, "Other Forms: Documenting the Vietnam War," investigates the representational strategies employed in documentary films about the Vietnam conflict.

Our organizational intent is to encourage a reading that registers the interrelations among the essays selected for inclusion in this volume.

Still, for all the shared or complementary thinking evident here, certain omissions nonetheless haunt this volume. The materials assembled here reflect our efforts to include a variety of perspectives and to bring attention to as many relevant films as possible. To some extent, our active efforts in this regard bore fruit: a number of important narrative and documentary films receive critical scrutiny, and the writers here include filmmakers, women, members of racial minorities, and Vietnam combat veterans. But, for all that, gaps persist. Most importantly, the marginalization of class, race, gender, and ethnicity in the discourse of the Vietnam War needs fuller analysis and theorizing than it receives here. In particular, we would have liked to include close readings of narrative films that are not the products of the major Hollywood studios. Among these are *The Trial of the Catonsville Nine* (1972), a courtroom drama based on the prosecution of antiwar activities; *Ashes and Embers*, which links the psychological trauma of a black Vietnam veteran to urban violence spawned by racial and economic inequities; and a great number of independently produced documentaries, such as *Requiem 29* (1971), which chronicles the first major Chicano antiwar protest in 1970 and the police riot that ensued. Even certain important but less publicized mainstream Hollywood films do not receive the attention they deserve. These include *Go Tell the Spartans* (1978), which provides an alternative view of the political, economic, and social divisions that were the basis of conflict within South Vietnam before U.S. escalation, and *The Boys in Company C* (1978), which demonstrates the cultural naiveté of young American soldiers who suddenly found themselves in Vietnam.

Though it is tempting to explain away these omissions as the result of bad luck or bad timing, the fact that essays on *Cutter's Way* and *Hearts and Minds* were not readily available while proposals for critiques of *Platoon*, *Full Metal Jacket*, and *Rambo: First Blood Part II* abounded argues differently. We share with you our editorial travail by way of cautioning against the risk that we, collectively, allow certain voices and visions to disappear. Calling attention to what does and does not enter the "canon" of films about the Vietnam War, we argue for critical engagement that questions our own priorities as viewers, writers, and readers. That the work within these pages most often concerns mainstream films says much about the ways the commercial film industry sets the agenda for scholarship. At the same time, the fact that the essays collected here refuse to accept these films at face value—that they refuse to leave unexamined precisely what these films present as unexaminable—affirms the usefulness of reading against the grain. In both respects, what we have here is more a "work-in-progress" than the final overview of the cinematic representation of Vietnam in American film.

Of course, reading the film industry's appropriations of the Vietnam war against the grain is not enough. Though it is indeed important that we continue to critique, theorize, and contextualize the films at hand, notably in terms of the way they guide audiences toward a spectatorship that accommodates a mystique of unintelligibility, it is also important to remember that this book's

Go Tell the Spartans . . . *provides an alternative view of the political, economic, and social divisions that were the basis of conflict within South Vietnam.*

address is itself inflected by an implied readership. In this respect we, the editors of this volume, note with considerable distress that the thinking gathered here will not reach more than a few of those for whom the issues it raises are most immediate: working-class men and women whose material circumstances make them most susceptible to the military's promises of opportunities for training, travel, and a better future. To recognize this problem of access and community is to uncover yet another aspect of the mystifying role of cultural processes. Seen in this light, the circulation of meaning taking place across the pages of this book is, itself, open to counter-reading. Awareness of this possibility, and of the responsibility it entails, is the final subtext for the work presented here.

NOTES

1. See Appendix A. In addition to the large number of films about World War II, numerous films about the Korean War tailored to fit the conventions and ideological dimensions established by World War II films were released during this period. Government and military officials were also aware of the important ideological capital that American feelings about World War II represented. *Why Vietnam?* (1965), a film produced by the Department of Defense and shown to all American military personnel before their departure to Vietnam, uses newsreel footage of Hitler and Mussolini to explicitly connect the U.S. involvement in Vietnam with the politics of World War II.

2. See also Richard Slotkin, "Gunfighters and Green Berets: *The Magnificent Seven* and the Myth of Counter-Insurgency," *Radical History Review* 44 (1989):65–90.

3. See Daniel Hallin, *The Uncensored War* (New York: Oxford, 1986).

4. Roland Barthes, "Rhetoric of the Image," *Image-Music-Text* (New York: Hill and Wang, 1977), pp. 32–51. See also Susan Sontag, "In Plato's Cave" and "The Heroism of Vision," in *On Photography* (New York: Dell, 1973), pp. 3–24 and 85–112; André Bazin, "The Ontology of the Photographic Image," *What Is Cinema?* vol. 1 (Berkeley and Los Angeles: University of California Press, 1967), pp. 9–16; and Philip Rosen, "History of Image, Image of History: Subject and Ontology in Bazin," *Wide Angle* 9, no. 4 (1985):7–34.

5. Bill Nichols, *Ideology and Image: Social Representation in the Cinema and Other Media* (Bloomington: Indiana University Press, 1981). See also Claudia Springer, "*Vietnam: A Television History* and the Equivocal Nature of Subjectivity," *Wide Angle* 7, no. 4 (1985):53–60.

6. Jeanine Bassinger, *The World War II Combat Film: Anatomy of a Genre* (New York: Columbia University Press, 1986); cf. Peter Rist, "*Platoon*: The World War II Combat Film Revisited" (Paper presented at "The War Film: Contexts and Images" conference, University of Massachusetts at Boston, March 25, 1988).

7. For more than four years, independent filmmaker Loretta Smith has been working on a documentary based on Ron Kovic's life, raising funds from private sources as the project progressed. The film is now in the final stages of production and is scheduled for release in the fall of 1990.

8. During both wars, of course, the Department of Defense and other U.S. government agencies produced documentaries that presented their version of "the Big Picture." But *Why Vietnam?* (1965) and *Know Your Enemy—The Viet Cong* (1966), for example, never enjoyed the popularity or large audiences of the *Why We Fight* series (1942–1945). See Claudia Springer, "Defense Department Films from World War II to Vietnam," *Cultural Critique* 3 (Spring 1986): 151–167.

9. Note ways that cinematography also registers address: *Apocalypse Now* and *The Deer Hunter* are clearly influenced by European and other "art" cinemas, while American antiwar documentaries are indebted to a rhetorical tradition extending from Dziga Vertov's work to Cuba's *The Seventy-nine Springtimes of Ho Chi Minh* (1969) and France's *Far from Vietnam* (1967) and *A Letter to Jane* (1972).

10. Carol Lynn Mithers, "Missing in Action: Women Warriors in Vietnam," *Cultural Critique* 3 (Spring 1986):79–90.

11. W. E. B. DuBois, *The Souls of Black Folk* (Chicago: McClung, 1903).

12. See, for example, Trinh T. Minh-Ha's documentary *Surname Viet Given Name Nam* (1989), which focuses specifically on women.

13. Fredric Jameson, *The Political Unconsciousness: Narrative as a Socially Symbolic Act* (Ithaca: Cornell University Press, 1981).

14. Peter Biskind, "The Local Hero: *My Darling Clementine* and the Doctor's Dilemma," in Biskind, *Seeing Is Believing: How Hollywood Taught Us to Stop Worrying and Love the Fifties* (New York: Pantheon, 1983).

15. See, for example, *Wide Angle* 7, no. 4 (1985), *Vietnam and the Media* special issue; *Cultural Critique* 3 (Spring 1986), *American Representations of Vietnam* special issues; and Carolyn Porter, "Are We Being Historical Yet?" *The South Atlantic Quarterly* 87, no. 4 (Fall 1988):743–786.

16. Robin Wood, *Hollywood from Vietnam to Reagan* (New York: Columbia University Press, 1986).

PART ONE

WIDE ANGLES
History in the Remaking

1

MICHAEL KLEIN

Historical Memory, Film, and the Vietnam Era

HOLLYWOOD AND HISTORICAL MEMORY: THE ROAD TO *PLATOON*

> We need to question discourse in order to identify not its deeper meaning, its concealed residue, but what is at stake in this or that interpretation.
> *Catherine Belsey,* The Politics of Meaning

After a war or significant social crisis that has been divisive, and especially during a period of conservatism following an era of radical social or cultural action, the history of the recent past is often reinterpreted. Those with access to the means of cultural production, in accordance with the new dominant political attitudes, are likeliest to be behind such major shifts in interpretation. Radical or oppositional moments in the history of a nation are effectively excised from the cultural memory. A process of organized forgetting takes people's complex past away, substituting comfortable myths that reinforce rather than challenge the status quo.

Thus, in the years after the American Civil War and the failure of radical Reconstruction, cultural production about the preceding period was dominated by revisionist myths, myths still apparent many years later in D. W. Griffith's *The Birth of a Nation* (1915), in *Gone With the Wind* (1939), and in the recent television series *North and South*.[1] Griffith's film is part of a thematic trend in popular narrative about the Civil War and Reconstruction, a trend governed by an ideology of reconciliation and national unity. Historians, novelists, and later filmmakers revised the history of the recent past in an attempt to heal national and class divisions that were rooted in still-unresolved social and political contradictions. After the radical forces that had achieved a certain degree of hegemony in the late 1860s were marginalized, compromised, or suppressed, the war that in a formal sense had ended slavery was reinterpreted from a conservative white Southern point of view by Southern Bourbons and the Ku Klux Klan with the tacit support of Northern business interests. They developed a reactionary Southern myth of a harmonious slave society and divisive war into a key aspect of the new national consensus. In time, the radicalism and achievements of the Civil War and Black Reconstruction eras were exorcised from historical memory.[2]

A series of historical narratives produced in the following decades shifted

sympathy from abolitionists, reformers, and Negro slaves to patriarchal former slave owners, Southern belles, and Confederate soldiers as victims of the
war and Reconstruction. For example, *The Birth of a Nation*, endorsed and
promoted by the U.S. president and the chief justice of the Supreme Court,
stereotypes Blacks and radicals as threats to law and order, sexual mortality,
and the social fabric; it celebrates the reestablishment of the nation on the
basis of the conservative prewar national consensus. The popularity of
Griffith's film, and later *Gone With the Wind*, are indexes of complacent acceptance of Jim Crow in the South and segregation elsewhere in insecure economic times. Later, scholarship and narratives that began to challenge the
revisionist interpretation of the Civil War and Reconstruction signalled a thaw
in American society and the start of the Civil Rights era.

An analogous process has taken place in our own period, through the reinterpretation of the American war in Vietnam. During the period of the war,
and of the movement against the war—which was part of a broad movement
whose concerns included equal rights and equal opportunities for Blacks,
other minorities, and women—the independent media produced a number of
works opposed to American military involvement, and in some cases were
sympathetic to the cause of the Vietnamese National Liberation Front. More
covert statements critical of U.S. intervention in Vietnam were also made
through Hollywood genre films. Subsequently, as America entered the Reagan era and began engaging in interventions in Central America, Grenada,
and the Middle East, Hollywood produced a series of films that glorified the
war in Vietnam. They have on the whole been permeated with macho-warrior
and racist ideology, reaffirming a neo–Cold War perspective of the world and
depicting radical and liberal-minded people as weak or deviant. Some recent
films have countered the excesses of this revisionism, but generally they have
failed to do justice to antiwar attitudes at home, within the army, or among
Vietnam veterans, and to the effect that this opposition had on people's consciousness of themselves and their society. They are therefore a distorted representation of the national past.

During the years of the Vietnam War and the protests against it, only one
Hollywood fiction film was set in Vietnam—John Wayne's *The Green Berets*
(1968). Drawing heavily upon established conventions of the World War II
and Korean War film and exploiting the image of its star, *The Green Berets*
was an unqualified defense of American military involvement in Vietnam. At
the same time, however, horrific images of the consequences of American
military presence and reports of worldwide antiwar protests were seen by the
American public on television news and in independently produced 16mm
documentary films such as *Inside North Vietnam* (1968), *In the Year of the Pig*
(1968), and *Hearts and Minds* (1974). Images and counterimages of the war
were an important aspect of the mid-sixties debate between doves and hawks
about the war and conscription.

Indirect criticism of the war also appeared in one established Hollywood
film genre, the Western, and expanded its conventions in new directions.[3]
Both Ralph Nelson's *Soldier Blue* (1970) and Arthur Penn's *Little Big Man*

Both Ralph Nelson's Soldier Blue *and Arthur Penn's* Little Big Man *suggest . . . allegories of the war in Vietnam.*

(1970) suggest in their condemnation of cavalry massacres and genocidal policy towards American Indians allegories of the war in Vietnam, perhaps with particular reference to the massacre of Vietnamese civilians in the village of My Lai and the U.S. Air Force's indiscriminate use of napalm in free-fire zones. Both films also offer a critique of white U.S. civilization as essentially colonialist, barbarous, hypocritical, and life-denying. Significantly, both films present Indian life, and by extension non-Anglo life, as more holistic and life-enhancing than competitive materialistic American society. In doing so they not only express a certain solidarity with the struggle of Third World people against cultural, military, and economic penetration but also affirm the social values of the Civil Rights movement and the counterculture, which were an integral aspect of the antiwar movement both within and outside the army.

Vietnam as a subject initially returned to the Hollywood screen after the conclusion of the war, in the form of a series of coming-home films that focused on the situation of the returning veteran. Again Hollywood only seemed able to confront the Vietnam experience by situating it within an established genre.[4] For example, *I Am a Fugitive from a Chain Gang* (1932) and *The Best Years of Our Lives* (1946) were post–World War I and post–World War II coming-home films that focused on a wounded, alienated, or rejected veteran's return to American society; such films have often been vehicles for social criticism and thus were a recognizable popular cultural form. Liberal and radical Vietnam-era coming-home films range from sympathetic portraits of the problem of rehabilitation that challenge mainstream American constructions of masculinity (*Coming Home* in 1978) to portraits of the vet as crazed protofascist victim (*Tracks* in 1976) to parables like *Cutter's Way* (1981), in which a mutilated veteran becomes an avenger, arrayed against semi-criminal capitalist establishment figures. One film in this genre, *Heroes* (1977), flashes back to the war, which is superimposed, in a horrifying hallucinatory scene, upon the landscape of Middle America. *Friendly Fire* (1979), which is set in the wheat belt, is concerned with developing political activism against the draft by the parents of a young soldier who has been killed by artillery fire from his own company, and with government surveillance and intimidation of their antiwar activity. The film incorporates several themes within its narrative about parents coming to terms with their son's death: campus teach-ins about the war; testimony by Vietnam Veterans Against the War before a congressional committee; peace demonstrations; criticisms of racism within the army, economic injustice in America, and unquestioning pro-establishment conformity. In the final sense these are films of closure: the war is exorcised and placed in the confines of the recent American past. These films' narratives generally advance from the war experience to criticize American society of the 1970s from alternative cultural perspectives. Their subject is not so much the war or combat experience—very few war scenes are presented—but the effect of the war on American veterans and the implications of the failure of the post-Vietnam United States to fully implement the countervision of the sixties at home or abroad.

The Deer Hunter (1978) initiates a different interpretation of the Vietnam era in Hollywood fiction film. Unlike, for example, *Go Tell the Spartans* (1978), which is set in Vietnam in 1964 at the start of the escalation of significant U.S. military presence, *The Deer Hunter* neither attempts a realistic recreation in fictional terms of the complexities of the war nor repudiates U.S. military involvement in Vietnam. Its subject is not the war, or the effect of the war and the antiwar movement upon American culture from 1964 to 1973, but American culture and society after the war as the 1970s drew to a close. Thus scenes set in Vietnam during the war are no more historically specific then depictions of Tombstone or the OK Corral in Westerns or of plantations and cotton fields in films about the Civil War and Reconstruction. They are nonetheless quite significant.

The Deer Hunter marks the beginning of a series of post-Vietnam films that negate the contradiction between doves and hawks and use the era as a period and a setting in order to construct parables that reinterpret the Vietnam experience in the context of the concerns and developing climate of opinion of the late 1970s and the 1980s. What is occurring in Hollywood narrative fiction film in the years after the war is that Vietnam, like the West in the days of Indians and cowboys or the South in the time of plantations, has become a setting within which ideological constructs are explored and contested. Given the illusionist power of the cinema and the technical skill of special effects teams, these fiction films may indeed seem to be detailed reenactments of history. They are, however, highly encoded generic melodramas and thus should be evaluated with an eye to their ideology and the ways they interpret a recent period of American history that is part of our national experience.[5]

For example, the Vietnam sections of *The Deer Hunter* are pervaded by racist and Cold War stereotypes: images of "the yellow peril," of "Russian roulette" as a routine form of Communist torture and an expression of Oriental decadence. At the conclusion of *The Deer Hunter* the characters, whose lives have been damaged by the Vietnam War, gather around a table and sing "God Bless America." Cimino's fable is fraught with contradiction and reveals more than it intends about the developing conservative climate of opinion in the United States in the late seventies. It is, perhaps, significant that it was screened on television by New York City's WOR-TV on the eve of Reagan's election. The film is permeated with a bewildered sense of nativist pride, bruised innocence and loss, a structure of feeling that is resolved in a vision of a beleagured but unified America—standing together, standing tall—in a hostile, evil, and incomprehensible world of Asian and Communist demons.

In the 1980s, as U.S. economic and political hegemony declined throughout most of the world, the decline was manifested, in excess, in a series of films that not only refight the Vietnam War and justify it on the basis of an anti-Asian racism and anti-Communist demonology, but create the illusion that the U.S. won the battle and in a sense the war (or that it won the battle but was betrayed, hence denied total victory in the war). Notable among these films were *Uncommon Valor* (1983); *Missing in Action* (1984); *Missing in Action 2: The Beginning* (1985); *Rambo: First Blood Part II* (1985); and *The Hanoi Hilton* (1987). In these films Vietnam has become the setting for fables that ideologically reproduce their time with clear implications for the direction of American foreign policy. This was recognized by President Reagan, who prepared the nation for the possibility of military intervention in the Middle East by commenting: "Boy, I saw *Rambo* last night; now I know what to do next time."[6] Fifty years earlier, President Wilson had also conflated revisionist fable and history when he praised *The Birth of a Nation* as "history written like lightning."[7] What is at stake in the interpretation is not only the memory of the past but the consciousness that will affect future policy.

Rambo and *The Birth of a Nation* revise history and justify vigilante-style military intervention (U.S. military/Ku Klux Klan) against alien peoples to sustain the construction of national consensus and the related discourse of them and us. Frantz Fanon, in writing about the literature and art of neocolonialism in *The Wretched of the Earth* (1961), has illustrated that the culture of the dominant forces in society tends to stereotype colonized peoples as "others"—as slaves (inferiors) or monsters (threats)—or simply to marginalize them beyond the fringes of society or historical memory. Excluded, they become invisible men and women.[8] In recent Hollywood fiction film narratives about the Vietnam era there is a tendency for both the Vietnamese, who fought in what they call the American war, and the majority of Americans, who ultimately came to oppose that war (in and out of the army), to be dematerialized or demonized. They are not the tellers of the tale any more than the slaves or abolitionists are in the conventional Civil War/Reconstruction film or the Indians in the traditional Western. These two separate but related dematerializations of the colonized or oppressed and their political allies work together to forward the interests of the dominant classes and their allies. The situation is thus fraught with contradiction. It is as if the recent past is being recounted by a victim of historical amnesia or by a narrator whose tunnel vision compels him/her to censor or repress certain material.

The narratives of films as diverse in quality as *Rambo: First Blood Part II* (1985), *Missing in Action* (1984), *American Commandos* (1985), *The Deer Hunter* (1978), and, as we will see, *Platoon* (1987), as well as those of popular novels such as J. C. Pollock's *Mission M.I.A.* (1982) and John Del Vecchio's *The Thirteenth Valley* (1982), reduce the complexities of the Vietnam era to the morality of soldiering. This is an effort to reconcile the ambiguities and silence the contradictions of a period that was a watershed in American politics—a period of opposition to the war and to the worldview that sustained it, as well as of challenge to racial and economic inequalities at home. In these works Vietnamese and other Third World people are dematerialized or stereotyped as dehumanized others, as shadowy aliens. The war is mystified as a tragic mistake or an existentialist adventure through which the White American hero discovers or realizes his identity. There is no sense of the existence of the significant antiwar movement at home—a broad movement for the transformation of American society—that ultimately gained a degree of hegemony, if only for a few years. The perspective of those soldiers who opposed the war, and in some cases fragged their officers, is silently erased from historical memory. There is no recognition that the war was hardly an accident but rather a historical development from long-standing and ultimately counterproductive French and American colonialist and imperialist policies.

PLATOON: EXPERIENCE UNENCUMBERED BY HISTORY

There, where a French legionnaire
once walked patrol . . .
Unencumbered by history
our own or that of 13-Century Mongol armies
long since fled or buried
by the Vietnamese
in Nha Trang in 1962, we just did our jobs . . .

Jan Barry, "In the Footsteps of Genghis Khan"

The advertisements for *Platoon* stressed that the film was authentic as its director was "a decorated infantryman who spent fifteen months in Vietnam." The film is well acted, conveys the tensions and discomforts of soldiering, and, although in visual terms it glorifies war as spectacle, the stated theme of the film is that wars in general are tragic experiences, grim rites of initiation and lost innocence. In these respects it counters the excesses of jingoistic films like *Rambo II* and *Missing in Action*. Yet, despite its critical stance, *Platoon* does not problematize or clarify the experience of the Vietnam era. It fails to situate the American military presence in Vietnam in political or historical perspective. Its critique of war in general is hermetic and exempts the U.S. government, military, and power elite from being called to account for their policies in the Vietnam War in particular, policies that included the strategic hamlet program, free-fire zones, and antipersonnel bombing. Its limitations are significant given the film's positive reception at the box office, and in Hollywood, where it was awarded four Oscars. As *Platoon*, in contrast to *Rambo II*, is a mainstream liberal meditation, the assumptions that underpin its construction of the Vietnam era are of special concern. My objections to the film involve its omissions and distortions, its orientation, its sense of "us" and "them," its lack of historical perspective.

The action of *Platoon* centers on Bravo Company in Vietnam. In particular, it focuses upon the war experience of Chris Taylor, a literate middle-class recruit in a company of grunts who takes on the role of a representative everyman, given the ideology of the film. Taylor's allegiance is split between two officers: Barnes, a brutal, effective killer and semifascist superpatriot who regards Vietnam as one big free-fire zone; Elias, an even more effective killer of the National Liberation Front (NLF), but a nonideologue and a person who adheres to the rules and laws of war as they have been established by the Geneva Convention. At one level the film is a repudiation of Barnes and the barbaric and genocidal war ethic, as Taylor gradually shifts his allegiance to Elias and finally avenges his death, which has resulted from Barnes's actions. By the end of the film Chris Taylor has undergone an experience of initiation (a familiar motif in war fiction) and achieved what the film would regard as maturity in his understanding of the evil excesses of war and human nature. At a deeper level, however, the film substitutes a psychological and metaphysical interpretation for a historical understanding of the genocidal aspects of the war.

Given the construction of *Platoon* as a tightly framed buddy film, we quickly identify with the group of American soldiers, sympathize with their losses, share their ideological perspective: fear and hate of the shadowy evil forces (the Vietnamese NLF) who are arrayed against them in the jungle and who constitute an ever present threat to their life and security. A subtle inversion has taken place. This is the aspect of the film that was foregrounded in the hard-sell advertisements shown on American television. It is carried through on the blurb of the jacket of the paperback novel that was written shortly after the film was released: "They were the men of Bravo Company. Officers and grunts . . . all of them Americans. It was war that brought them together—and it was war that would tear them apart. This is their war—a war of camaraderie forged in violence and of brutality born of madness. This is their story—gritty, unflinching and real."[9]

What tears the group of American soldiers apart are tensions that emerge after the company massacres a group of civilians, Vietnamese villagers. However, given the widespread public condemnation of the My Lai massacre and similar atrocities that took place during the war in the latter 1960s and early 1970s, the film's critique of analogous events seems extremely mild, both in its visualization of the events and as it abstracts them from government policies and hence from the politics of the war, substituting a grim and mystifying humanism for clarity on the events of the period. *Platoon* does not so much condemn the massacre of Vietnamese civilians as minimize and explain it. The explanation offered to the audience fails to situate the massacre in the context of genocidal U.S. policies that were pursued throughout the war (search and destroy missions, strategic hamlets, free-fire zones, and so on) and were underpinned by socially constructed assumptions of racial and national superiority. Instead it is decontextualized, mystified as merely an example of the dark side of human nature under stress.

The scenes that are the key to the cultural politics of *Platoon* merit detailed consideration. Bravo Company, consisting of raw recruits and seasoned officers, has begun to coalesce as a fighting force. The company is out on patrol in the Vietnamese countryside. It may be part of a regional pacification program involving the destruction and resettling of villages, but if so we are not provided with this information. Given the discourse of the film we simply share the soldier's perspective: somewhere out in the jungle we, like the soldiers, are being hunted by an alien and evil antagonist; we are surrounded, as perhaps in a larger sense America is by Third World and Communist aliens. Two members of the platoon, with whom we have begun to identify, are killed by the Vietcong while they are out on patrol. One youth is killed by a booby trap bomb, a cowardly terrorist act, given the rhetoric of the film. The other, a likable Black soldier, is strung up on a tree as a warning to the Americans, a primitive barbaric act, given the construction of the narrative. As no other perspective has been admitted into the film's discourse, we, the audience, continue to share the point of view of Chris and the other recruits. Shortly afterward Bravo Company discovers a village that seems to be a hiding place for the Vietcong. It is put to the torch. The inhabitants are interrogated. Two are killed, at the instigation of Barnes and his henchmen.

The massacre scene is fraught with tension and the potential of significant contradiction. Given the construction of the narrative we comprehend Chris and the other young recruits' anger, grief, and desire for revenge. That is, at the start of the scene the reprisals against the village are rendered plausible, given the deaths of the two American soldiers, the grief and fatigue of the company, and the participation in the reprisals of Chris, who is our window on the film. Note also that only two Vietnamese have been killed, which, in a sense, equals the deaths of the two unfortunate young Americans and thus signifies that the reprisals have not been carried to the point of Rambo-like excess. Suddenly at this point Elias bursts onto the scene and prevents Barnes from killing any more civilians. As the two soldiers confront each other initially it appears as if the dramatic conflict will be expanded into an ideological conflict. However, his intervention—a moment of great dramatic intensity—

also serves to deflect the film from any significant political critique to concerns that are primarily psychological and metaphysical. Elias quickly brings the matter to the attention of the commanding officer of the unit who orders an investigation, commenting that acts of war against Vietnamese civilians are contrary to U.S. policy. Elias and the commanding officer's interventions limit the massacre and isolate the actions that have occurred against Vietnamese civilians from any potential critique of U.S. policy in the war.[10] At worst the reprisals are exceptional acts, performed under stress in special circumstances that release the dark side of human nature, perhaps understandable but certainly neither sanctioned nor related to the general thrust of U.S. counterinsurgency strategy in Vietnam. Moreover, once the commanding officer appears order is restored. The system works, it would seem. This further deflects the disturbing material in the narrative from potentially serving as a critique of U.S. military policy in Vietnam. Ideology is dramatically reproduced as a unity without contradiction.

Tensions are further dissipated as Bravo Company help evacuate the Vietnamese peasants from the ruins of their village. The scene concludes with a panoramic shot of U.S. troops walking through fields in the bright sunlight carrying Vietnamese children on their shoulders. It is elegiac and self-congratulatory. This last sequence, which affirms the essential humanity of the occupying American military force, is reminiscent of some of the worst moments of British or French colonialist cinema or of the cinema of Coca-Cola imperialism. Two emblematic scenes come to mind from other U.S. films about Vietnam and the Vietnam era. The first is the affirmation of national unity, reconciliation, and healing at the conclusion of *The Deer Hunter*, when the survivors of what has been portrayed as a war against Asian Red demons gather with their friends and families around the table and sing "God Bless America." The second is the extension of affection to the colonized and hence subordinate "other" at the conclusion of *The Green Berets*—rendered through John Wayne's paternalist concern for a Vietnamese orphan. Such scenes exploit our most generous sentiments, for who can be against kindness? Their effect is seriously flawed, however, given the context in which they occur. Americanism that fails to extend the vision of the Declaration of Independence to other nations is a dubious creed. A candy bar or a hug are not adequate reparations for the imperialistic occupation and destruction of a hamlet, or of a country, its people, and its culture.

As the film draws to a close Chris Taylor kills Barnes to avenge Barnes's shooting of Elias. This in one sense is a radical act, as Barnes is a protofascist figure who is certainly guilty of intending to murder Elias and who will not otherwise be brought to justice. However, the narrative of the film is carefully constructed to abort any possible conclusion that in killing a sadistic soldier Taylor was taking a stand against the war in Vietnam: although Barnes is a representative prowar figure, Elias is not a symbol of antiwar resistance. Indeed, this option of resistance is never present in the film. Thus Taylor is not picking up the fallen banner of opposition to the war in avenging Elias's death. It is more a ritualistic attempt to exorcise the dark side of human nature.

Elias was shot by Barnes while he was engaged in the midst of a rapturous and delirious jungle fight, zapping numerous gooks in individual combat, the White American hunter beating the Vietnamese jungle fighters at their own game fair and square. The shoot-out is rendered with great intensity in a series of tracking shots. It is a scene that signifies that although Elias is a liberal figure, insofar as he took a stand against excess in pursuit of victory in Vietnam, he is certainly not an antiwar pacifist; he is man enough to fight in a fashion as spectacular as Rambo/Stallone or Braddock/Chuck Norris against the Vietnamese enemy. In a sense Barnes's real crime in bringing about Elias's death is transgression of the law, in this case not "thou shalt not kill civilians" but "thou shalt not kill members of thine own army." Barnes's shooting of Elias marks Barnes as an extremist, perhaps an inverted soulmate of the radical antiwar soldiers who fragged their officers and whose existence is repressed by the discourse of the film. Indeed, the subject of fragging is sufficiently taboo that after Barnes shoots at Elias the film introduces an evasive element of ambiguity about the degree of his responsibility for Elias's death. This is a further case of the film repressing the ideological implications of issues raised by its own narrative. Chris Taylor's killing of Barnes is, then, merely an affirmation of the middle way, of privatistic resolution of the moral crises of the Vietnam era, of recognition and hence victory over one's own potential for excess and evil. In killing Barnes he has recognized and exorcised the evil in himself. He has now passed through a rite of initiation and can return to society a wiser man. Given that Chris is hardly a typical recruit, but representative instead of the middle stratum in U.S. who on the whole did not support the war, his nonoppositional stance at the end of the film is, in a sense, a rewriting of the movement generation's experience of the Vietnam era.

What does the film tell us at the moment of closure? "That in the end . . . we did not fight the enemy. The only enemy is within man himself."[11] Put simply, that the atrocities of war are caused by the sadistic nature of some of the combatants. All war is hell, the film says, but the Vietnamese war was in most respects no worse than any other war, and then only in moments of excess when conditions were created that licensed the darker, sadistic side of human nature to emerge. And then—as the village massacre scene illustrated—it was counter to official military policy. However, U.S. policy in the war, which was legitimized by racist and neocolonial assumptions about the value that can be placed upon Asian life, included: marking free-fire zones in which any civilian was fair game; the strategic hamlet policy of forced evacuation from and destruction of ancestral villages; the defoliation of the countryside; search and destroy missions; the use of napalm, Agent Orange, and antipersonnel bombs; condoning rape, torture, and mutilation of prisoners under interrogation; collecting various parts of the human anatomy as verification of kill ratios; the bombing of hospitals and schools and civilian areas of cities in the North Vietnam.[12] Thus, given the dialectic of people's war, it was U.S. military policy and its ideological assumptions that structured the degradation and genocide that took place in Vietnam. *Platoon* erases the context of the war from historical memory. Foreground-

ing an American soldier's myopic perspective on the morality of several decontextualized moments of combat, it blots out the history of Mongol,
French, and U.S. occupation of Vietnam and centuries of Vietnamese resistance, as well as the general thrust of U.S. military counterinsurgence
policy and the genocidal actions that it sanctioned.

FULL METAL JACKET: PAINT IT BLACK

> If you would see the horizon from a forest, you must first build a
> tower. . . . Of course the tower is crooked, and the telescopes
> warped. . . . What supports our use of them, now, is that our intimacy
> with the master-builder of the tower . . . has given some advantage for
> correcting the error of his instruments.
>
> *Norman Mailer,* The Armies of the Night

Stanley Kubrick's *Full Metal Jacket* (1987) presents a very different vision
of the Vietnam War, one with enhanced perspective. While in general critics
have been quite favorable to well-made films in the new war genre—*Platoon*
and *Hamburger Hill* (1987)—their evaluation of Kubrick's important work
has been tempered by political sniping. For example, Philip French, in the 13
September issue of the British publication *Observer,* concludes that viewers
of the film "receive our regular, liberal anti-war inoculation." Pauline Kael,
writing in an August 1987 issue of the *New Yorker,* contrasts *Hamburger Hill*
and *Full Metal Jacket. Hamburger Hill* merits praise as a good example of the
buddy combat film genre: "They fight because their country tells them to
fight . . . and the movie respects their loyalty to each other." This is in contrast to "the neat parcel of guilt supplied by *Full Metal Jacket.*" When critics,
writing in somewhat establishment periodicals, adopt a patronizing tone, dis-
missing the political stance of a film as a matter of bad taste, often as "simply
liberal" or "too neat," I often take it as a sign that something interesting is
happening in the work.
    In general, praise of the technical brilliance of *Full Metal Jacket* has also
been tempered by criticism of the film as being too "cold." Critics tend to like
the first section of the film (Kubrick's savage parody of the brutality of boot
camp military indoctrination) but feel uneasy about the second half of the film
(his portrait of the disintegration of the American war machine in combat). In
the first section of the film our sympathies are directed against a brutal, mid-
dle-aged, and extremely unattractive right-wing drill sergeant, a figure few in
the audience would identify with. But in the second section of the film the war
machine that the sergeant molded in the confines of a training camp at home
in America is demystified: when tested in battle in Vietnam the recruits are
panic-stricken, ill-disciplined, and decidedly unheroic. What makes some
critics and spectators in the audience uncomfortable is that Kubrick inverts the
combat film genre of *Platoon* and *Hamburger Hill,* in the process critiquing
the chauvinism—both national and male—that often negates or undermines

the antiwar stance of explicitly critical Vietnam films. The emotional distance of the film and its departures from naturalistic presentation of the war enhance the film's critique. Invoking Brecht's "alienation" effect (the formal distanciation and self-reflexivity he calls *Verfremdung*, or "strange-making"), *Full Metal Jacket* elicits the kind of multilayered dialectical reception Brecht called "complex seeing," as it guides its audience to contextualize, to look at the specifics in the locus of the narrative in relation to larger questions on the intellectual horizon.

For example, let us review several key scenes in *Full Metal Jacket*. Early in the Vietnam section of the film, when the new marine division is being flown into battle in a helicopter, we witness an incident of genocide: an air cavalry machine-gunner, dressed in a flamboyant Hawaiian sport shirt, casually leans out of the helicopter and fires at civilians scurrying to cover on the ground below. Corporal Joker, our protagonist in the film, asks: "How can you shoot women, children . . ." The machine-gunner replies: "Easy—you just don't lead them so much." He laughs and then adds: "Ain't war hell." We have encountered similar "war is hell" statements before in combat films that claim to be critiques of the war effort: in the midst of Vietnam War sequences that affirm the tragic vitality of American servicemen in battle while denying Vietnamese any significant human presence. Kubrick's parody is a chilling indictment of the complacent Cold War liberalism of that kind of film, for he is saying that unless we adopt another perspective we are no more than helicopter machine-gunners who have suffered or, in retrospect, have regrets. Thus it is significant that he begins the film with an extended inquiry into how the consciousness of the helicopter gunner was created.

The opening section or prologue of *Full Metal Jacket* is set in a marine boot camp at Parris Island, South Carolina. Kubrick records in great detail the process of training a recruit to be a member of an elite corps of the U.S. fighting forces. However, this section of the film is far more than simply a critique of the sadistic and dehumanizing process of training that strips young men of their identities and shapes them into robotlike killing machines. U.S. military policy in the Vietnam land war was based upon a draconian strategy of counterinsurgency: search and destroy missions; free-fire zones; destruction of the countryside and/or of the NLF's base areas; attainment of kill quotas. This strategy necessitated the production of a special kind of soldier, one who would not relate to potential objects of genocide (male or female) as fellow human beings. This in turn required the production of soldiers inculcated with conceptions of national and racial superiority and the inferiority of Third World peoples and with a warriorlike conception of masculine misogyny committed to rooting out the other-directed—that is "female"—aspects of their personality. Kubrick illustrates that these qualities are not inherent in the dark side of human nature (the perspective of *Platoon*) but are instead socially produced.

The boot camp is a microcosm of a society being trained and educated in national chauvinism, racism, and sexism. This takes the form of lessons assimilated passively from lectures or learned by rote and repeated in the forms of songs. The drill instructor calls out the lines that the young school-age student-soldiers repeat or sing while they march. They acknowledge his lectures by assent ("Yes, sir!") while standing at attention. These devices allow Kubrick to foreground the ideological aspects of the training process while maintaining the dramatic flow of the narrative. The lectures and drill songs coalesce into a curriculum: For example: "I love working for Uncle Sam/Let's me know just who I am." "You will be a weapon/You will be a minister of death." "I don't want no teenage queen/I just want my M-14." "Niggers, wops, gooks, or greasers. Here you are all equally worthless." "What makes the grass grow?"/"Blood, blood, blood." "What do we do for a living?"/"Kill, kill, kill." The violence of the process—the shouting, the punishments, the sadism—is also part of the curriculum. The young men are molded into gook-hating, misogynist, robotlike killers during their period of basic training. They graduate as U.S. marines. They know what they are fighting against but have little sense of what they are fighting for. As one marine says: "Do you think we waste gooks for 'freedom'? If I'm gonna get my balls shot off for a word, my word is 'poon-tang.' "

The main section of the film duplicates the structure of the conventional war film: we follow the lives of the recruits from boot camp in the United States to Vietnam. As in the prologue, however, Kubrick reproduces the outline of the war-film narrative to deconstruct the convention. In the remainder of the film he continues to develop his critique of racism and sexism in the armed forces—of attitudes that effectively stereotype and dehumanize Vietnamese women and men as alien, as "others." In addition he challenges the national-chauvinist assumption that, given the superiority of the U.S. troops, most battles, if not the war, were won (or were winable). In these respects *Full Metal Jacket* is a significant corrective to films as diverse as *Rambo II* or *Platoon.*

The Vietnam section of the film starts in Da Nang and moves on to the ancient city of Hue during the 1968 NLF Tet offensive. In Da Nang we begin with a scene that is set away from the war zone. We quickly sense that the culture of Vietnam has also become a casualty of the war, a parody of the consumer capitalism of its foreign occupiers. In the foreground are several of the troops from the marine company, including Rafter Man and Joker; the latter is somewhat similar in education and background to Chris Taylor and witnesses the key events in the film. They are passing the time sitting at a table in a café talking with a Vietnamese prostitute, trying to get her to lower her price.[13] Her identity has been reduced to a Western sexual commodity. She is dressed in U.S.-style streetwalker clothes—a short tight skirt, high boots—and does her best to negotiate in American: "You want fuckee? Me so horny. Me fuckee, fuckee." In the background an enormous advertising billboard rises from the top of a building. It looks something like the Camel cigarette billboard in Times Square in New York City. On the left of the billboard there is a large cartooned face of a man, in this case semi-Asian and smiling, with a lot of teeth. The rest of the billboard is covered with advertising copy in Vietnamese. On the sound track of the film Nancy Sinatra's "These Boots Are Made for Walking" is blasting.

The scene, rendered for the most part in a long shot so all the signifiers are equally present, is a perfect icon of Coca-Cola imperialism. Both the prostitute and the Asian face are grotesque parodies of materialist American culture reminiscent of the Dr. T. J. Eckleburg billboard that overlooks the wasteland of the Valley of Ashes in F. Scott Fitzgerald's novel about the American Dream, *The Great Gatsby*. Kubrick's juxtaposition signifies that Third World and colonized people can only be conceptualized by the colonizer insofar as they attempt to assimilate his culture (in this case by becoming commodities). They are only valued insofar as they accommodate to imperialist prerogatives. As a marine commanding officer says: "We are here to help the Vietnamese because inside every gook there is an American." The boots in the song signify America's presence in Vietnam, walking all over the country and the culture. As the scene draws to a close the screen fades to black and in the darkness the concluding words of the chorus are repeated by the female voice of the singer: "These boots are gonna walk all over you." It is an indication—almost subliminal—that some sort of reversal is going to take place.

The reversal occurs when the squad of marines, led by Sergeant Cowboy, panics and loses discipline when it comes under NLF sniper fire. This is the group that we observed being molded into a fanatic fighting force, confident of its inherent national superiority. (They were told in basic training that "God has a hard-on for the U.S. marines.") The battle scene is overlooked and anchored by the image of the Americanized Asian face that was present on the billboard in Da Nang, as the shattered remnants of a duplicate billboard are on the side of a building that has been blasted in the battle. In this context his gaze signifies that the seemingly colonized culture is more resilient than the occupiers realize. Moreover, when the marines are pinned down by a sniper and four are killed, the discipline of the macho war machine breaks down in panic and recrimination and they abandon the object of their mission. Somewhere in the distance a Vietnamese person has intervened to destroy the confidence and cohesion of the elite fighting force of *ubermenschen*. When the lone sniper is revealed to us to be a Vietnamese woman, the ideological mold of the conventional combat film is shattered.

The sniper is a woman. As such, she represents the object of the twisted sexuality that has been articulated in the basic training marching songs and demonstrated in the soldiers' brutal encounters with Vietnamese prostitutes. She is also nonwhite, and thus falls into the category of human beings the drill sergeant specifically designates as "worthless" in the first section of the film. She is also a Communist and, by implication, a non-Christian. She is as "other" as "other" can get to the representatives of American culture who encounter her presence. Her appearance shatters not only the conventions of the combat film—and the expectations of the audience—but also the ideology of the larger culture from which these conventions spring.

Equally important, she is the avenger of the imperialized and chauvinized prostitute who took center stage when the squad of marines first arrived in Vietnam. The bravest and most skillful representative of the other side is a woman. She is thin, even skinny, in contrast to the bare-armed, grotesque, muscle-bound grunts. She thus appropriates the male warrior role of the marines and in a sense of all the U.S. soldiers whose presence dominates the mid-eighties crop of buddy war films that are set in Vietnam and whose exploits often reduce the conflagration to a boy's own military adventure. It is significant, however, that Kubrick's critique of the war ethic extends beyond mere role reversal. The scene is shot in slow motion so we attend carefully to every detail of what happens. In the midst of the fight in which, very much outnumbered, the young woman is surrounded and shot by the marines who have managed to survive her attack, there is fear in her eyes *and* in the eyes of our figure of reference, Corporal Joker, who has by now come to doubt the war. They are bonded in common humanity, in contrast to the other marines, whose eyes blaze with sadistic energy as they blast their weapons. The look in her eyes and in the eyes of Corporal Joker is the only glimmer of potential redemption in Kubrick's bleak and savage film.

In the next and concluding scene the marines march off through the burning city of Hue into the darkness. They are singing. However, it is not the confident and affirmative marines' "Battle Hymn"—"from the halls of Montezuma to the shores of Tripoli . . . the streets are guarded by the United States Marines"—that they practiced in boot camp in the early part of the film and that has been sung in triumph at the moment of closure in many Hollywood war films. Instead, the marines sing "Mickey Mouse is the leader of our club . . . /Mickey Mouse, Mickey Mouse/Forever let us hold our banners high," as they march into the sunset on the road to nowhere. *Full Metal Jacket*, in contrast to the rhetoric of *Rambo II* and its appropriation by the commander-in-chief in the White House, asserts that after Vietnam the ideal of easy military conquest of a Third World nation cannot be simply affirmed in conventional discourse as relatively unproblematic. Its sound and image fuse into a complex trope: an army that sought world hegemony is linked with an ersatz culture, itself an aspect of that hegemony. There is an ironic ersatz glee in Kubrick's construction of the scene; his reduction of sacred heroic marine ritual to kitsch brings to mind the horrific banalities of Nazi culture. The analysis is further historicized through the implied ironic association with film images of the U.S. cavalry going into the sunset, in this case the glow of the flames of the city the marines are protecting. The reference to Mickey Mouse as the leader of the club/army/society is not only surprising but suggestive. Mickey Mouse, of course, is a Hollywood artifact. At one level this may be a reference to the Hollywood antecedents of the incumbent commander-in-chief in 1987 when the film was made. More important, the cluster of associations—Mickey Mouse, U.S. film representations of the cavalry in Westerns, the marines in Vietnam—suggest that the hegemony of an ideology that incorporates national chauvinism, racism, and sexism in the media and culture as a whole, can be a key factor in constructing a consensus of popular support for war or domination of Third World nations or peoples. The film ends on a bleak note. As the final image fades we hear the Rolling Stones' "Paint It Black" on the sound track. Kubrick is far from optimistic about the possibility of change.

Although the raw material for the film *Full Metal Jacket* comes from the novel *The Short Timers* (1979) by Gustav Hasford, the key sequences are essentially Kubrick's. He has constructed *Full Metal Jacket* by conflating two chapters of the book: in the first chapter, in Hasford's version, the Marines kill a woman NLF fighter, then butcher her corpse with a machete; in the next chapter they are pinned down by sniper fire and are on the verge of a suicidal attempt to save the lives of four wounded and dying marines when Corporal Joker shoots his buddies to put them out of their misery and abort a futile attack that would have resulted in additional loss of life. Instead Kubrick foregrounds the figure of the woman NLF fighter and concludes with the ironic scene of the marine Mouseketeers marching into the sunset. The rhetorical and often parodic use of background music on the sound track—"These Boots Are Made for Walking" and "The Mouseketeers' Song," as well as the Stones' "Paint It Black"—are also Kubrick's contribution. Equally important are the inclusion of songs in the background to the narrative that are examples of a debased culture whose artifacts are displays of hypocritical sentiment: "The Chapel of Love"; "Surfer Bird"; "Hello Vietnam," the country/ western song heard at the beginning of the film. This illustrates how painstakingly Kubrick has constructed a critique of the chauvinist assumptions, sense of national superiority, and moral complacency of the conventional combat genre film set in Vietnam—and of the larger culture that the discourse of these films represents.

The achievement of *Full Metal Jacket* is incomplete, however, insofar as it is rendered through the structured absence of the *potential* for resistance to the war or of information about that resistance, which is part of the historical record. That is, the film is problematic in that it does not recognize that a counter-hegemonic ideology existed, that acts of resistance to the war were possible and when achieved were often heroic and significant. From perceptions of despair and anguish many who lived through the Vietnam years wrestled with the facts and transformed their hearts and minds in the process.

Thus, impressive as *Full Metal Jacket* is, it does have certain limitations. Some of these become apparent if we set it in comparison with *Paths of Glory* (1957), Kubrick's first antiwar film, which is set during World War I. In that film a woman also appears at the conclusion to symbolize an alternative conception of humanity: a captured German woman whose song (which the French troops join in singing) for a brief moment unites nationalities who are trapped in an absurd and brutal interimperialist conflict. In *Paths of Glory*, the action of the narrative shifts back and forth from the grim field of battle to the plush and ornate marble-walled centers of military command. The generals in crisp dress uniforms who order the attacks are contrasted to the tired, dirt-encrusted soldiers. In this way the film explores related issues of class domination and privilege while it indicts a military caste system for its role in bringing about and perpetuating the war. This kind of analysis is rarely pursued in *Full Metal Jacket*.

In several important respects, *Full Metal Jacket* also shares the historical amnesia of other Reagan era Hollywood productions that are set in Vietnam.

Although the first half of the film occurs in the United States in 1967 and 1968, one has no sense that significant opposition to the war and the draft existed and was being expressed in teach-ins and demonstrations, as well as by soldiers in the coffeehouse antiwar movement on the fringes of armed forces bases in the U.S. Nor after seeing the film would one realize that in 1968, shortly after the Tet offensive, a squad of marines mutinied at Da Nang, or that marines and other members of the armed forces were active in opposition to the war, both in 'Nam and at bases on the Pacific Rim (for example the U.S. 1st Marine Air Wing at Iwakumi Air Base),[14] or that they published the *Grunt Free Press* and an estimated 144 other alternative newspapers to counter the propaganda of the *Stars and Stripes*, and as the war continued organized the Vietnam Veterans Against the War (VVAW) in the U.S.[15] From seeing the film one would not be aware that at Christmas 1968 30,000 troops at Long Binh demonstrated their opposition to the war by giving a peace salute to General Creighton Adams.[16] Or that from 1966 to 1973 191,840 young men refused to respond to draft notices, that 503,926 U.S. soldiers deserted the armed service,[17] and that by 1970 over 200 officially verified fraggings were taking place per year.[18]

There are brief moments when the ideological mind-set molded in the boot camp cracks, but the consciousness of the marines in *Full Metal Jacket* does not coalesce into a viable alternative perspective: we do not, for example, sense that it is possible that some may return home and join the VVAW and organize protest against the war, although that course of action was taken up as the conflict continued. Joker, our guide throughout the film, begins to distance himself from the war, at first through wry remarks (for example: "I wanted to meet interesting and stimulating people of an ancient culture and kill them") and gestures (combining a peace symbol with his military gear) that simultaneously express the contradictions in his situation and attempt to hold it in stasis. Later, after the experience of affinity with the Vietnamese woman fighter, Joker appears to be developing a fragile humanist anti-imperialist discourse that might be a source of renewal and resistance.

This faint glimmer of possible change does not finally rescue the film from its Hobbesian pessimism, however. There is nothing to replace the deconstructed ideology of the boot camp, nothing to indicate that people could progress in consciousness beyond recognition of their complicity and entrapment in a policy of genocide. As the final image of the film, the march of the marine Mouseketeers, fades, Joker concludes, "I *am* in a world of shit," and wills his mind to focus on a wet dream about a misogynist homecoming "fuck fantasy with Mary Jean Rottencrotch." This too will be unfulfilling and is viewed with a sense of self-disgust. Then, as the credits begin, our ears are invaded by a cry of anguish. It is like a hitherto repressed interior narrative or submerged authorial voice. And as the anguished intervention through song begins just as Kubrick's name comes up on the final credits of the film, it not only qualifies the stoicism and amplifies the horror in Joker's sense of experience of his role in the Vietnam War but also expresses Kubrick's sense of rage and overarching tragic vision of history as socially produced nightmare.

I have to turn my head until my darkness goes . . .
I look inside myself and see my heart is black . . .
Maybe I'll fade away and not have to face the facts
It's not easy when your whole world is black . . .
Paint it black! . . . Paint it black! . . . Paint it black!

The final moments of *Full Metal Jacket* have a wastelandlike intensity that echoes Lear's cry of despair and Kurtz's howl of recognition in the heart of darkness. Yet in one sense the conclusion of the film is incomplete. For a more comprehensive interpretation of the Vietnam era, that is, for perspectives that Kubrick's film excludes, we have to turn to the record of independent film production in the period.

Pierre Macherey, in *A Theory of Literary Production* (1966), has called our attention to the phenomenon of structured absence in art and other forms of communication, to the significance of what is left out of an account of an event, to what has been forgotten, suppressed, repressed, or decontextualized as memory of the past is revised in accord with the prevailing ideological drift. These images can be recovered from the record of independent counter-hegemonic documentary films made in the Vietnam era. They remind us that there was a good deal of resistance to the war and to aspects of American culture and society that sustained the war, both outside and within the armed forces. They correct not only the jingoistic excesses of *The Deer Hunter*, *Rambo II*, and so on, but also the Hobbesian pessimism that is often expressed in *Full Metal Jacket*.

During the Vietnam era, radical films critical of the war or of the injustices of racism and poverty in American society, or sympathetic to Third World revolutions, were widely seen at teach-ins and antiwar cultural events, on campuses, in 16mm cinemas, on television. It was a period in which alienation often led to commitment. The war and the civil rights movement and liberation movements at home and abroad sparked a reevaluation of the premises of life in America that was far more critical than the perspectives of recent Hollywood films about the Vietnam era. The issues were contextualized and interrelated. A general analysis emerges from these films in which the U.S. is seen as having reached a critical point in its development: social happiness, economic democracy, community, equality, freedom, and justice at home and peace in the world could only be attained in the future through a new politics based upon a set of values and priorities very different from those that prevailed in the period of the Cold War and U.S. hegemony in the Third World. The independent film record is one index of the consciousness of the broad and representative movement that flowered in the 1960s and early 1970s. At least 164 16mm documentary films circulating in the U.S. in 1975 focused on the politics and events of the time from a counter-hegemonic perspective.[19] They can be divided into the following subject topics:

1. Films that took as their subject what was called the war at home—the Civil Rights and Black Power Movements, trade union and workers' struggles, prison revolts, student struggles on a range of anticapitalist issues. For example:

. . . a period that was a watershed in American politics—a period of opposition to the war and to the worldview that sustained it.

Angela: Portrait of a Revolutionary; Attica; The Columbia Revolt; Finally Got the News; Don't Bank on America; The Black Panther Party.

2. Films that focused on the antiwar movement within the United States *and* within the Army in Vietnam. For example: *Vietnam Day Berkeley: 1964; The Confrontation at Kent State; The Trial of the Chicago Seven; The Day We Seized the Streets of Oakland; F.T.A.; No Vietnamese Ever Called Me a Nigger.*

3. Films that focused on cultural, economic, and political events in the Third World from a socialist or anti-imperialist perspective. For example: Felix Greene's *China; The Hour of the Furnaces; The Bay of Pigs*, an indictment of the U.S.-sponsored invasion of Cuba.

4. Films that viewed the war in Vietnam from an anti-imperialist perspective. For example: *In the Year of the Pig; Interview with Ho Chi Minh; Interviews with My Lai Vets; Introduction to the Enemy; For a Vietnamese Vietnam.* In some cases documentary films highly critical of the U.S. war in Vietnam were shown on national television: *Inside North Vietnam; The Selling of the Pentagon; Hearts and Minds.*

5. In addition, at least twenty-three films in distribution in the U.S. in 1975 were made by filmmakers in the Democratic Republic of Vietnam or in the liberated zones in the South. They presented the National Liberation Front's and Hanoi's perspective on the war. For example: *Hanoi Tuesday the 13th*; *Our Children Accuse*; *Toxic General Warfare in South Vietnam*; *Ten Girls of Nai Mountain*; *The Tet Offensive*. These communicated the perspective of "the other side" to American audiences.

Thus, during the height of the war, when the Vietnam issue was most controversial, and at the height of the struggle against the war, a large body of films critical of U.S. intervention was in circulation. It focused upon resistance to the war at home and within the armed forces, and included consideration of the Vietnamese perspective.

Films like *Platoon* or *Rambo II* or *The Deer Hunter* cannot heal the American psyche, cannot reconcile lingering divisions in the American people about U.S. involvement in the war in Vietnam or prepare us for the challenges of the 1990s. They do little to enhance our consciousness of history or to clarify our understanding of the political, economic, and ideological factors that sustained the war or that brought the war to an end. Film and television can, however, play a role in this process as they did in the antiwar period. This will require a new language, a new set of images, and a new politics. Recovering the images of the 1960s and deconstructing 1980s Hollywood representations of the Vietnam era is part of a dialectical process through which attempts to create a better America and a better world can progress with a sense of social memory.

NOTES

1. All three films were based upon popular novels. They not only shaped attitudes but also reflected existing conceptions about American history. After the repression and abandonment of Reconstruction, the system of Jim Crow and segregation was established on a legal basis. By the mid-1880s joint memorial services for Civil War veterans North and South were being held. In this period revisionist histories and novels about the Civil War began to be produced. By the end of the century the revisionist interpretation of the Civil War and Reconstruction was hegemonic; by 1912 one of the leading revisionist historians was president of the United States, the chief justice of the U.S. could openly boast that he was a member of the KKK, and the system of white supremecy had been securely reestablished North and South.

2. For example, in *The Birth of a Nation* history is inverted: a black Reconstruction leader is named "Lynch," although it was the KKK that engaged in lynch mob terrorism. The white leader of the abolitionists is named "Stoneman." A set of negative stereotypes defines radicals and Blacks in post-Reconstruction cultural production. There are parallels with the portrayal of radicals and Vietnamese in post-Vietnam era cultural production about the Vietnam war.

3. The term "genre" is used here not to indicate the broad classes of literature (poetry, fiction, and drama) or the modes of tragedy, comedy, and satire but to designate types of popular narratives (print or cinematic) with certain established conventions. For example: the Western, the War Film, and so on. Within each there are subcategories according to the subject (the

Civil War Film, the Vietnam War film) as well as theme (the coming-home film, the antiwar film). For purposes of convenience I will refer to both the major categories and subcategories as "genre films."

4. Analyses of popular culture in the Vietnam era have often proceeded from the concept of "genre." For example: "Formerly hegemonic genres such as the War film and the Western would seem to bear out the argument that the Vietnam War threw established discourse into crisis—certainly the traditional war film had difficulties in representing Vietnam. . . . Douglas Pye, in a seminal article, has argued that a similar fate overtook the Western." See Jeffrey Walsh and Alf Louvre, *Tell Me Lies about Vietnam* (Milton Keynes: Open University Press, 1989), p. 5.

5. For studies of the social implications of the Western as genre see: Will Wright, *Sixguns and Society: A Structural Study of the Western* (Berkeley and Los Angeles: The University of California Press, 1975); Philip French, *Westerns* (New York: Vintage, 1977); John Cawelti, *The Six Gun Mystique* (Bowling Green, Ohio: Bowling Green Press, 1971). For a study of Westerns and the Vietnam era see Michael Klein, "Images From the Movement in the Fast Lane: Radical Protest and the Experience of Defeat," in William Riches, ed., *The Turbulent Decade: The United States in the 1960s* (Coleraine: Irish Association for American Studies Papers, 1988), pp. 69–83.

6. President Ronald Reagan, quoted in the *New York Times*, 1 July 1985.

7. President Woodrow Wilson quoted in Thomas Cripps, "The Reaction of the Negro to the Motion Picture 'The Birth of a Nation,' " in Fred Silva, ed., *Focus on The Birth of a Nation* (Englewood Cliffs, N.J.: Prentice-Hall, 1971), p. 115.

8. Frantz Fanon's best-known writings were published as *The Wretched of the Earth* in translation in English in 1965 and were very influential in the 1960s. Seamus Deane has applied a similar analysis to Irish Catholics in the North of Ireland in "Civilians and Barbarians" in Deane, ed., *Ireland's Field Day* (London: Hutchinson, 1985). Also see Ralph Ellison, *Invisible Man* (New York: Signet, 1952), which explores the marginality of race in the U.S.

9. Dale Dye and Oliver Stone, *Platoon* (New York: Berkley, 1986), back cover.

10. Contrast the representation of the massacre in *Platoon* with the reports of the events given in Joseph Strick's documentary film, *Interviews with My Lai Veterans* (1970).

11. The statement by Chris at the end of the film is reproduced in the Dye and Stone novel of *Platoon*, p. 247.

12. For accounts of the genocidal aspects of U.S. policy in the Vietnam war see: Bertrand Russell, *On the War in Vietnam* (New York: Student Peace Union pamphlet, 1964); Seymour Hersh, *My Lai 4: A Report On the Massacre and Its Aftermath* (New York: Random House, 1970); Jonathan Schell, *The Military Half: An Account of Destruction in Quang Tri and Quant Tin* (New York: Knopf, 1968); *The Failure of Special War* (Hanoi: Vietnamese Studies no. 11, 1966).

13. Vietnamese sources estimate that three-hundred-thousand women became prostitutes in the south of Vietnam under French and U.S. occupation. *The Indochina Newsletter* (U.S.: November/December 1982) estimate is two-hundred-thousand prostitutes. In either case it illustrates how disruptive and decadent the process of neocolonization was.

14. The scenes are recorded in Francine Parker's documentary film *FTA*. We have no sense of this in the film *Full Metal Jacket*, or in the novel from which the film derived: Gustav Hasford, *The Short Timers* (New York: Bantam, 1985).

15. Steve Rees, "A Questioning Spirit: GI's Against the War," in Dick Cluster, ed., *They Should Have Served That Cup of Coffee* (Boston: South End Press, 1977), p. 150, estimates that 200 G.I. antiwar alternative newspapers were published during the war. Colonel Robert D. Heinl, in "The Collapse of the Armed Forces," *Armed Forces Journal*, 7 June 1971, pp. 22–30 estimates 144. In either case it illustrates the scope of opposition and resistance to the war in the U.S. armed forces. This is what the films excise from historical memory. Pierre Macherey calls

attention to the process of "structured absence" in *A Theory of Literary Production* (London: Routledge, 1978). To retrieve some of the alternative counter-hegemonic cultural work produced by the antiwar movement see: Jan Barry, ed., *Winning Hearts and Minds: War Poems by Vietnam Veterans* (Brooklyn: First Casualty Press, 1971); Susan Sontag, "Trip to Hanoi," in Sontag, *Styles of Radical Will* (New York: Delta, 1969), pp. 204–274; Norman Mailer, *The Armies of the Night: History as a Novel/The Novel as History* (London: Weidenfeld and Nicolson, 1968).

16. Reported in the *San Francisco Chronicle,* 23 December 1968.

17. Reported in *The New York Times*, 20 August 1974. These are official U.S. government figures and may understate draft resistance and desertion. Again, the Hollywood post-Vietnam construction of the Vietnam era gives no sense that this took place.

18. Heinl, "The Collapse of the Armed Forces," pp. 30–31: "By every conceivable indicator, our army that now remains in Vietnam is in a state approaching collapse . . . dispirited where not near mutinous."

19. Kathleen Weaver and Linda Artel, eds., *Film Programmers Guide to 16mm Rentals: Third Edition* (California: Reel Research, 1975).

2

RICK BERG

Losing Vietnam:
Covering the War
in an Age of Technology

> What does it mean to win or lose a war? How striking the double meaning
> is in both the words! The first, manifest meaning, certainly refers to the
> outcome of the war, but the second meaning—which creates that peculiar
> hollow space, the sounding board in these words—refers to the totality of
> the war and suggests how the war's outcome also alters the enduring
> significance it holds for us. This meaning says, so to speak, the winner
> keeps the war in hand, it leaves the hands of the loser; it says the winner
> conquers the war for himself, makes it his own property, the loser no
> longer possesses it and must live without it. And he must live not only
> without the war per se but without everyone of its slightest ups and
> downs, every subtlest one of its chess moves, every one of its remotest
> actions. To win or lose a war reaches so deeply, if we follow the
> language, into the fabric of our existence that our whole lives become
> that much richer or poorer in symbols, images, and sources.
>
> *Walter Benjamin, "Theories of German Fascism"*

America won no hearts or minds in Vietnam—it lost them. They went the
way of the war and the country. After April 30, 1975, when the North Vietnamese Army (NVA) unfurled a flag from what had once been the presidential
palace in what had once been Saigon, Vietnam became part of our past. Our
history inherited every escalating incident, and Vietnam, which for the U.S.
had always been more a war than a country, faded from our national collective
attention. Little remained of the war that had been an enduring aspect of many
lives during the 1960s and early 1970s. Still less remained of the country we
wasted to preserve. For Americans, the experience of Vietnam was one of
loss. We lost the war in 1973 and the country in 1975. This loss haunts us.[1]

But the absence that haunted us in the seventies is lost to the eighties. The
war's remains have been resurrected and, like Frankenstein's monster, given
new life. Ten years after Saigon's fall and liberation, Vietnam has become, if
not a commodity, then a resource for the American culture industry. Publishers and producers are working it for all it is worth. Books on Vietnam,
once almost impossible to find in any major chain, now are almost impossible
to avoid. New books appear regularly; older works, long out of print, have
reappeared with glossy new covers, and mass-market publishers distribute
them nationwide.

Editors' Note: Though the issues raised in this article apply to all recent American films about
the Vietnam War, it was written for a special issue of *Cultural Critique* in the spring of 1986.
Consequently, its discussion of specific films focuses on those released prior to that time.

Nor have TV and film producers been slow to exploit the resource. Although TV has been unable to find an agreeable fictional format for the Vietnam War, other than the thinly veiled *M*∗*A*∗*S*∗*H*, it has, since 1975, aired a number of documentaries and news specials. But while it waits for the right fictional vehicle, TV has added the Vietnam vet to its lineup. Via the magic of the flashback, TV heroes from *Miami Vice* to *Magnum, P.I.* have gained a past as well as a quick justification for mayhem and irreverence. There is even, thanks to Coors beer, a television commercial for those "who paid the price."

Film producers are also cashing in on the expanding market. Hollywood is no longer looking away. Capitalizing on the synonymity of "lost" and "missing," *Uncommon Valor* (1983), *Missing in Action* (1984), and *Rambo: First Blood Part II* (1985) have recovered Vietnam, and film audiences everywhere have discovered that what they once imagined lost was only MIA. Hollywood has even recalled the veterans. But, as the recently proposed sequel for *Billy Jack* (1971) implies, the ones they remember are their own creations. The vets in such films as *Search and Destroy* (1981), *First Blood* (1982), *Exterminator I* (1983), and *Fleshburn* (1983) only reflect the vets of earlier films like *The Losers* (1970) or *The Visitors* (1972).

Even music producers have joined in.[2] Although no Britten or Penderecki has composed a *Vietnam Requiem,* country, rock, punk, and New Wave have all made their contributions. From The Clash's "Charlie Don't Surf" to Paul Hardcastle's "19," from Charlie Daniels's ode to the flashback, "Still in Saigon," and Billy Joel's "Goodnight Saigon" to Stevie Wonder's embittered "Front Line," the music industry sings its sad song of Vietnam to a generation that, because of a long silence, knows little more about Vietnam and its victims than the media's revised images. And often the music seems to sing that dependence on past media images. Other media and their images are the subject of the music and their videos. The subject of Paul Hardcastle's "19" video, for example, is not age but just this interdependence of past and present representations of the War.[3] The subject of John Sayles's video for "Born in the U.S.A." negates the media-made myths and supports Springsteen's lyric by wrenching an image of Vietnam away from the former media-made doxa and wedding it to a class perspective.

In Country, the most recent addition to the growing body of fiction on Vietnam, exploits this awareness of our dependence on the media.[4] Samantha Hughes, the seventeen-year-old heroine, finds herself trying to come to terms with a Vietnam that she only experiences as a loss. Almost twenty years after, like a female Telemachus, she attempts to find her lost father and his war, but ends, like Penelope, weaving and unravelling her inherited texts. Like the child in *Tender Mercies* (1983), Sam Hughes has a lost a father, KIAed in his irresponsible adolescence, and has a disturbed Uncle Emmett, ailing from the probable effects of Agent Orange, and an impotent vet lover. She knows nothing of 'Nam other than the multitude of representations that signify our loss: her father's letters and his journal, Springsteen's lyrics and their accompanying video. Nothing is authentic. Even the *M*∗*A*∗*S*∗*H* episodes are reruns. She is the subject of distances and displacements. When Emmett finally tells her a war story—one of those ever present horror stories authenticating the vet while it drives a wedge between him and the community—Sam can respond only by comparing it to pictures she has seen. In short, Sam Hughes is today's child suffering yesterday's trauma. She suffers a modernist nostalgia for authentic experience. Desiring to know and experience the lost war, she remains unsatisfied with her representations. Mason has bequeathed our desire for 'Nam to the next generation.

Vietnam *remains,* then, regardless of the ritual cleansings and willed suspensions of memory, regardless of the scope memorials for the unknown dead and the parades for the soldiers who should have known better. And while it remains, it stays a problem, or to be more precise, the remains of Vietnam are problematic. What is left of the war, its fragments and its ruins, stays unrepressible and endlessly recuperable. The many mutations mark not merely the continuing effort to misrepresent what has been lost as merely missing and possibly recoverable; they also mark the failure of our modes of cultural representation. None of the transformations satisfy. The illusion, so necessary to particular values, fails. Vietnam succeeds in challenging and foiling the ideological apparatus's modes of production. These ruins and fragments of Vietnam—these mutable, protean images—compose a history of recuperation that signifies not only our desperate desire to win the lost war, to conquer and possess it, to make it our own property, as Benjamin suggests, but also Vietnam's continuing liberation. Our fetishized desire to win defeats us. With each imagined success, we only picture our loss.

At first America took its loss on the chin, recovering with the slogan "peace with honor." And as we watched the POWs emerge from the plane in 1973, no one even noticed that America had lost her first war. Like the POWs, the country was released, and the release signified an end, not a loss. The country, warweary like the returning vets and POWs, needed to heal its wounds and forget the trauma—or so the official and popular rhetoric ran. For the national health and welfare, Vietnam and its effects, the war and its remains, were to be decently repressed and forgotten, buried like the three-hundred-dollar aluminum coffins.[5]

At this time, and it seems peculiar now, the war's loss was marked by its absence from the marketplace. Vietnam was gone. It was unavailable in either of the two contending clearinghouses of information: neither the academy nor the culture industry, neither pedagogues nor producers, classrooms nor TV recalled Vietnam. Whether because of a lack of commitment on the part of the culture industry or because of a sense of "good taste" on the part of the academy, information about Vietnam prior to 1980 was spotty. What had been all too present, almost omnipresent, seemed to disappear. Vietnam's apparent absence from both markets, the sigh of its end, became a simulacrum of its loss.

For years homes all over the country had been flooded with scenes from Vietnam.[6] TV news shows like *ABC Scope*, NBC's *Vietnam Weekly Review*, and CBS's *Vietnam Perspective* brought the war home.[7] It rushed into living rooms. But wars in the living room are not unusual. World War II had been a radio war.[8] Like radio, TV brought the war home, but unlike radio it did not so much report the war or even dramatize it as witness the event actually happening. The family at home watched the front (not altogether a negligible, geographic metaphor, since it displays our desire to map the war even as we blocked and subdivided the country) and witnessed the firefights. Parents had the pleasure of seeing their children or the children of others blown away right before the weather and just after the sports roundup (or so we who were fighting the war often imagined this grotesque evening ritual). The family had what appeared to be an intimate acquaintance with Vietnam, even though the correspondent's reportage (which would change during the course of the war) mediated it all.

But what the viewer saw on the nightly news only passed itself off as direct and objective, and therefore, by the logic of association, unmediated and real. The medium of television journalism, with its quality of self-effacement, created an illusion of reality, an illusion so stylized that it could be re-created for the TV film *Special Bulletin* (1983).[9]

The trick is in the photography. The photographer's *cinéma vérité* style effaces its technology and intervention, thus translating the production of the "real," the real production, into a "capturing of reality."[10] By means of this TV magic—which conjured up and transmitted the "real" war to the "World"—Vietnam, the war and the country, became for the American viewer a set of transparent signs, signifying at one and the same time "reality" and Vietnam. They were interlocked, especially when TV's master authorized each evening's fare with his signature—"and that's the way it was."[11]

After 1973, Vietnam faded from the screen. The living room war was gone: the major networks took it off the air. It was as if TV cancelled the war, and then the president recalled the actors. Between 1973 and 1977 a respectful silence seemed to reign. At this time, journalists wrote a number of articles about the forgotten war. According to many, the culture industries seemed to have called a moratorium on works dealing with Vietnam, unless they dealt with the fact that it was forgotten. Vietnam, however, made a brief return on April 29, 1975, when the three networks aired *Vietnam: A War That Is Finished*; *Special Report: Seven Thousand, Three Hundred Eighty-two Days in Vietnam*; and *Vietnam: Lessons Learned, Prices Paid*. They were received, however, as interesting but unwarranted interruptions.

In 1985, the crews returned. Ted Koppel, perched on a balcony overlooking Ho Chi Minh City, attempted to interview Le Duc Tho. The TV cameras watched the troops parade down a major thoroughfare, and newscasters, those insipid heroes of Vietnam, continued to exploit the Vietnamese. Between commercials, television even touted its own technological achievements, showing the viewer how it was receiving a direct and immediate image from Vietnam via the miracle of satellites, while also showing those who were looking how television was again selling itself as an unmediated, therefore objective, window onto the world. Not many troubled to look, least of all newsmen.

Nor did it seem to trouble newscasters, during most of the ten-year-anniversary news specials, that although there seemed to be a major revision of the history of the war, the war we saw "beneath" all those omniscient voice-overs was the same war we had always seen. The same nameless man was summarily executed on the same nameless street in Saigon. The same nameless bodies were dragged by their heels from the Embassy, and the same nameless marines fought in the streets of Hue. Although the words of the faceless narrators declared a new understanding, it was obviously one that had little to do with how the cameras saw and defined the war. According to TV's revisions, the correspondents might have misunderstood the war, but they understood brilliantly the nature of representations. In the process, TV displayed yet another forgotten lesson, learned by Michael Herr, who, like other journalists, had gone to 'Nam to "watch": "You were as responsible for everything you saw as you were for everything you did."[12]

The television news had attempted to rewrite its original take on Vietnam, but TV producers seem unable to come up with the right formula for fictionalizing the "living room war," even though *M*A*S*H* kept the war on TV ten years after it was lost. Films like *A Rumor of War* (1980) and *Friendly Fire* (1979) were made for TV and aired, but network shows concerning Vietnam have been scarce.[13] In 1985, for example, CBS spent a million dollars attempting to turn Anthony Grey's *Saigon* into a miniseries before it cancelled the project, just as the networks toyed with projects for sitcoms in the early eighties. But little came of them: 'Nam is still an anathema.

During the war, programs like *Combat, The Rat Patrol, Garrison's Gorillas*, and *Gomer Pyle, U.S.M.C.*, plus the usual fare of World War II flicks, aired nightly. Only such a rare exception as *The Final War of Ollie Winter* (1967) dared compete with the nightly news version of the war in Vietnam, and it flopped.[14] TV, then, took a lesson from Hollywood. Instead of airing 'Nam directly, it pictured Vietnam by representing the veteran. For instance, in 1969 ABC aired the TV film *The Ballad of Andy Crocker*, a story about a returning vet who discovers that the "World" has changed.[15] The film was unpretentious but unusual. Unlike the POW (Martin Landau) in *Welcome Home, Johnny Bristol* (1971) or the three crippled veterans in *Beg, Borrow, or Steal* (1974), who pull off the perfect heist, Andy Crocker was neither psychotic nor criminal, merely alienated and marginalized.

For a number of years that was the TV vet. Like his film counterpart, he would play a strung-out, criminal psychotic who could go off at the sound of a backfire. During the 1974 TV season, for instance, the vet was seen as a hired killer on *Colombo*, as a drug-dealing sadistic murderer on *Mannix*, as a suspected yet innocent murderer on *The Streets of San Francisco*, as a shakedown artist on *Cannon*, and as a "returned hero" who "blew up himself, his father and a narcotics lab" on *Hawaii Five-O*.[16] In each instance, the vet threatens law and order, with a criminality founded on his tour in 'Nam.

Some time would elapse before intervening veterans groups persuaded TV to stop confusing the veteran with the war; even as the more offensive aspects were muted in the media, the character of the Vietnam vet had been drawn and determined.

Where the early 1970s had depicted him—never her—as a mad threat to law and order, the late 1970s turned him into an always irreverent, slightly crazed eccentric who was subject to the occasional flashback. The professional soldiers of a film like *Welcome Home, Soldier Boys* (1972), who massacred the town of Hope, New Mexico, became the *A-Team*. Now the TV vet works either as a cop, a private eye or, in the case of *Lou Grant*, as a photographer for a large metropolitan newspaper, where diagnosed as the mild-mannered "Animal," he photographs the "World." The former object of representation has become the representer. *Simon and Simon* can even turn the original crazed vet stereotype into a plot device: the "Phantom" vandalizing an American theme park is not a demented vet carrying out a psychotic vendetta against his old commanding officer; on the contrary, the phantom vet has so-called *good reasons* for destroying the park. The criminal threat to law and order of the early 1970s has become, by the early 1980s, a vigilante hero, a true "Victor" Charlie, committed to truth and justice.

By the late seventies, TV's attitude toward 'Nam had waffled. The networks even considered projects for sitcoms.[17] MTM developed *The Bureau* for CBS.[18] CBS had been interested in an earlier project, *Mike Freit*.[19] NBC developed *The 6:00 Follies*, and ABC tried with *Bringing It Home*, which went nowhere, and again with *Fly Away Home*, which ended as a summer movie.[20] These projects have a number of similarities. With one exception, *The 416*, "a comedy pilot about a group of misfit reserves called to active duty in Vietnam," none dealt with troops fighting the war.[21] When it came time to find a pilot for a Vietnam sitcom, TV turned, in narcissistic fashion, to the makers of the living room war. Most of the pilots included not only a major black character (*Mike Freit* and *The 6:00 Follies*) but several photojournalists (*Mike Freit* and *Fly Away Home*) or news service reporters who were "a conduit for getting the word out." What doctors had done for Korea, journalists would do for Vietnam—display the unvarnished, liberal truth.

But the initial paradox, the ground for all of *M*A*S*H*'s liberal outrage, is not present. It is one thing to be a doctor in the service of the military, since saving lives and taking them are at odds, but it is another thing to be a correspondent in the service of a war, where journalists made reputations reporting that truth had become the "first casualty." For instance, the central character in the pilot *Fly Away Home*, Carl Danton (Bruce Boxleitner), a newsreel cameraman, is told: "Forget the big picture. We're into miniatures. Combat footage is a cinch for the 6 o'clock news."[22] Besides the obvious reference to TV's displacement of film (big picture by miniatures) or even the implied critique of military propaganda, "The Big Picture," there is also a recognition that TV news produced a vision of the Vietnam War. Once TV began to represent what was being reported in Vietnam as untrue, the stereotype of the committed war correspondent began to unravel.

But for all their failures, these shows offer an insight into TV's understanding of its relation to Vietnam and its participation in the war. In these shows, we see TV defining its own flaws, creating its own dimensions, signifying its own place in history, willing to picture itself as a technology of production, but not as a site of distribution, or an intrusion into living rooms where participants become passive viewers and eyewitnesses. *The 6:00 Follies*, for instance, a sitcom about the Armed Forces TV network in Saigon, is about television watching itself. It is TV seeing itself covering Vietnam and being covered by the war. According to the show's writers, "The characters oppose the war, but their opportunities to express that opposition on the air are limited. They're generally confined to reporting the Army point of view, even when they know the truth. They do manage to get off a word now and then but generally their conduit for getting the truth out will be a news service reporter."[23] In this case, TV pictures itself as a maligned and manipulated technology sending out a version of the war, but not to some estranged public back "in the World," fixed by TV's evil eye and turned into voyeurs, but to those "in country." The misinformed viewers become those fighting the war, already understood as uninformed: "The soldiers could actually get instant replay. They could fight in a battle and see it on the news that night" (occasionally true, but hardly the rule, a situation more relevant to antiwar demonstrators than to combat troops). By 1979, TV had tried to rewrite the war, its combatants, and its role. The theater of war ironically became the living room, an inversion that David Rabe had already exploited in *Sticks and Bones*. The dirty work of war was lost in its spectacle.

If television producers floundered and quit, film producers fared somewhat better. During the war they seemed unwilling to compete with the nightly news. Unlike World War II, when the film industry could serve both itself and the country by placing a screen between the war and the viewer, a screen that veiled the war as it displayed it, Vietnam could not be readily accommodated by such a framing. Television had apparently eliminated the distance between the "World" and the war, rending the veil so necessary for producing and screening war films, rescinding the license for fictional re-creation.[24]

Throughout the war, film companies and publishers seemed to follow TV's example, or at least its impulse, toward documentary realism. A number of books, for instance, published during and just after the war bear the imprint of either a diary or a simple chronology. Their titles give the impression that they are catalogues of events recorded as they occurred: *365 Days*, *Vietnam Diary*, and *The War Year*. A reading proves the first impression wrong. Film producers, also appearing to compete with television's realistic version, invested in documentaries. Some, like the *Anderson Platoon* (1966), were shown on TV. Others, like the fictional *P.O.W.* (1973), used a documentary style. Still others, like *A Face of War* (1967) and *Hearts and Minds* (1975), revealed television's influence because they insisted on documenting the real war, the one seen on TV, whether it was the Big Picture—the history of American involvement in Vietnam—or the day-to-day grind of a marine grunt company.

Unlike the nightly news, however, *A Face of War* and *Hearts and Minds* unwittingly reveal the devices of their intervention. The anthropomorphism of their titles, for example, signals their mediation. What we see more clearly here than on TV is how the directors, Eugene Jones and Peter Davis respectively, wanted the war to look (as if the war had *looks*, or could ever be an object of sight). And it was to look like TV. For example, *Hearts and Minds*, unlike *In The Year of the Pig* (1969) or Nick MacDonald's *The Liberal War* (1972), contextualizes Vietnam not only within TV's purview but also within a sentimental understanding of American history.[25] It finds the failures in the brightest and the best, as well as in certain cultural predilections—in our "hearts and minds," as it were. The film never suggests that the best and the brightest are hardly separable from the failures and the predilections. People make history out of conditions they inherit, and often the conditions are as responsible for the people as the people are for the failures. Hence a simple changing of people's minds or hearts, as the film suggests, does not insure success. This absence of an historical understanding from a film wedded to the lessons of history is troubling, especially when the film ends worrying the question, Will the lessons of Vietnam be recalled in the future?

The future has proven that they have not. As a historical document, an ideological product, not simply an historical documentary, *Hearts and Minds* records some of the reasons why. Witness the film's final minutes. It ends several seconds after the credits roll over a parade: the state triumphs—its forces are marshalled and its power flaunted—children in uniform, Uncle Sam in red, white, and blue all go up the road; viewers cheer. During this triumph, an incident occurs: some people on the sidelines are demonstrating—the crowd jeers, paraders flip off the demonstrators, and the cops roust the protestors by busting heads. At the film's end, after the credits, we discover that a veterans' group was protesting for jobs. We see the forces of the state win back the war by beating back the losers. Vietnam's countermemory (which oral narratives like *Nam and Bloods* will later recover) is marginalized as the state obscures the "voice" of those who fought in the war.

But *Hearts and Minds* is not innocent. It helped legitimize revisionary tactics by, for example, placing the vets *after* the credits and on the *margin* of the screen and film, where few if any will hear what they say. For instance, throughout the film anyone in uniform is portrayed as vulgar, politically naive, or reactionary. Ask a grunt during a firefight whether he thinks the war is right or not, then forget that he has his mind on something else. Picture two servicemen in a whorehouse treating women as commodities and ignore the various mutinies and the two brig riots that occurred in country in 1968.[26] Never bother to recall those who "found the guts to just call it all off and refuse to ever go out anymore."[27] These omissions mark the uniformed as the uninformed. At best, the soldier, according to *Hearts and Minds*, is a young, ignorant victim, barely able to think for himself, and not the victim of class and economic deprivation. Only upon release or after he had been wounded beyond repair could the vet, according to the film, let his hair down in the manner of the antiwar demonstrators and come to his right mind. But even these moments, with a glimpse of Dewey Canyon III, are all too brief. There is no awareness in *Hearts and Minds* that the soldier is a victim of class and economic deprivation. *Hearts and Minds* retains its enlightened perspective, then, because of clichés and at the expense of what those who "fought *in* the war" already knew. Hence the lessons from war end by justifying this film's perspective. And those soldiers who speak that point of view become eccentric and marginal because they are untypical.

But if *Hearts and Minds* sees 'Nam this way, *A Face of War* sees it in another way. In this film, the marines of Mike Company are well-meaning young heroes, curing the old and presiding over births only to get killed or wounded for their pains. In our time of *Rambo*, *A Face of War* stands as a needed corrective, asserting its view of way against Stallone's silly spectacle of glory. But instead of picturing the war with all its tediousness and dirty work, *A Face of War* unwittingly documents nothing less than a documentary's inability to see the war in Vietnam. At a loss to see Vietnam, or even its own inability to see it, as Godard did in *Far from Vietnam* (1967), it can only record a group of marines acting as the Corps would have marines act if they were playing in a classic Hollywood war film. *A Face of War* becomes, then, a real live training film with real live dead.

Its narrative is not unlike World War II films. Each scene is part of a series of ever escalating incidents in which the marines start out as moving targets and end up destroying the "no-name" ville. In a final scene, Amtracs arrive to evacuate the people. As they plow onto the screen, an old woman scurries out of their way. The might of our technology towers over the tiny people. The Amtracs neatly swallow the villagers, and when the latter are taken away, the collective might of our technology destroys their homes. The action that leads to this final conflagration is framed by "the patrol"—a metaphor drawn from World War II films. In the beginning, we see a patrol forming up; at the end we see the same patrol going out. The film closes with the credits rolling over a close-up of each marine: his name, rank, and hometown listed on the bottom of the screen. All this is coupled with a whistled tune supplementing the credits and helps turn *A Face of War* into the typical Hollywood war film, in which the name of the actor and his character are given as he marches off screen.

A Face of War, then, is hardly the documentary it pretends to be. With its final sequence (flames spewing from the barrel of a flame tank, E-1 Amtracs launching missiles with a quarter-ton of C-4 trailing behind like a kite tail), its focused camera work, and its almost seamless suturing, *A Face of War* becomes a Hollywood film singing the praises of American *techne*. The war never even intrudes on the film. Even when the war's sudden explosions mar the immaculate focus, it does not rupture the film's suturing. These outbursts are neatly folded back into the film. As they are repeated, they become a sign, a transition from peace and quiet to sudden death and maiming. The loss of Vietnam is apparent. And *Face of War* declares itself to be merely the surface of war, which, no doubt, is the only face it has.

Yet it is a surface audiences seem to crave. Fed a steady diet of TV's illusion of realism, audiences seem unwilling to suspend their belief where Vietnam is concerned. Fictional accounts and devices seem forbidden. The conveniences of fictional representation are not tolerated. Reviewers did not tolerate Wayne's *Green Berets* (1968) tampering with the real for the sake of production values (for example, sun setting in the South China Sea), nor did they tolerate the poetic license of Russian roulette in *The Deer Hunter* (1978). "Capturing the reality" of Vietnam on film, as if it were always escaping, is a necessary claim of the Vietnam War film. With the loss of the war, however, the camera lost its object. Unable to re-create the proper aspects that audiences seemed to demand, filmmakers resorted to inserting old news footage. In 'Nam films, this tradition goes back at least to Fuller's *China Gate* (1957). It is reported that in *Full Metal Jacket*, Stanley Kubrick's and Michael Herr's adaptation of Gustave Hasford's *The Short-Timers*, Kubrick is going to use the same special effects Woody Allen used in *Zelig*. Scheduled to be released late in 1986, the movie, instead of using location shots, is being filmed in a deserted London gasworks against a backdrop of news footage with the actors placed into historical footage of the actual events.

This continuing desire to see what we take for the real war, the real Vietnam, obscures any other understanding of Vietnam, as well as any other form of understanding. Our revisions are not rewritings or resightings, merely repetitions that sublate difference. With every repetition of these real TV images from Vietnam, we witness a continued insistence on sublimating an unstable historical understanding by means of a violated ideology. Our fidelity to certain pictures and certain modes of picturing underwrite what we know as well as how we know. The recurring TV images stabilize our understanding and fix the past with known images. They reassert a naive epistemology that ignores and mystifies technology's role in their production and maintenance. Seeing is still knowing. We leave the films not only assured that we still know what Vietnam was and what it was all about, but also that our ways of knowing are still intact.

Hence Hollywood did and did not look away from the war in Vietnam. For Hollywood, Vietnam—both the country and the war—seemed to be just off-screen, at the edge and on the frontier, always about to be found. As in most other things, Hollywood helped discover it for the American public. But in the early films, Vietnam is like Morocco in *Casablanca* (1942), exotic and marginal, the end of the earth where criminals and soldiers of fortune retreat, a place without an indigenous population, culture, history, or politics, never a nation, hardly a peninsula, not even a domino, merely a space on a map signifying imperialism's history and its frayed ends. Some twenty years before John Wayne landed with his Green Berets, Alan Ladd met Veronica Lake in

Not a complimentary picture of Vietnamese women, "Lucky Legs" is a half-caste whore.

Saigon (1948). But from all accounts, the film is little more than an extended version of *Terry and the Pirates*. The next year Dick Powell in *Rogues' Regiment* (1948) joined the Foreign Legion to track down a German war criminal. But even a brief battle with guerilla forces failed to demystify either Vietnam or the enemy.[28]

Like the war, this enemy is not fully discovered until 1952, when Sam Katzman's *A Yank in Indo-China* was released. We fought in this war against this enemy for the next twelve years, sometimes *as* the French in *Jump into Hell* (1955), sometimes *with* the French in *China Gate* (1957), and finally alone in *Five Gates To Hell* (1959), *Brushfire* (1961), and *A Yank in Viet-Nam* (1964). As inhabitants of this hell, the enemy is duly depicted. Like the Centaurs of Dante's *Inferno* or Caliban of the Enchanted Isle, they are known by their irrepressible sexual habits. Hence the guerilla leader, Neville Brand, in *Five Gates to Hell* lets his men rape the five nurses he has captured, even as the enemy leader in *Brushfire* rapes Easter, the wife of an American planter, just as six years later the VC in *The Green Berets* (1968) will rape and torture the young Moi girl.

These dozen years also witnessed Hollywood's initial responses to history's changes, and, as it would in the future, Hollywood responded by changing its signs, not its mind. After the Vietnamese liberated themselves from the French, the Yank who had been in "Indo-China" in 1952 returned to "Viet-Nam" in 1964; *The Quiet American* of 1958 became *The Ugly American* of

In the early films, Vietnam is . . . exotic and marginal, the end of the earth. . . . Alan Ladd met Veronica Lake in Saigon.

1963, and finally the *Brushfire* of 1961 became a full-scale Hell no longer encompassed in a small place. By 1965, after the French had *Lost Command* (1966), the Yank in Viet-Nam, Marshall Thompson, returned *To the Shores of Hell* (1966) with the marines. Like the films that had come before *Brushfire* and *China Gate* and those that would follow *The Green Berets*, such as *Apocalypse Now* and *Rambo*, he arrived with a mission and a definite goal in mind: he sets out on a patrol to rescue his brother.

Regardless of the changes, then, Hollywood continued to imagine and still remembers U.S. involvement in Vietnam according to a particular paradigm—the patrol with a definite mission. Hence it imagined the conflict occurring not in a particular place or landscape with a particular population, history, and politics, but in a cinematic frame with a beginning and an end. The patrol mounts up at some safe origin and proceeds through enemy territory until it reaches its goal: sometimes a rescue mission, often a surprise attack on an unsuspecting enemy. Vietnam, for Hollywood and hence for us, became something to walk through.

Samuel Fuller's *China Gate* (1957) has a patrol with a mission and an object: blow up the Commie ammunition dump at China Gate. It also has Communists with barely repressible sexual habits, an international French unit, and a small native child and his puppy seeking refuge with the military. It even has a political endorsement disguised as a history lesson. *China Gate* opens with documentary footage of peasants working in rice fields. A voice-over tells us: "This motion picture is dedicated to France. More than three hundred years ago, French missionaries were sent to Indochina to teach love of God and love of fellow man. Gradually French influence took shape in the Vietnamese land. Despite many hardships, they advanced their way of living and the thriving nation became the rice bowl of Asia." Then we are told that this prosperous country is now under attack by Moscow's puppet, Ho Chi Minh. The rest of the film follows the politics of this opening lesson. Vietnam, like Korea, is a state under siege, where professional soldiers like the Americans Brock (Gene Barry) and Goldie (Nat "King" Cole) go to continue their fight against communism.

China Gate also has a woman: Lia, or "Lucky Legs" (Angie Dickinson) as the French call her, is a half-caste hustler with a child, son of the American Brock. Both she and the boy are caught in the struggle. She wants the boy to go to America, because she doesn't want him "killed, carrying a gun at fifteen, or becoming a Communist." In order to assure his safe passage, she agrees to lead a patrol of French Legionnaires to China Gate, the hidden ammunition dump. Part Asian, part Western, Lucky Legs can "pass," and she does so easily, moving through the two worlds of French-occupied towns and Communist fortresses. On the one hand, she is Lia, wife and mother; on the other, she is "Lucky Legs," object of desire, signified by particular parts of her body. She is not the dependent she ought to be. Too often she is pictured as resourceful, independent, and intelligent—walking point and leading the patrol. As her American husband Brock had discovered, she looked one way but turned out to be another—Lucky Legs is dangerous. Like the young Vietnamese girl in *Go Tell the Spartans* (1978), she is the monstrous unknown "other" whose looks tell us nothing more than that looks deceive.

Not a complementary picture of Vietnamese women, "Lucky Legs" is a half-caste whore, with intelligence and a willed independence; but considering the history of women in Vietnam films, Lia is unusual, since she anticipates not our continued misunderstanding of the Vietnamese but the signs of our misunderstanding.[29] On the one hand, she is both the object and the subject of sight; on the other, she is the site of its ambivalence. Lucky Legs undermines epistemology's tropes of sight. Through her we learn not to trust what we see while we learn to look at the seen and our ways of seeing.

She teaches us, then, how to read the film, for what we see is not what we get. In one scene, the patrol must pass a Moi village, friendly to the Communists. Lucky Legs will lead them through. She enters the ville while the patrol waits. In their last ambush the Moi have captured a phonograph along with a record of "La Marseillaise." She asks the Moi chief if he knows what he is playing; he says he does not, but that it makes him feel good. He asks, "What is it?" "The song of the people," she replies. While the patrol passes in the night, Lucky Legs, standing on a platform beneath pictures of Mao, Stalin, and Ho, leads the villagers in the song of the people. The pictured three would no doubt be pleased with the ambiguity.

Almost ten years later John Wayne, with the same politics yet with less assurance and ambiguity, will tell the same story in *The Green Berets*. One of the two episodes in the film uses a woman as lure and a VC general as the object of the hunt. The story, an odd coda, is tagged onto what is already a two-hour "Western." Its authority is no doubt Robin Moore's book. Still it bears a remarkable resemblance to *China Gate*. But Lin (Irene Tsu) in *The Green Berets* is hardly Fuller's Lia. In short, Lin fulfills the role of all women in *The Green Berets*, as well as in most Vietnam narratives. She is an object of desire, one of the South's "top models" (unlike her counterpart in Moore's book, who is a schoolteacher), and a potential victim. Like his World War I Creel Committee predecessors (for example, D. W. Griffith *Hearts of the World* [1917]), Wayne gives women a strict role in war. Either the allies protect them or the enemy rapes them. In either case, women signify not only the enemy's unnatural desires and natural inferiority but also that war is always man's work.

The Green Berets's failures are legendary. Renata Adler, then of *The New York Times,* saw it as a "pivotal event" representing "the end of the traditional war picture and a tremendous breakdown of the fantasy-making apparatus in this country."[30] She was wrong. It did not take the glamor out of war, only the romance out of war films. There was no suspension of disbelief. It was, as Herr says, "a film about Santa Monica," or, as Joker, Hasford's protagonist in *The Short Timers*, puts it when he sees the film in Da Nang on Freedom Hill, "it is a soap opera about the love of guns." In short, like Hasford's marines, we saw *The Green Berets* as a movie: "The audience of Marines roars with laughter. This is the funniest movie we have seen in a long time. . . . At the end of the movie, John Wayne walks off into the sunset with a spunky little orphan. The grunts laugh and threaten to pee all over themselves. The sun is setting in the South China Sea—in the East—which makes the end of the movie as accurate as the rest of it."[31] Like its sign, the green beret, which the Vietnamese always associated with the French, the film flaunts the marks of its own breakdown. Hence its ultimate success. What in essence failed was the viewer, not the ideological apparatus, for the film itself calls attention to the means of its making.

The Green Berets is nothing if not a lecture on the failings of representations and the necessity of "seeing for oneself." From the opening scene at Fort Bragg, when the squad marches on to instruct the audience on the "capabilities of the Green Beret," to the briefing scene that follows, the film insists upon the primacy of sight and the authority of experience. Colonel Kirby (John Wayne) tells Beckworth (David Janssen) on at least two occasions that one cannot really understand Vietnam or know the war until one sees it. What the film represents and teaches—for, after all, it is only a long lecture— is that the war can be seen (although what can be seen is left off the screen) and we can know nothing until we see it for ourselves. Seeing is knowing. *The Green Berets* claims to tell us, then, that representations are fraudulent, even as it requires us to look at it *as* a representation. The film sacrifices its own validity for its belief in the primacy of experience, and ends by representing the "failure of the fantasy-making apparatus."

With the failure (or success) of *The Green Berets*, the search for knowledge supplants the earlier films' assured sense of a mission. The earlier films had a direct goal in mind. They knew where they were headed, and what they wanted. The later films do not even know where they are, much less why they are. After Wayne's folly, the films become epistemological dramas. Each attempts to find a means for knowing and understanding the war. *The Boys in Company C* (1978), *Go Tell the Spartans* (1978), and *Apocalypse Now* (1979) all turn, each in its own way, on the notion of war as an arena of maturation and education, a place where boys become men, and a realm where lessons are learned, surely in contradiction with the first lesson learned in war: many boys never mature into anything other than dead souls. From the imperative of Ted Post's title (*Go Tell The Spartans*) to the voice-over monologue that begins *The Boys in Company C*, the films seem determined to inform and instruct the audience. But all they tell us, all they can teach is that the tropes of epistemology fail. Seeing is not knowing. The inexplicable grunt tic, "there it is," sums up all that is seen and known. Like the enemy, the war in Vietnam dissipates as an object of sight. It is lost to the eye, even as our films assert the authority of the eyewitness. Even in *Apocalypse Now,* where the war becomes spectacle and the warrior both voyeur and voyager (hence a metonymy for the camera), there is nothing in sight but the end. In grand operatic terms complete with the appropriate apocalyptic tone, we witness the twilight of the idols of sight. Post's *Go Tell The Spartans* does the same thing less pretentiously. Nothing in this film remains unquestioned, unexamined, or unknown. Everyone asks questions; everyone receives answers. Before the film is over, we know why aging Major Barker (Burt Lancaster) is still a major, although his old aide is now a general. We find out why the draftee Courcey (Craig Wesson) has, in 1964, volunteered for a tour in Vietnam: like Philip Caputo's protagonist in *A Rumor of War*, he just wanted to know "what a war was like." We even find out where we are.

> Barker asks his Adjunct, "Where are we?"
> The Adjunct answers, "Penang Vietnam."
> "You sure it's not a loony bin," Barker replies.
> "Sometimes I think we're in a goddam loony bin."

Nothing remains unknown, except the nature of the enemy and the Vietnamese people. We see them—often. They charge the garrison at Muc Wa in the full light of flares. Courcey even spots a VC scout, who becomes nothing less than his own "secret sharer."[32] We even see the friendly Vietnamese, but we learn that the young female refugee's longing looks are hardly loving: the interpreter, Cowboy (Evan Kim), tells us "she is VC." But in fact, according to the film, we do not know them at all, even though "the VC know everything we're going to do." According to the company medic, the Vietnamese do not know why they are fighting. There is no reason why one should fight and die for the South or one should fight and die for the North. They are interchangeable because neither side cares or knows why they are fighting. This piece of wisdom becomes the film's central lacuna: we know everything, including the fact that the enemy knows everything about us but nothing about politics. Hardly the facts, but an extremely telling characterization of ourselves and our understanding. Unlike the Australian film on Vietnam, *The Odd Angry Shot* (1979), Post's film suggests that our cinematic imaginations are incapable of dealing with the politics of war. The troops in these American films are at best tourists, while the VC remain an invisible enemy. They only become visible and political for the American public when the U.S. government controls the ideological apparatus, as in *Know Your Enemy—The Viet Cong.*[33]

Thus we often leave the films of the war in Vietnam as Willard (Martin Sheen) leaves the besieged bridge in *Apocalypse Now*, refusing to hear or understand. As Willard moves through the trenches, he keeps asking if anyone knows who is in charge. No one answers. But at the end, immediately after Roach, the black grenadier, knocks out the noisy but unseen VC, Willard asks, "Do you know who is in charge?" "Yes," Roach answers, then sits down. The answers have always been lucid, but never clear.

At the end of *Go Tell the Spartans*, Courcey looks at the wounded VC, his secret sharer, in the treeline and says, "I'm going home, Charlie." He turns his back on his other and drags his wounded leg off the screen. After the defeat of *The Green Berets*, Hollywood, like Courcey, returned home. Filmmakers moved the war and relocated it in a more tractable environment. Since the usual mode for producing the war—documentary as simulacrum—was restrictive at best, the ever resourceful image-makers found another means of (re)presenting the war to the Americans. As the war continued to escalate, Hollywood discovered the returning vet, and this synecdoche became the major means of reproducing the war. The Vietnam vet came to stand for the prejudices and contradictions that the home folks had about the war, for, after all, the essential quality of the veteran is that he has internalized the war and with a stiff upper lip carries it around with him. Thus Hollywood could take the notion of the returning vet and fill it with the country's sense of Vietnam. In this way, it freed itself from making pictures about the war that only reproduced what TV had already shown, while it maintained the essential characteristic of both the war film and TV journalism—the eyewitness.

By displacing the war and locating it in the veteran, however, these films eventually took a peculiar turn. For unlike such films as *The Best Years of Our Lives* (1946) or *Till the End of Time* (1946), which imply that violence is merely part of the returning vet's readjustment period, films about returning Vietnam vets made in the late sixties and early seventies share a dominant structural feature: "In each case, he [the vet] is a catalyst for violence if not violent himself."[34] Although films like *I'll Be Seeing You* (1944), John Huston's suppressed *Let There Be Light* (1945), or Abraham Polonsky's radio play *The Case of David Smith* (1945),[35] written for *Reunion U.S.A.*, suggest that psychoneurosis was a problem, it is not the World War II vet who is remembered as suffering.[36] (Hollywood would wait until 1985 before making a film about a World War II vet suffering from flashbacks, and even then *Desert Bloom* was not released). It is the vet from Vietnam whom Hollywood represents as essentially a maladjusted sociopath. Film titles like *The Born Losers* (1967), *Angels from Hell* (1968), and *The Stone Killer* (1973) not only convey the country's ambivalent attitude toward Vietnam, they also show what others thought of the "Vietnam vet." In the beginning, the vet is associated with outlaw bikers. The position these gangs hold within popular culture explains the relation. Since *The Wild One* (1954), biker gangs have come to signify a marginal and irreconcilable counterculture whose members work within the dominant culture but are hardly part of it. Hence the gang films signify and sublate class differences for sociopathic behavior. In early films like *The Angry Breed* (1969) or *Chrome and Hot Leather* (1971), when the vet opposes the gang, or in *Angels From Hell* (1968), when he rides with them, the vet is merely being placed in a marginal world where he "fights with the gang," as it were. For instance, *The Born Losers* (1967) presents Tom Laughlin as Billy Jack (soon to become a sixties folk hero), a Native American Green Beret veteran who single-handedly takes on and defeats a gang of motorcyclists who, à la *The Wild One*, have terrorized a California town and, like their VC counterparts, have raped four women. The vet's marginal status is confirmed, since he reflects the values of this "other." Neither for nor against, he is marked as a classless threat to the dominant values. By 1970, *The Losers* erases the illusion of difference. Biker and combat vet are one: "A motorcycle gang [is] recruited to rescue a presidential advisor held prisoner by the Viet Cong. The five bikers succeed, but all die violently and in gory slow motion in the process."[37]

By 1972, the veteran is no longer simply marginal; he moves into mainstream culture, where he has become, at best, a passive decoy and target, as in *Clay Pigeon* (1971), or a professionally trained killer for hire, as in *The Stone Killer*, where a psychologist tells us after Lipper, one of the killers, is caught: "Vietnam doesn't make heroes—it makes a generation of Lippers."

By now the massacre at My Lai had infected the image of the vet. A film like Elia Kazan's *The Visitors* (1972) carries its mark: two vets, Tony Rodriguez (Chico Martinez) and Mike Nickerson (Steve Railsback), visit Bill Schmidt (James Woods), a former friend and also a veteran. The two vets threaten Bill Schmidt and Martha Wayne (Patricia Joyce), the unwed mother of his baby, because Bill had presented evidence of war crimes against them. While in country, the two had raped a Vietnamese woman. These two visitors enter the white house of Harry Wayne (Patrick McVey), noted writer of Westerns, father of the unwed mother, and supposed World War II vet (we never know for sure since at one time he talks about being in Europe and at another about being in the Pacific). Before the day is over, the two vets have helped Harry Wayne kill a neighbor's dog, have beaten the informer, and with a deliberate casualness have raped the daughter. Then they drive away.

Kazan called the film a "home movie." No other label could be more exact. It not only describes the style and the economics of this independent production; it also fixes the source of its values. Not since Peckinpah's *Straw Dogs* (1971) has the home and what it signifies been so threatened or so casually wasted. The film establishes its source of values with the opening shot, a picture of a large white house in the snow, and with stunning clarity, Kazan portrays the fears of the viewers. The vet is pictured as an ominous threat to the living room, sign of the home and place of the family. Like their VC counterparts and those other outlaws, the bikers, the vets are rapists, the irrepressibly uncivilized who violently intrude on our peace and quiet. They have returned, crossed over the threshold, and violated the sanctuary of the American dream.

In *Welcome Home, Soldier Boys* (1972) four discharged Green Berets, Danny (Joe Don Baker), Shooter (Paul Koslo), Kid (Alan Vint), and Fatback (Elliot Street), come back to the "World," only to find they do not fit—anywhere. After they buy a second-hand Cadillac and set off for the California Dream, they discover that, although a Cadillac is large enough for the four to live and love in, a white house, Danny's home, is far too small to hold one returning son, much less him and his three parents. Even Texas is too small. When the Cadillac throws a rod, they are confronted with not only the customary dishonest mechanic but a possible barroom brawl with some World War II vets, who insist that these veterans were not fighting a war but "just killing civilians." Finally out of money and gas, the four erupt into violence. Working as a whole unit with an inexplicable language of their own, they destroy the town of Hope, New Mexico, and massacre its eighty-one citizens with a professional élan that underscores their alienation as it highlights their camaraderie. Their potential for violence grows with their awareness of their alienation, usually the mark of education in war films. In a final shot that obviously alludes to the Kent State massacre, the vets confront the National Guard, gasmasked, weapons at the ready. The four veterans from Vietnam die in black-and-white slow motion, killed on the street of a western town. John Wayne's and John Ford's Western vision of 'Nam has come home.

The vet, by 1972, has become the V(i)et Cong. No longer just an ominous threat and rapist, his potential for destruction and mayhem is fully realized. Vietnam's veterans have become indistinguishable from the outlaw bikers of *The Born Losers*. But what the vet has become is hardly of his own making. In *Welcome Home, Soldier Boys*, one "waitress" tells Danny, "You are what you do." And this film elaborates, like others, on the spectator's view. For the viewer, the vet *has* become what he has done. According to the viewer, the vets' tour had drawn a line between them and their culture. The Vietnam veteran has become a transient loser, a marginal, who has toured Hell and returned, not wiser or maturer, but a threat to the American dream. Always a killer, the vet is seen as one who is infected spiritually and mentally—never politically—by the senseless genocide in Vietnam, the continuing murder of women and children. In a war of containment, he has failed and is contaminated. He is now part of the problem, a carrier who must be sterilized: "The stewardess comes through the [airplane] cabin, spraying a mist of invisible sterility into the pressurized, scrubbed, filtered temperature-controlled air, killing the mosquitoes and unknown diseases, protecting herself and American from Asian evils, cleansing us all forever."[38]

In order to perform this ritual cleansing, Hollywood has had to sublate another vision of the veteran, which an alternative film practice such as California Newsreel has documented. In Newsreel's unfinished *Winter Soldier* (1971) or its completed *DC III* (1971), the veteran is pictured not as the psychotic killer of the country's extravagant imagination, but as organized and politically astute. The former documents the "winter soldier" investigations in Detroit, in which combat vets addressed the issue of war crimes and atrocities; the latter documents the VVAW's 1971 march on Washington, "Dewey Canyon III," where they went so far as to advocate the violent overthrow of the government: "We don't want to fight anymore," says one nameless vet, "but if we do it'll be to take these steps."[39] Both films show vets taking up politics and directing it, along with their medals, at the nation's Capitol steps. Not until *The War at Home* (1979) would this suppressed image of the politicized veteran be seen again. In 1980, Hollywood attempted to recover this image, but *The Line* (1980), a fictionalized version of the Presidio Mutiny, is seldom seen. By the mid-1980s Hollywood adds a political twist to the ominous threat of the veteran's violence when the heroes of *First Blood*, *Missing in Action*, and *Rambo* take on not only the Vietnamese but also the American politicians.

Between 1972 and 1978 veterans and Vietnam, it seemed, disappeared from the screen. They made only cameo appearances, as it were (for example, *American Graffiti* [1973]). In 1978, veterans reappeared, but were noticeably changed. As Hollywood had reacted to changes in history, it now responded to veteran politics; it changed its signs, not its mind. The vets in *Heroes* (1977), *Who'll Stop The Rain?* (1978), and *Coming Home* (1978) bear a likeness to their former incarnations. In *Heroes*, for instance, the motifs of films like *Welcome Home Johnny Bristol* (1971) reemerge, but now the veteran, Jack Dunne (Henry Winkler), is a comic madman, suffering from the hallucinatory effects of post-traumatic stress syndrome. Although he is primarily a comic figure and, to all intents, harmless, there is the obligatory violent confrontation between the vet and the biker. The veteran is still an undecidable figure, capable of disrupting any setting, but seen now through comedy this potential for excess is diffused. In *Who'll Stop the Rain?*, the character of the veteran is split, a technique repeated in other films, like *Cutter's Way* (1981) and *Birdy* (1984). On the other hand, there is Jonathan Converse (Michael Moriarty)— "the asshole"—the sensitive vet and correspondent who has sent home a load of heroin, enough to hook his wife, Madge (Tuesday Weld); on the other hand, there is Ray (Nick Nolte), the student of Nietzsche, the *Übermensch*—violent, unpredictable, heroic, and a threat to the order of culture. The latter dies, and the former lives on with the junkie who was once his wife but now is the sign of his guilt and the burden he must bear. In short, by the late 1970s, there are two kinds of veterans—killers and moral killers (as an academic once told me).

In *Coming Home* (1978), the diverse strands of the earlier clichés converge, for this film owes more to the media's production of images and to the history of Vietnam films than it does to the Vietnam War. Hardly the "achingly accurate representation of Vietnam" that Peter Arnett, Michael Arlen, and others would claim, *Coming Home* not only represents the plight of the disabled veteran, as the earlier film *The Men* (1950) did, it also (re)presents the already produced version of Vietnam and its veterans.[40] As in *Who'll Stop the Rain?*, there are two types of veterans in *Coming Home*: the hero, Bob Hyde (Bruce Dern), violent and irrepressible, and the wounded, castrated victim, Luke (Jon Voight). Both are potential agents of unrestrained violence who must be arrested, retrained, and removed. *Coming Home* does all three: it represses the potential for violence by re(s)training the wounded vet and drowning the other. Thanks to the insight of a woman, Sally Hyde (Jane Fonda) ("What makes you such a bastard?"), Luke, like most other images of wounded vets, comes to terms with his disability and guilt, while Bruce Dern, who in an earlier version of the screenplay was to have taken his rifle to a nearby hill to snipe at passersby, is put to rest because, no doubt, he refuses Sally's healing aid.[41] Just as Dern takes off his uniform, the sign of his profession, in order to free himself, Voight confesses before a group of students, professing publicly that he has killed for his country. One veteran confesses; the other drowns. Like the Germans at the end of World War I, Americans have turned "defeat into inner victory by means of confessions of guilt which [are] hysterically elevated to the universally human."[42]

The Deer Hunter (1978) was released the same year as *Coming Home*, and both came up for an Academy Award. There was an immediate controversy. In his syndicated editorial, Peter Arnett compared the two, calling the latter "an honest attempt to come to terms with the war in Vietnam" and calling *The Deer Hunter* "Fascist trash," another fraudulent Hollywood view of Vietnam that he feared the public was "interpreting as a deep historical truth."[43] The point of the controversy was clear: one of the two competing films was to be understood as the "proper" view of Vietnam, because it was approved by Vietnam's foremost war correspondent; the other was to be disregarded on account of its apparent politics and propaganda. Like John Wayne, Arnett condemned one point of view and sanctified the other based upon what he had seen "in country." Hence *The Deer Hunter* was dishonest, because neither Vietnam nor the Vietnamese "looked" that way, at least to a liberal reporter.

But what Arnett failed to comment on in his defense of the Vietnamese was that this film was less about Vietnam and more about the American community that fought the war. *The Deer Hunter* was a new twist in the history of Vietnam films. No one prior to Cimino had bothered to look at the effects the war had on that community. Admittedly, Cimino's is a vulgar vision, neither idyllic nor middle-class, and founded on a particular reading of American working-class literature. It begins, for instance, like Upton Sinclair's *The Jungle*, with a wedding and a reception. Like Sinclair's butchers or Dahlberg's bottomdogs, Cimino's steelworkers are brutal, often racist, always sexist, and rooted in the myths of America and its past. Like Tressall's raged philanthropists, who suffer because they cannot see that they are starving because they are giving away their livelihood, Cimino's workers unwittingly bear the contradictions of their class rather than fulfilling its potential. They are hardly class-conscious. They come from a particular community fraught with contradictions, at a particular time with a peculiar history, where the desired "unpalatable data relating to the subjective consciousness of the characters and the objective lines of force acting on and within the community [which] would insist on expression" can only be expressed by the viewer, not the viewee.[44] Such an expression from such a community is purely a utopian hope and a middle-class aspiration, hardly congruent with our dedication to a "naturalistic" cinematic practice.

In *The Deer Hunter*, the vet is portrayed neither as a psychotic killer nor as some secret sharer doubling for someone else's vision of the VC nor as some moral killer needing to confess his crimes. He is not a marginal or a homeless transient, alienated because of some secret initiation rite called combat that separates him from others because of a higher plane of knowledge. Mike (Robert DeNiro), Steve (John Savage), and Nick (Christopher Walken) are members of a community—second-generation Ukrainian steelworkers— whose homes and histories militate against any form of choice. As the children of Ukrainian immigrants, they are almost destined to fight against communism. They suffer, like the Vietnamese, the effects of the war, for the community is shattered. The film ends with a funeral, where the last survivor, Mike, sees his reflection on Nick's coffin (just as other vets would see themselves reflected off black marble), and with a wake, that apocalyptic moment, when the ruined community nostalgically attempts to regain its former intimacy, but must awaken to its present conditions and possible futures.

Nothing reigns for them now but alienation. Their day of mourning ends with "God Bless America," a song that many read as just another attempt to recuperate the patriotic myths that led into the war. Yet it should be understood within its cinematic context: it is not an attempt to reiterate the shoddy values of a hollow patriotism. What we see is a community shattered by Vietnam, trying to express a deeply rooted nationalism, with all its ironies and contradictions, and founded on such events as the Homestead Riots. These people, then, are not merely the inheritors of simple freedoms, but the constructors of a history that has both made and unmade them. Like the Vietnamese, they are the ignorant and innocent victims of a war being waged against exploited peoples by exploited people. No doubt this is not the same "honest" and attractive view of the Vietnam War that *Coming Home* was, but it is nonetheless valid.

In *Rolling Thunder* (1977), the POW Charlie Rane (William Devane) comes home. He returns to the States a hero complete with groupie and receives his reward: one thousand silver dollars. A gang of thieves looking for the money feeds the obstinate Charlie's hand to the garbage disposal and kills his wife and son. When Charlie recovers, he sets out with his groupie to hunt down the killers. He finds them in a whorehouse south of the border. With another POW, he infiltrates the house and wreaks havoc on house, gang, and hookers. In *First Blood* (1982), John Rambo (Sylvester Stallone), long out of the service, returns to a small town after its sheriff has escorted him out. The sheriff arrests him for vagrancy, and the deputies brutalize him. As Charlie Ranes did before him, Rambo flashes back to his wartime experience as a tortured POW. Crazed, he jumps jail and heads for the woods, where he wreaks havoc on the posse. By the end of the film, Rambo has destroyed most of the downtown real estate and returns to the waiting arms of his onetime commander, who just happens to betray him at least twice before the film ends.

By 1984, then, Charlie is no longer the enemy, or just a perfume or even a tuna; like the character in the film *Charly* (1968), he has suffered a sea change. He is now the veteran gone from bone-dumb grunt to superguerilla. The Vietnam veteran of the eighties, unlike his earlier incarnations, is a retired, barely re(s)trained, mostly misunderstood, asexual, Green Beret hero occasionally called Charlie. No longer the enemy of *Welcome Home, Soldier Boys* or the ominous rapists of *The Visitors*, the vet has come home and is now recognized for what he is: the long-suffering hero apotheosized into Victor Charlie, complete with politics. The secret sharer of films like *Apocalypse Now* and *Go Tell the Spartans* has emerged not as an "other" but as an emanation of the combat vet. In good shaman fashion, we have stolen, if not the magic of our enemy, at least his signs.

Take John Rambo. In *First Blood*, after his escape from jail, he runs off to the forest, Indian country, where, almost always unseen, he leads the posse a merry chase. In the sequel, *Rambo: First Blood Part II* (1985), he is again sprung from jail and is returned to 'Nam with his bow and arrows. The Indian (like Billy Jack, Rambo is both a Green Beret and part Native American) is returned to "Indian country," the legendary bad bush where Charlie, in all his invisibility, once ran free, and where he again, disguised as John Rambo, will wreak destruction, only this time on Soviet troops. And we will know him by these signs. First—sweat ("no sweat" is the sign of a bygone era). Today the "good guys" sweat, but back in 1957 when Fuller sent Lucky Legs and her patrol upriver, the only people who looked at all as if they were sweating were the crude Commies. Rambo, however, sweats throughout the film. Second— camouflage; as all the major texts admit, Charlie was invisible, could not be seen, turned the ground against us— "Forget the Cong, the *trees* could kill you, the elephant grass grew up homicidal, the ground you were walking over possessed malignant intelligence, your whole environment was a bath."[45] Who can forget our American poet, Rambo, running free in the American forest or rising up out of the Vietnamese mud or coming out of the bark of a tree, and not marvel at how literal he has become?

In these recent twists on Vietnam, we imagine the vet as fully (re)covered, re(s)trained, and returned to his rightful place, where he will continue to run through the jungle looking for what America lost. He will continue to fight until he gets it right. The vet of the Vietnam War, now almost ageless, yet well developed, returns to 'Nam to retrieve his lost buddies and our lost honor and return them to the United States. What we see in films like *Missing in Action*, *Rambo*, and *Uncommon Valor* (as well as *Red Dawn* [1984], another Vietnam variation, only well-trained American high school football players are the VC) is not merely the same old marginal vet, unable to make it in America, exiled and returned to 'Nam where he is "really himself." These films dramatize the mechanisms of our cultural repression. What is presented is our cultural obsession with "returning."

In the late 1960s we silenced Vietnam; in the 1970s we defended ourselves from it; and in the mid-1980s we return to it, or it returns to us. Like the characters in *Cease Fire* (1985), the country is suffering a collective flashback. In films like *Rambo* and *Streamers* (1983), we again prepare for it (and if Paul Mazursky fulfills his options on *Joyride*, we will, in the future, return to 'Nam from the West on bicycles). In others, like *The Killing Fields* (1984) and *Search and Destroy* (1981), our past, in the form of Southeast Asians, hunts us up.

By 1984, Hollywood has recuperated the veteran, Vietnam, and the War. Like other systems of representation, it has traced its own process of recovery. *The Stunt Man* (1980), one of those Hollywood products compromising Brechtian self-consciousness, represents how the Dream Factory recovered both the war and the veteran. In short, we see a film not merely about filmmaking, but one that displays the fantasy-making apparatus. Vietnam will be revised, hence lost and won, because it will be remade, *The Stunt Man* says, in the image of an older war. From the beginning, when Cameron (Steve Railsback, the actor who played the brooding rapist in *the Visitors*) escapes from the cops, until he confesses his crime to his lover in terms of the usual cinematic clichés, we see the already established image of the Viet vet. But this film is a variation, for the vet finds himself in a movie, one about World War I. To hide form the police, he becomes a blond stuntman, someone who not only does other people's dirty work but also, as another's double, is invisible while he is translated into a body of work. The irreality of film will capture the alienated vet and his war, translating him and it into something else, something hardly recognizable, hardly himself, merely a "blond" shadow warrior, standing in not only for an actor but also the image of a warrior. No longer alienated, he will come to stand for our culture's desires and foibles.

An entire history and countermemory, however, is lost in such a translation. In 1966 the Puerto Rican artist Jaime Carrero wrote a play called *Flag Inside*.[46] It is about a Puerto Rican family and the death of a son in Vietnam. In the beginning, the family receives word that the casket will be returned. They prepare a space at home. Around this space marking the family's loss, the drama takes place. For me, this play seems paradigmatic of the discourse I have tried to map, as well as the problems that the discourse as a whole presents. Formally, for example, the play fuels any number of interests, everything from the Heideggerian notion of the metaphysical presence of absence to the deconstructionist recognition that the breathing in and out of presence and absence is less important than the play it seems to generate—the permutations and changes that take place as the discourse attempts to mute the unavoidable lacuna. But finally the drama's absence from 'Nam discourse is itself significant because it represents what has been lost. With rare exceptions, Vietnam has not been presented as an aspect of working-class life. It is seldom seen as an experiential and historical fact in the lives of many working-class and ethnic families. It is hardly an innocent oversight that the working-class gave up the most soldiers to the war.

This is not to say that there are no alternative discourses. Far from it. Alternative videos like Dan Reeve's *Smothering Dreams* (1981) and independent film productions like Michael Uno's *The Silence* (1983),[47] Haile Gerima's *Ashes and Embers* (1982),[48] and Haskel Wexler's *Latino* (1985) have attempted in a variety of ways to picture this countermemory. Unlike recent Hollywood productions that turn the vet into a sign of our repression and its constant return, these films have inserted Vietnam into an historical continuum. The vet is returned not merely to the history of historians, but to a class history spoken by the oppressed, a countermemory lost to the dominant discourse.

For instance, *Ashes and Embers* and *Latino* turn on the recognition engendered, yet hardly voiced, in *The Deer Hunter*: the oppressed have been killing those who were helping to fight against oppression. In each film a character must deal with the fact that he has been used to further imperialism. In *Ashes and Embers*, the black veteran (John Anderson), like all black veterans from all American wars, must deal with the fact that "the man" has exploited him, and like other Vietnam vets he suffers from a psychological trauma. Unlike his Hollywood contemporaries, the director has understood that the traumas are as much a product of the state of society, and the vets' place in it, as they are of the war. Hence while *Ashes and Embers* is an uncompromising psychological drama, it is construed according to a political and historical imagination. The film records not merely the vet's alienation but his place in history and his return to it. For it is not about a lone, troubled psyche, but about history and its varieties: personal history, cultural history, and ethnic history are the subjects of the film. In a series of dialectical encounters signifying the vet's

The film records not merely the veteran's alienation but his place in history and his return to it.

troubled psyche and unstable relationship to society, it narrates the means of a healthy return.

The major moment in the film occurs when once again the alienated vet feels compelled to tell one more horror story. As usual, when the vet tells the tale, he finds that he has only deepened his alienation. As he authenticates his grief and rage, he also drives a wedge between himself and others. As long as the war is understood as a combat zone where unique events occur, no genuine return for the vet can be achieved. The vet was born elsewhere, as it were, outside history, beyond the world and its culture—so the stories say. But in this film, Gerima subverts this understanding. When the vet is through screaming his tale at his lover, Liza Jane (Kathy Flewellen), her young son, Kimathi (Uwezo Flewellen), enters the scene and says: "My father was killed in Vietnam." Hardly earthshaking, but the timing is immaculate; it dissipates the tension between speaker and hearer, between the black veteran and his lover, between the viewer and the film, because it suggests that Vietnam is suffered by an entire working class. It is not a singular event in a few select persons' lives; its consequences range throughout a community. With that recognition, the vet can begin to overcome his alienation.

Latino, while not about Vietnam, addresses the same question as *Ashes and Embers*. In this film, Captain Eddie Guerrero (Robert Beltran), a Green Beret who fought in Vietnam, has stayed on in the military. As a career soldier, he finds he is now part of a Spanish-speaking contingent of American soldiers sent to Honduras to train and work with the Contras. He finds himself leading raids into Nicaragua. Guerrero discovers that he has to come to terms with the fact that the people he is killing look like his own family. The crisis occurs when he confronts his complicity with oppression. Like others, Guerrero must quit or repress his growing awareness that he is fighting for "the man." We witness the moment of repression; when Guerrero expresses his doubts and growing awareness to his partner, Ruben (Tony Plana), he is answered with "Forget the shit," and this refrain is picked up and changed by the other G.I.'s in the bar. The noise literally drives out his newfound awareness and figuratively drives him back to Nicaragua, where he is captured, humiliated, and led off in disgrace.

Trudeau has written recently: "This just in from Hollywood; we won in Vietnam." But our desire to forget and to win through representation continues to defeat us. *Rambo* and his ilk, with their emphasis on winning, signify nothing more than "American lost and forgot." They would never have been made without that awareness, and, as they attempt to forget and recuperate our loss, they revise our tactics, our politics, and our history. In the process, we lose the element of the war that *Latino* and *Ashes and Embers* display. What is lost and forgotten with each imagined win are those who fought and suffered. It is all well and good to desire to turn Vietnam vets into heroes, but not at the expense of their children and their history. As Brecht's *Mother Courage* reminds us, war profiteering has a long, honorable, and expensive history. I wonder if Stallone and his fellow revisionists are wiling to pay the price.

NOTES

1. Other than some minor changes in the notes, I have decided not to update this essay. This does not mean that I think the essay is flawless. On the contrary, there are a number of flaws. But any major revision would not only correct the errors but also undo a number of insights. Besides, both the errors and the insights are signs of their time; history impinges on this paper. So I have left it as it is.

2. Robert Hilburn, "Pop Breaks Vietnam Silence," *Los Angeles Times*, 3 October 1982, "Calendar." But these, of course, are only the most recent additions to the list of songs about Vietnam. If we return to the 1960s, there are the antiwar songs, for example, Phil Ochs, "Talking Vietnam," The Fugs, "Kill for Peace," and Country Joe and The Fish, "Fish Chant."

3. "Dancing to the Vietnam Beat," *Newsweek*, 27 May 1985, p. 61.

4. Bobbie Ann Mason, *In Country* (New York: Harper and Row, 1985).

5. For a sense of this rhetoric, see the various contemporaneous articles in *Time*: for example, "The Anatomy of a Debacle," *Time*, 14 April 1975, pp. 16–19; "How Americans Should Feel," *Time*, 14 April 1975, p. 27; or "Fed Up and Turned Off," *Time*, 14 April 1975, p. 22.

6. Michael J. Arlen. *The Living Room War* (New York: Penguin Books, 1982), and Arlen, *The View From Highway 1: Essays on Television* (New York: Farrar, Straus, & Giroux, 1976).

7. Charles Montgomery Hammond, Jr., *The Image Decade: Television Documentary: 1965–1975* (New York: Hasting House, 1981), *passim*.

8. J. Fred McDonald, *Don't Touch That Dial: Radio Programming in American Life, 1920–1960* (Chicago: Nelson-Hall, 1979).

9. See Steve Bognar, "The Omnipresent Eye: Television News and *Special Bulletin*," *Filament* 4 (1983):28–46. Cf. J. G. Ballard's short story, "Theatre of War," *Myths of the Near Future* (London: Jonathan Cape, 1982), pp. 118–140.

10. I should make it clear that what I am calling *cinéma vérité* style is a combination of direct cinema and *cinema vérité*. Direct cinema is that of the observer-documentarist; it is a form of documentary. The "direct cinema documentarist took his camera to a situation of tension . . . ; he aspired to invisibility and played the role of uninvolved bystander." Direct cinema found its truth in events available to the camera. However, one of the problems hanging over the observer-documentarist was the extent to which the presence of the camera influenced events before it. Therefore practitioners of *cinéma vérité* in France "maintained that the presence of the camera made people act in ways truer to their nature than might otherwise be the case." Thus they acknowledged the impact of the camera, but instead of considering it a liability, they looked on it as a "valuable catalytic agent, a revealer of inner truth." Erik Barnouw, *Documentary: A History of Non-Fiction film* (London: Oxford, 1974), pp. 229–262.

11. "Except for rare instances, what is seen on network news is not the event itself unfolding before the live camera, or even a filmed record, but a story about the event reconstructed on film selected from fragments from it. . . . Despite the hackneyed maxim that television news 'tells it like it is,' presenting events exactly as they occur does not fit in with the requisites of network news. . . . A former Saigon bureau chief pointed out that it is considered standard operating procedure for troops to fire their weapons for the benefit of cameramen. If our cameramen had to wait until a fire fight with the Viet Cong broke out, we'd have less footage—and perhaps cameramen." Edward Jay Epstein, *News From Nowhere* (New York: Random House, 1973), pp. 152–158.

12. Michael Herr, *Dispatches* (New York: Avon, 1980), p. 21.

13. Arlen, "Surprised in Iowa, Surprised in Nam," *The Camera Age: Essays on Television* (New York: Farrar, Straus & Giroux, 1981), p. 96.

14. Arlen, "The Networks Continue to Give Us What We Really Want. We are Immeasurably Grateful & Utter Little Cries of Help," *The Living Room War* (New York: Penguin Books, 1982), pp. 40–45.

15. Tony Lawrence, "Television Review," *Daily Variety*, 18 November 1969, p. 29.

16. R. Brewin, "TV's Newest Villain: The Vietnam Veteran," *TV Guide*, 19 July 1975, p. 4; Julian Smith, *Looking Away: Hollywood and Vietnam* (New York: Scribner, 1975), p. 164.

17. Todd Gitlin, *Inside Prime Time* (New York: Pantheon, 1983), pp. 223–243.

18. Howard Rosenberg, "Mixing Humor with Vietnam," *Los Angeles Times*, 11 January 1980.

19. Rosenberg, "*Mike Freit*: The Saga of a Failed Concept," *Los Angeles Times*, 3 March 1980.

20. Marvin Kitman, "*Fly Away Home*, A Story That Won't Quit," *Daily Variety*, 24 September 1981, p. 23.

21. Rosenberg, "Mixing Humor with Vietnam."

22. John J. O'Connor, "These Productions Struggle to be Provocative," *The New York Times*, 13 September 1981.

23. "Six O'Clock Follies," *Daily Variety*, 28 April 1980, p. 6; Jerry Buck, "A Comedy Based on Vietnam?" *Alabama Journal* 19 (April 1980): 20.

24. At this point it is worth noting a number of other documentaries; the war, it seems, was fought not only with bombs and booby traps but documentaries as well. In 1954 Roman Karmin filmed *Vietnam*; the NLF did *Hun Tho Speaks to The American People* (1965) and *The Way to the Front* (1969). The North Vietnamese did *Some Evidence* (1969). The Cuban director Santiago Alvarex did *Hanoi, Tuesday the 13th* (1967), *79 Springtimes* (1969), and *Laos: The Forgotten War* (1967). Another Cuban director, Julio Garcia Espinosa, did *Third World Third World War* (1970). Two East German documentaries were *The Job* and *Pilots in Pyjamas*. Other documentaries were Joris Ivens's *17th Parallel* (1967); Poland's *Fire* (1968), directed by Andrzej Brzozowski; Canada's *Sad Song of Yellow Skin* (1970); and the Syrian film *Napalm* (1970). For a more complete discussion of these films, see Barnouw, *Documentary*, pp. 268–281.

25. See David James, *Allegories of Cinema: American Film in the Sixties* (Princeton, N.J.: Princeton University Press, 1989).

26. See David Cortright, *Soldiers in Revolt: The American Military Today* (New York: Doubleday, 1975), pp. 29–49.

27. Herr, *Dispatches*, p. 69.

28. See Smith, *Looking Away*, and Gilbert Adair, *Vietnam on Film* (New York: Proteus Publishing, 1981).

29. See Susan Jeffords, *The Remasculinization of America: Gender and the Vietnam War* (Bloomington and Indianapolis: Indiana University Press, 1989). As for women in Vietnam, there are two films: *Don't Cry, It's Only Thunder* (1982) and *Purple Hearts* (1984). And several books on the way: for example, Chris Noel's autobiography and Kathryn Marshall *In the Combat Zone: An Oral History of American Women in Vietnam* (Boston: Little, Brown, 1987).

30. Quoted in Smith, *Looking Away*, p. 136.

31. Gustav Hasford, *The Short Timers* (New York: Bantam Books, 1980), p. 38.

32. William J. Palmer, "*Go Tell the Spartans*: The Forgotten Vietnam Film," unpublished paper.

33. Cf. Guy Hennebelle, "Le Cinéma Vietnamien," *Ecran 73*; and Peters Gessner, "Films from the Vietcong," *The Nation*, 24 January 1966, pp. 110–111.

34. Smith, *Looking Away*, p. 143.

35. Abraham Polonsky, "*The Case of David Smith*: A Script by Abraham Polonsky," *Hollywood Quarterly* 1 (1945–1946): 185–195.

36. Cf. Franklin Fearning, "Warriors Return: Normal or Neurotic?" *Hollywood Quarterly* 1 (1945–1946): 97–109.

37. Smith, *Looking Away*, p. 160.

38. Tim O'Brien, *If I Die In A Combat Zone Box Me Up and Ship Me Home* (New York: Dell, 1979), p. 203.

39. See John Kerry et al., *The New Soldier* (New York: Macmillan, 1971).

40. Arlen, *The Camera Age*, p. 101.

41. Cf. Leonard Quart and Albert Auster, "The Wounded Vet in Postwar Film," *Social Policy*, Fall 1982, pp. 25–31.

42. Walter Benjamin, "Theories of German Fascism," trans. Jerolf Wikoff, *New German Critique* 17 (Spring 1979): 122.

43. Peter Arnett, "Vietnam's Last Atrocity," *Los Angeles Times* 4 April 1979.

44. Andrew Britten, "Sideshows: Hollywood in Vietnam," *Movie* 27/28 (Winter 1980/Spring 1981): 2–23.

45. Herr, *Dispatches*, p. 69.

46. Jaime Carrero, *Flag Inside*, in *Teatro: Flag Inside, Captain F4C, El Caballo Pipo Subway No Sabe Reir* (Rio Piedras: Ediciones Puerto, 1973), pp. 7–55.

47. "A dramatic story set in the period of the Vietnam War. An American soldier is stranded in the jungle with a Vietnamese woman who buries the dead": Program notes, 1983 *Asian American International Film Festival*.

48. Haile Gerima, *Ashes and Embers*, a Mypheduh Films, Inc., release, 1982.

The War about the War:
Vietnam Films and American Myth

During the Iranian hostage crisis, I was teaching a class on the economics of less developed countries at Georgetown University. There was a warlike mood in Washington in those fading days of Carter "wimpishness." I had been a marine infantryman in Vietnam and I wanted to know how many supported a war with Iran. The show of hands was sixty to three in favor of war. Then I asked how many thought the United States ought to go back to a universal military draft. The vote was fifty-nine to four against it. The one who switched was an Iranian student. I have cherished this incident as proof of the mindless military rambunctiousness that grows up among the comfortable when they feel secure from the sobering threat of the draft. A few short years after the fall of Saigon, the nation's youth, the Future Veterans of Foreign Wars, or FVFW, as I like to think of them, were raring to go again.

The Hollywood Vietnam film has done its bit in bringing about this state of affairs. A census of the whole Vietnam film library, from right to left or from militarist to antimilitarist, would show a lopsided count with the right-wing, militarist end badly overcrowded. It is not even clear that any recent example of a 100 percent antimilitary, anti-imperialist film exists. Ivan Passer's veteran film, *Cutter's Way* (1981), comes close. But the film's perspective is so unusual that critics misunderstood even the basic plot elements. Cutter, an embittered veteran, learns of a murder by a powerful businessman, a symbol of corporate power and militarism. The plot revolves around Cutter's attempt to convict the businessman and validate the longing for heroism that drove him to Vietnam. Several critics decided, in contradiction to what the film says, that Cutter is paranoid and that his efforts to put things right, however sympathetic, are products of a delusion. Less critical views than Passer's are more common.

For example, in *The Deer Hunter* (1978) and *Go Tell the Spartans* (1978) the problem is that bad leaders or mistaken or misguided policy had led to an unworthy or an overly cruel war. In films that have a more promilitary slant, there is a heavy reliance on a "war is hell" message until, at the farthest right and most populated end of the spectrum, the Rambo and Chuck Norris part, war becomes exciting and fun. But locating Vietnam movies according to their position on a political spectrum of attitudes toward the war or militarism is oddly uninformative. Much more is going on.

Editors' Note: This is a revised version of an article that originally appeared in *The Village Voice* in September 1987.

It is in films that the important work is going to be done of forcing the facts of the Vietnam War into the mold of national myth and reconciling the country to its first defeat in war. So far, the broadest generalization about the Vietnam movies is that they show how trapped the country is in the perceptions of World War II. We liked that war and are reluctant to surrender the sense of unity and righteousness it brought. The Vietnam films share with the World War II films ingredients like the following:

> A moral impulse is behind every American war. Wars are undertaken by Americans, even if the cause is mistaken, as crusades.
> Individuals "prove" themselves by personally participating in combat, which teaches truths impossible to learn elsewhere.
> The foreignness of the enemy is a sign of evil, although "foreignness" needn't be evil if the foreigners have acquired the cultural traits of Americans.
> Americans themselves are better, friendlier than other nationalities, and want nothing selfish in their relations with foreigners.
> But if there is conflict, Americans are inherently better at violence and will win. And so on.

The Vietnam film continues the World War II film tradition of portraying war as an arena for the display of a man's ferocity, courage, capacity for sacrifice, altruism, and the like. But these martial qualities are now treated as though they had important, even decisive, military consequences. The World War II movie showed Germans and Japanese with ferocious or sadistic traits, but these films did not insist, the way the more recent films do, that viciousness confers real military advantage. This new wrinkle, which meshes with the right-wing theory of the defeat in Vietnam, could be called "the doctrine of restrained ferocity." The doctrine, most explicit in *Rambo*, holds that the United States fights according to rules, while its opponents don't. Vietnam movies suggest that refraining from brutality is an important disadvantage in war. Rambo explains, in one of his rare utterances, that he was made to lose by having to observe rules. Clint Eastwood has observed, "I disagree with the [John] Wayne concept. . . . I play bigger than life characters, but I'll shoot a guy in the back. I go by the expediency of the moment."

In films on the World War II era, the brutal Germans and Japanese were contrasted with the personally decent Americans. Is there any Hollywood film scene where enemy troops are shown assisting their own wounded? We always try to help ours and we lacked the icy sadists of the German and Japanese officer corps. But there was no implication then that Americans could not beat them anyway without imitating them. American audiences are now being told that they have been disadvantaged by their past decency, whether real or imagined. But they no longer have to suffer this disadvantage if they are prepared to get mean themselves.

There have been films in the past that advocated a Cold War struggle in the Third World where America's task was long and demanding. In *The Ugly American* (1963), a Kennedy-era movie based on the Lederer and Burdick novel, the problem was one of alerting America to the need for complex tactics and political stamina. Americans in Asia, in particular those in the mythical Southeast Asian country of Sarkhan, were lazy, thoughtless about other cultures, and unaware that the global stakes of the struggle with the Soviet Union required a strategy of strength and intelligence. There is emphatically no patience nowadays for this kind of strategy. Insofar as a policy is now being advocated, it is that Americans should give vent to a spasm of retributive rage.

Another key feature of the film falsification of war is the importance of the individual, the solitary hero of American myth whose lineage goes back to James Fenimore Cooper's *Deerslayer*. Not only do Rambo and Chuck Norris go into the fight alone, but so too do Martin Sheen in *Apocalypse Now* (1979) and Robert DeNiro in *The Deer Hunter*. We should not underestimate the extreme effort of imagination and will that is necessary to come up with plots that allow military men to undertake these solitary missions in total opposition to the doctrine and practice of the United States military. Portrayals of military units of men at war like *Pork Chop Hill* (1959), at which Hollywood has a very respectable tradition, seemed to stop with the Vietnam war film. The peculiar realistic quality of *Platoon* (1986) depended largely on the fact that it did not contain a preposterous military mission concocted by a scriptwriter to display a central character's solitary daring. Americans admire heroes who act alone, and they are encouraged in this by movies to a ridiculous degree. Even Jon Voight's character, the paraplegic sergeant in *Coming Home* (1978), carries out a one-man antiwar protest at a time in United States history when this was normally a group activity.

There is almost no human activity that is as intensely social as modern warfare. This is thought to be so essential that modern battle doctrine concentrates on destroying the ability of the enemy force to interact organizationally as a prelude to destroying those forces. When a military unit loses its internal coherence and starts to fight as individuals there is such a radical and unfavorable change in the casualty ratio that it is almost always decisive. So there is something appalling in the relentless depiction of the importance of individual bravery when every general staff in the world since 1914 has known that the bravery of individual soldiers in modern war is about as essential as whether they are handsome. Like the bayonet, personal courage has little relevance in modern battle. And like bayonet training, it is one of the archaisms whose cult is preserved by militarist culture so that potential recruits will see war as psychologically satisfying.

The American war film requires that the twin deities of individualism and populism be served. In the Vietnam movie the myth of the solitary combatant or lonesome cowboy seems to be stronger. This could be the result of greater ignorance of the mechanics of war on the part of producers, directors, and writers. The class background of the Vietnam-era draftees compared to those of other wars saw to this. Oliver Stone is an exception, and *Platoon* is in a category by itself as a result. The democratic mystique of American political culture is so strong that we have acquired an empire describing it to ourselves, all the while, as aid to "the people" in their liberation struggles. American myth likes the enemy to be big and powerful and established. We like a sense that the technological and material advantages of war are on the enemy's side, while the moral advantage and the sympathy of the people are on ours. Hollywood reflects and reinforces this popular yearning. George Lucas's *Star Wars* (1977) even plagiarized the Vietcong when he created a race of furry forest dwellers, the Ewoks, who fight against the Imperial Storm Troopers of the Galactic Empire. And in the Vietnam movie, the American martial spirit sees itself as the Special Forces soldier fighting with the partisans and not as the B-52 pilot or the military aide in the palace.

The emphasis on the Special Forces soldier suggests that survival and success in war are the result of skill and mastery. There is a fetish about the skills of the warrior. Substantial dialogue is dedicated to explaining how formidable a combatant the central character is. From *Rambo* to *Platoon*, the convention is rarely violated, and sometimes it is the chief substance of the film. This is an important part of the make-believe. There is a conspiracy on the part of professional soldiers, veterans, and even troops in combat, to assist in the pretence that you can substantially affect your destiny by your efforts, that it is not all just dumb luck. It is true that bad luck seems to follow incompetents around, but the John Wayne super-trooper stereotype is an object of contempt among troops in combat for good reasons. Everyone learns very soon in combat that modern war kills very, very tough guys in much the same way that it kills everybody else. Mortar rounds in the sky, fired by people miles away, do not know and do not care how fast your reflexes are or how good your marksmanship is or whether you are brave. Grunts in combat believe that being savvy and alert can improve their chances, but everyone agrees it is a lot better to be lucky than to be smart or tough. In every unit, tough, capable guys get killed all the time and everybody knows it.

A crypto discussion of the Vietnam war, *M*∗*A*∗*S*∗*H* started a trend that can be labelled "the devolution of personal loyalties." The *M*∗*A*∗*S*∗*H* movie and television series deal with a helicopter medevac unit in the Korean War, where there was no such thing except as a brief experiment. The resentment of military bureaucracy in the main characters is a trivializing surrogate for the rebellion and antiwar feeling of the Vietnam years. But antibureaucratic struggle keeps cropping up in *M*∗*A*∗*S*∗*H* and elsewhere as little folks discover they don't like the system. Their squabbles with superiors serve as a surrogate for more principled conflict. Among other things, this acts as a surrogate for conflict over principle.

In *Rambo* (1985), on the other hand, proletarian rage sweeps away other allegiances. Rambo is the soldier without a cause, although the militarist stupidity of the Rambo films obscures the startling antipatriotism of the character. Stallone's hero has been betrayed by his government, the army, and even the Special Forces. The only claim still recognized by the inarticulate and inaccessible Rambo is the claim of his fellow veterans and MIAs. He still hates the Vietnamese, but he also hates his nation and his government because, having started the war and expended American lives, they quit. Nearly everything in national life is contaminated by the dishonesty of politics and bureaucracy and therefore unworthy of loyalty.

In the Vietnam films, the rise of "lesser" loyalties supplants such older causes as anticommunism or the loyalties of the World War II film to nation and democratic principle. Cimino's *The Deer Hunter* and Coppola's *Gardens of Stone* (1987) are mainly concerned with characters who are in the process of transferring allegiance away from the older ideals. On the right and on the left, the war is seen to have tainted the nation-state in people's minds, and they reject it. A host of other loyalties has rushed in to fill the gap. These include self, family, friends, ethnic groups and religions, and, in *Gardens of Stone*, the United States Army. Some of these same loyalties had to be explicitly condemned in the older tradition. Gary Cooper as Sergeant York had to learn to discard his Tennessee fundamentalist religion so that he could be an effective member of the national army. The World War II film often showed ethnic prejudice in army units as the enemy of military effectiveness. To serve the higher cause of army unity, urban micks like James Cagney in *The Fighting 69th* (1940) have to suppress their antagonism toward the Alabamans in a rival unit. The classic Hollywood infantry platoon is portrayed as a basket of antagonistic ethnicities that is transformed and elevated by American democracy when it forgets its differences and dedicates itself to defending that democracy, usually by destroying, say, the Japanese.

With the Vietnam film, we see loyalties devolving down to small groups like the work unit, the family, the circle of friends or buddies, or the ethnic group. This parallels what was actually happening to the United States Army in the field during the war. Coppola and Cimino, in particular, have laid on with a trowel the idea that family or ethnicity or fidelity to the army are fine successor loyalties to the World War II standards of democracy and nation.

The hostage, the exile, the person separated unwillingly from home and family is another recurring theme. The longing for recovery, retrieval, and reconciliation is so pervasive that it cannot be due merely to claims of some people, especially family members, that Vietnam is still holding MIAs in prison. It can only signify some deeper sense of loss associated with the war, a nostalgia for our short-lived global preeminence and for a national unity now wrecked. LBJ told us, "Make no mistake. America wins the war she undertakes." We hated losing and still hate the Vietnamese for it. Nobody knows how much. Gene Hackman, Chuck Norris, and Sylvester Stallone have all infiltrated Indochina to bring back POWs. Is this a way of bringing back the dead we lost in the first war we lost? Is Rambo going back to retrieve the dead or to retrieve victory? Or is he helping us blame the Vietnamese for the dead not being here?

These emotional obsessions coexist with a fascination for military hardware. In the American system of military Keynesianism, the army is mostly a vehicle for weapons sales. American generals think more about budgets than about battlefields. Consuming the goods of military industry is an end in itself, nearly the only end. As a result, weapons are constantly replaced and tactics are constantly adjusted so that more weapons are needed. In the field in Vietnam this led to bitter complaining among enlisted men. In February of '66, marines near Da Nang, while on Operation Long Bow, raged over having their M-14s taken away and replaced with M-15s. This weapon had a rate of fire that, as is now famous, guaranteed jamming. There was grumbling and even real revolts over vehicles like the Amtrac helicopter and the tactics that came with them.

Platoon is a rare exception, with its incident where the artillery lands on the American troops; the implication is that the United States tactics are, with their reliance on firepower, self-defeating. The sergeants know the enemy is deliberately staying too close for fire missions. In North Vietnam, General Vo Nguyen Giap had set down a dictum for his troops: "You fight Americans by holding on to their belt buckles." But in the South only enlisted men realized that the style of close-quarter fighting had made American war technology irrelevant. The film industry's default has let these matters go unquestioned. American filmmakers have done little more than act as the passive beneficiaries of the "visuals" of the helicopter and air strike, and they are steered in this direction by a military trussed up in its own technology.

The Pentagon has an active hand in film production. Congressman Benjamin Rosenthal (D-N.Y.) estimated the cost to the Pentagon for assistance in the making of *The Green Berets* to be over a million dollars. Wayne was billed $18,623.64 for help, which included 85 hours of helicopter flying time and 3,800 man days of borrowed military personnel. Army cooperation was "extensive" in the making of *Gardens of Stone*. The price of this cooperation was a series of script changes to depict army personnel favorably. The result of this gold thumb on the scales has permitted the production of a whole clutch of propagandistic films that would have otherwise been strangled in the cradle by the magic of the marketplace.

The Pentagon's direct role goes back at least as far as the golden age of the war film during World War II. The War Department's propaganda films established much of the basic worldview of the war film. During the war, the Army rejected several of the scripts for Frank Capra's *Why We Fight* because the scripts blamed the emperor and the ruling elite of Japan and were therefore likely to elicit "too much sympathy for Jap people." Finally Joris Ivens, the writer who was the chief offender, was fired and a script written that blamed the culture, history, institutions, and people of Japan for the war. This seems to be the origin of the film convention whereby Germans and other Europeans are evil because of their wicked ideology whereas Asians are wicked because they are Japanese or Chinese or Vietnamese. Lionel Chetwynd's *Hanoi Hilton* (1987) is a simple World War II Japanese prison camp movie, unusual only in that there is an explicit statement of this racist ethic in the film.

In the Vietnam War one of the main public relations concerns of the Pentagon was to promote the Special Forces' irregular warfare. John Wayne (who else?) rose to the challenge. In *The Green Berets* Wayne showed what a difficult time America was having in disentangling from its World War II self. The film boiled special warfare down into a formula that is basically a Western combined with elements from Wayne's earlier *Back to Bataan* (1945). The Americans are the good guys, the Vietcong are the bad guys, and the peasants are the frightened townsfolk who need protection and the rule of law. The Spe-

In The Green Berets *Wayne showed what a difficult time America was having in disentangling from its World War II self.*

cial Forces compound is very like a fort in Indian territory. The Vietcong give war whoops.

In the war film, new experience is continually being masticated into the form that can be most easily incorporated into American mythology. We are now finding it difficult to tell the difference. In a sense the American experience in Asia began as a continuation of the American frontier, the centerpiece of national myth. The lieutenants and captains in the wars against the Sioux and Apache became the colonels and generals who put down the Philippine insurrection after the Spanish-American War. The means they used were the same they used in the American West, reservations, fortified hamlets, the search and destroy mission. Most figures in public life, like Teddy Roosevelt, the Rough Rider, used the rhetoric of Manifest Destiny in expressing their approval. Comparisons were explicitly made to the conquest of the West. Accusations of imperialism came especially from the intelligentsia in the East, from people who had never been keen about westward expansion and who thought even less of grabbing the Philippines as a result of a dispute over Cuba. In short, there was an antiwar movement among "effete easterners" and alienated intellectuals like Mark Twain and William James. An American officer, Major Waller, was tried and convicted of a massacre atrocity. Boston intellectuals lamented the Wild West values that seemed to be driving the country west toward empire with dark implications for democratic traditions. Their patriotism was attacked. The Philippines became a colony anyway.

The conviction exists in many places that television has obviated novels and films, having already brought to the public everything there is to know about the Vietnam War. The most common misconception is that the war was on television every night in all its violence and gore. Of the forty-one hundred network news stories about the war during those years, about 10 percent actually had "bang, bang" in them. The bulk of the stories were the body counts, the pacification programs, Westmoreland inspecting the ARVN. Nevertheless, the public remembers the violence it saw and thinks it was put through a living hell even though these scenes were not usually very horrific, since the TV crews obviously could not get into the places that were really hot.

Platoon demonstrated an interesting side of the illusion that the war was "brought into the living room." In the scene some critics called "the My Lai scene," the audience is shown the familiar images of the Vietnam war—the peasant huts, the water buffaloes, the conical hats. You can almost sense the audience's feeling of being at home with the images, of thinking, "I know, I know," until the United States soldiers start to kill villagers. At this point there is a palpable wincing and turning away, as if to say, "No! This isn't how it goes. It goes some other way." But that was how it went too often, more often than any of us will ever know.

Vietnam films are famous for having stars as combat infantrymen who are much too old to be realistic. In *The Deer Hunter*, Michael Cimino had the gall to show a thirtyish Robert DeNiro leave a good job in a steel mill to go fight in Vietnam. *Platoon* is the first film not to make the mistake of featuring men the age of DeNiro, Sylvester Stallone, or Chuck Norris, who are far too old to withstand the rigors of jungle war. But this use of overage stars depicts war as the business of "real" men, mature men rather than the star-crossed adolescents who actually fight it. The Vietnam War, like nearly all wars, was fought by teenage males. After all, the most undesirable person in society is a teenage male. On this Reagan and Gorbachev and Ayatollah all agree. The Future Veterans of Foreign Wars are economically and socially expendable. In addition, their systems are simmering with the hormones usually associated with homicide. But war films shrewdly do not show this. Instead they show combat veterans as valued and indispensable members of an exclusive society within society. This makes it possible to compress "the horrors of war" and treat them as a rite of passage. The films understand the psychology of the teenager underclass. While the films show gratifying fantasies of power and rage to the least powerful, they also show them that war is a way of escaping their despised status. It was, of course, no accident that the teenagers who fought the Vietnam War were disproportionately the high school dropouts, the poor, black, and Hispanic. These are the people for whom the recruitment slogan that the army lets you "be all that you can be" is the literal and pathetic truth.

Among the recent Vietnam War films, two in particular focus on the war and its relation to young males. Eastwood's *Heartbreak Ridge* (1986) is cute and coy about what happens to your head in the Marine Corps and how it in-

Full Metal Jacket *gets at the specific craziness in the military's way of remaking teenagers into "killing machines."*

volves forfeiting bonds with women. The Eastwood character the teenager is being asked to admire and emulate is the usual semicomic "roughest, meanest, whore-banging, whiskey-guzzling hornswoggler in this man's [insert relevant military unit]." The film is adoringly approving. Kubrick's *Full Metal Jacket* (1987) gets at the specific craziness in the military's way of remaking teenagers into "killing machines," and the film does a good job bringing it to life. Any monk or marine can tell you that the most effective way an institution can dominate a young person's inner life is for it to dominate his (or her) sexuality. The recruits are abused with a weird litany of images of sex, aggression, and dismemberment. The script underlines the way the recruits are feminized by this abuse as a way of enhancing their contemptibility. I could tell from the laughter in the theater that this was a novelty for the preview audience. All of this is accurate, but the script neglects the element of power and real fear involved in being at the mercy of three sergeants charged with convincing you that life is cheap and killing is pleasurable. Deformed sexuality and hatred of women are necessary inputs in the production of cannon folder. They are not its cause.

With Private Joker in *Full Metal Jacket* Kubrick shows evil being borne by a character so odd and insignificant that he does not seem worthy of the monstrosities he commits. American culture is a kind of generalized Eichmann problem where the wretched little chips of humanity who bear historical evil are bland and boring, as in the case of Eichmann, or, in *Full Metal Jacket*, merely jerks. This is the way Kubrick's world ends, not with a bang but a giggle. This film might be the one America needs right now.

If film is going to tear itself away from the contemplation of American mythic obsessions and tell what happened in Vietnam, here are some of the incidents it will see when it opens its eyes. This list is conceived with the FVFW in mind. With this list we turn away from the war that the brass wanted to fight and toward the one the privates actually did fight. In this war the air strikes are as dangerous to us as to the people who are shooting at the infantrymen. The helicopters don't come promptly when there are wounded. You hear on the sound track guys who have been tough in the earlier reels screaming, expecially the ones who have lost limbs. They've been shot up with morphine and the corpsmen have begged them to shut up because they are giving away their position. But the morphine won't work for twenty minutes and they don't care who hears them. Their legs are gone at the knees and they're howling and thrashing around, crying for their mothers, yelling "Mommy! Mommy!" over and over again at the top of their lungs. No shame. They don't care any more. The others wish they'd shut up. The others wouldn't mind if they'd die, if only they'd shut up. It's not so much that they're giving the position away. It's the howling, the bottomless woe. Those wounded are only ten to twenty meters away in the dark, but they're signalling how horrible it can be, how anybody can sound, if their luck runs out, when "it" finally happens. This would be a whole different order of screaming from the kind you'd need later in the hospital ward scenes. (There is a striking absence of hospital scenes in the Vietnam genre film). The screaming in the hospital wards on the day the corpsmen come to clean the stumps would present new challenges to the audio engineers.

Not all of these overlooked incidents have to be horrific. Some could be subtle. There could be a depiction of the quiet vomiting of members of an infantry squad before they leave the perimeter for a night patrol. Previous movies have missed the small ways that fear affects you. The way it grinds you down, and diminishes and degrades you. And they have missed fear's aftereffects, like the screaming nightmares of G.I.'s in the field hospitals, who rave about "gooks," G.I.s who have been wounded and the ones who now would like to kill all of "them," even the Vietnamese who sweep the ward.

And, of course, there are the Vietnamese. It would seem lopsided if the films kept focusing exclusively on our story. Will we keep thinking the tragedy is that of the invader, of his losses, of his painful self-knowledge, his loss of innocence, his recognition of limits? This suits the national character so depressingly well. It would be interesting to take other lives into account. There should be scenes about the little circle of laundresses and whores and barbers and spies that the American troops knew, who were all of Vietnam most Americans ever knew. And what about our "allies," the ones we went there to defend? Who were those people whose daughters wore white ao dais and rode bicycles to the Lycée Blaise Pascal on Doc Lap Street? Who were the families with the Citroëns? One day in the spring of '66, some of them were going in to Da Nang, dressed in their best clothes, to protest something or other. Some ARVN soldiers fired an antitank weapon at their bus. A horrible mess, all those bright clothes covered with blood. We were ordered to fire on the ones who fired the antitank weapon, if they fired again. It was a national controversy. We could learn about it in a film that could be made one day when, after growing curious about what we were like, and then after learning about ourselves made us acquire an interest in other lives including Vietnamese. There could be a film about their experience. Our memorial wall in Washington has fifty-eight-thousand or so dead on it. The Vietnamese suffered more than 2 million dead. Because their country is smaller than our country, one fifth the size, their wall, if they had one and we allowed for these differences, would be two hundred times larger than ours.

But it is not easy to go against a culture of not wanting to know, or even identify where in the circle of not knowing we need to break in. The columnist Anthony Lewis, who wrote a good deal about Vietnam, stated that *Platoon* told him things he hadn't known about the war. How did he not know these things? And the great American mass has its own convictions about "offensive incidents." At the end of the war, Richard Nixon was using the need to prevent a bloodbath as the only excuse for continuing the war and citing the "Hue massacre" as proof that this would happen should the other side gain control. At the time, I was active in Vietnam Veterans Against the War (VVAW). A CBS file clerk sent to the offices of VVAW an outline of a documentary project that had been killed. The proposed project had located a number of credible (that is, non-Vietnamese) sources who said that what the Marine Corps claimed were massacre victims were in fact killed by the Marine Corps bombing raids during the retaking of Hue. As the Vietnamese forces held out against the Marines for weeks after Tet, the corpses became a health hazard and the city's residents pushed the dead into mass graves. It was these mass graves that the Marine Corps used in its massacre claims and still stands by. Kubrick's antiwar *Full Metal Jacket* shows the uncovering of these graves and naively offers the Marine Corps's version of how they came to be. Armed with the internal documents, VVAW staged a sit-in at CBS headquarters at "Black Rock," where it became clear that CBS would give no ground and would soon call the police. We gave in. But the episode exposed me to the thinking at CBS. I was told that they "had taken so much heat over My Lai" that it was just impossible to go with another story like the one we were then proposing. As Barry Richardson, then vice-president for public relations, told me, "One of those is enough." So one of those was all America was permitted to have. With *Platoon* there is the suggestion that a hidden history of "offensive incidents" lies like a lost continent under the waters of the media images of the war. *Platoon*'s popularity may mean that the national wish to not know is waning.

It is to protect America's fabled innocence and sense of benevolence that the country's editorialists, since America's defeat in Vietnam, have begun to speak of these qualities as though they were national treasures to be preserved as ends in themselves. There is no sense that these might be qualities or virtues

Innocence is something awful if you are committing crimes.

that have to be maintained through effort, that innocence is something awful if you are committing crimes, that optimism is self-destruction if it hides real dangers, or that faith in your own benevolence can be a disguise for evil. Film producers and politicians and our other merchants of moral comfort may produce and sell new walls of spiritual insulation. But almost certainly sooner rather than later, and at a time of its choosing and not ours, history will destroy the mythic insulation with which we are presently protecting ourselves from its "offensive incidents."

"They Were Called and They Went":
The Political Rehabilitation
of the Vietnam Veteran

A commercial message precedes the film *Platoon* (1986) on the Home Box Office (HBO) videocassette release. The "institutional" ad establishes a particular image for a major American automobile corporation, and it provides a position from which to make sense of the film that follows. Chrysler chairman Lee Iacocca, wearing a suit and a trench coat, walks slowly through a wooded area and comes across an army jeep in a clearing. Iacocca is pensive, lost in thought. The camera pans across the front of the jeep, finally framing Iacocca within the windshield as he speaks:

> This jeep is a museum piece, a relic of war. Normandy, Anzio, Guadalcanal, Korea, Vietnam. I hope we will never have to build another jeep for war. This film *Platoon* is a memorial not to war but to all the men and women who fought in a time and in a place nobody really understood, who knew only one thing: they were called and they went. It was the same from the first musket fired at Concord to the rice paddies of the Mekong Delta: they were called and they went. That in the truest sense is the spirit of America. The more we understand it, the more we honor those who kept it alive. I'm Lee Iacocca.

The ad functions in at least two ways. First, it provides an appropriately sober introduction to the film. *Platoon*, advertised as "the first *real* film about Vietnam," received widespread critical and public attention at the time of its theatrical release. A publicized dispute over ownership delayed the film's release on videocassette, increasing the sense of anticipation reflected even in news reports. In short, *Platoon* achieved legendary status prior to its videocassette release, and the ad acknowledges and exploits this status while establishing a reverential mood. The ad underscores *Platoon*'s media-generated aura of authenticity.

Second, the ad associates an implied political rehabilitation of the Vietnam veteran with the economic rejuvenation of the Chrysler Corporation, a vulgar cooptation achieved by powerful imagery and a strategically crafted script that engulfs the memory of the Vietnam War with the memory of World War II. The visual elements suggest a European battlefield overgrown with vegetation, and Iacocca's clothing suggests the image of a war correspondent returned to the site of fighting. As he speaks, he runs his hand across the hood of the jeep, and the camera pans across the jeep's grill when he is finished. Finally, a slow dissolve reveals a red, white, and blue Chrysler logo with the words "Jeep" and "Eagle."

The image of the Chrysler jeep signifies ideological continuity extending through time, as if the specific historical conditions of World War II battles illuminate later wars of containment, as if the American sacrifices at Normandy give heroic meaning to death in Vietnam. The ad communicates a transcendent vision of sacrifice detached from any historical context. The scripted narration develops the theme of continuity by collapsing American combat experiences onto one timeless battlefield where Concord and the Mekong Delta merge in the "same" continuum of rational, ideologically explicable sacrifice. This commercial message hails the Vietnam veteran's doubtful *willingness* to serve in an inexplicable war. Simultaneously, the message implies that the Chrysler Corporation, just as the ahistorically defined "men and women," stands ready to answer the call "to build another jeep."

The ad demonstrates even more explicitly than *Platoon* and other recent war films the extent to which cultural forms now produce a vision of the Vietnam War that obliterates the lived social experience of ideological crisis. The ad, like many films and television dramas about the war, helps produce Vietnam as an inexplicable terrain and the Vietnam veteran as a World War II poser. The thirty-second ad is an instance of ideological condensation, facilitating the successful reassertion of cultural patterns rendered problematic by the war. Viewers are clearly expected to react respectfully to Iacocca's statement; *they are not expected to laugh* at the absurd associations of World War II, the American Revolution, and the production capability of strategic industries with the Vietnam War and its veterans.

During the last ten years, the Vietnam veteran has undergone a kind of miraculous transformation, facilitated by the historical revision of the war and signified by mass-mediated rituals. Functioning to repress what Lloyd Lewis calls a shattered belief system,[1] immediate postwar representations of the veteran depicted him as either a violent psychotic or a victim, prompting Rick Berg to conclude that cultural forms have simply failed to deal adequately with the soldier's experience of the war.[2] Berg, writing from the perspective of a combat veteran, laments the apparent inability of mass media to represent the soldier's lived social experience of ideological crisis and to link that experience to concrete political conditions. In his important essay, "Losing Vietnam," Berg attempts to reclaim his Vietnam experience ideologically from the mediated process of revision, and he implies that Vietnam veterans are losing the opportunity to bear witness to the war's contradictions. In short, mass media representations are coopting the very experience that makes Vietnam veterans, for better or worse, unique in the national story. Shifting away from themes of victimization and psychosis, more recent representations function therapeutically to rehabilitate the Vietnam veteran, positioning him as a warrior hero whose experience can now be used to justify a continuation of a modified form of the Truman Doctrine: intervention by proxy and internal subversion.

Berg reflects the anger and disappointment shared by many Vietnam veterans who now see their war experience called into service for the very objectives that brought so much needless misery to the peoples of Indochina and, to a far lesser degree, the United States. But there is another way of looking at the ideological process now unfolding in our mass media and in other sites of ritual, including the ubiquitous "homecoming" parades that Michael Clark calls examples of "historical surrealism."[3] While many media representations of the war *repress* ideological contradictions, they also *produce* a general frame of reference that assigns particular meanings to the Vietnam War experience. The question now becomes "how" and "why" have ideological apparatuses, including the mass media, succeeded in producing the Vietnam veteran as a warrior hero, potentially usable in the further development of American imperialism.

REINTEGRATION AND IDEOLOGICAL STRUGGLE

Mass media interpretations of the war have political significance. Film, television, and other cultural forms provide sites of ideological struggle and assign meaning to the war experience and to veterans in an attempt to reintegrate both into the ongoing national story. Anthropologist Victor Turner locates this political process within the so-called social drama, a ritualized form of conflict management characterizing all cultures.[4] Social dramas erupt when norms are breached, prompting a crisis stage that requires a subsequent redress of grievances. The final stage of a social drama is reintegrative, characterized by the attempt of cultural forms—what Louis Althusser calls "ideological state apparatuses"—to make sense of the social drama in terms consistent with previous social experience and established cultural patterns.[5]

Although the social drama may prompt cultural patterns to change to some degree, the process is essentially conservative.[6] Change must be accommodated within already established frames of reference, otherwise reintegration will fail and the social drama's outcome will result in social fragmentation or revolution. Turner conceptualizes cultural forms as sites of ritual where social meaning is enacted or performed and where distressed subcultures and societies find "healing" in the aftermath of crisis. Turner provides an anthropological explanation of ideological struggle, the ongoing contest among conflicting groups laying claim to the meaning of the nation and to state power.

Our culture is now experiencing the reintegrative phase in the aftermath of an ideological crisis that polarized the nation. The 1982 construction of the Vietnam Veterans Memorial—The Wall—prompted the current reintegrative phase by returning veterans to public discourse and facilitating a rich array of rituals in which pilgrims enacted their relationships to the war dead.[7] Mass media gave widespread attention to these rituals and reproduced The Wall's image as the war's embodiment. Encouraged by The Wall's unexpected critical and popular success, other cultural forms quickly focused on the veteran and on the war dead as objects of ideological struggle, necessarily involving conflicting visions of the nation.[8] The truly remarkable characteristic of the current reintegrative process is the extent to which mass media and other cultural forms obliterate much of the soldier's lived social experience of the war and generate representations of Vietnam consistent with the reassertion of military containment as a credible policy.

In Vietnam, many Americans experienced the structural contradictions of imperialism and recognized those contradictions in their own contacts with the Vietnamese. *Winning Hearts and Minds*, the first major collection of poems by American combat veterans, reflects the soldier's sense of complicity in needless brutality.[9] In his analysis of American strategy, *The Perfect War*, James William Gibson explains how U.S. war managers succeeded by discursive means in subjugating knowledge of Vietnam's social reality.[10] This strategy implemented the policy of military containment and positioned the Vietnamese peasant (always the key to victory) as a mere statistic whose subjectivity—or sense of self—meant nothing. A similar strategy discounted the lived social reality of American soldiers whose experience developed as an ideological crisis originating in the contradictions between stated objectives and their dysfunctional deployment. For many troops, the war ceased to be understandable in terms compatible with American values and beliefs, and this unique perspective threatened not only the specific objectives in Vietnam but the viability—the good sense—of intervention based solely on an overdetermined, hyperpositivist commitment to what Gibson calls "mechanistic anticommunism." Vietnam's social reality had no place in the equation whereby American war managers attempted to produce the nation of South Vietnam, but American troops could not so easily ignore the structural conditions of their own environment. U.S. policy put American troops in a position where traditional values and explanations ceased to make sense and where the resulting ideological crisis made them potentially oppositional. The soldier's ideological crisis operates on a deeply political level, as some of the oral histories of the war reveal: "Vietnam taught you to be a liar. To be a thief. To be dishonest. To go against everything you ever learned. It taught you everything you did not need to know, because you were livin' a lie. And the lie was you ain't have no business bein' there in the first place. You wasn't protecting your homeland. And that was what wear you down."[11]

Knowledge of the "lie" of Vietnam positioned Vietnam veterans as politically volatile persons in American culture, anomalies within the prevailing arguments of mechanistic anticommunism. Again, the Chrysler ad illuminates the ideological process that now dislocates the veteran's political volatility. The ad identifies the Vietnam War as "a place nobody really understood," mystifying the circumstances of the soldier's ideological crisis while simultaneously absolving him of responsibility. The ability of the dominant ideology to reprocess the soldier's knowledge, to represent his experience of ideological crisis in ways advantageous to the very objectives that produced the crisis, demonstrates the productive power of hegemony, the process by which an ideological bloc attains "progressive ascendancy over the apparatuses of opinion formation" so that the bloc's narrow interests gain wide acceptance as natural.[12] The veteran's transformation is a product of successful ideological struggle waged throughout social institutions.

REVISING THE WAR IN SOCIAL INSTITUTIONS

Current representations of the war emerge within a cultural context of revisionism, a New Right project whereby cultural forms (including academic writing) reassert the consensus discredited by the war. The revisionist process takes form in the postwar readjustment strategies observable in several social institutions. These strategies provide the structural evidence of an ideological bloc's claim to state power and the structural context of mass media representations of the war. For example, elite policy-making organizations, reacting to a perceived loss of American global power, developed and implemented strategies aimed at reasserting the authority and credibility unmasked by the war's social reality. Joseph Peschek, in his study of several influential policy and research organizations, concluded that in the aftermath of Vietnam and subsequent "crises" of the 1970s, "[American political] elites saw the expansion of liberal democracy [in the United States] as endangering the social order and the economic system they presided over. In differing ways, this contradiction established the terms in which the policy-planners of the center and the right approached the task of rescuing a system in decline."[13]

James Boylan shows that a similar ideological adjustment occurred within the organizational structures of news media.[14] News content became less critical, and "balance" was negotiated in favor of the emerging ideological bloc.[15] Network television news content shifted as an organizational accommodation to conservative electoral victories.[16] As Lee Iacocca's Chrysler ad demonstrates, advertising agencies began recognizing an emerging set of circumstances and developed numerous campaigns associating products with a revived national spirit. These structural adjustments reflect the attainment of hegemony by an ideological bloc fearful of the war's effect on the viability of U.S. intervention. Hegemony establishes the bloc's legitimacy by producing politically useful subjectivities, or positions from which individuals might view social reality. This process requires the political rehabilitation of the Vietnam veteran for reasons identified in Marilyn Young's critique of revisionist historical analysis of the war:

> I believe that the treatment of Indochina in the postwar period is a vital part of the effort to create a new ideological consensus, one that will preserve the possibility of counter-revolutionary interventions when and how they become necessary. For the fundamental institutions which gave rise to the Vietnam war have hardly changed; what has changed is the *credibility* of the imperialist ideology which justified that war. From the viewpoint of the State, that is the wound that must be healed.[17]

Young's emphasis on credibility focuses attention on how the war revealed, finally, the ruthless nature of American imperialism and the failure of American political elites to adequately understand Vietnamese society. The revelations implied that Americans were fighting and dying in Vietnam for an unworthy cause. Antiwar soldiers, reacting to their experience of ideological crisis in Vietnam, aided in the destruction of administrative credibility by mounting several widely televised demonstrations and other events.

Joshua Meyrowitz observes that "hierarchies will be undermined by new media that expose what were once the private spheres of authorities."[18] The same can be said of already established media, which reveal flaws in policy-making normally hidden from public view. Antiwar Vietnam veterans, by their presence in news reports, signified the failure of policymakers to generate explanations for the necessity of the war consistent with American political ideology. Returning soldiers unavoidably embodied the war's ideological crisis, and this explains why many veterans remained silent about their service. Significantly, the first major academic attempt to revise the war's history focused directly on the experience of soldiers and attempted to obliterate it.

Guenter Lewy's *America in Vietnam* is a classic revisionist interpretation of the war and has influenced subsequent attempts to discount the soldier's experience of ideological crisis in Vietnam.[19] One chapter, "Atrocities: Fiction and Fact," establishes the ideological basis for the transformation of the Vietnam veteran into a World War II hero. Lewy discounts most atrocity stories as exaggerations of stories fabricated by bored troops, and he explains "actual" atrocities as an outcome of "callousness caused by . . . American journalists and politicians who, while seeking to end the American involvement, for years exaggerated the faults of the South Vietnamese government and nation and gradually created an image of people not worth defending, if not altogether worthless."[20] Lewy's book shows the extent to which the soldier's lived experience must be discounted to accommodate the war's revision and the resurrection of a discredited foreign policy.

The significance of atrocity stories is not, of course, that all Americans participated in or condoned such action. Lloyd Lewis demonstrates that the experience of actual atrocities was merely one very compelling example in an array of social experiences that disconfirmed the soldiers' belief system[21] and generated what Robert Lifton identified very early as Vietnam's "counterfeit"-reality.[22] Lewis and Lifton provide, respectively, the sociological and psychological explanations for the soldier's ideological crisis in Vietnam, a crisis generated by the absence of a viable explanation for the American presence. The specific conditions of Vietnam produced survival as the only explanation of the soldier's action, and this made the Vietnam War unique in the American experience. The domestic political polarization experienced at home had a tragic parallel among the troops in Vietnam. As the war exposed the contradictions of mechanistic anticommunism and the American dependency on brutality, the soldier's lived social experience of war developed as an ideological crisis, interpreted by commanders as a morale problem. For example, Colonel Robert D. Heinl, Jr., observed, "The morale, discipline and battleworthiness of the U.S. Armed Forces are, with a few salient exceptions, lower and worse than at any time in this century and possibly in the history of the United States."[23]

The near-mutinous conditions identified by Heinl reflected the troop's recognition, in varying degrees, of the "lie" of Vietnam, including what Gibson describes as the Saigon government's "institutionalized corruption," underwritten by U.S. war managers as a necessary component of rapid modernization.[24] Significantly, New Right ideologues avoid the undependability of American troops as a factor in the litany of why the United States lost the war.[25] By obliterating the soldiers' most dramatic experience of ideological contradictions (unjustifiable killing), Lewy helped initiate an interpolation—or "hailing"—of Vietnam veterans within the form of previous wars.[26] Heroic self-sacrifice and ideological commitment emerged as components in a therapeutic strategy that produced a new subjectivity reflected in the eager responses of some veterans with access to opinion magazines.

The revisionist strategy reduces the Vietnam War experience to a merely aesthetic issue, suggested by William Broyles's widely quoted *Esquire* article, "Why Men Love War," in which he observes that "war is the only utopian experience most of us ever have."[27] Broyles celebrates war's erotic appeal and dramatic grandeur, revealing that he "preferred white phosphorous, which exploded with a fulsome elegance, wreathing its target in intense and billowing white smoke."[28] A full-page photograph shows Broyles seated and holding his son within the monumental legs of soldiers depicted in the Iwo Jima statue at Arlington, underscoring Broyles's imagery of war as the male equivalent of childbirth.

Broyles's article is a political marker, another instance of ideological condensation in which the rehabilitated veteran serves the interests of patriarchy, antifeminism, *and* imperialism. Following its publication, Broyles appeared in several network television interviews that focused superficially on the nature of masculinity. Like Marinetti's Futurist interpretation of war's beauty, Broyles's essay introduces "aesthetics into political life."[29] Here, in the process whereby an ideological bloc achieves dominance, several subjective positions intersect. The embattled male, reacting to the onslaught of feminism, intersects with the ideologically tainted soldier. The dramatic nature of combat links the veteran to the timeless, and ahistorical, essence of masculinity. The ideological crisis of Vietnam is obliterated by the bizarre reorientation of signs, but the specific conditions of hegemony prevent the television interviewers from asking him: "Why did you pose with your infant son at a war memorial which has nothing to do with your generation's experience in Vietnam?" By 1984, such a question would have implied an "unbalanced" approach to news reporting; the interviewer would have seemed inexplicably opposed to the reintegration of Vietnam veterans. Hegemony assures that ideological contradictions seem natural and right. Explicit identification often seems petty, stridently partisan, or simply idiosyncratic when it occurs within journalistic forms. By 1984, the visual convergence of World War II and the Vietnam War seemed natural or true enough. As in the Chrysler ad, this interpretation increasingly celebrates the transcendent glory of war and the soldier's commitment, while discounting the specific factors that produced the Vietnam experience as an ideological crisis. Young men are "called" to combat by the irresistible forces of nature, not by selective service boards. The interpretation's strength rests in its ability to discount critics as "antimale" or "antiveteran," opposed to the reintegrative process veterans deserve. The revival of mechanistic anticommunism as a credible policy required a new position for the veteran, and mass media helped provide it.

THE VETERAN'S TRANSFORMATION

Like Broyles's celebration of war's erotic and timeless appeal, *Rambo* helped remove the Vietnam veteran from any specific historical context. The film expresses the veteran's discontent while decontextualizing its origin, contributing to the therapeutic strategy that positions the veteran as a warrior hero. *Rambo* identifies the veteran's source of estrangement in too narrow terms, in terms conducive to the revisionist project but in terms that avoid the soldier's experience with the Vietnamese. *Rambo* avoids the soldier's knowledge of the peasant's suffering and focuses only on the soldier's knowledge of a generalized suffering that originates in an effete, antimilitarist bureaucracy. It is not the lived social experience of ideological crisis that produces Rambo's pathology but rather the betrayal of his cause by a venal bureaucracy that seeks to contain the natural expression of his masculinity. Rambo is doubly betrayed. When he ignores orders and rescues an American prisoner of war (POW), he is abandoned atop a dangerous hill. *Rambo* offers a position from which to understand the veteran's postwar silencing in terms consistent with the revisionist interpretation of the war. As a ritual enactment, *Rambo* helped rehabilitate the Vietnam veteran politically by purging him of ideological taint. Here, the veteran emerges as a usable sign of postwar consensus, serving the needs of the ideological bloc that assigns particular meanings to the war throughout an array of social institutions. In *Rambo*—as in the widely reported homecoming parades—the veteran serves as a sign of ideological certainty and thereby helps establish credibility for a discredited policy. The price of reintegration is the strategic forgetting of ideological crisis, demonstrated by the film's naturalized destruction of Vietnamese village life.

Rambo has limited but disastrous contact with Vietnamese peasants, and here the film echoes Lewy's attempt to explain atrocities in terms consistent with the revisionist interpretation of the war. Rambo merely collides with villagers, and he only *incidentally* destroys them and their homes as an unfortunate—but entirely natural—outcome of war. In one sequence, for example, Rambo flees through a hillside village and tricks the pursuing Russians and Vietnamese into following him into a nearby field of tall, dry grass and bamboo. Demonstrating his natural cunning (a product of his German and Native American origins), he traps his pursuers with a wall of fire, which chases them toward the village. Rambo's well-placed explosive arrow engulfs the village, incinerating his enemies. The villagers pay the seemingly rational, albeit regrettable, price of destruction.

In another sequence, Rambo pilots a damaged helicopter filled with liberated POWs. His Russian enemy pursues in another helicopter and an exchange of fire erupts over a village. Rambo returns fire only when the Russian demonstrates his disregard for the villagers by firing first. Rambo's counterattack causes a sheet of armor to fall from the Russian craft, and it bounces on the Vietnamese terrain, eventually smashing a tree and igniting a home. The event occurs within the much longer aerial chase sequence, and it signifies the veteran's ritualized reintegration by absolving him of responsibility for civilian suffering, which it simultaneously projects upon the hated Russian (portrayed in the conventions of a wartime German Nazi) with whom Rambo shares a sadomasochistic relationship.

Soon after its release, *Rambo* generated a debate over "fascist aesthetics." Hoberman, drawing upon Susan Sontag's criteria of fascist aesthetics, saw parallels between *Rambo* and Nazi documentaries.[30] The film brings to mind Benjamin's observation that "fascism sees its salvation in giving . . . [the] masses not their right, but instead a chance to express themselves."[31] In *Rambo*, hegemony dislocates the veteran's *source* of ideological crisis while expressing his lost sense of a coherent belief system. In the film, as in the homecoming parades, the veteran is "subjected, used, transformed and improved" through disciplinary and therapeutic measures.[32] The Vietnam veteran is contained, made manageable, reprocessed by a specific ideological bloc that, as we have seen, deploys its strategy throughout the institutions of civil society. Other films in the return-trip cycle contribute to the process, as do several television spin-offs.

The return trip to Vietnam appeared in the CBS series *Magnum, P.I.* soon after *Rambo*'s success. *Magnum, P.I.* explores the limits of its genre by focusing on the process of recollection.[33] The audience follows the postwar reconstruction of a veteran's identity in the weekly coping of its lead character, Thomas Magnum, whose self-reflexive sense-making emerges in his continuing voice-over comments about the action. Even when the program is not "about" the war, Vietnam frames the story line, because regular viewers understand that Magnum, a former Navy intelligence officer who operates a private investigation business in Hawaii, works to maintain his relatively functional adjustment. Television's episodic nature provides a broad range of formulaic circumstances within which the veteran's reintegration is ritualized. The emphasis on Magnum's unfolding psychological condition serves to unify the series and is explicitly therapeutic. In an ambitious two-part episode titled "All for One" (originally aired on January 31 and February 7, 1985), Magnum and his buddies return to Southeast Asia, ostensibly to rescue a captured American soldier. But they soon learn that Tyler Peabody McKinney, a new character, has tricked them. The real mission centers on rescuing the "George freakin' Washington of Cambodia," a medical doctor who serves as "the Provisional President of a Confederation of Democratic Resistance Groups," which now fights, simultaneously, the Vietnamese occupation army and the Khmer Rouge.

The provisional president has no basis in the actual historical circumstances of Southeast Asia except, perhaps, in the wildest dreams of U.S. policymakers and their apologists. He signifies the imagined presence of a viable

Third Force in Cambodia and, more importantly, the imagined presence of a democratic bloc in wartime Saigon. The character and story line reflect the revisionist convergence of the Vietnamese defeat of the United States with the genocidal policy of Cambodia's Pol Pot. Moreover, the conventions of representation are highly recombinant, an example of how television's production methods endlessly rework established images and themes in new configurations.[34] The *Magnum, P.I.* series generally, and the two-part episode especially, draw upon the formal characteristics of television and film to develop a pastichelike representation. Although the action is set in contemporary Cambodia, the episode draws upon the conventions of World War II combat films, *Rambo* and similar back-to-'Nam films, imagery and music of the 1960s, and television news coverage of the war. As the episode unfolds, distinctions blur between contemporary Cambodia and the Vietnam of mass-mediated memory. Magnum and his war buddies are relocated in an ongoing, timeless Vietnam War so that viewers may examine the origins of Magnum's postwar relationships. The recombinant nature of network TV programming coalesces an imagined Cambodia of the mid-1980s with a reimagined Vietnam of the late 1960s so that Magnum enters an utterly ahistorical and timeless war.

The provisional president facilitates the Vietnam veteran's rehabilitation by providing a rationale for American sacrifices consistent with the needs of mechanistic anticommunism. Tyler admits that he lied about the captured American in order to get Magnum and his buddies to help rescue the president, and Tyler explains his lie in terms of freedom: "I think it's about time we stopped puttin' conditions on the words freedom and commitment. You live 'em or you don't. That's why we're here." The provisional president reinforces Tyler's use of "freedom" as a euphemism for military containment, and he explains to Magnum why Tyler's lie was necessary:

> PRESIDENT: But the lie itself was based on a truth. And I think that truth is one that you and he and your friends ultimately share.
> MAGNUM: What truth is that?
> PRESIDENT: The most basic one of them all. The belief in freedom. Sometimes I think people just have to be reminded of it. And sometimes it doesn't particularly matter how. Thank you.

Here, the episode transposes "lie" with "truth" to generate agreement on the war's heroic nature. The "lie" of Vietnam—the soldier's experience of ideological crisis—becomes the "truth" of freedom, contingent on Magnum's commitment to values that transcend the specific details of history.

Magnum and his buddies befriend villagers who are forced by the Vietnamese to grow poppies for the opium trade. In a final shoot-out, an evil Vietnamese officer tosses a grenade at two children, and Tyler makes the ultimate sacrifice to save them. Magnum, forced to support "freedom" by Tyler's heroic act, guns down the Vietnamese. Tyler's heroic self-sacrifice, like Lewy's revisionist history, expiates the worst memory of the war—the killing of noncombatants—and rationalizes the purpose of American policy. Americans died for freedom and to prevent Vietnamese soldiers from performing heinous acts against civilians. Here, Lewy's denial of atrocities takes the form of projection. As in *Rambo*, the process of representation produces ideological contradictions in the concrete examples of role reversal. Tyler's death reduces the contradictions of American policy to a matter of tactics. Rather than questioning the efficacy of military containment, "All for One" represents the policy as a misapplication. Tyler atones for a tactical error, not for structural contradictions inherent to the intervention.

In *Magnum, P.I.*, the war's meaning is explorable but, in the end, inexplicable. Magnum provides a concluding statement intended to frame the action and conflict within the veteran's need for therapeutic self-discipline. Returning to Hawaii, Magnum and his buddies walk along the beach, sharing the mundane problems they must solve as a result of their absence from work. Rick stands with the Pacific as a backdrop and asks: "What if we hadn't o' gone?" Viewers familiar with the series understand that Rick's question refers not only to the recent return trip but to the broader issue of the Vietnam War itself. Magnum and the other characters stop and remain silent for several seconds until Magnum provides an answer: "We did." Like *Rambo*, the episode decontextualizes the veteran's experience while expressing his discontent and hailing his commitment to a generalized, ahistorical "freedom," as Magnum reveals in his closing voice-over narration:

> We wound up going to Cham Kur and Bang Lai for that most basic truth. Freedom. But did Tyler? I don't know. Ultimately, it didn't matter. What mattered was we were faithful to that truth. And so was Tyler Peabody McKinney.

What "matters" is the veteran's action based on his internalized commitment to the truth of freedom; Vietnam's meaning resides in the imagined history of the veteran, which displaces the history of the war. Hegemony produces identical messages in the ruminations of Magnum and his buddies as they walk on the beach and Iacocca as he walks through the overgrown meadow. In each case, the veteran remains faithful to values that transcend the specific and inexplicable circumstances of Vietnam.

Given the simplistic quality of the return-trip scenarios, it was not surprising that a more determined "realistic" representation of the war would emerge. Representations like *Rambo* and *Magnum, P.I.* successfully removed the veteran from the specific historic circumstances of the war, opening the way for close examination of what had remained a Hollywood taboo: small-unit combat. *Rambo* helped generate the circumstances in which *Platoon* could win popular acceptance as the "real" story of Vietnam, what *Time* would label as "the way it really was."[35] Doubtless the film's status as "the first commercial feature about Vietnam written and directed by a vet" helped produce an aura of authenticity, emphasized in studio press releases and advertisements.[36] Two important sets of images, or visual paradigms, underscore *Platoon*'s realism. *Platoon* focuses on the relatively mundane aspects of daily life in the bush and, more importantly, on death.[37]

Platoon is the first Vietnam War film to provide extensive visual representation of the "hump," the physically demanding and often fearful movement through dense jungle. These highly detailed scenes accompany the representation of base-camp life. Soldiers swap stories, eat, brush their teeth, shave, bathe, write letters home, smoke dope, play poker, and burn feces. These scenes provide *Platoon* with an element of authenticity missing in films like *Rambo*, which rely solely on action. And they draw upon an already established familiarity with the "look" of Vietnam developed over the years by television news stories and documentaries. Indeed, one scene originates in the famous CBS news story about the burning of Vietnamese hootches by American soldiers using Zippo lighters. These scenes are detailed reminders of what we've already experienced in a variety of mass-mediated settings during the last twenty years.

More importantly, *Platoon* is the first Vietnam War film to represent extensive combat and the process of dying, a direct result of the popular and critical success of The Wall. The ideological crisis of the war prevented the widespread depiction of fighting and casualties, one reason why film and television developed the formulaic representation of veterans as victims or psychotics following their return from Vietnam. The war was seen as an effect, not a process. Contrary to popular misconceptions, Vietnam did not unfold on television as "the living room war," if that phrase means the nightly exposure to combat and casualties. Content analyses of network news programs reveal that American audiences rarely saw the suffering of soldiers in the field. Most often, audiences saw the movement of soldiers as they jumped off helicopters in secured landing zones. By acknowledging death, The Wall generated rituals of remembrance, opening the way for the representation of combat and for tentative attempts to assign meaning to the loss of American lives. *Platoon* contributes to the reintegrative phase of the Vietnam social drama by representing death, and this underscores the film's realism.

Platoon provides the elegy for the Vietnam War dead that cultural forms, including the political speech, avoided during the postwar "trance of collective amnesia."[38] The film parallels the rituals of remembrance performed at The Wall and uses Samuel Barber's "Adagio for Strings" in conjunction with images of the dead to emphasize this ritual function.[39] Because the film avoids the specific circumstances of ideological crisis and instead develops the theme of lost innocence, it facilitates a broad range of interpretations, as does The Wall. Attention is given to the dead in the first few moments of the film. As Chris (Charlie Sheen) steps off the plane that brought him to Vietnam, he sees body bags loaded for shipment home and hears another soldier ask: "Aw, man, is that what I think it is?" In other scenes, the dead are loaded on helicopters. Chopper blades blow away a tarp, revealing corpses. The representation of injury is graphic, painful, and bloody. The camera focuses on the eyes of casualties as medics take extreme measures to save them. And the brutal killing of two American soldiers establishes the context for later atrocities at a village (recalling the conditions of the My Lai massacre). In one action sequence, Sergeant Elias is chased by enemy troops from the jungle toward a destroyed church. Unable to rescue him, Chris and others watch helplessly from a hovering helicopter as Elias, his body hit by enemy fire, extends his arms in a futile gesture toward the sky. This image, similar to the image of Rambo's abandonment, is used in promotion and draws attention to the film's ritualized acknowledgement of suffering. The concluding sequence shows death in a variety of forms, lingering over corpses piled on the jungle floor. Like The Wall, *Platoon* introduces the dead as an object of ideological struggle in the reintegrative phase.

Other films released after The Wall's construction share *Platoon*'s emphasis on graphic depiction of combat injury and death. *Full Metal Jacket* (1987), set in the 1968 Tet Offensive, uses slow-motion techniques to show the killing of American soldiers. The death of one character, Cowboy, provides the context of the "payback" killing of a Vietnamese sniper. *Hamburger Hill* (1987), set in the 1969 Ashau Valley fighting, opens with images of The Wall, which quickly overlap with images of American troops carrying a dead soldier to a waiting helicopter. An injured soldier, tossed through the air by an explosion, suffers a stomach wound shown in a lengthy foreground shot. One character, Doc, bears responsibility for identifying the dead and thereby provides the element that unifies the several death scenes. The film visualizes the sacrifices signified by the names on The Wall. *Hamburger Hill*, like *Platoon* and *Full Metal Jacket*, uses a familiar plot device from World War II combat films: characters, developed as members of a platoon on a mission, are killed in pursuit of their objective. *Hamburger Hill* claims the dead for the revisionist agenda. American troops, all of whom are identified as "niggers" by Doc, are located in Vietnam because of the antiwar movement back home. The soldiers' struggle against the Vietnamese is also a struggle against critics of American policy. Like *Rambo*, *Hamburger Hill* dislocates the source of the veteran's shattered belief system; the source resides not in the lived social experience of the war's contradictions but in the actions of "college kids," "hairheads," and "pretty little things" who toss "bags of dogshit" at returning troops. "That's why I'm here," explains one soldier. A sergeant gives his opinion of draft resisters: "You don't have to like it [the war], but you have to show up." Like Broyles's article, *Hamburger Hill* celebrates war as a rite of manhood but locates responsibility for the soldiers' suffering specifically in the actions of the antiwar movement. In *Platoon*, the war is simply inexplicable.

Despite its powerful imagery and claims of authenticity, *Platoon* decontextualizes the ideological crisis it represents. Subcultures, classes, and races are locked in inexplicable conflict, and Chris concludes that "we fought ourselves" without questioning how, why, and in whose interest he fought the Vietnamese. Similar to Broyles's celebration of war as a ritual of masculinity, *Platoon* subsumes the soldier's experience of ideological crisis in the theme of lost innocence and the transformation of youth into manhood. Chris is the "cherry," "dip-shit," "fresh meat," "lame-ass," "sorry cheese-dick,"

Hamburger Hill *claims the dead for a revisionist agenda. American troops, all of whom are identified as "niggers" by Doc, are located in Vietnam because of the antiwar movement back home.*

"shit-for-brains," and "boy" until he receives a minor wound that transforms him into a man. By avoiding the political significance of the soldier's experience of ideological crisis, *Platoon* is especially susceptible to Lee Iacocca's cooptation on behalf of the Chrysler Corporation. Iacocca neatly summarizes the strategy employed to transform the Vietnam veteran into a usable sign of anticommunist consensus. Vietnam was simply inexplicable, "a place nobody really understood," least of all the men who fought there and who maintained their commitment to "the spirit of America" while others lapsed. The Vietnam veteran emerges as a new and improved model of ideological commitment, usable in the selling of cars and usable in encouraging others to answer the next call when it comes.

The therapeutic nature of the revisionist strategy makes the question of cultural resistance problematic. The strategy's success is based in its ability to culturally reproduce Vietnam veterans as signs of ideological certainty and continuity, every bit as "good" as World War II veterans. Given the marginal position of Vietnam veterans in American society following the war, their need for acknowledgement and acceptance is understandable. But the current reintegrative phase unfolding in mass media assigns an extraordinarily narrow meaning to the broad range of American experience in Vietnam and requires veterans to abandon their historical position in favor of an ahistorical pose. Hegemony easily defines critics of the process as unreasonably opposed not merely to the reassertion of mechanistic anticommunism as a credible policy but to the overdue reintegration of the veteran into civilian life. The strategy adjusts the veteran's subjectivity to the requirements of the revisionist agenda. Veterans who resist the therapeutic fix are subject to marginalization. They are not merely bitter. By their own choice, they remain "burdened" by the war. In the reintegrative phase, hegemony mystifies the ideological crisis remembered in this excerpt from W. D. Ehrhart's poem, "A Relative Thing":

> *We have seen the pacified supporters*
> *of the Saigon government*
> *sitting in their jampacked cardboard towns,*
> *their wasted hands placed limply in their laps,*
> *their empty bellies waiting for the rice*
> *some district chief has sold*
> *for profit to the Vietcong.*
>
> *We have been Democracy on Zippo raids,*
> *burning houses to the ground,*
> *driving eager amtracs through new-sown fields.*[40]

Ehrhart, a Marine combat veteran, focuses on images of rapid and bru-tal modernization and the uncritical use of American power in the interests of mechanistic anticommunism. Refusing the role of warrior hero in an inexplicable war, Ehrhart seeks to make explicable his own experience of

"We have been Democracy on Zippo raids."

ideological crisis. He grounds his experience in the encounter with another culture. He performs the role of witness, and his poetry communicates astonishment over the American policy in Vietnam. As the revisionist strategy reworks the meaning of the war, as mass-mediated rituals reintegrate veterans as timeless heroes in an inexplicable cause, our culture risks losing this sense of astonishment. We risk the easy acceptance of future Zippo raids.

NOTES

1. Lloyd Lewis, "The Thousand-Yard-Stare: A Socio-Cultural Interpretation of Vietnam Narratives" (Ph.D. dissertation, University of Connecticut, 1982).

2. Rick Berg, "Losing Vietnam: Covering the War in an Age of Technology," *Cultural Critique* 3 (1986):92–125.

3. Michael Clark, "Remembering Vietnam," *Cultural Critique* 3 (1986):46–78.

4. Victor Turner, *From Ritual to Theatre: The Human Seriousness of Play* (New York: Performing Arts Journal Publications, 1982).

5. Louis Althusser, *Lenin and Philosophy and Other Essays* (London: New Left, 1971).

6. Stuart Hall, "Signification, Representation, Ideology: Althusser and the Post-Structuralist Debates," *Critical Studies in Mass Communication* 2 (1985):91–114.

7. Peter Ehrenhaus, "Silence and Symbolic Expression," *Communication Monographs* 55 (1988):41–57; "The Wall," *Critical Studies in Mass Communication* 6 (1989):94–98; "The Vietnam Veterans Memorial, An Invitation to Argument," *Argumentation and Advocacy* 25, no. 2 (Fall 1988):54–64.

8. I have discussed the revisionist claim to The Wall in "'What Kind of War?': An Analysis of the Vietnam Veterans Memorial," *Critical Studies in Mass Communication* 3 (1986):1–20.

9. Larry Rottmann, Jan Barry, and Basil T. Paquet, eds., *Winning Hearts and Minds: War Poems by Vietnam Veterans* (Brooklyn, N.Y.: First Casualty Press, 1972).

10. James William Gibson, *The Perfect War* (New York: Vintage, 1988).

11. Wallace Terry, *Bloods* (New York: Random House, 1984).

12. Hall, "The Toad in the Garden: Thatcherism Among the Theorists," in *Marxism and the Interpretation of Culture*, ed. Cary Nelson and Lawrence Grossberg (Urbana, Ill.: University of Illinois Press, 1986), pp. 35–73.

13. Joseph Peschek, *Policy-Planning Organizations: Elite Agendas and America's Rightward Turn* (Philadelphia: Temple University Press, 1987), p. 241.

14. James Boylan, "Declarations of Independence," *Columbia Journalism Review* (November/December, 1986):29–45.

15. Michael Hertsgaard, *On Bended Knee: The Press and the Reagan Presidency* (New York: Farrar Straus Giroux, 1988).

16. Daniel Hallin, "We Keep America on Top of the World," in *Watching Television*, ed. Todd Gitlin (New York: Pantheon, 1987), pp. 9–41.

17. Marilyn Young, "Revisionists Revised: The Case of Vietnam," *Newsletter of the Society of Historians of American Foreign Relations* (Summer, 1979):1–10.

18. Joshua Meyerowitz, *No Sense of Place: The Impact of Electronic Media on Social Behavior* (New York: Oxford University Press, 1985).

19. Guenter Lewy, *America in Vietnam* (New York: Oxford University Press, 1978).

20. Ibid., p. 310.

21. Lewis, "Thousand-Yard Stare."

22. Robert Lifton, *Home from the War* (New York: Simon and Schuster, 1973), pp. 168–188.

23. Heinl, Robert, "The Collapse of the Armed Forces," *Armed Forces Magazine*, June 1971, pp. 22–30.

24. Gibson, *Perfect War*, p. 82.

25. Jeffrey Kimball, "The Stab-in-the-Back Legend and the Vietnam War," *Armed Forces and Society* 14, no. 3 (1988):433–458.

26. Althusser, *Lenin and Philosophy*.

27. William Broyles, "Why Men Love War," *Esquire*, November 1984, pp. 55–65.

28. Ibid., p. 62.

29. Walter Benjamin, *Illuminations* (New York: Schocken, 1969).

30. James Hoberman, "The Fascist Guns in the West," *American Film*, March 1986, pp. 42–48;
Susan Sontag, *A Susan Sontag Reader* (New York: Farrar Straus Giroux, 1982), pp. 305–325.

31. Benjamin, *Illuminations*, p. 241.

32. Michel Foucault, *Discipline and Punish* (New York: Vintage, 1979).

33. Horace Newcomb, "Magnum: The Champagne of TV?" *Channels of Communications*, May/June, 1985, pp. 23–26.

34. Todd Gitlin, *Inside Prime Time* (New York: Pantheon, 1983).

35. Richard Corliss, "Platoon: Viet Nam, The Way it Really Was, on Film," *Time*, 26 January 1987, pp. 54–61.

36. Oliver Stone, "One From the Heart," *American Film,* January/February 1987, pp. 17–19.

37. *Platoon's* success spawned several spin-offs, including two television series, *Tour of Duty* and *China Beach* (a representation of nurses' experience at the American rest-and-relaxation center near Da Nang), and at least two all-male pornographic videos set in Vietnam-like environments. *Stryker Force*, featuring porn star Jeff Stryker, was produced in 1987 by Matt Sterling and Huge Video Productions (Los Angeles). *The Platoon: More Than a Company of Men* was produced in 1988 by Dirk Yates and Seabag Productions (San Diego) and made use of actual Vietnam combat film in conjunction with videotaped episodes of explicit sex among Marine corpsmen.

38. Fox Butterfield, "The New Vietnam Scholarship," *The New York Times Magazine,* 13 February 1983, pp. 26–32.

39. Barber's "Adagio for Strings" has a discomfiting association with the origins of American policy in Vietnam. The piece was performed on network television by the New York Philharmonic on the night President John F. Kennedy was assassinated.

40. W. D. Ehrhart, "A Relative Thing," in *To These Who Have Gone Home Tired* (New York: Thunder's Mouth Press, 1984).

PART TWO

CLOSE-UPS
Representation in Detail

5 GAYLYN STUDLAR AND DAVID DESSER

Never Having to Say You're Sorry:
Rambo's Rewriting of
the Vietnam War

CULTURAL TRAUMA AND "THE WILL TO MYTH"

"History is what hurts," writes Fredric Jameson in *The Political Uncon-scious,* "It is what refuses desire and sets inexorable limits to individual as well as collective praxis."[1] The pain of history, its delimiting effect on action, is often seen as a political, cultural, and national liability. Therefore, contemporary history has been the subject of an ideological battle that seeks to rewrite, to rehabilitate, controversial and ambiguous events through the use of symbols. One arena of ongoing cultural concern in the United States is U.S. involvement in Vietnam. It seems clear that reconstituting an image—a "memory"—of Vietnam under the impetus of Reaganism appears to fulfill a specific ideological mission. Yet the complexity of this reconstitution or rewriting has not been fully realized, either in film studies or in political discourse. Neither has the manner in which the Reaganite right coopted often contradictory and competing discourses surrounding the rehabilitation of Vietnam been adequately addressed. A string of "right-wing" Vietnam films has been much discussed, but their reliance on the specific mechanism of displacement to achieve a symbolic or mythic reworking of the war has not been recognized. Also insufficiently acknowledged is the fact that, far from being a unique occurrence, the current attempt to rewrite Vietnam, and, more broadly the era of the 1960s, follows a well-established pattern of reworking the past in postwar Japan and Germany. Although it would be naive to advance a simple parallelist conception of history that foregrounds obvious analogies at the expense of important historical differences, the rewriting of the Vietnam War evidences a real, if complicated, link to previous situations where nations have moved beyond revising history to rewriting it through specific cultural processes.

That the U.S. "rewriting" of the Vietnam war is ideological in nature, of a particular political postwar moment, is clear a priori. But the site at which it is occurring is perhaps less clear and therefore more significant. For what is being rewritten might justifiably be called a trauma, a shock to the cultural system. Commonly used phrases such as "healing the wounds of Vietnam" are quite revelatory of this idea but do not grasp the difficulty of any cultural recuperation from shock. In reality, the attempt to cope with the national trauma of Vietnam confronts less a physical than a psychic trauma. The mechanisms through which healing can occur, therefore, are more devious, more in need, if you will, of "analysis."

The central question in the problem of the Vietnam War in history is: How can the U.S. deal with not only its defeat in Vietnam, but with the fact that it never should have been there in the first place? By answering this question, the United States would confront the potentially painful revelations of its involvement in Vietnam, which is reminiscent of those questions faced by other nations: How can Japan cope with its role in the Pacific aggression of World War II? How can the Germans resolve the Nazi era? These questions are virtually unanswerable without admission of guilt. But if, as Freud maintained, individuals find guilt intolerable and attempt to repress it, why should cultures be any different?[2] And if guilt, in spite of repression, always finds an unconscious avenue of expression in the individual's life, we must similarly mark a return of the repressed in cultural discourse as well.

In one respect, the return of the repressed explains the number of Vietnam films appearing simultaneously, or at least in waves of films during the 1980s. Given the nature of film production, the box-office success of any individual film cannot account for so many Vietnam films appearing within a short period of time. Nor can the popularity of such films, left and right, automatically be taken as an indicator of psychic healing. On the contrary, their coexistence might be read as a register of the nation's ambivalent feelings about the war, and ambivalence, Freud tells us, is one of the necessary ingredients in the creation of guilt feelings.[3]

Psychoanalytic therapy maintains that to be healed, one must recall the memory of the trauma that has been repressed by a sense of guilt. Otherwise, a "faulty" memory or outright amnesia covers the truth, which lies somewhere deep in the unconscious. The more recent the trauma, the more quickly the memory can be recalled; the more severe the original trauma, the more deeply the memory is buried, the more completely it is repressed. In this respect, cultures can be said to act like individuals—they simply cannot live with overwhelming guilt. Like individual trauma, cultural trauma must be "forgotten," but the guilt of such traumas continues to grow. As Freud notes, however, the mechanism of repression is inevitably flawed: the obstinately repressed material ultimately breaks through and manifests itself in unwelcome symptoms.[4] In 1959, Theodor Adorno, calling upon the psychoanalytic explanation of psychic trauma in his discussion of postwar Germany, observed that the psychological damage of a repressed collective past often emerges through dangerous political gestures: defensive overreaction to situations that do not really constitute attacks, "lack of affect" in response to serious issues, and repression of "what was known or half-known."[5] Popular discourse often equates forgetting the past with mastering it, says Adorno, but an unmastered past cannot remain safely buried: the mechanisms of repression will bring it into the present in a form that may very well lead to "the politics of catastrophe."[6]

One example of the politics of catastrophe was Germany's own unmastered response to World War I. Although Hitler's rise to power was complex (as is

America's rewriting of the Vietnam War), there was a crucial element of psychic trauma that enabled Hitler to step in and "heal" the nation. In *The Weimar Chronicle*, Alex de Jonge offers a telling account of an element of this trauma. At the end of the war, the Germans were unable to comprehend that their army, which proudly marched through the Brandenburg Gate, had been defeated. Instead of blaming the enemy, or the imperial regime's failed policy of militarism, the Germans embraced the myth of the "stab in the back." Defeat was explained as a conspiracy concocted by those Germans who signed the surrender.[7] William Shirer has noted that the widespread "fanatical" belief in this postwar myth was maintained even though "the facts which exposed its deceit lay all around."[8] This act of "scapegoating" evidences the desire both to rewrite history and to repress collective cultural guilt and responsibility. Resistance to the truth meant that, for Nazi Germany, ideology functioned as "memory," fantasy substituted for historical discourse, and the welcome simplicity of myth replaced the ambiguity of past experience. While World War I should have logically signalled an end to German militarist impulses, it served as merely a prelude, a "founding myth," for their most virulent expression.[9]

This example, replayed in many more contemporary realms, including the current discourse surrounding Vietnam, allows us to posit a "will to myth"—a communal need, a cultural drive—for a reconstruction of the national past in light of the present, which is, by definition of necessity, better. Claude Lévi-Strauss has suggested that primitive cultures that have no past (that is, do not conceive of or distinguish between past and present) use myth as the primary means of dealing with cultural contradictions. Modern societies, of course, are cognizant of a past but frequently find it filled with unpleasant truths and half-known facts, so they set about rewriting it. The mass media, including cinema and television, have proven to be important mechanisms whereby this rewriting or reimaging of the past can occur. Indeed, it was Hitler's far-reaching use of the media that allowed him to solidify the National Socialist state and set his nation on its monstrous course in a carefully orchestrated exploitation of the will to myth.[10]

A common strategy by which the will to myth asserts itself is through the substitution of one question for another. This mechanism is invoked by Lévi-Strauss as he notes how frequently one question or problem mythically substitutes for another concept by the narrative patterns of the myths. In dream interpretation, psychoanalysis calls this strategy displacement. If we allow the notion that cultures are like individuals (and recall the commonplace analogy that films are "like" dreams), we should not be surprised to find displacement occurring in popular discourse. Displacement accounts for the phenomenon of scapegoating, for instance, on both individual and cultural levels. But there are more devious examples, more complex situations in which the displacement goes almost unrecognized, as has been the case thus far with the current wave of Vietnam films and the project of rewriting the image of the war.

In the case of the recent right-wing Vietnam war films, the fundamental textual mechanism of displacement that has not been recognized is that the question "Were we right to fight in Vietnam?" has been replaced (displaced) by the question "What is our obligation to the veterans of the war?" Responsibility to and validation of the veterans is not the same as validating our participation in the conflict in the first place. Yet answering the second question mythically rewrites the answer to the first.

One of the key strategies in this displacement of the crucial question of America's Vietnam involvement is that of victimization. The Japanese have used this method of coping with their role as aggressor in World War II, just as the Nazis used it to rewrite World War I. The Japanese soldiers who fought in the war now are regarded as victims of a military government that betrayed the soldiers and the populace. The Japanese do not try to justify their actions in the war or even deal with the fact that their policies started the war in the first place. Rather, they try to shift (displace) blame for the war onto wartime leaders who are no longer alive. Contemporary Germany, too, relies on this strategy in an attempt now to rehabilitate its Nazi past. Strangely enough, its appropriation was given public sanction by President Reagan in his visit to Bitburg cemetery.

That America's problem of/with the Vietnam War might be related to Germany's Nazi past and the controversy over Reagan's visit to Bitburg is addressed in an interesting if disturbing way in a letter quoted by Alvin Rosenfeld. The letter writer claimed that Reagan's trip to Bitburg signified "that we are beginning to forgive the German people for their past sins, in much the same way that American has begun to seek forgiveness for Vietnam."[11] But is America (or, for that matter, West Germany) actually seeking "forgiveness" for the past? Reagan told the Germans at Bitburg what they wanted to hear, that the German soldiers buried in the military cemetery were themselves victims of the Nazis "just as surely as the victims of the concentration camps."[12] The American resistance to admitting culpability for Vietnam, like the Bitburg affair, revolves around a collective cultural drama of memory and forgetting. In essence, what we find in Japan's revision of its wartime history, Reagan's Bitburg speech, and many of the Vietnam films of the 1980s is that the appeal to victimization via the will to myth is a powerful rhetorical tool to apply to the problem of guilt. To be a victim means never having to say you're sorry.

MIAS; OR, I AM A FUGITIVE FROM BUREAUCRACY

As of this writing, two waves of Vietnam war films in the 1980s have been claimed: the right-wing revisionism of *Uncommon Valor* (1983), *Missing in Action* (1984), and *Rambo: First Blood Part II* (1985); and the ostensibly more realistic strain of Vietnam films emerging with *Platoon* (1986), *Hamburger Hill* (1987), and *Full Metal Jacket* (1987). At first glance, the comic-book heroics of the earlier films seem antithetical to the "realism" of the later ones, but in spite of such differences the films are actually very much alike in their dependence on the strategy of victimization. The films all work to evoke sympathy for the American G.I. (today's veteran) and pay tribute to the act of remembering the war as private hell. While the right-wing films, especially *Rambo*, justify a private war of national retribution for the personal sacrifice of vets, the realistic films demonstrate the process of victimization of the draftee or enlisted man. *Platoon* even goes so far as to transpose its conflict from the specificity of Vietnam into the realm of the transcendental: the two sergeants, Barnes and Elias, become mythic figures, warrior archetypes, battling for the soul of Chris (Christ?). The crucifixion image as Barnes kills Elias is too clear to miss, while Chris becomes the sacrificial victim who survives.

The right-wing films, especially *Rambo*, most clearly demonstrate the strategy of mythic substitution or displacement in the use of an oft-repeated rumor: that American MIAs are still being held captive in Southeast Asia. That *Rambo* was not only the most commercially successful of all the Vietnam films thus far but also became culturally ubiquitous (a television cartoon series, formidable tie-in merchandise sales, and, like *Star Wars*, becoming part of political discourse) speaks to the power of the will to myth. The need to believe in the MIAs gives credence to the view that the Vietnamese are now and *therefore have always been* an inhuman and cruel enemy. Vietnam's alleged actions in *presently* holding American prisoners serves as an index of our essential rightness in fighting such an enemy *in the past*. Moreover, our alleged unwillingness to confront Vietnam on the MIA issues is taken to be an index of the government's cowardice in its Vietnam policy: confrontation would mean confirmation. The American bureaucracy remains spineless: they didn't let us win then, and they won't let us win again.

Consequently, while it appears to embrace the militaristic ideology of the radical right, *Rambo* simultaneously delegitimizes governmental authority and questions the ideological norms of many other Vietnam films. Within its formula of militaristic zeal, *Rambo* sustains an atmosphere of post-Watergate distrust of government. The MIAs, John Rambo's captive comrades, are regarded only as "a couple of ghosts" by the cynical official representative of the government, Murdock, who lies about his service in Vietnam. He is willing to sacrifice the MIAs to maintain the status quo of international relations. President Reagan's portrait graces the wall behind Murdock's desk, but Murdock is a "committee" member, aligned, it seems, with Congress, not with the avowed conservatism of the executive branch. Colonel Trautman, Rambo's Special Forces commander and surrogate father figure, reminds Murdock that the United States reneged on reparations to the Vietnamese, who retaliated by keeping the unransomed captive Americans. Failure to rescue the MIAs is the direct result of their economic expendability. Murdock says the situation has not changed; Congress will not appropriate billions to rescue these "ghosts."

Abandoned once by their country (or rather, "government"), the POWs/MIAs are abandoned yet again in a highly symbolic scene: air-dropped into Vietnam to find and photograph any living MIAs/POWs, Rambo locates

While it appears to embrace the militaristic ideology of the radical right, Rambo *simultaneously delegitimizes governmental authority and questions the ideological norms of many other Vietnam films.*

an American; the rescue helicopter hovers above them as Vietnamese soldiers close in. Murdock abruptly aborts the mission. Rambo is captured and submitted to shocking (literally) tortures. His Russian interrogators taunt him with the intercepted radio message in which he was ordered abandoned. Rambo escapes, but not before he swears revenge against Murdock.

The mythical MIA prisoner may represent the ultimate American victims of the war, but *Rambo: First Blood Part II* also draws on the victimization strategy on yet another level, through the continued exploitation of its vet hero, John Rambo. The film opens with an explosion of rock at a quarry. A tilt down reveals inmates at forced labor. Colonel Trautman arrives to recruit Rambo for a special mission. Separated by an imposing prison yard fence, Rambo tells Trautman that he would rather stay in prison than be released, because "at least in here I know where I stand." The Vietnam vet is the eighties version of the World War I vet, the "forgotten man" of the Depression era. Like James Allen in Warner Brothers most famous social consciousness film, *I Am a Fugitive from a Chain Gang* (1932), Rambo is a Congressional Medal of Honor winner who feels "out of step" with a society that has used and discarded him. Condemned as a common criminal, Rambo is released from military prison and promised a pardon because his unique combat skills are again required by the government. He does not realize that he is also needed for political purposes. He will provide the gloss of a veteran's testimonial to the mission's findings, which have been predetermined: no Americans will be found.

As far removed from an appeal to victimization as Rambo's aggressive received myth-image might appear to be, his personal mission of victory and vengeance crucially hinges on his status as present and past victim, as neglected, misunderstood, and exploited veteran. Ironically, in a film that has no memory of the historical complexities of the Vietnam War, Rambo's personal obsession with the traumatic past of Vietnam is cited as the truest measure of his unswerving patriotism. Even Colonel Trautman feels compelled to tell him to forget the war. Rambo replies: ". . . as long as I'm alive—it's still alive."

Stallone explained the film in an interview: "I stand for ordinary Americans, losers a lot of them. They don't understand big, international politics. Their country tells them to fight in Vietnam? They fight."[13] Rambo and the captive MIAs are the innocent victims of wartime and postwar government machinations that preclude victories. By implicating American policy and government bureaucracy in past defeat and current inaction, the film exonerates the regular soldier from culpability in American defeat as it pointedly criticizes a technologically obsessed, mercenary American military establishment. This echoes both the Japanese strategy of blaming dead leaders for World War II and Reagan's declaration at Bitburg that the Holocaust was not the responsibility of a nation or an electorate, but an "awful evil started by one man."[14] Similarly, in his statements on Vietnam, Reagan has employed a strategy of blaming Vietnam defeat on those who cannot be named: "We are just beginning to realize how we were led astray when it came to Vietnam."[15]

"Are they going to let us win this time?" Rambo first asks Trautman when the colonel comes to pull Rambo out of the stockade rock pile for sins committed in the prequel. Trautman says that it is up to Rambo, but the colonel is unaware that Murdock is merely using Rambo to prove to the American public that there are no POWs. As the film's ad proclaims: "They sent him on a mission and set him up to fail." Rambo, setting the ideological precedent for Ollie North, is the fall guy forced into extraordinary "moral" action by the ordinary immoral inaction of bureaucrats. According to official standards, Rambo is an aberration, the loose cannon on the deck who subverts the official system, but in doing so he affirms the long-cherished American cult of the individual who goes outside the law to get the job done. He ignores the "artificial" restraints of the law to uphold a higher moral law, but (unlike Ollie) Rambo manages to avoid the final irony of conspiracy-making.

CONFRONTING THE OTHERNESS OF FRONTIER ASIA

In rewriting the Vietnam defeat, *Rambo* attempts to solve the contradiction posed by its portrayal of the Vietnam vet as powerless victim *and* supremacist warrior by reviving the powerful American mythos of a "regeneration through violence." Identified by Richard Slotkin as the basis of many frontier tales, this inter-text illuminates the way in which Rambo's narrative structure resembles that of the archetypal captivity narrative described by Timothy

Flint, whose *Indian Wars of the West, Biographical Memoir of Daniel Boone (1828–33)* typified this form of early frontier story. In this formula, a lone frontier adventurer is ambushed and held captive by Indians. They recognize his superior abilities and wish to adopt him, but he escapes, reaches an outpost, and with the help of a handful of other settlers wins a gruesome siege against hundreds of his former captors.[16] Sanctified by the trial of captivity, the hunter confronts an Otherness, represented by the wilderness and the Indians, that threatens to assimilate him into barbarism. Through vengeance, he finds his identity—as a white, civilized, Christian male.

Rambo's war of selective extermination inverts the wartime situation of Vietnam into a hallucinated frontier revenge fantasy that literalizes Marx's description of ideology: "circumstances appear upside down."[17] Rambo is an imperialist guerrilla, an agent of technocrats, who rejects computer-age technology to obliterate truckloads of the enemy with bow and arrow. Emerging from the mud of the jungle, from the trees, rivers, and waterfalls, Rambo displays a privileged, magical relationship with the Third World wilderness not evidenced even by the Vietnamese. As Trautman remarks: "What others call hell, he calls home."

Charmed against nature and enemy weapons, Rambo retaliates in Indian-style warfare for the captivity of the POWs, the death of his Vietnamese love interest, and his own wartime trauma. He stands against a waterfall, magically immune to a barrage of gunfire. His detonator-tipped arrows literally blow apart the enemy—who is subhuman, the propagandist's variation on the Hun, the Nip, the Nazi. Held in contempt even by their Russian advisors, the Vietnamese are weak, sweating, repulsive in their gratuitous cruelty and sexual lasciviousness. Rambo annihilates an enemy whose evil makes American culpability in any wartime atrocities a moot point. In *The Searchers* (1956), Ethan Edwards says: "There are humans and then there are comanch." In *Rambo*, there are humans and then there are gooks who populate a jungle that is not a wilderness to be transformed into a garden, but an unredeemable hell that automatically refutes any accusation of America's imperialistic designs.

With regard to the captivity narrative, it is also significant that Rambo is described as a half-breed, half German and half American Indian, a "hell of a combination," says Murdock. The Vietnam's vet's otherness of class and race is displaced solely onto race. The Indianness of costume signifiers—long hair, bare chest, headband, and necklace/pendant—ironically reverses the appropriation of Native American iconography by the sixties counterculture as symbolic of a radical alternative to oppressive cultural norms.[18] Ironically, the film's appropriation of the iconography of the noble savage also permits Rambo to symbolically evoke the Indian as the romanticized victim of past government deceitfulness disguised as progress (that is, genocide). These invocations of Indianness should not overshadow the fact that Rambo is perceived to be a white male, as are most of the men he rescues. Thus the film elides the other question of color—the fact that "half the average combat rifle company . . . consisted of blacks and Hispanics."[19] American racism and the class bias of the culture found the U.S. armed services in Vietnam consisting of a majority of poor whites and blacks, especially among the combat soldiers, the "grunts." The captivity narrative overshadows the historical narrative of rebellion in the ranks of the grunts (for example, fragging—the killing of officers) and the feeling of solidarity that soldiers of color felt for their Vietnamese opponents.

The reliance on the captivity narrative and Indian iconography evidences a desperate impulse to disarticulate a sign—the Vietnam veteran—from one meaning (psychopathic misfit, murderer of women and children) to another (the noble savage). Stallone admitted in an interview that the rushes of the film made Rambo look "nihilistic, almost psychopathic."[20] The film cannot repress an ambivalence toward the Vietnam veteran, in spite of the noble-savage iconography. By emphasizing the efficiency of Rambo as a "killing machine" created by Trautman, Stallone's protagonist becomes an American version of Frankenstein's monster. In his sheer implacability and indestructibility, he begins to evoke figures from genre films such as the Terminator, or Jason in *Friday the 13th*. One critic has written that Michael, the hero of *The Deer Hunter*, confronts the perversity of Vietnam's violence "with grace."[21] Rambo, as the embodiment of the return of the repressed, can only confront perversity with perversity.

Through the castrated/castrating dialectic of sacrifice and sadistic violence, Rambo redeems the MIAs and American manhood, but in spite of his triumph of revenge, he has not been freed of his victim status at the end of the film. Trautman tells him: "Don't hate your country." Rambo's impassioned

Through the castrated/castrating dialectic of sacrifice and sadistic violence Rambo redeems the MIAs and American manhood.

final plea states that all he wants is for his country to love the vets as much as they have loved their country. Trautman asks, "How will you live, John?" Rambo replies, "Day by day." The ending suggests that the screenwriters absorbed much from Warner Brothers' *I Am a Fugitive from a Chain Gang* in which veteran Allen, duped by bureaucrats, is returned to prison and denied his promised pardon. He escapes a second time to tell his fiancée, "I hate everything but you . . ." She asks, "How do you live?" Allen: "I steal." While Allen disappears into darkness, Rambo's walk into the Thai sunset also serves to recall the ending of numerous Westerns in which the hero's ambivalence toward civilization and the community's ambivalence toward the hero's violence precludes their reconciliation. Like Ethan Edwards, Rambo is doomed to wander between the two winds, but to a 1980s audience, no doubt, the ending did not signal the awareness of the tragic consequences of unreasoning violence and racial hatred as in Ford's film, but the exhilarating possibility of yet another Stallone sequel.

LUXURIATING IN THEIR PATRIOTIC SYMPTOMS

Like populist discourses such as Bruce Springsteen's "Born in the U.S.A.," *Rambo* plays upon a profound ambivalence toward the Vietnam vet, the war, and the U.S. government, but, like Springsteen's song, *Rambo* has been incorporated into the popular discourse as a celebration of Americanism. In its obvious preferred reading, the film is decoded by its predominantly post-Vietnam male audience as a unified, noncontradictory system.[22] This kind of integration into the cultural discourse is possible because the will to myth overrides the ideological tensions that threaten the coherence of the film's textual system. The film does not require a belief in history, only a belief in the history, conventions, and myth-making capacity of the movies.

In a challenging essay in *Postmodernism and Politics*, Dana Polan speaks of cinema's "will-to-spectacle," the banishment of background, the assertion that "a world of foreground is the only world that matters or is the only world that *is*."[23] If one eliminates the past as background, events can be transformed into satisfying spectacle, hurtful history into pleasurable myth. Drawing on this will-to-spectacle, the mythogenesis of *Rambo* lies not in history but in the *ur*-texts of fiction that provide its mythic resonance as a genre film and its vocabulary for exercising the will to myth.

In fact, virtually all background is eliminated in *Rambo*, and the spectacle becomes the half-clad, muscle-bound body of Sylvester Stallone: the inflated body of the male as the castrated and castrating monster. John Rambo is the body politic offered up as the anatomically incorrect action doll; John Ellis describes an ad for the film showing Rambo holding "his machine gun where his penis ought to be."[24] Rambo declares that "the mind is the best weapon," but Stallone's glistening hypermasculinity, emphasized in the kind of languid camera movements and fetishizing close-up usually reserved for female "flashdancers," visually insists otherwise.

Rambo's narcissistic cult of the fetishized male body redresses a perceived loss of personal and political power at a most primitive level, at the site of the body, which often defined the division of labor between male and female in pretechnological, patriarchal societies. The male body as weapon functions as a bulwark against feelings of powerlessness engendered by technology, minority rights, feminism; this helps explain the film's popularity not only in the U.S. but overseas as well, where it similarly appealed to working-class male audiences.[25] Most of all, however, the film speaks to post-Vietnam/post-Watergate America's devastating loss of confidence in its status as the world's most powerful, most respected, most moral nation. Our judgment and ability to fight the "good" war as a total war of commitment without guilt has been eroded by our involvement in Vietnam, as surely as a sense of personal power has been eroded by a society increasingly bewildering in its technological complexity.

Attempting to deliver its audience from the anxiety of the present, *Rambo* would seek to restore an unreflective lost Eden of primitive masculine power. Yet Rambo must supplement his physical prowess with high-tech weapons adapted to the use of the lone warrior-hero. A contradictory distinction is maintained between his more "primitive" use of technology and that of the bureaucracy. Rambo's most hysterical, uncontrollable act of revenge is against Murdock and Murdock's technology. He machine-guns the computers and sophisticated equipment in operations headquarters. Uttering a primal scream, he then turns his weapon to the ceiling in a last outburst of uncontrollable rage. Such an outburst is the predictable result of the dynamics of repression, for the film cannot reconstitute institutional norms except through the mythological presence of the superfetishized superman, who functions as the mediator between the threatened patriarchal ideology and the viewer/subject desperately seeking to identify with a powerful figure. As a reaction formation against feelings of powerlessness too painful to be admitted or articulated, Rambo's violent reprisals, dependent on the power of the overfetishized male body, may be read as a symptomatic expression, a psychosomatic signifier of the return of the repressed, suggesting profound ideological crisis in the patriarchy.

Freud warned that within the context of repression and unconscious acting out, the young and childish tend to "luxuriate in their symptoms."[26] *Rambo* demonstrates a cultural parallel, a luxuriating in the symptoms of desperate ideological repression manifested in the ability to speak of or remember the painful past, a cultural hysteria in which violence must substitute for understanding, victimization for responsibility, the personal for the political. While *Rambo* reflects ambiguous and often inchoate drives to rewrite the Vietnam War, it also shows how in the will to myth the original traumatic experience is compulsively acted out in a contradictory form that leaves the origins of ideological anxiety untouched: the need to reconcile repressed material remains.

NOTES

1. Fredric Jameson, *The Political Unconscious: Narrative as a Socially Symbolic Act* (Ithaca: Cornell University Press, 1981), p. 102.

2. Sigmund Freud, "Repression," in *General Psychological Theory*, ed. Philip Rieff (New York-Macmillan-Collier, 1963), p. 112.

3. Ibid., pp. 114–115.

4. Ibid., pp. 112–113.

5. Theodor W. Adorno, "What Does Coming to Terms with the Past mean?" in *Bitburg in Moral and Political Perspective*, ed. Geoffrey H. Hartman (Bloomington: Indiana University Press, 1986), p. 116.

6. Ibid., p. 128.

7. Alex de Jonge, *The Wiemar Chronicle* (London: Paddington Press, 1978), p. 32.

8. William Shirer, *The Rise and Fall of the Third Reich* (Greenwich, Conn.: Fawcett, 1960), p. 55–56.

9. De Jonge, *Wiemar Chronicle*, p. 32.

10. Robert Edwin Hertstein, *The War That Hitler Won: The Most Famous Propaganda Campaign in History* (New York: Putnam, 1978).

11. Alvin H. Rosenfeld, "Another Revisionism: Popular Culture and the Changing Image of the Holocaust," in *Bitburg*, ed. Hartman, p. 96.

12. Ibid., p. 94.

13. Richard Grenier, "Stallone on Patriotism and 'Rambo,'" *New York Times*, 6 June 1985.

14. Ronald Reagan, "Never Again . . . ," *Bitburg and Beyond*, ed, Ilya Levkov (New York: Shapolsky, 1987), p. 131.

15. Francis X. Clines, "Tribute to Vietnam Dead: Words, A Wall," *New York Times*, 11 November 1982.

16. Richard Slotkin, *Regeneration Through Violence: The Mythology of the American Frontier, 1600–1860* (Middletown, Conn.: Wesleyan University Press, 1973), p. 421.

17. Karl Marx and Frederick Engels, *The German Ideology* (London: Lawrence and Wishart, 1965), pp. 37–38.

18. Slotkin, *Regeneration*, p. 558.

19. Gabriel Kolko, *Anatomy of a War: Vietnam, the United States, and the Modern Historical Experience* (New York: Pantheon, 1985), p. 360.

20. Grenier, "Stallone on Patriotism."

21. Judy S. Kinney, "The Mythical Method: Fictionalizing the Vietnam War," *Wide Angle* 7, no. 4 (1985):40.

22. John Ellis, "Rambollocks' is the Order of the Day," *New Statesman* 8 (November 1985): 15.

23. Dana Polan, "'Above All Else to Make You See': Cinema and the Ideology of Spectacle," in *Postmodernism and Politics*, ed. Jonathan Arac (Minneapolis: University of Minnesota Press, 1986), p. 60 (emphasis in original).

24. Ellis, "Rambollocks," p. 15.

25. Ibid.

26. Sigmund Freud, "Remembering, Repeating, and Working-Through," in *The Standard Edition of the Complete Psychological Works*, ed. and trans. James Strachey, 23 vols. (London: Hogarth Press, 1953–66), 12:152.

6

GREGORY A. WALLER

Rambo:
Getting to Win This Time

In this essay I seek neither to praise nor to bury *Rambo: First Blood Part II* (1985). Keeping in mind the immense commercial success of the film and the overwhelmingly negative response to the film by what *Newsweek* calls "critics, cinematic or social," the following close textual and ideological analysis focuses on *Rambo*'s narration, the hero the film constructs, and the topical, "political" points it explicitly addresses.[1] Several general questions inform my discussion: What is the place of *Rambo* in the Age of Reagan? What sort of active work does it require of its viewer? What position or role would it have the viewer assume? And, finally, to what extent does it verify Fredric Jameson's argument that "even the most degraded type of mass culture" must offer some trace of a "utopian" potential, some tapping of "genuine social and historical content," some "dimension . . . which remains implicitly, and no matter how faintly, negative and critical of the social order from which, as a product and a commodity, it springs"?[2] If, as Scott Forsyth proposes, "the ideological text is one level of a complex interaction in any art (including media) amongst production, form, reception, social moment—a process not simply homogeneous and monolithic," what precise configuration does this "interaction" take in *Rambo*?[3]

THE NARRATION OF WINNING THIS TIME

In a manner that apparently could not be more straightforward and more typical of what David Bordwell identifies as the "canonical" goal-directed story format, *Rambo*'s opening exposition sequence announces this narrative's primary enigma or goal.[4] Rambo's former commanding officer, Colonel Trautman, appears at a heavily guarded prison work detail, calls for Rambo, and, speaking through the barrier of a cyclone fence, offers him a special mission: "recon for POWs in 'Nam." Rambo accepts the offer, then asks Trautman: "Do we get to win this time?" Rambo is thus granted the privilege of articulating the question that the rest of the film will seek to answer; he tells us what we should desire (victory), and we assume that through his actions he will bring about the gratification of this desire.

Rambo's initial question—more rhetorical than interrogative—is hardly unique in contemporary popular culture.[5] A similar question informs almost all sports films released since *Rocky* (1976) and *Breaking Away* (1979); crossing genre boundaries, it is equally central for contest-filled teen comedies in the wake of *National Lampoon's Animal House* (1978) and *Porky's* (1981), whose pleasure to a large extent arises from the poetically just victory of likable misfits or gutsy underdogs. In the post-Vietnam era marked by one "hostage crisis" and terrorist attack after another, such films rather transparently attest to a once-again widespread desire for clear-cut confrontations in which easily identified-with protagonists earn much-deserved victories rather than suffer through hollow triumphs, stand-offs, or outright defeats.[6]

What does Rambo's question—so familiar and so readily answered—entail? Given that he alone is chosen for this mission and that the film's title, like its advertising campaign, quite accurately affirms his singularity and preeminence, his use of the plural pronoun is noteworthy. "We," Rambo later declares, are the still underappreciated, heroic, rank-and-file soldiers who fought in Vietnam. Rambo will carry their mantle and in so doing he will let us share in the pleasures of victory as well. The question he poses to Trautman is an exhortation to and definition of the film's spectators, who are very much addressed as a collective audience, the "we." Like the flag-draped Rocky in *Rocky IV*, Rambo will become the symbol, representative, and creator of a renewed, true America to which "we" unquestionably aspire. ("Rambo—symbol of the American spirit" proclaimed one prominent newspaper ad for the film.) In addition, by holding out the promise of winning *this time,* Rambo reminds us of still memorable defeats—explicitly the Vietnam War, implicitly the entire course of American foreign policy during the 1970s. He presupposes that we are still engaged in confrontation, still at war. Like the Reagan administration, with its highly publicized war on terrorism and war on drugs, *Rambo* offers a reassuringly well-defined image of the enemy as other, a life-or-death cause, and a satisfying, righteous display of might. Only in *Rambo* we get to win this time.

Guiding the audience from rhetorical question to foregone conclusion, the work of narration in *Rambo* is to negotiate the long delay—filled with disappointment and partial gratification—between promise and delivery, wish and fulfillment. Forsyth suggests that *Rambo* can perhaps be understood as something of a musical, in that like other recent "blockbusters" it is structured as a series of special effects sequences, each having "the status of the 'number' in a musical."[7] But *Rambo*'s narrative organization, it seems to me, does not simply provide the occasion for displaying its hero or incorporating a string of "numbers." Rambo is a hero only insofar as he can make good on his opening promise by creating or causing a story of winning this time. The spectacular "numbers," which prominently feature Rambo as star (and often as directorial figure), all arise out of and advance the film's narrative chain of causal relations. With its reliance on a causality whose principal agent is a goal-directed protagonist, *Rambo* quite clearly falls within the bounds of "classical [Hollywood] narration," a mode of narration that, in Bordwell's words, "tends to be omniscient, highly communicative, and only moderately self-conscious" as it avoids disorientation and "moves steadily toward a growing awareness of absolute truth."[8] In its classicism, *Rambo* resembles the *Rocky* series, *Uncommon Valor* (1983), and *Missing in Action* (1984), and it provides an alternative, formally as well as thematically, to, say, *Apocalypse Now* (1979)—

and also to the most critically acclaimed writing about Vietnam, including *Dispatches*, *Going After Cacciato*, and *A Rumor of War*.

As any number of recent commentators have noted, classical Hollywood narration is ideologically charged entertainment. And in the most general terms, we might say that *Rambo*, with its goal-directed narration centering on the actions of an individualized protagonist, is but one more product and producer of the "false consciousness" so necessary for hegemonic capitalism. However, as Bill Nichols notes, "not all classical narrative films are equally complicitous with . . . the dominant ideology of their time."[9] To begin to get at the ideological significance of *Rambo*—its degree of "complicity" and what Jameson would call its utopian or critical dimension—it is necessary to look more closely at precisely how *Rambo* tells its story of winning this time by recombining three different narrative schemata (all variants of the adventure story) traditionally designated as "masculine" in and by American popular culture: the quest, the story of escape, and the revenge story. This narrational strategy becomes, in effect, a means of setting priorities and redefining values and goals.

Rambo begins quite unmistakably as the story of a quest, with Rambo being directed and acted upon (he is initially "patient" rather than "actant").[10] He is called forth by Trautman; freed from prison; reinstated in the service of his country; flown to Thailand; briefed by "special ops designate" Murdock about the recon operation he is to undertake; and armed by his government with "the most advanced weapons in the world." The familiar conventions of the romance quest are explicitly evoked: Rambo is dubbed the "chosen one"; his task is a "mission" of national importance behind enemy lines in search of an all-important object (photographic proof of the existence of American POWs in Vietnam); his personal preparations assume through close-ups the status of the ritualized arming of the questing warrior; and his dangerous journey will take him on a perilous harrowing of "Hell" (as Vietnam is called in the film).

What is striking about the opening sequences of the film is how quickly and how thoroughly Rambo redefines his role and his mission, thereby breaking his contract with the superior official agency that would dictate his fate. All the high-tech paraphernalia proves to be a potentially deadly encumbrance, and Rambo literally cuts himself loose and so must rely on his own weapons (and, later, on those he steals from the enemy) and remain out of contact with Murdock's computerized central command post. Most important, Rambo, in an affirmation of individual power and morality, transforms the goal of the quest itself: he will attempt to bring home the POWs rather than be merely a photographer—a recorder of evidence, finally no better than a journalist.[11] Overcoming great odds, assisted solely by Co, his "indigenous agent" contact, Rambo is on the verge of completing the quest on his own terms when he is betrayed by Murdock. This "special ops designate" aborts what was intended to be simply a government-sponsored public relations ploy designed to misinform those citizens still foolish enough to trust the government after Vietnam and Watergate.

Rambo himself is never guilty of such foolish blind faith. Before leaving the Thailand base, after listening to Murdock's briefing, Rambo tells Trautman: "You're the only one I trust." Murdock's—and the government's—subsequent act of betrayal is thus not only a case of narrational redundancy, but also proof of Rambo's privileged access to the truth and therefore of his role as interpretive guide as well as casual agent. By announcing the importance of "trust," Rambo underscores the film's commitment to translating the political into moral, personal terms. His suspiciousness concerning official authorities and government-initiated "missions" can be read less as paranoia than as the residual effect of Lyndon Johnson's and Richard Nixon's duplicity and Jimmy Carter's failure to be sufficiently experienced or "strong" enough to warrant trust as a leader. Faced with this legacy, the Reagan presidency presented itself as supremely trustworthy and promoted the image of a righteous, missionary America. Rambo does not find Reagan—as one might find Christ—but at least he does come to trust Co, and in so doing he discovers the possibility of trustworthiness in the mid-1980s.[12] The spectator, in turn, finds Rambo, who does not betray his or her trust.

With Murdock's betrayal and Rambo's subsequent capture by Vietnamese troops, history repeats itself. The danger of granting power to the untrustworthy is that again U.S. soldiers will be exploited and deserted by their government and that the U.S. will sink even deeper into the morass of merely expedient politics. No simple quest in the name of obligation and repatriation will suffice to restore America. Once Murdock has effectively reduced Rambo from actant to patient—returning him to prison and, thus, short-circuiting the connection between wish and fulfillment—the film becomes for a time principally concerned with how the hero will endure punishment and effect his escape. This supremely personal test is appropriately grueling and graphic: Rambo is humiliated, electro-shocked, virtually crucified, and branded by his Vietnamese and Soviet captors. At issue here is less the prospect of winning this time than the capacity of the hero to survive his brutal captivity.

Having taken all that the enemy can dish out—the cornerstone of Rocky's pugilistic strategy—Rambo fights his way to freedom, again with the notable assistance of Co, who now acts purely on the basis of personal motives (admiration, sympathy, love for Rambo) rather than official orders. If individual freedom and the prospect of a new or a newly restored life were Rambo's true goals, *Rambo* would end here. Yet as in the film's opening prison work-detail sequence, freedom is posited as a means, not an end. It is necessary but not in itself sufficient to assure victory. Once he is again free, Rambo seems for an idyllic instant to be willing to flee to the United States with Co. But the unfinished war and the inescapable past intrude in the form of a Vietnamese officer who ambushes Co. Propelled as if by destiny and with his own betrayal and torture and the murder of Co now providing added motivation, Rambo turns back to his doubly redefined mission—winning this time becomes inseparable from gaining personal vengeance. And from this point on, *Rambo*, like *Rocky IV* and like the bombing of Libya as produced and marketed by the Reagan administration, reenacts the extraordinarily durable fantasy of revenge.[13]

Rambo . . . *reenacts the extraordinarily durable fantasy of revenge.*

With the death of Co (she has served her purpose of aiding Rambo in his escape, humanizing the hero, and demonstrating that trust is still possible) and the quick termination of the romance subplot, Rambo is free to win, which means, initially at least, that he can make good his desire to refight the Vietnam War. Finally become the literal one-man army that was so much emphasized in the advertising for the film, Rambo ambushes Soviet and Vietnamese troops, then commandeers a Soviet helicopter and transforms a POW camp into a corpse-strewn inferno. His vengeance generates the film's most spectacular pyrotechnics, a display all the more gratifying given the fact that Murdock's mission was designed to lead to nothing except photographs of a deserted POW camp.

However, decimating Vietnam, piling up the Communist body count, and even rescuing POWs do not in themselves constitute the victory toward which Rambo aspires. In keeping with a tradition that moves from Mickey Spillane's Mike Hammer novels through *Death Wish* and into the 1980s, Rambo's vengeance must be personal, an expression of the individual hero's prowess and righteous fixation on *lex talonis* justice. For Rambo, military action—which is to say, true *political* action—is nothing if not personally motivated and conducted. And it is memory that drives the hero who drives the narrative. In exalting the importance of not forgetting, *Rambo* implies that memory should determine our actions as individuals and as a nation. In this way alone can we hope to win *this* time, which is what the film names as our most basic desire.

In short order Rambo kills Co's murderer with an explosive-tipped arrow, overcomes the brutal Soviet torturer in hand-to-hand combat, destroys the chief Soviet officer in a duel of helicopters, and then confronts his most insidious antagonist, Murdock. Before dealing with the cowardly, cynical "special ops designate," whom he has vowed to "get," Rambo fires round after round of machine gun bullets into Murdock's computerized control center—symbol here of technocratic bureaucracy, covert politics, and governmental overseeing. Murdock himself becomes hardly worth killing; he need only be suitably terrified, humiliated, and left to relay Rambo's threats to his superiors. This final, tantalizing act of restraint underscores the film's racism and Sovietphobia (after all, Murdock, for all his faults, is still a white American). More explicitly, it proves that Rambo is no homicidal veteran or newborn revolutionary.

As the end of the film demonstrates, Rambo's war is against both the enemy in Southeast Asia and the untrustworthy, exploitive government represented by Murdock. And winning this time can only be achieved by the passionate, wrathful avenger—surely not by any diplomatic or legalistic means. In addition to linking Rambo to a long line of heroic avengers in American popular culture, the narrative privileging of actions undertaken in the name of personal revenge implies that repatriating lost Americans or achieving individual freedom (not to speak of attaining social prosperity or stability) is far less important than striving for a just victory, which is the ultimate goal of Rambo's mission.

RAMBO AS HERO

In the lead-in to a December 1985 feature article about the success of *Rambo* and *Rocky IV*, *Newsweek* affirmed that "Sylvester Stallone has brought the hero back to the forefront of American mythology," and it went on to link

Rambo, the "warrior hero," with both John Wayne and the "noble savage."[14] Rambo as embodiment of the heroic figured prominently in other reviews and print commentaries on *Rambo*'s "message," in comic monologues and satirical editorial cartoons, and, not least of all, in the merchandising of ancillary *Rambo*-inspired products (such as toys, comic books, a "kid-vid" animated series).[15] Following these cues and bearing in mind the connotative flexibility of "hero" as a term of approbation and estimation of value (among the ranks of recent "heroes" are Indiana Jones, Ronald Reagan, the Road Warrior, Sonny Crockett of *Miami Vice*, and Ripley of *Alien* and *Aliens*), I would like to examine how the hero is constructed for and by the viewer in *Rambo*.

Given the production and marketing strategies of the American culture industry, even "brand-new" texts, as Jameson notes, "come before us as the always-already-read."[16] Thus, to the extent that we are familiar with Sylvester Stallone, *First Blood*, and the discourse surrounding the sequel, we "know" Rambo apart from *Rambo*. For example, since Rambo is Sylvester Stallone, there seems to be little doubt that he (and we) will win, only at what cost and by what means. Rocky Balboa, of course, is nothing if not a winner, and so, too, is "Stallone"—that is, the sum total of film performances, interviews, press releases, and celebrity portraits.[17] "Stallone" is one of our preeminent self-made men (sic), possessor of enviable material success and enormous public reknown. Like his muscularity, his status—so the story goes—has been the product of hard work as well as "natural" gifts. He survived *Paradise Alley* (1978), *F.I.S.T.* (1978), and *Rhinestone* (1984) with his celebrityhood and his persona intact, much as he survived his potentially crippling lower-class beginnings. In the time-honored tradition of star biography, he tasted the bitter fruits of success, for as *People* put it, "Stallone [like Rocky] too has battles he won't stop fighting."[18] Through it all, "Stallone" persevered, took on more missions, and won—can there be any doubt that Rambo will do the same, particularly since *Rambo: First Blood Part II* gives Rambo a new opportunity to prove himself after his emotional breakdown/surrender at the end of *First Blood*?

One principal function of the advertising campaign for *Rambo* was to sharpen the audience's expectations concerning this new incarnation of "Stallone." For example, in the newspaper ad that accompanied the film's initial release, "STALLONE" appears centered in bold-face block letters at the top edge, symmetrically balanced against the film's title at the bottom of the ad. In between—linking star and film, as it were—stands the dominating figure of Rambo in a frontal medium shot. To assure the full prominence of Rambo, the background is nondescript, except for three brief sentences in the right-hand corner of the ad that preview the narrative situation: "They sent him on a mission and set him up to fail. But they made one mistake. They forgot they were dealing with Rambo." The ad as a whole and the image of Rambo it offers will not allow us to make the same mistake "they" do. Rambo stands poised for battle, wielding a rocket launcher whose explosive tip breaks through the frame of the image. His weapon, muscular shirtless torso, unemotional facial expression, and rock-steady pose all exude strength, readiness, dominance, and determination as he stares at the reader. Of such stuff, the ad affirms, is the individual hero made.

The film delivers the goods its advertising promises by bringing to "life" this powerful, unshakable, exceedingly capable hero. Yet however self-evident Rambo's stature is supposed to be, high on the film's agenda is the need to prove conclusively that Rambo is not merely an "expendable" operative (this is how Rambo describes his own plight to Co and how Murdock conceives of Rambo); a "piece of meat" (the view of one of his Soviet torturers); or a "pure fighting machine" (Trautman's definition of his former pupil and a phrase picked up by many reviewers of the film). [19] In other words, while the narrative requires that Rambo be freed from an American prison and that he escape from a Vietnamese POW camp, an equally pressing task—a story within the story—is to free Rambo from the ranks of exploited ("expendable"), dehumanized ("meat," "machine") labor, which is defined and used by the bureaucratic overseers who manage society. Outside of and in spite of the system—never called capitalism—Rambo successfully asserts his own integrity, independence, and right of self-determination. Thus, in recognition of his worth, Co declares her love for Rambo by telling him: "You not expendable [sic]." The hero's victory and unqualified vindication are ideologically charged, especially in light of Stallone's assertion that what he tries to do "is to interpret the longings of the everyday proletariat, the blue-collar man"[20] or Newsweek's contention that Stallone is "a filmmaker to a damn-mad blue-collar America."[21] Rambo could be said to tap essential "longings" and apprehensions of labor under the domination of monopoly capital, while at the same time, Stallone's "interpretation"—that is, Rambo's spectacular, single-handed victory—fulfills what Jameson describes as the "function of inventing imaginary or formal 'solutions' to unresolvable social contradictions."[22]

Contributing to this "solution" is the fact that although Rambo is marked as one of the expendable and exploited, his singularity removes him from the anonymous ranks of the "everyday proletariat." The ad I discussed earlier tells us as much by foregrounding Rambo, and in the opening sequence of the film he is literally called forth from his place among his fellow convicts/manual laborers. His utter uniqueness is emphasized and hallowed throughout the film; when spoken by Co or Trautman, "Rambo" is a name to conjure with. Whatever difficulties he faces, whatever victimization he suffers, he remains—unlike the overheated, thirsty, weak Murdock—impervious to pain and to the merely ordinary demands of the body for food, shelter, and sleep. His work transcends dehumanizing, repetitive labor because he alone among the film's male characters is capable of valorous individual action well beyond what is demanded by official orders (hence his role as causal agent in the narration). Thus Stallone "solves" the problem of exploited labor by providing us with a nonpareil superman with whom to identify. The larger unacknowledged irony, of course, is that Rambo was a highly profitable commodity, if not for Murdock, then for Stallone, Tri-Star Pictures, Thorn EMI/HBO Video, Coleco, et al.

Though Rambo rises above the social conditions of Murdock's world by virtue of his singularity and prowess, he remains an exploitable "piece of meat" to the extent that the camera reverently scans his body, exhibiting Stallone's sculptured physique for the viewer's benefit and pleasure. These rippling muscles signify self-discipline, concentrated strength, and heroism—or, rather, a potential for heroism. For all the narcissistic attention it bestows on this well-honed, unexpendable body, the film, in fact, accords the greatest number of close-ups to Rambo's face and alert eyes—windows not to the soul but to the "mind" within, the mind being, in Rambo's words, "the best weapon."[23] Rambo's mind is signified so often by his face, rather than his speech, because the film shows how readily language functions as a tool of oppression and an assertion of authoritarian prerogative (whether via the "official" jargon of Murdock or the ironic flourishes of Pudovsky). To some degree, Rambo's haltingly articulated, heartfelt, unembellished, unintellectual speech redeems language, which can, in fact, express what Rambo knows to be the truth about the world and about correct political and ethical conduct. That such truth, *the* truth, is readily discernible, even self-evident to the hero, is one fundamental assumption that harkens back to *The Green Berets* (1968) and sets *Rambo* off from the critically acclaimed wave of Vietnam War narratives that appeared in the late 1970s.

Singular, privy to the truth, and almost superhumanly skilled and durable in body and mind, Rambo seems close indeed to being the "pure fighting machine" that Trautman so admires. "Rambo has the skills of a thousand men crammed into one," Stallone told a *New York Times* interviewer.[24] He must, the film insists, be humanized, though this dilution of his "purity" does not render him weak or flawed or unheroic. Hence the significance of Rambo's ill-fated fall into love with Co. This subplot reveals new "depths" to Rambo—a heretofore suppressed capacity for tenderness and "normal" (hetero)sexuality that marks Rambo as man not machine, and, once again, sets him apart from all the other male characters in the film. This capacity also seems designed to correct or at least to neutralize any suspicions we might have about Rambo's affinity for (and obsession with) the sadomasochistic pleasures of administering and enduring physical pain.[25]

In addition, Rambo's alliance with a Vietnamese woman (albeit a woman who is conventionally beautiful in Western terms and so is a legitimate object of desire according to the film's racist logic), coupled with his position as parolee and disenfranchised Vietnam vet, identifies him as being outside contemporary American society. No longer the ethnic, lower-class Rocky who can rise by his own efforts within society, "Stallone" in *Rambo* is the outsider in conflict with a state that seeks to exploit his labor only as long as it remains profitable. He is the outsider as *native* American—blooded in battle, wilderness-tested, preternaturally cunning.[26] His code name is "Lone Wolf"; his hair hangs to his shoulders; he wears no military uniform or simulacrum of an official uniform. Along with his Special Forces training, it is presumably his American Indian descent that accounts for his being completely at one with the natural environment ("What you call Hell, he calls home," Trautman declares) and makes him as adept with a knife and a bow as with an automatic rifle and a helicopter. While

Ronald Reagan's characteristic "Western" pose had been that of sheriff (paternalistic preserver of law and the social order) or rancher (capitalist or feudal overlord of the frontier), Rambo is the renegade half-breed who can only suffer from his dealings with powerful white men.

And suffer he does. Yet regardless of the fact that he has once again been exploited and abandoned by the system and that his own self-sufficiency and individual prowess have enabled him to win this time, Rambo still desires to be reintegrated into the nation, "loved" by his country. "I want," he confesses to Trautman in his final speech, "what they [the rescued POWs] want, and every other guy who came over here and spilt his guts and gave everything he had wants. For our country to love us as much as we love it. That's what I want." With this scene the film attempts to fully resolve its contradictions and recuperate its hero: being outside is not freedom but curse; winning this time *over there*, even being "Rambo," is not enough. According to *Rambo*, no citizen, not even the most disillusioned and exploited, would in his or her deepest dreams hatefully give up or give up on America.

THE TOPICALITY OF *RAMBO*

In the sense that ideology is the "reproduction of the existing relations of production . . . the image a society gives of itself in order to perpetuate itself,"[27] *Rambo* could be said to perpetuate ruling-class hegemony by solving the problem of the disenfranchised outsider whose labor is exploited for profit by a system that regards him or her as expendable. In the course of presenting this social allegory, *Rambo* endorses a particular view of heroism, which emphasizes, in addition to valor and prowess, the importance of *lex talonis* justice, trustworthiness, humanization, individuality, and memory in its personalization of political, military, international action. This view, I believe, is no less ideologically significant and no less worthy of critical attention for being more manifest than the film's relatively latent allegory of class relations. The same can be said for *Rambo*'s explicit, highly topical representation of the current geopolitical situation, the plight of Vietnam vets, and the nature of "true" militarism and patriotism in the 1980s.[28]

Unlike *First Blood*, *Rambo* is in line with the much-commented upon post-detente belligerence and nouveau Cold War sentiments of the early and mid-1980s—the "growing anti-Communist fervor," in *Time*'s phrase[29]—in that it unequivocally posits the existence of the Enemy, in this case those "Russian bastards."[30] In his sadistic villainy and overweening egotism, Soviet Lieutenant Colonel Pudovsky more than a little resembles Hollywood's stereotypical Nazis, while his troops are as interchangeable as the Vietnamese, who themselves are dressed in the manner of World War II Japanese soldiers.[31] Having identified an Enemy whose goals seem to be imperialism and the sheer assertion of power, *Rambo* demonstrates that the Soviets can and should be defeated and that—regardless of the "lesson" of Vietnam and the widespread early 1980s anxiety about thermonuclear war—war is winnable. In part by rendering Rambo's style of combat so exciting and visually spectacular, the film redeems war, paving the way for an acceptance of armed intervention as a viable strategic and political alternative in U.S. foreign policy, provided that the commanders and the warriors themselves are trustworthy men who can when necessary back up their words with suitably efficient and violent deeds.[32] More generally, Rambo's condemnation and unmasking of Murdock suggests that geopolitics need not be a messy, calculatedly pragmatic affair.

The arena for conflict in *Rambo* is Vietnam, which serves as a synecdoche for the Third World.[33] In the film's depiction of Vietnam, the Communist ruling class is utterly dependent on and subservient to the Soviet military forces, and there are no politicized masses that either support the Communist regime or struggle for Western-style democracy. The English-speaking Co is the sole counterrevolutionary in the film. Working for some unspecified "intelligence agency," she is characterized as being intelligent enough to want to leave her homeland for America and for Rambo. (However, as Co's death suggests, there is no place in *Rambo* for a woman of color except as yet another victim.) The peasants in *Rambo* are distanced, passive, innocent bystanders to all political struggles; they endure, the film suggests, so let us leave them to their harmlessly premodern, agrarian destiny. In contrast, the greedy, scavenging, corrupt river pirates who are paid to transport Rambo and Co to the prison camp must be eliminated. And so they are, after they attempt to sell out Rambo. Stained by their desire for money, these proto-capitalists profit from the plight of the Third World and exemplify the mercenary spirit (thereby linking the pirates with Murdock's henchmen, who are also explicitly dubbed "mercenaries"). The pirates underscore, by way of contrast, the moral rightness and political legitimacy of Rambo's version of American intervention.

Rambo's representation of the Third World works ideologically by positing a thoroughly entrenched Soviet presence and by denying the existence of politicized "native" masses. By foregrounding the plight of MIAs, POWs, and Vietnam vets—all victims who seek only to be repatriated literally or figuratively—*Rambo* masks the possibility that the United States might have any vested interest in exploiting the Third World.[34] In this way the film corroborates aspects of the Reagan administration's public posture, while still remaining "critical" of America's treatment of Vietnam vets. It is, after all, Rambo's status as Vietnam vet, not his status as "average" citizen, that makes him an expendable, exploitable commodity. Released to coincide with the tenth anniversary of the fall of Saigon, *Rambo* implies that the much publicized memorializing of the American casualties in Vietnam must be backed up with an outpouring of love for Vietnam vets and, more crucially, a willingness to actively win this time. Thus the film is at most only peripherally concerned with offering a revisionist (or mythic) view of what Murdock calls the "mess" that was the Vietnam War; unlike *First Blood*, in the sequel Rambo's wartime experiences are neither recounted in dialogue nor reenacted in flashbacks. *Rambo*'s emphasis is on the present—this time is 1985, as Rambo tells a dazed POW.

By foregrounding the plight of MIAs, POWs, and Vietnam vets, . . . Rambo *masks the possibility that the U.S. might have any vested interest in exploiting the Third World.*

With its present-tense call to arms and its picture of the Third World as a superpower battle zone, *Rambo* obviously speaks of and to the resurgence of militarism in the early 1980s.[35] Given the role of the "Russian bastards" in the film, military action is the only viable American recourse. Yet it is precisely in its glamorization and vindication of militarism that *Rambo* departs from the public agenda of the Reagan administration, for the film is critical of any simple equation of military prowess and national strength with increases in the budget of the Department of Defense or advances in high-tech weapon systems (Star Wars or otherwise). *Rambo* categorically rejects the idea of a bureaucratic, hierarchically organized military establishment that stakes its faith in technology and relies on mercenaries and the work of committees in an attempt to manipulate public opinion rather than to win wars. All who participate in this deeply flawed system fail. This is the lesson exemplified in the fate of Colonel Trautman, who still wears his Special Forces uniform. Potentially an avatar of the Father (his role in *First Blood*), Trautman is trustworthy, courageous, right-thinking, and fully sympathetic with Rambo's plight, but ultimately he is, in Murdock's words, "just a tool."[36]

Of course, *Rambo*'s critique of the political-military complex is neither groundbreaking nor incisive, though it does seem to tap into a long-standing American anxiety about government bureaucracy and behind-the-scenes Realpolitik. By focusing this critique on the character of Murdock and then dramatizing Rambo's much desired, absolute victory over the "special ops designate," the film in effect neutralizes its attack on the system. In the end we are left no longer prey to Murdock but instead beholden to Rambo, the superman whom we must simply trust to do the right thing.

Rambo's double-edged war against the Communists and against Murdock's brand of politics and militarism is conducted in the name of personal vengeance that is at the same time an expression of self-confessed love for America. This is the America that Co dreams of escaping to and that is praised in the rock song heard over the film's end credits. *Rambo* would thus seem to be perfectly in line with the exhibitionistic patriotism so prominent in the Age of Reagan. But Rambo is no flag-draped Rocky, and the America he loves and forsakes is more a matter of hope or memory than fact. For Murdock, too, is an American, as the Coca Cola machine, photo of Ronald Reagan, and decorative American flag in his office continually remind us. The presence of Murdock—and the system he represents—prevents a wholehearted endorsement of "My Country, Right or Wrong"; the defeat of Murdock signals the necessity for and the possibility of righting America.

After winning, Rambo is not accorded a long-overdue victory celebration signifying his country's esteem and gratitude and his own personal reintegration into the workaday United States. Echoing *I Am a Fugitive from a Chain Gang* (1932), *Rambo*'s final scene has Trautman imploring Rambo to return home and asking, "How will you live, John?" To which Rambo responds, "Day by day," and walks off in self-imposed exile—not "America, love it or leave it," but love it and leave it. (Here, however, unlike *I Am a Fugitive*, no darkness swallows up the solitary hero/victim.) This lack of closure rather blatantly leaves room for a *First Blood Part III*, while it also raises—at least momentarily—the problem of life-after-war (even after victorious war) and evokes the familiar image of the singular hero excluded from the body politic he has valiantly purged or defended. America, it would seem, has no place for Rambo, no love to bestow on him. And *Rambo* does not explicitly propose a solution to this dilemma, except perhaps in calling for a further reawakening of the country's collective memory, a resurgence of bona fide patriotism, and a heroic assault on our enemies within and without. But if Rambo in the diegesis remains displaced and unloved, no matter. A good number of Americans, led by the president (who, in a widely publicized statement made on the eve of the release of American hostages hijacked to Lebanon, declared that "I saw *Rambo* last night, and next time I'll know what to do"[37]), welcomed this hero with open arms, expressing patriotism and bestowing love in the form of adulation, imitation, and hard cash. Rambo wins. "Stallone" wins (yet again). And so also does the sympathetic viewer, whose anxieties and apprehensions are superseded by the pleasure of winning this time and whose "critical" misgivings are voiced then drowned out by the victory chants for the triumphant and just avenger.[38]

NOTES

1. Peter Goldman, "Rocky & Rambo," *Newsweek*, 23 December 1985, p. 58.
2. Fredric Jameson, "Reification and Utopia in Mass Culture," *Social Text* 1 (1979): 144.

3. Scott Forsyth, "Fathers, Feminism and Domination: Marxist Theory on Ideology in *Popular Film*," *Cineaction!* 2 (Fall 1985): 29.

4. David Bordwell, *Narration in the Fiction Film* (Madison: University of Wisconsin Press, 1985), pp. 33–40.

5. The most telling comparison with *Rambo* in this regard might well be *Year of the Dragon* (1985), in which the racist police captain/Vietnam vet protagonist challenges his superiors, who have given in to political pressure and tried to end his investigation of organized crime in Chinatown: "This is a fuckin' war, and I'm not gonna lose it, not this one, not over politics. This is Vietnam all over again. Nobody wants to win this thing, do you, just flat-out win?"

6. Even regarding this desire for a winnable confrontation, popular culture is hardly univocal. For example, a good many contemporary horror films, from *Dawn of the Dead* (1979) and *The Funhouse* (1981) to the *Nightmare on Elm Street* series, could be said to answer comic teenpix and the films of Chuck Norris and Stallone by depicting a well-nigh interminable struggle, by underscoring the weighty cost of victory, or—less frequently—by casting doubt on the efficacy of winner-take-all confrontation.

7. Forsyth, "Capital at Play: Form in Popular Film," *Cineaction!* 3–4 (Winter 1986): 93. See also Michael Wilmington, "Why a *Rambo II*? For Muddiest of Reasons," *Los Angeles Times*, 22 May 1985; Wilmington calls the film "a series of exhortations punctuated by bomb bursts."

8. Bordwell, *Narration in the Fiction Film*, pp. 159–160.

9. Bill Nichols, *Ideology and the Image* (Bloomington: Indiana University Press, 1981), p. 84. Furthermore, as Forsyth quite correctly puts it, "to assume the pleasures of narrative are automatically reactionary poses a singular reading of a film, and thus a singular notion of spectatorship, ignoring the tactics of appropriation and play an audience may bring to a film" ("Fathers, Feminism and Domination," p. 32).

10. Judy Lee Kinney, "The Mythical Method: Fictionalizing the Vietnam War," *Wide Angle* 7, no. 4 (1985): 35–40, offers a rather reductive account of the distancing and depoliticizing use of "warrior myths of the hero" in previous Vietnam films.

11. Here *Rambo* obliquely responds to left-liberal films like *Under Fire* (1983) and *The Killing Fields* (1984), which take as their central concern the moral and political dilemma of the American journalist in the civil-war-torn Third World.

12. In a typical interview, Stallone left no doubt that he trusted Reagan: "President Reagan has provided this country with a lot of incentives to feel better. When you think about what it was coming off of with the last three presidents, Reagan has been a godsend" (Nancy Collins, "The *Rolling Stone* Interview: Sylvester Stallone," *Rolling Stone*, 19 December 1985, p. 166).

13. Vincent Canby's Sunday *New York Times* column for 26 May 1985 was entitled "*Rambo* Delivers a Revenge Fantasy."

14. Goldman, "Rocky & Rambo," p. 58.

15. In explaining the decision to produce a line of *Rambo* "male action figures," a spokesperson for Coleco Industries declared: "We believe the character is emerging as a new American hero, a hero that has a high degree of excitement and patriotism and a thirst for justice associated with him" (quoted in Todd S. Purdum, "Coleco Smitten by *Rambo*," *New York Times*, 1 August 1985). See also Susan Spillman, "Rambomania: Action Dolls, Other Tie-ins Spark Toy War," *Advertising Age*, 5 August 1985, pp. 3, 63.

16. Jameson, *The Political Unconscious: Narrative as a Socially Symbolic Act* (Ithaca: Cornell University Press, 1981), p. 9.

17. See Richard Dyer, *Stars* (London: British Film Institute, 1979), pp. 68–98. A more thorough analysis of the construction of "Stallone" would take into account not only magazine "profiles"—like Charles Leerhsen, "Blood, Sweat and Cheers," *Newsweek*, 3 June 1985, pp.

62–64—but also television talk shows, *Entertainment Tonight*-style reporting, and mass market biographies.

18. Carl Arrington. "The Fight of Sly Stallone's Life," *People*, 3 June 1985, p. 99. See also Pat H. Broeske, "Sly Stallone's Rocky Road," *Washington Post*, 22 May 1985.

19. See, for example, Michael Sragow, "Heroes We Don't Deserve," *Atlantic* 256 (October 1985): 89–91.

20. Quoted in Collins, "The *Rolling Stone* Interview," p. 167.

21. Goldman, "Rocky & Rambo," p. 58.

22. Jameson, *Political Unconscious*, p. 79.

23. And in Stallone's words: "I don't think people understand that my life is much more cerebral than physical. I've gotten where I am today only because of mental plan [sic]" (quoted in Collins, "The *Rolling Stone* Interview," p. 168).

24. Quoted in Richard Grenier, "Stallone on Patriotism and *Rambo*," *New York Times*, 6 June 1985.

25. Rambo is humanized, but not rendered "passive, fearful, manipulable, submissive," as Susan Jeffords argues is the case with the "feminized" male protagonists of *Apocalypse Now*, *Coming Home*, and *First Blood* ("Friendly Civilians: Images of Women and the Feminization of the Audience in Vietnam Films," *Wide Angle* 7, no. 4 [1985]: 13–22).

26. *Rambo*'s "Indian motif" is mentioned by various reviewers, including Stanley Kauffmann, "Now about Rambo . . . ," *New Republic* 193 (1 July 1985): 16; and Tom O'Brien, "Birth of Legends: Unchaining Loss & History," *Commonweal* 112 (21 June 1985): 375.

27. Nichols, *Ideology and the Image*, p. 1.

28. No doubt the topicality of much popular art is a transparent marketing ploy (designed to entice us with a much-diluted verisimilitude and "relevance"). And few viewers of *Rambo* would accord a fictional feature film starring Sylvester Stallone the same "factual" status as TV network news or official government proclamations. Nonetheless, the film's topical messages should not be dismissed as "cheap and superficial references to dangerous, live moral issues" (Richard Schickel, "Danger: Live Moral Issues," *Time*, 24 June 1985, p. 91), nor should they be treated as simply a veneer to be stripped off so as to reveal a more important, latent subtext.

29. Richard Zoglin, "An Outbreak of Rambomania," *Time*, 24 June 1985, p. 73.

30. Most closely allied with *Rambo* in this regard are *Red Dawn* (1984), *Invasion U.S.A.* (1985), and, predictably enough, *Rocky IV* (1985), though Marcia Pally places *Rambo* in the company of a wide range of recent films that represent the Communist Enemy ("Red Faces," *Film Comment* 22 [January–February 1986]: 32–36).

31. One extremely curious and telling testament to the iconographic coding of the Enemy in *Rambo* is the pirated version of the film widely circulated in the Middle East. According to Mounir B. Abboud, "Pirated *Rambo* Tapes Tell a Different Tale: WWII Replaces 'Nam," *Variety*, 27 November 1985, pp. 1, 156, the French and Arabic subtitles in this version include no references to Vietnam and the Soviet Union and identify the story as taking place in the Philippines in 1943.

32. J. Hoberman, in "The Fascist Guns in the West," *American Film* 11 (March 1986): 48, argues that it is particularly in its view of war as "regenerative, if not hygenic" that *Rambo*—along with John Milius's films and Chuck Norris vehicles like *Invasion U.S.A.*—is incipiently fascist. Reviewers like Paul Attanasio ("*Rambo*: New Blood, Old Moves," *Washington Post*, 22 May 1985) and David Denby ("Blood Simple," *New York*, 3 June 1985, pp. 72–73) also emphasize the film's "neo-Nazi" or fascist values.

33. For columnists like Richard Cohen, *Rambo*'s Vietnam is transparently analogous with Nicaragua ("Next: Rambo Goes to Nicaragua?" *Washington Post*, 4 June 1985).

34. See Ellen Farley, "The U.S. Has Surrendered—Now *Rambo* is Taking the World by

Storm," *Business Week*, 26 August 1985, p. 109, for a discussion of the way the promotional strategy for selling *Rambo* very much emphasized playing up the Vietnam vet/MIA "angle." For responses by veterans to the film, see Jonathan Karp, "How Real Is *Rambo*: Vets Dubious but Approve of Film's MIA Focus," *Washington Post*, 8 July 1985; and Mike Felker, "*Rambo*: 'I Remember It Differently,' " *Jump Cut* 31 (March 1986): 4, 28.

35. One point that clearly merits more attention is *Rambo*'s place in the context of other expressions of the "new" militarism in, for example, ad campaigns for the Armed Forces, "G.I. Joe" war toys, and films from *Stripes* (1981) and *An Officer and a Gentleman* (1982) to *Top Gun* (1986) and *Heartbreak Ridge* (1986).

36. On the basis of its "antagonism" to bureaucracy and the "government machine," Russell A. Berman identifies *Rambo* as "an indication of a basic shift in the strategy of the culture industry which has abandoned the imagery of mass conformism and uniform identity while replacing them with the artificial negativity of a valorized deviance" ("Rambo: From Counter-Culture to Contra," *Telos* 64 [Summer 1985]: 145).

37. *Sixty Minutes* made much of this comment in a 15 December 1985 segment produced by Suzanne St. Pierre, entitled "Ronald Reagan: The Movie."

38. In this essay I have posited a "constantly active" viewer, who, in Bordwell's words, "takes as a central goal the carving out of an intelligible story," by applying "narrative schemata" and using "incoming clues" to "make assumptions, draw inferences" (*Narration in the Fiction Film*, p. 39). Cued—by the advertising and promotion of the film, by some familiarity with "Stallone," and by the text itself—about what to expect and what to desire, this viewer is positioned but not passive and is "sympathetic" to the degree that he/she identifies with the hero and pays due heed to the film's clues in constructing a privileged meaning. The important thing to be kept in mind is that any notion of "subject positioning" must take into account the incisive points raised by Dave Morley: conceptualizing reading/viewing as the positioning of a subject too often "serves to isolate the encounter of text and reader from all social and historical structures *and* from other texts"; and "it does not follow that because the reader has 'taken the position' most fully inscribed in the text, sufficient for the text to be intelligible, he/she will, for that reason alone, subscribe to the ideological problematic of that text" ("Texts, Readers, Subjects," in *Culture, Media, Language*, ed. Stuart Hall, Dorothy Hobson, Andrew Lowe, and Paul Willis [London: Hutchinson, 1980], pp. 163, 167).

Missing in Action: The Vietnam Construction of the Movie Star

> While the strategic implications of the war for the future of American
> military power in local conflicts was the most obvious dimension of its
> defeat, it had confronted these issues often since 1946. What was truly
> distinctive was the collapse of a national consensus on the broad contours
> of America's role in the world. The trauma was intense: the war ended
> without glory and with profound remorse for tens of millions of Ameri-
> cans. Successive administrations fought the war so energetically because
> of these earlier frustrations of which they were especially conscious in the
> early 1960s, scarcely suspecting that rather than resolving them, they
> would only leave the nation with a far larger set of military, political and
> economic dilemmas to face for the remainder of this century. But by 1975
> the United States was weaker than it had been at the inception of the war
> in the early 1960s, a lesson hardly any advocate of new interventions
> could afford to ignore.[1]

The Vietnam War's aftermath left deep scars upon the American psyche.
This prevented any common consensus about the trauma's implications,
whether on the political or artistic level.[2] Nearly a decade passed before Hollywood began making large numbers of Vietnam war movies. However, most
productions lacked any understanding of the war's socio-historical complexity. The Norris/Cannon *Missing in Action* series is no exception.

It is easy to dismiss the populist, imaginary Norris-Stallone Vietnam constructs as moneymaking artifacts beneath the contempt of serious scholars.
Although these films are not (and make no claim to be) accurate or artistic,
they do offer important insights into how a traumatic conflict becomes fictionalized for a later generation. The *Missing in Action* films are significant. They
reveal the operation of a mythical ideological superstructure reinterpreting a
past trauma to echo the contemporary conservative mood that resulted in Reagan's landslide victory in 1984.

In contrast to the generally positive reception enjoyed by American films of
the preceding decades, certain critics have rejected the productions of 1980s
Hollywood.[3] But the former are significant in articulating important contemporary ideological manifestations. Eighties films belong to the same social
and industrial system that generated their predecessors. This system is never
static. It constantly evolves in the context of changing historical circumstances. We see a utilization of previous motifs within the classical Hollywood cinema such as the cultural figure of Cooper's Deerslayer within
Cimino's *The Deer Hunter* (1978). But the director undermines any heroic

associations, showing their redundancy in the light of Vietnam's historical trauma.[4] Other films, such as *Uncommon Valor* (1983), *Rambo: First Blood Part II* (1985), and the *Rocky* cycle (1976 and after), attempt to restore the patriarchal male hero as a conservative response to changing social conditions. Vietnam is now subject to the same revisionist processes that reinvented the American West. The *Missing in Action* series significantly fuses mythological archetypes from the American collective unconscious to represent Vietnam in terms of eighties right-wing populist mentality.[5] In this formation the star system is of strategic importance. Norris and Stallone continue the fight begun by John Wayne both on screen and off.

A star image is often an ideologically governed construction relevant to the historical period of its formation. It may help to suture a complicit audience within a dominant narrative structure, particularly in terms of gender representation. Certain psychological mechanisms occur. They may involve basic common-sense ideas of the male as active, tough, lacking feminine qualities of sensitivity, and dominating the female by the force of his personality. Norris's attitude toward his female costars in *Missing in Action* (1984) and *Invasion U.S.A.* (1985) show him acting according to patriarchal attitudes. No star construction is ever natural. There are pertinent social, historical, and ideological processes at work within its formation.

One key function of the star system may relate to wish-fulfillment factors governing a fantastic resolution of a nation's historical trauma. We find this in Cannon's treatment of the Vietnam experience. In this respect the Norris image is a perfect example of Richard Dyer's concept of a star attempting to reconcile dominant tensions in social life and affirm "that it is possible to triumph over, transcend, successfully live out contradictions."[6] In both his personal and celluloid life Norris has attempted such a reconciliation. Product of an unhappy marriage between a Cherokee Indian father and a mother of Irish-English descent, he transcended personal and economic difficulties, becoming a three-time undefeated world karate champion before entering films.[7] Married for thirty years, fiercely patriotic even before the Reagan era, Norris appeared in a variety of genre films—all relying on his martial arts audience—before achieving recognized stardom in the Cannon box-office successes *Missing in Action* and *Missing in Action 2—The Beginning* (1985). Even before his major stardom, the Vietnam association always formed some aspect of his star persona, either explicitly or implicitly.

Set in Watergate's pessimistic aftermath, *The Good Guys Wear Black* (1979) featured Norris as a Vietnam veteran victimized by a bureaucracy that had betrayed the war. *A Force of One* (1979) stressed his Special Forces connection in a *film policier*, while *The Octagon* (1980) briefly mentioned his Vietnam service. Steve Carver's cop movie *An Eye for an Eye* (1981) assumed a Vietnam background for his character. *Forced Vengeance* (1982) identified him as an ex-member of the 101st "Screaming Eagles" Airborne Division, restoring the Vietnam motif to a prominent role in the narrative. McQuade's Silver Star in *Lone Wolf McQuade* (1983) could only have been won in Vietnam. The film's publicized significance arose from the conflict between Norris and David Carradine—men on both sides of the martial arts

CONSTRUCTION OF THE MOVIE STAR   131

and political spectrum. Carradine's anti–Vietnam War sentiments must have influenced the casting, although he later went on to star in Cannon's *P.O.W.: The Escape* (1986). There were clearly elements dormant within Norris's earlier films that made him an ideal candidate for the 1984 Vietnam revisionism of winning the war on celluloid. His cinematic heroism in triumphing over all odds made him an ideal candidate. Although, like Stallone, he never served in Vietnam, unlike Stallone he had done his military service and had lost a brother in Vietnam.

It was not accidental that Norris's star image took on a definitive Vietnam association with *Missing in Action*. In both *Silent Rage* (1982) and *Forced Vengeance* he appears as an anachronistic "cowboy" in a complicated modern world. This anachronistic invocation of the Western, combined with Vietnam associations (and sometimes emphasis) in the earlier films, enabled him to elide the humiliating Southeast Asia historical contradictions within the escapist confines of *Missing in Action*.

The development of Norris's image parallels three important phases of the star persona: the period of "immaturity" when the star experiments in creating different images; the "mature" stage when identifiable star imagery results; and the final phase of self-reflexivity and parody usually associated with the star's aging.[8] Since Norris has frequently spoken of the cinematic influence of classical Hollywood stars as patriarchal substitutes for his absent father in his formative years, John Wayne and Humphrey Bogart are appropriate models. Wayne's performances from *The Big Trail* (1930) to *They Were Expendable* (1945) and Bogart's from *A Devil with Women* (1930) to *Across the Pacific* (1942) are good illustrations of the first tendency. During this period a star has associations with the genre in which he will later achieve success. Examples are Wayne with the Western and Bogart with the gangster film. In the meantime stars experiment with different roles, some of which are appropriate to their later development. Others are not. Wayne's Republic Western "singing cowboy" roles and Bogart's mad scientist in *The Return of Dr. X* (1936) are relevant examples.

Wayne's *Fort Apache* and *Red River* (both 1948) to *The Alamo* (1960), and Bogart's *Casablanca* (1942) to *Key Largo* (1948) roles reveal the stars' attainment of distinctive screen characteristics in periods that are both historically and politically significant. Wayne becomes a popular star in authoritarian roles in the Cold War era especially in Westerns and in blatantly McCarthyite vehicles, for example, *Big Jim McClain* (1952) and *Blood Alley* (1955). Bogart's star association is as Rick, *Casablanca*'s disillusioned romantic American individualist who finally makes the appropriate personal and political commitment during World War II.

Wayne in *The Comancheros* (1961) to *The Shootist* (1976) and Bogart in *Knock on Any Door* (1949) to *The Harder They Fall* (1956) represent the final phase. During this period, assured of a fixed identity, the star attempts different roles. He may either parody the familiar image (Wayne's Hawks trilogy— *Rio Bravo*, *El Dorado*, *Rio Lobo*—and *True Grit*) or self-reflexively muse on previous roles (Bogart's criminal persona in *The Desperate Hours*).

Obviously, there may be fusions between the three phases. The preceding model is useful in analyzing Norris's significance. Leaving aside his brief appearance in *The Wrecking Crew* (1968), his early phase runs from *Return of the Dragon* (1973) to *Lone Wolf McQuade* (1983). The middle period includes the two *Missing in Action* films, *Invasion U.S.A.* (1985), and *Braddock—Missing in Action Part Three* (1988). It is far too early for the latter phase to emerge.

Like his cinematic father figure, John Wayne, Norris has significant Western connections. In its later phase the genre gained Vietnam associations in films such as *Soldier Blue*, *Little Big Man* (both 1970), and *Ulzana's Raid* (1972). The frontier mythology was always there as a potential ideological theme for reinterpreting Vietnam. Norris's first major film appearance was as the villain Colt in *Return of the Dragon* (1973). The film's sound track used as leitmotif Frank's theme in *Once Upon a Time in the West*. In *Breaker! Breaker!* (1977), Norris's trucker, John D. Dawes, was clearly the Westerner's twentieth-century descendant. The final martial arts duel occurs in a corral. *Forced Vengeance* combined Norris's Vietnam persona with the Western by naming his character after Steve McQueen's Josh Randall in *Wanted—Dead or Alive*.[9] John Wayne's Western associations were also a crucial feature of *The Green Berets* (1968). Both the horror film *Silent Rage* (1982) and *Forced Vengeance* have Norris's character taunted with the term "cowboy." *Lone Wolf McQuade* blatantly parodied Italian Western conventions in visuals and sound track.

All these relevant generic signifiers—martial arts, Western, and Vietnam—merged in 1984 with the release of *Missing in Action*. This election year was one of popular enthusiasm for Ronald Reagan. He had made America "feel good," reinterpreted Vietnam as a "noble crusade," and restored leadership to the Oval Office. The year 1984 was also when the MIA issue received widespread publicity. Norris's fervent patriotism, his heroic leadership qualities in *Missing in Action*, his championship of the MIA issue, and his non-antihero image all benefited from the charismatic shadow of Ronald Reagan. In a year in which all these factors dominated the public mind it was hardly accidental that *Missing in Action* proved a contemporary box-office (if not critical) success. Like the characters he played, Norris believed fervently in the action movie with its single hero overcoming all odds. His 1984 stardom was not entirely accidental.

Norris's status resembles Jonathan Culler's description of the sign: "Because it is arbitrary the sign is totally subject to history, and the combination at a particular moment of a given signifier and signified is a contingent result of the historical process."[10] In this case, the given signifier is the eighties revisionist Vietnam interpretation that becomes fixed in popular consciousness. It combines with the patriarchal star signifier of individual heroism (most exemplified by John Wayne) to present an imaginary wish-fulfillment cinematic scenario of America winning the Vietnam conflict. Any star's communication with a contemporary audience occurs in a given historical moment.[11] This happens to be the early 1980s. Tony Bennett's argument concerning literary effectiveness parallels Norris's dominance as a star in 1984. He states that "it

All these relevant generic signifiers—martial arts, Western, and Vietnam—merged in 1984 with the release of Missing in Action.

is not the text's origins or its purely formal properties which determine its literariness but its mode of functioning within a society's culture as determined by its contingent and therefore historical and changing relations with other cultural forms."[12]

Similar cultural forms operate in association with the developing Norris star persona. They reach their fullest expression if they are in tune with the contemporary ideological tendencies that move any audience. Three such tendencies are influential: the cult of the individual hero, particularly exemplified in the *Rambo* films;[13] ideological revisionism of the Vietnam humiliation into a "noble crusade"; and right-wing populist wish-fulfillment feelings about winning the war, if only on celluloid.

Norris's rise to stardom in 1984 as individual hero belongs to a Hollywood cinema responding to what was seen as strong, patriarchal, leadership emerging from the White House from a president intent on making America feel good after the traumatic post-Watergate years. In an era that approved masculine aggressiveness as a solution to political problems such as the "evil Empire" and international terrorism, it is hardly surprising that a karate champion forms part of a contemporary star triumvirate with Stallone and Schwarzenegger. All three have waged an imaginary cinematic war on the real-life political antagonists of Ronald Reagan.

North Vietnam is one of these antagonists. Of the three, Norris and Stallone have actively championed "the noble crusade" on screen. Their Vietnam films fulfill what Lévi-Strauss calls "the will to myth," displacing Vietnam's historical trauma from popular memory to achieve a "symbolic or mythic reworking of the war" closely related to American culture.[14]

The American cultural tradition is an important influence on the Norris star persona, especially in the *Missing in Action* films. Since the early eighties he has developed the image of the strong, silent Westerner mixing the classical and contemporary star components of John Wayne and Clint Eastwood, themselves offshoots of the solitary frontier hero. The Puritan captivity narrative occupies a functional role in the MIA films. This narrative involved an isolated hunter figure who ventured into the Indian-inhabited wilderness to rescue captive white women. The community viewed the loss of its female members as divine punishment for sins. Once the successful hunter restored the captives he would return once more to the wilderness, since the community no longer had need of him. This archetypal symbolic structure has dominated American consciousness from its earliest days and has both a past and a contemporary relevance.[15] It is easy to recognize this myth not only in the works of James Fenimore Cooper but also in classic American Westerns such as *Shane* (1953) and *The Searchers* (1956). This myth has also survived in the devalued cartoon formats of the Stallone-Norris films.

A seeming contradiction of the original myth lies in the fact that the MIAs are all male. But if we further examine mythic cultural motifs this objection vanishes. Feminization is the major fear within this masculine tradition in both literature and film.[16] The MIAs are all reduced to passivity either by physical debilitation or sexual humiliation.[17] Betrayed by a political establishment relying on the computer (*Rambo*) and futile diplomacy (*Missing in Action*) rather than brute force, the MIAs are scapegoats for the national disgrace. As a result, these new captivity victims become as impotent and passive as their female Puritan ancestors, symbolic substitutes for a government demasculinized as a result of military defeat. The only figure capable of a rescue mission is the anachronistic hero who embodies masculinity to its highest extent. He may be either the muscular John Rambo or the "Good Joe" officer figure of Colonel James T. Braddock.[18] In their MIA films Stallone and Norris embody the ultimate masculine image. This image results not only from the denial of feminine qualities within the hero but through the disappearance, death, or masculinization of the heroine.[19] Whenever any gentleness appears it does so strictly within the confines of the traditional patriarchal father or mother role.[20] With its frontier connotations this eighties masculinity represents a return to "true American values" associated with a president elected to represent a strong nation and reverse America's internal weakness and international humiliation. The documentary footage of Reagan's appearance at the beginning of *Missing in Action 2—The Beginning* thus crudely lays bare the ideological devices of these films in relation to contemporary history. These new heroic values are not only comprehensible as specific forms of gender construction; they also reinvest the old captivity narrative formula with specific ideological considerations.

Richard Slotkin states that myth is central to any society's cultural functioning. It may metaphorically contain historical lessons reinterpreted according to any national *Weltanschauung*.[21] Myth has an ideological relationship to cultural activity. In *The Eighteenth Brumaire of Louis Napoleon* Marx commented on the process of historical mythologization arising from circumstantial constraints and past traditions limiting the creative powers of historical figures. He also noted the tendency of men in social crises to "anxiously conjure up the spirits of the past to their service and borrow from them names, battle-cries and costumes in order to present the new scene of world history in this time-honored disguise and this borrowed language."[22] The relationship to contemporary Reaganite speeches and eighties Hollywood cinema needs no further emphasis.[23]

It is easy for sophisticated viewers to be self-congratulatory in recognizing these cultural forms and their misuse. But the *Missing in Action* films were box-office successes. To disdain them as cinematic constructions exhibits the most blinkered prejudices of academic isolation from social context. In fact, these films influenced contemporary audiences much as earlier Hollywood war movies seduced the Vietnam generation into support for the Vietnam War and reconciliation to its aftermath. They successfully seduced their unsophisticated male audience by providing an imaginary wish-fulfillment hero. But they also achieved this by utilizing the cinematic "suture" mechanism.

According to Kaja Silverman, "Suture is the name given to the procedures by means of which cinema texts confer subjectivity upon their viewers."[24] It is a term that compares the cinema audience's manipulation into the dominant ideology to the stitching performed during a surgical operation. Although this concept has been criticized for its original rigid formulations, it is a useful definition as long as we also consider audience reception, ideology, class, and social formation.[25] Naturally, some spectators immediately recognize the impoverished narrative structure and ludicrous heroics of the Norris-Stallone films. Certainly, this is true of Vietnam veterans. But for impressionable, unsophisticated youngsters, descendants of those immature sixties males seduced into Vietnam by the John Wayne "wet dream," it is a different matter.[26] They are the audience Cannon aims at.

The powerful cinematic mechanisms at work on the *Missing in Action* audiences deserve close analysis. The suture process is one such device, particularly in its association with the psychoanalytic theories of Jacques Lacan. These theories reveal much about ways *Missing in Action*'s ideological operations conceal "the categories of real responsibility and punctuation in socioeconomic communication."[27] At issue here are mechanisms that disavow the political significance of Vietnam and manipulate their chosen audience in an ahistorical, mythic manner. Lacanian cinematic concepts can show us how a particular audience becomes manipulated. As Anthony Wilden points out, if we use Lacan from an extrapsychoanalytic perspective we may get valuable information about cinematic processes of manipulation, particularly if "we want fully to understand the controlling functions of this principle of 'divide and rule' in contemporary society—the real existence of this form of the societal manipulation of learned insecurity."[28]

Jacques-Alain Miller believes that suture is an essential component in

Lacan's theory of subjective formation.[29] In one way or another it responds to a "lack," either some unanswered question in language or society or a child's traumatic separation from the mother. Its original formulation is solipsistic and ahistorical. But when we refer the "lack" to Wilden's important historical and extrapsychoanalytical dimensions, we may draw some interesting conclusions.

Lacan's "lack" is the first loss in the history of the subject, happening at the moment of birth.[30] It initially refers to the impossibility of being both male and female and occurs outside the realm of signification. Lack also anticipates further divisions experienced by the subject within signification in the symbolic Oedipal order. One consequence of this initial lack is an attempt to substitute something else to symbolize the lost object. This may be not merely sexual but also ideological, especially when it refers to some crisis in the national psyche left consciously unresolved in politics or art. The linguistic level may attempt resolution by renaming the trauma as the "noble cause." Consequently, substitutionary historical wish-fulfillment fantasies could emerge as another way of denying the tragedy's threatening consequences.

These substitutionary objects are Lacan's *objets petit a.* "This rubric designates objects which are not clearly distinguished from the self and are not fully grasped as other (*autre*). The object (a) . . . derives its value from its identification with some missing component of the subject's self, whether that loss is seen as primordial, *or as the result of a bodily organization, or as the consequence of some other division*" (italics added).[31] This "other division" may be an ideological crisis in the social formation in which codes, formerly relevant to the construction of subjectivity,[32] become irrelevant to the real conditions of existence.[33] Their validity becomes questionable.

The Norris films show the operation of the suture process as it attempts to repair an ideological crisis in the social formation.[34] When related to Emile Benveniste's model of a discontinuous subject, suture reveals an important construction of human subjectivity relevant both to cinema and ideology. According to Benveniste, a discontinuous subject is coherently constructed when linguistic signifiers "I" and "you" are matched to ideal representations within which the subject finds itself. In "Language and Freudian Theory" Benveniste describes a particular discursive operation. The viewer may begin to question a representation affecting a previously unquestioned subject position. He then calls on an "other" to observe him: "His discourse is appeal and recourse: a sometimes vehement solicitation of the other through the discourse in which he figures himself desperately, and an often mendacious recourse to the other in order to individualize himself in his own eyes."[35]

This Other, or the Absent One, has attributes of the mythically potent symbolic father possessing virility, knowledge, transcendental vision, and power. Naturally the feminine is excluded. The viewer may identify either with this Law of the Father or his symbolic representative on the screen (for example, Norris) in a conservative entertainment production.

Desire is connected to "lack." The subject attempts to fill in whatever lack emerges by the suture process. Like "lack," desire is continuous, occurring at

The viewer may identify either with this Law of the Father or his symbolic representative on the screen (for example, Norris) in a conservative entertainment film.

several points in the subject's life.[36] Beginning at birth, it takes the form of individual alienation, whether from a previously accepted personal identity or aspects of the status quo. As treated in Ron Kovic's autobiography, *Born on the Fourth of July* (1976), the author's paraplegic status alienates him both from his former self and from identification with the status quo. He falls into individual anguish, but he does not desire reintegration, a return of the "lack." Discovering the ideological contradictions within his subjectivity he becomes a politicized antiwar demonstrator. There is no "desire" to return to his former self and turn the clock back. Unfortunately, this extra-individual political dimension is lacking in the Lacanian formulation. Nevertheless, Lacan's ideas enable us to understand the conservative nature of certain suturing mechanisms at work within *Missing in Action*. Instead of being moved into opposition like Kovic, the manipulated viewer is now put into a position of desiring the now mythically displaced Vietnam victory. He identifies with both the Law of the Father and the masculine hero now taking John Wayne's place. America has historically lost the war. A real victory is impossible. Hence a substitutionary wish-fulfillment fantasy has to take the place of the originally desired victory.

In the Lacanian framework, desire can never be realized. It is directed toward an ideal representation forever beyond the subject's reach. Confronted with need, the primary process produces an imaginary gratification. The

opening ten minutes of *Missing in Action* present a hallucinatory fantasy involving dreams of death and humiliation. This segment represents the impossibility of a historical American victory in Vietnam. As a result, the remainder
of the film offers a secondary process supplying an ingenious resolution of the
fantasy. The fictional narrative compensates to some extent for American defeat. But, despite its emotional, wish-fulfillment aspects, desire is still subject
to lack and impossible to realize. Hence, narrative resolution can only be an
unrealistic fiction. All the film can offer is an imaginary suture demanding
complacency nourished by fantasy. Indeed, the whole structure of *Missing in
Action* attempts ideologically to answer this historical "lack." If we broaden
Lacan's original individualistic formulation to include this extrapsychoanalytic dimension, we may see how cinematic mechanisms suture certain
eighties audiences into an ideal uncritical subjectivity.

Lacan points out that whenever a subject confronts any lack an "*image
comes to the position of bearing all the cost of desire.*"[37] *Missing in Action*
has two major introductory sequences that contain images that attempt to fill
in a lack. The first occurs in the opening four minutes, in which the desiring
spectator's initial insecurity is answered by an appeal to the "Absent One"
who enters the frame in the form of the spectator's fictional representative. We
are introduced to a dormant jungle environment. There is, at first, no movement. The viewer clearly feels unpleasure locked within the cluster of technological apparatus. The camera slowly dollys right along a jungle area. No
human being is in the frame. The only sounds are natural. A pregnant silence
of danger falls. As viewers we become conscious of looking. Then the camera
slowly turns left. An explosion erupts, This "violence" leads to a montage
series of explosions.[38] The film sound track begins. Then Norris enters the
frame *from the direction the camera was turning.*

Before Norris's entry, insecurity reigns. Like Daniel Dayan's spectator, the
viewer "discovers that he is only authorized to see what happens to be in the
axis of the gaze of another spectator, who is ghostly or absent."[39] In this sequence the viewer feels a sense of "lack," a desire to see more than the speaking subject withholds. One of the ways in which the classic film text cancels
this position of passivity, a feeling of loss or castration, can be by the classical
Hollywood editing pattern of shot–reverse shot. A gaze within the fiction may
step in to conceal the castrating gaze outside the fiction. However, the subject
may decide to become absent to itself by permitting a fictional character to
stand in for it. The moment the viewing subject accepts the fiction or identifies
with the male character (I primarily speak of male audiences who accept the
ideology of both discourse and character), suture becomes successful. In
Missing in Action this moment occurs with the introduction of Norris into the
frame toward which the camera was moving. He is the patriarchal salvation
offered by the Absent One in instituting a historical wish-fulfillment dream
fantasy sequence. His entry as star is both ideological and historical. Indeed,
Missing in Action 2—The Beginning is significant for emphasizing this feature. In the opening postcredit scenes the documentary footage of Ronald

Reagan dissolves to reveal the fictional Vietnam prison camp where Norris becomes the textual production of the presidential discourse. It is therefore not surprising, again, that Lacan's own use of the term *suture* defines it as a "junction of the imaginary and symbolic."[40]

In the images following the dream sequence both Braddock and the viewer are offered a subject position, one of identification with militaristic male gendered subjectivity. Now, however, the film begins to lay bare its ideological device of constructing the Norris star format, by reference not to any real event but to an imaginary cartoon formation. After his symbolic death in the introductory dream sequence we see Braddock lying prone on a hotel bed. A television set broadcasts the MIA issue. Braddock switches channels. A Spiderman cartoon appears. Torn between reclusiveness and his designated role as MIA hunter-savior Braddock moves slowly into the next room. As the cartoon continues he falls prey to another memory. He is powerless to stop a sadistic guard from executing a fellow prisoner. The sequence finishes. Looking absently at the set he turns it back to the news channel. Angered at the report of his nonparticipation in a government MIA mission, he kicks the set over. Braddock then picks up the phone and utters the first words in the film as he agrees to participate.

The Spiderman sequence is crucial here. It naturally leads to Norris's activity in the film, which will make him a star. Braddock moves from a "feminine" prone position into an active "masculine" one. Braddock's activity is an ideological operation of desire designed to fill a humiliating historical lack that can never be filled. The Spiderman sequence represents Lacan's idea of the image coming to the "position of bearing all the cost of desire." In this respect, Steve Fore's analysis of the relationship of Kuntzel's law and the vast majority of Hollywood films is relevant also to *Missing in Action*'s Vietnam dilemma, except that here the "film work" occurs not at the film's beginning but rather in the succeeding brief cartoon sequence.[41] Fore's observations deserve emphasizing.

> Ostensibly, the beginning of the film (or any narrative text) typically supplies the viewer with some kind of avenue of entry, a way into the story. A problem is presented through means which may vary from film to film but which serve the same universal functions: "centering the narrative" on a character or characters and establishing the terms of the problem itself, which Kuntzel calls "the terror enigmas, trails, menace and horror" and is "inscribed in the diegesis: the spectator, for his part, already *knows* what awaits him; a *difference* will never erupt in the film: from now on, there will be nothing but the fulfillment of expectations." The main body of a film, then, primarily (though not merely) elaborates the world and world view established at its very beginning—and in the case of a genre film both the narrative genesis and the narrative elaboration are likely to be structured in a strongly conventionalized fashion, providing the viewer with further, semi-continuous intratextual and culturally based signposts of meaning.[42]

These observations are particularly relevant to the opening sequence's ideological project. It provides an imaginary answer to the traumatic Vietnam defeat and the MIA issue by an infantile fantasy of American prowess. Myth is at the service of suture. A new star in the John Wayne mold emerges to present Vietnam in mythological modes similar to those of *The Green Berets*.[43] The selection of Spiderman, however, serves to lay bare the excessive nature of the film's project. Does not the origin of this cartoon lie in adolescent insecurity and a yearning for the fantasy male role?[44] Braddock occupies this role when he picks up the phone, answering the call to his new tour of duty in the laconic Eastwood manner.

It is not accidental that a reviewer described this film as a "threadbare Action Man fantasy."[45] *Missing in Action* answers a desire that can never be filled, utilizing imaginary adolescent icons from American popular culture in a comic-strip manner. Roger Manvell's observations on animated film's unreality are pertinent to *Missing in Action*'s conscious and unconscious operations. Manvell points out that any animated film introduces "no extraneous qualities from actuality, or from the complicated psychology of the real human being, who, like the actor, can never possess the utter singleness of purpose of an artist."[46] It is the ideal format for representing any noncontradictory ideologically governed message. Such is the case of *Missing in Action*'s Spiderman cartoon in this Cannon production.

The Spiderman sequence uses key signifiers that will later appear in the film such as the prison camp, helicopter, American flag, and Spiderman's rope. Within the episodic cartoon narrative Spiderman confronts the Shocker who has escaped from prison, as Braddock has also. Spiderman puts a mask over his face and swings toward the camera, blocking the image with the black emblem on his costume. Braddock wears a black costume when he goes on a night mission to interrogate General Tran. Spiderman swings on a rope around the American flag. Braddock has to slide on a rope to return to his hotel. The Shocker represents an animated, clean-shaven version of Norris.

The cartoon presents an animated version of the Manichean conflict in Braddock's own mind: the individual who has escaped from prison and wishes to hide (Shocker), and the patriot (Spiderman). This latter persona in Braddock's form will soon occupy the position of the captivity narrative hunter who will rescue the MIAs from the forces of darkness. Therefore, the Spiderman sequence and the *Missing in Action* films form an apt parallel to how politicians manipulatively use American Western mythology. As Slotkin points out, "Myth is invoked as a means of deriving usable values from history, and of putting these values beyond the reach of critical demystification. Its primary appeal is to ritualized emotions, established beliefs, habitual associations, memory nostalgia. Its representations are symbolic and metaphoric, depending for their force on an intuitive recognition and acceptance of the symbol by the audience."[47]

Thus, it is by no means accidental that the *Missing in Action* films use the cartoon format of Westerns and the World War II films. They are part of a popular American tradition of mythical narratives whose "formal qualities and structures are increasingly conventionalized and abstracted, until they are reduced to a set of powerfully evocative and resonant 'icons' . . . in which history becomes a cliché. At the same time that their form is being simplified and abstracted, the range of reference of these stories is being expanded."[48]

Slotkin further points out that myth-based children's games such as cowboys and Indians have historical bases that change continually in response to "ideological cues provided by the adult culture." They are a "set of forms generated by a particular set of cultural producers in a particular historical moment."[49] One historical moment, 1984, led to Cannon's production of the *Missing in Action* films—works dominated by the Reagan era's Vietnam revisionism. The films' uncomplex narrative formats used classical cinematic techniques for subject production, providing a fabricated star in a bastardized version of the American cultural tradition. Seen in these terms, Norris's long hair and beard represent a Barthesian, inoculated version of features that once symbolized the anti–Vietnam War generation. A right-wing populist revolt operates against government bureaucracy led by John Rambo and James T. Braddock, the new descendants of James Fenimore Cooper's military aristocrats.[50]

In the 1960s the hippy opposition used Native American symbols and Thoreau's civil disobedience to affirm forgotten free American traditions. Vietnam films of the 1980s see the classic dualities of American literature (Huck and Jim, Ishmael and Queequeg, Natty and Chingachgook) combined into single male figures. Rambo is as at home in the forest as his Indian predecessor. Braddock combines opposites in his persona; he has the martial arts technique of his Vietnamese opponents as well as an American patriotism disdainful of both phony Washington diplomats and enemy aliens. Rescuing the captives he implicitly invokes that Puritan war of extermination present in the captivity narratives. His persona mixes mythic-cultural patterns and suturing cinematic processes in a way designed to lure the unwary spectator into accepting ideologically proscribed roles. Despite inadequate acting ability, he is the successor to the popular audience's need for the traditional hero role left vacant by John Wayne. The cinematic mechanisms behind the construction of his star persona are important devices to understand, particularly in a historical era in danger of repeating past mistakes.

NOTES

1. Gabriel Kolko, *Anatomy of a War* (New York: Patheon Books, 1985), p. 548.

2. For a brief survey see: Fox Butterfield, "The New Vietnam Scholarship," *New York Times Magazine*, 13 February 1983, pp. 26–34, 45–60; Peter C. Rollins, "The Vietnam War: Perspectives Through Literature, Film and Television," *American Quarterly*, 36, no. 3 (1984): 419–439; Tim O'Brien, *If I Die in a Combat Zone* (New York: Delache Press, 1973); and Kolko, *Anatomy of a War*. I am grateful to Professor Rollins for these references.

3. See Robin Wood, "80s Hollywood: Dominant Tendencies," *CineAction!* 1 (Spring 1985): 2–5; Andrew Britton, "Blissing Out: The Politics of Reaganite Entertainment," *Movie* 31/32 (Winter 1986/87): 1–42.

4. For contrasting analyses of this film see Britton, "Sideshows: Hollywood in Vietnam," *Movie* 27/28 (Winter 1980/81): 2–5, 15–20; Wood, *Hollywood: From Vietnam to Reagan* (New York: Columbia University Press, 1986), pp. 270–298.

5. The use of *archetype* needs qualification, since its usual inflections are generally ahistorical. We can apply the concept in relation to "historically specific terms with . . . demonstrable connection to events, and to the processes of recall" that allow us to test in a more concrete and historical manner our ideas about the ways in which mythologies are created. See here Richard Slotkin, *The Fatal Environment: The Myth of the Frontier in the Age of Industrialization 1800–1890* (New York: Athenaeum Press, 1985), p. 28.

6. Richard Dyer, "Four Films of Lana Turner," *Movie* 25 (Winter 1977/78): 30. See also his monograph, *Stars* (London: British Film Institute, 1979).

7. For relevant publicity-oriented biographical information see Byron Coley, *Chuck Norris* (New York: St. Martin's Press 1986); Chuck Norris with Joe Hyams, *The Secret of Inner Strength* (Boston: Little Brown, 1988).

8. This formulation parallels Christian Metz's interpretation of genres in *Language and Cinema* (New York: Praeger, 1975). For an informative discussion of both genres and stars in relation to audiences see Graeme Turner, *Film As Social Practice* (London: Routledge, 1988), pp. 83–86, 94–126.

9. I am grateful to David Raines for this information.

10. Jonathan Culler, *Saussure* (London: Fontana, 1976), p. 36.

11. On the star as "sign" see also Dyer, *Stars*, pp. 99–172.

12. Tony Bennett, *Formalism and Marxism* (London and New York: Methuen, 1979), p. 60.

13. See J. Hoberman, "The Fascist Guns in the West," *American Film*, 11, no. 5 (March 1986): 53–59, for a survey of these contemporary individualist cult movies.

14. See also Louis J. Kern, "MIA's, Myth, and Macho Magic: Post Apocalyptic Cinematic Visions of Vietnam," in William J. Searle, ed., *Search and Clear: Critical Responses to Selected Literature and Films of the Vietnam War* (Bowling Green, Ohio: Popular Press, 1988), pp. 37–54.

15. For further information see Slotkin, *Regeneration Through Violence: The Mythology of the American Frontier 1600–1815* (Middletown, Conn.: Wesleyan University Press, 1973).

16. For significant examples see Paul Seydor, *Peckinpah: The Western Films* (Urbana: University of Illinois Press, 1980), pp. 229–241; Slotkin, *Fatal Environment*, pp. 139–140.

17. In *Missing in Action 2—The Beginning*, the North Vietnamese sexually humiliate a captured South Vietnamese officer before prostitutes. Since he is made a spectacle for the American prisoners, they are also involved in this humiliation process.

18. For the use of the "Good Joe" concept in the star system see Orrin E. Klapp, *Heroes, Villains and Fools* (Englewood Cliffs, N.J.: Prentice-Hall, 1962), pp. 108–123; Dyer *Stars*, pp. 53–56. In terms of Norris's firm views on his audience's need for a hero and his refusal to portray negative images, he definitely belongs to the traditional type of hero noted by Klapp, a contradiction in the climate of the 1980s.

19. From *Missing in Action* to *Invasion U.S.A.*, Norris's female partner was usually a "macha-female" such as Lenore Kasdan or Melissa Prophet, whose grotesque masculinization paralleled the developing violent side of Norris's changing image. Since Norris's recent attempts to change his image to a gentler character (*Firewalker* (1986), *Braddock* (1988), and *Hero and the Terror* (1988), the female partner has reverted to a much softer, "feminine," dependent role. For an analysis of male insecurities concerning the female in recent 1980s military movies, see Tania Modleski, "A Father is Being Beaten: Male Feminism and the War Film," *Discourse*, 10, no. 2 (Spring-Summer 1988): 62–77.

20. This is most obvious in *Braddock*, where Norris rescues the captive Amerasians from the Vietnamese "Indians." The film unsuccessfully attempts an intra-generic cross-fertilization between the 1980s Vietnam genre and the recent baby movies such as *Baby Boom* (1987), *She's Having A Baby* (1988), and *Three Men and A Baby* (1988) through experiments with slightly changing Norris's persona and utilizing successful audience formulas. For Ripley's develop- menty of a maternal instinct in *Aliens* see Harvey R. Greenberg, "Reimagining the Gargoyle: Psychoanalytic Notes on *Alien*," *Camera Obscura* 15 (Fall 1986): 77.

21. Slotkin, *Fatal Environment*, p. 536.

22. Quoted, ibid., p. 537.

23. Ibid., pp. 18, 537.

24. Kaja Silverman, *The Subject of Semiotics* (New York and Oxford: Oxford University Press 1983), p. 195.

25. See Britton, "The Ideology of Screen," *Movie* 26 (Winter 1978/79): 15–17, for criticisms concerning early definitions, and Silverman's observations on the complex develop- ment of this concept (*Semiotics*, p. 200). The concept has recently come under attack by the cognitive group of theorists. See David Bordwell, *Narration in the Fiction Film* (Madison, Wis.: University of Wisconsin Press, 1985), pp. 110–113, 325, and Noel Carroll, *Mystifying Movies: Fads and Fallacies in Contemporary Film Theory* (New York: Columbia University Press, 1988), pp. 183–99. As will be pointed out, the *Missing in Action* films do not presuppose the active spectator demanded by perceptual cognitive theory. They rely instead on the uncon- scious mechanisms instilled within the viewer as a result of immersion within the ideological social-historical *Weltanschauung*. The suture mechanisms operate in the few specific introduc- tory instances within the film text which seek to determine spectator assent. Neither suture nor psychoanalysis is relevant to *every* viewing experience. The same could be said for cognition theories.

26. For a useful discussion on the significance of John Wayne to the Vietnam generation, see Tobey C. Herzog, "John Wayne in A Modern Heart of Darkness: The American Soldier in Vietnam," in Searle, *Search and Clear*, pp. 16–26.

27. Anthony Wilden, *System and Structure: Essays in Communication and Exchange*, 2nd ed. (London: Tavistock Publications, 1984), p. 474; see also his highly relevant conclu- sions on society and gender identity, ibid., pp. 278–301.

28. Ibid., p. 477.

29. Jacques-Alain Miller, "Suture (elements of the logic of the signifier)," *Screen*, 18, no. 4 (Winter 1977/78): 25–26.

30. Jacques Lacan, *The Four Fundamental Concepts of Psychoanalysis,* trans. Alan Sheridan (New York: Norton, 1978), pp. 204–205.

31. Silverman, *Semiotics*, p. 156.

32. Relevant works include Ron Kovic, *Born on the Fourth of July* (New York: McGraw- Hill, 1976); Michael Herr, *Dispatches* (New York: Alfred A. Knopf, 1977); Philip Caputo, *A Rumor of War* (New York: Richard and Winston, 1977); Mark Baker, *Nam* (New York: William Morrow, 1981); Al Santoli, *Everything We Had* (New York: Random House, 1981); and Wal- lace Terry, ed., *Bloods: An Oral History of the Vietnam War by Black Veterans* (New York: Random House, 1984). Note also Vietnam fiction such as Charles Durden, *No Bugles, No Drums* (New York: Viking Press, 1976), and Gustav Hasford, *The Short Timers* (New York: Harper and Row, 1979). For two useful surveys of Vietnam in literature and film see Julian Smith, *Looking Away: Hollywood and Vietnam* (New York: Charles Scribner and Sons, 1975), and James C. Wilson, *Vietnam in Prose and Films* (Jefferson, N.C.: McFarland, 1982). See also Albert Auster and Leonard Quart, *How the War was Remembered: Hollywood & Vietnam* (New York: Praeger, 1988), which arrived when this article was in the process of completion.

33. See Kolko, *Anatomy of a War*, chapter 13.

34. For much of the following material I am indebted to Silverman, *Semiotics*, pp. 194–236.

35. Emile Benyeniste, *Problems in General Linguistics,* trans. Mary Elizabeth Meek (Coral Gables, Fla.: University of Miami Press, 1971), p. 67.

36. Silverman, *Semiotics*, p. 176.

37. Lacan, *Ecrits* (original French edition Paris: Seuil, 1966), p. 655, quoted by Stephen Heath, "Notes on Suture," *Screen* 18, no. 4 (Winter 1977/78): 54.

38. For a discussion of the role of violence in initiating a narrative see Heath, "Film and System: Terms of Analysis," *Screen* 16, no. 1 (Spring 1975): 49–50. Again, in contrast to Carroll (*Mystifying Movies,* p. 166), Heath's concept of violence as initiating the narrative in this specific instance is relevant since the powerful masculine prowess equilibrium we see in the beginning (as well as in the silent jungle scene) is disturbed.

39. Daniel Dayan, "The Tutor Code of Class Cinema" in Bill Nichols, ed., *Movies and Methods* (Berkeley and Los Angeles: University of California Press, 1976), p. 448.

40. Heath, "Film and System," pp. 55–56.

41. Thierry Kuntzel, "The Film Work 2," originally appeared in the French journal *Communications* 23 (1975): 136–90. The English translation is in *Camera Obscura* 5 (1980): 6–69.

42. Steve Fore, "Kuntzel's Law and *Uncommon Valor*, or Reshaping the National Consciousness in Six Minutes Flat," *Wide Angle* 7, no. 4 (1985): 26.

43. For evidence that *The Green Berets* succeeded at the American box office due to its manipulative use of American cultural and mythological codes see John Hellmann, *American Myth and the Legacy of Vietnam* (New York: Columbia University Press, 1986), pp. 90–93.

44. See Jim McFarlin, "An Off-the-Wall Superhero," *Chicago Tribune,* 2 June 1986.

45. Tim Pulleine, "Missing in Action," *Monthly Film Bulletin* 52, no. 615 (April 1985): 117.

46. Roger Manvell, *The Animated Film* (London: Sylvan Press, 1954), p. 9.

47. Slotkin, *Fatal Environment*, p. 19.

48. Ibid., p. 16.

49. Ibid., p. 20. We may view Cannon Films as a 1980s parallel to Slotkin's concept of "cultural producers." As well as aspiring to the role of a classical Hollywood major studio, this company has actively produced action movies catering to the developing conservative tastes of the Reagan era. Charles Bronson's ailing career gained a new lease of life beginning from *Death Wish III* (1985) and continuing to *Messenger of Death* (1988). Much work remains to be done on the ideological significance of Cannon beyond the cursory reviews in *Variety* and *American Film*. Cannon's films built up the Vietnam signifier already present in the Norris persona, signing him up for a $21-million seven-year contract in 1984. Robert Friedman, "Will Cannon Boom or Bust?" *American Film* 7 (July–August 1986): 53–59, represents the usual uncritical promotional material.

50. On the military aristocrat see Slotkin, *Fatal Environment*, pp. 103–106, 347–348, 501–502.

The Politics of Ambivalence:
Apocalypse Now as Prowar and Antiwar Film

> The opposition between nature and culture which I have insisted on
> seems today to offer a value which is above all methodological.
> > *Claude Lévi-Strauss,* La pensée sauvage

With the advent of poststructuralism, deconstructionism, the new historic-ism, feminism, and other theoretical paradigms, the insights of structuralism and semiotics as conceived by the French anthropologist Claude Lévi-Strauss are fast fading from film and literary studies. The new methodologies have challenged the idea that film and literature, as symbolic systems like myth, can be viewed in terms of how codes consciously or unconsciously establish aesthetic and social meaning in a text. But before consigning Lévi-Strauss's method to the ash heap of outmoded critical thought, it might prove useful to reexamine what use-value can be gleaned from the structuralist project. In particular, one aspect of Lévi-Strauss's system—his mode of analysis of my-thic structuration—may still prove fruitful for understanding our modern myths and epics: our national cinemas. The basic assumption that cultural products such as film and literature can be viewed as epiphenomenal man-ifestations of an underlying system of textual and social relations is too valu-able a tool to abandon to the vertiginous vortex of recent theory.

Lévi-Strauss made a lifelong study of the kinship, mating, and mythologi-cal systems in so-called primitive cultures. His anthropological data revealed that the complex rituals of many societies could be reduced to a system of rules or codes, and that those rules and codes were themselves variants of a limited set of elemental binary oppositions: nature/culture, raw/cooked, ani-mal/human being, and peace/war. Further, his mythological data suggested that the ostensible chaos of myths could be ordered if they were considered as aspects of a social language whose fundamental units and oppositions could be identified. More important, Lévi-Strauss spelled out the ultimate reason for such structures: "to insure the permanency of the social group."[1]

This universal, ahistorical, and essentialist grid obviously needs to be re-vised and applied to the specificity of various artistic texts, cultures, and ep-ochs. In a way, then, every text transmogrifies Lévi-Strauss's universal dichotomies to speak of and to its own nation and era, within a particular so-cial formation. Historicizing these cosmic concepts and concretizing them in a given film text helps clarify the role of myth in artistic construction and so-cial reception. The concern here is with the extent to which the structures of myth are formative as well as reflective of our collective attitudes: the degree to which myths construct and uphold particular worldviews and ideologies. Lévi-Strauss was well aware of this problem when he said, "I do not aim to show how people think in myths, but how myths think in people, unbeknownst to them."[2]

One of the most important binary oppositions in any myth or film is that between the social representations in the text (its social imaginary) and the social realities from which those representations are derived and with which they interact. In general, myths consist of binary polarizations of certain social realities and tendencies that are familiar and important to a given culture. The myth ultimately produces the impression of resolving those dichotomies, of sublating the dialectic. As Lévi-Strauss said, "Myth . . . provides an interpretive grid, a matrix of relations which filters and organizes life experience and produces the blessed illusion that contradictions can be overcome and difficulties resolved."[3] Such a "blessed illusion" can be very satisfying to a troubled culture and its citizens. Indeed, Lévi-Strauss saw this ameliorating social function as crucial: "Through their myths, people try to hide or to justify the discrepancies between their society and the ideal image of it which they harbour."[4]

Regardless of whether Lévi-Strauss was correct that the source of binary language structures is inherent in the human mind or whether binarism in structural anthropology reflects a Western ideology imposed on native cultures, the dramatic art of the West has relied on oppositional syntax and construction since time immemorial. These patterns are as evident in the contemporary products of "civilized" cultures as they are in "primitive" myths. Indeed, the former often rely on the latter for their general structuration and specific "mythologemes." Whether consciously intended by their authors or unconsciously appropriated from the culture by an artist, the repositories of modern cultural myths—such as contemporary films—often rely on binary oppositions. These artistic antinomies, then, arise from the real contradictions of a historical period and serve specific sociopolitical ends. As Bronislaw Malinowski stated, "Myth is not symbolic, but a *direct* expression of its subject matter. . . . Myth fulfills in primitive culture an indispensable function: it expresses, enhances, and codifies belief; it safeguards and enforces morality; it vouches for the efficiency and contains practical rules for the guidance of man."[5]

A MODERN MYTH: *APOCALYPSE NOW*

Francis Ford Coppola's stated reason for making *Apocalypse Now* (1978) was to assist Americans in "putting the Vietnam experience behind them."[6] In the context of Lévi-Strauss's and Malinowski's analyses, then, this statement of authorial intentionality reveals much about almost all the post–Vietnam War Hollywood films, the film in question, and American society in general. Only a handful of U.S. films about Vietnam—*The Green Berets* (1968), *In the Year of the Pig* (1969), and *Hearts and Minds* (1974) being the most notable—

were made during the Indochina conflict. Those that followed tended to depoliticize the struggle, turning it into a test of manhood, a rite of passage, or a personal trial. Many dealt with the valid issue of "Vieterans' " return to postwar American civilian life (*Rolling Thunder* [1977], *Coming Home* [1978], *The Deer Hunter* [1978], *First Blood* [1982]) but avoided overt commentary on the moral and political questions of the war itself. Instead, they tended to focus on an individual's personal reaction to his Vietnam experience and subsequent readjustment.

Apocalypse Now turned the real-life specificity of U.S. imperialism into an abstract and philosophical cinematic meditation on good and evil, light and dark. In the process, American society was treated to a film that represented not so much Vietnam-era America as America's idealized view of itself post-Vietnam, that is, from the enlightened perspective of a historical hindsight that could sublate contradictions. As such, *Apocalypse Now* might be categorized as both a prowar movie and an antiwar movie in that the film's cinematic and political ambiguity both conceals and reveals a national ambivalence toward the Vietnam War.

Francis Coppola was no stranger to the concept of an ambivalent war movie. He was the screenwriter of *Patton* (1970), which portrayed the World War II field commander as, on the one hand, a raving megalomaniac who loved war, slapped his own soldiers, strutted around and cursed pathologically, and had an odd penchant for pearl-handled revolvers and, on the other hand, a determined military hero who took strong, decisive action to win the war in North Africa, Sicily, and Europe. It is a common marketing strategy of the American cinema to attempt to deal with controversial subject matter by having it both ways, so as not to alienate segments of the mass audience who have strong feelings on one side or another of a particular issue. *Patton* offended neither doves nor hawks, since each group could read into the film (like a national Rorschach test) its own preconceived ideas about the World War II general and the then-raging Vietnam conflict.

Indeed, one hawkish viewer of *Patton*, President Richard Nixon, watched the film twice at Camp David. Nixon publicly stated, after watching the film, that he realized that the solution to the Vietnam quagmire was strong, decisive military action, and he immediately ordered the invasion and bombing of Cambodia. Despite Nixon's one-sided "reading," dovish viewers saw the film as extremely critical of hypermilitarism. In short, through its contradictory themes and techniques, *Patton* was able to appeal to viewers of every political stripe. No segment of the box office was alienated, and *Patton* went on to win Academy awards for best picture and best screenplay, as well as the best actor award for George C. Scott.

When a nation (or, rather, its film industry) "nominates" such a divided hero-villain to explain itself to itself, that fictive representative and the entire representational process become implicated in the way that nation signifies its own conflicted view of its role in the contemporaneous real war (Vietnam), as opposed to the relatively unconflicted, historically depicted, reimagined war (World War II). Thus, *Patton* appropriated the reigning sociocultural

Patton was, to some, a brave and resourceful warrior fighting in a just cause and, to others, a vain, imperious martinet.

divisiveness and national disunity about the Indochina conflict and grafted it onto a less troubling military endeavor from the past, World War II. The negative contemporary ramifications were displaced and dispersed onto a more remote and more popular era of national unity. At the same time, the depiction of the hero, General George S. Patton, did bear the marks of the divided political realities of the contemporary national debate. Patton was, to some, a brave and resourceful warrior fighting in a just cause and, to others, a vain, imperious martinet.

This same strategy of "having it both ways" can be seen in *Apocalypse Now*. Having been rewarded with an Oscar, financial success, and increased professional prestige for his articulation of national divisions in *Patton*, Francis Coppola seemed to have learned his lesson well when he came to make the equally ambivalent *Apocalypse Now*. In the latter project, however, he enlisted the aid of cowriter John Milius, who is well known for his right-wing jingoistic predilections (*Dirty Harry* [1971], *Magnum Force* [1973], *The Wind and the Lion* [1975], *Conan the Barbarian* [1982], *Red Dawn* [1984]). This divided authorship may account for some of the film's unresolved combinations of dovish and hawkish elements. On the one hand, *Apocalypse Now* has been read as an antiwar statement because many scenes depict the absurdity and outright lunacy of America's Vietnam policies, as well as the machinations of high-level military commanders. On the other, certain elements of its content and style work against this dovish reading. For instance, the title, *Apocalypse Now*, seems to emphasize the destructive, prowar side of the film, derived as it was from the *anti*war slogan "*Peace* Now!" Yet it is also possible that the title is an ironic warning of the ultimate dangers of extended conflict.

Not all of the film's elements are so ambiguous. Many scenes and cinematic techniques work to further a promilitary, prowar interpretation. For example, by showing the U.S. winning all the battles, the film provides the American audience with a victorious rush that is accentuated by the lack of concern for Vietnamese lives. During the battle scene at "Charlie's Point," a peaceful Vietnamese village is destroyed, photographed so as to excite the viewer viscerally and to glorify war and its godlike heroes. The sheer kinesthetic excitement of this sequence—especially its sweeping and majestic helicopter shots—might even provoke a "gung-ho" response from those who revel in deeds of derring-do (or, in fact, from *most* viewers because the glory of war is a built-in code of the combat genre). The editing is quick and fast-paced, simulating the highly charged emotional state of the aptly named Colonel Kilgore and his men. The scene is synchronized to a triumphant musical score, Richard Wagner's "Ride of the Valkyries," which monumentalizes the passage of dead heroes into Valhalla. Further, point-of-view camera angles inscribe the viewer in the helicopter looking down on the Vietnamese villagers, making them faceless and tiny in the frame as they are gunned down, but the camera moves in to isolate the agony of one wounded *American* soldier. The audience is thus cinematically implicated in the exhilarating superiority of the American attack.

This aestheticization of violence contributes greatly to the film's appeal to a twisted patriotism. The use of wide-screen, low-angle long shots of helicopters in tight formation flying up from the horizon into a rising sun creates a grandiose, romanticized, and even heavenly aura of battle that changes destruction and death from acts of horror into Armageddon-like sights of awe-inspiring beauty. In some ways, *Apocalypse Now* shows the war not as immoral, only mishandled. It may be saying that had Americans made war with the passion of Colonel Kilgore, the cool of Captain Willard, and the brutal honesty of Colonel Kurtz, the United States would have won. The film pays tribute to our heroes' ability to *search* and to our technology's ability to *destroy*. As one viewer put it,

"In an age of liberal moralism and bureaucratic fear, *Apocalypse Now* made a daringly reactionary statement: War is a beautiful and vital human experience."[7]

Finally, on the prowar side of the ledger, the narrative goes out of its way to justify the actions of Colonel Kurtz, the ostensibly brutal martinet whose methods are labeled unsound by his superiors. In fact, Kurtz is actually portrayed as correct in all his judgments. Although he became an outlaw to the generals by summarily executing four supposedly friendly Vietnamese, all enemy espionage activity immediately stopped after those murders. The victims were obviously Vietcong double agents (Willard: "I guess he must've hit the right four people"). In addition, Kurtz's many citations and commendations are elaborately displayed throughout the journey upriver so that he is revered even before he is first seen by the audience. Willard's voice-over narration, his aural point of view, expresses his admiration for the colonel's accomplishments: "Third-generation West Point, top of his class . . . a thousand decorations," "He had an impressive career," "Kurtz staged Operation Archangel . . . rated a major success," ". . . passed jump school at age thirty-eight," "The more I read . . . the more I admired him."

Cinematically, Kurtz's gold-star dossier is shown to us directly through Willard's eyes, through our identification figure's visual point of view. Despite Willard's indeterminate, tabula rasa facial expressions and "man without qualities" persona (qualities that would normally militate *against* emotional empathy with a character), audience identification is achieved through a fairly strict point-of-view regimen that involves Willard's detached observation of the world around him combined with overtly subjective shots (for example, the early sequence in which Willard looks through the Venetian blinds in his hotel room ["Saigon. Shit, I'm still in Saigon"] or the shrimp and cigarettes offered directly to the camera [Willard] in the general's quarters). Filmmakers often use subjective angles to establish perceptual, conceptual, and emotional rapport with their characters. In this case, the rigorous point-of-view structure facilitates identification with a half-psychotic, alcoholic CIA assassin.

Throughout the narrative, Willard is closely identified with his prey, Colonel Kurtz. Both are introduced reclining in bed, heavily shadowed but lit by an odd orange light. The photograph of Willard's wife at his bedside closely resembles that of Kurtz's spouse, seen in his dossier. Similarly, Willard grasps at a fly in his opening scene and Kurtz repeats the gesture later on. Willard becomes more like Kurtz as the film progresses, his gradual immersion into physical darkness (including black camouflage makeup) corresponding to Kurtz's silhouetted or darkly shadowed physiognomy. Indeed, Willard makes their doppelgänger status explicit: "There is no way to tell his story without telling my own." After "terminating" his superior, Willard rubs his face in his hands, mimicking a gesture Kurtz used earlier.

These doppelgänger motifs imply the father-son nature of their roles and their transubstantiation in the last scene, but the growing similarity between Willard and Kurtz had been preordained from the very beginning. Both men were defined as psychotic military officers from the outset. The politics of this characterological similarity are obvious: Willard's supplanting of Kurtz (his "termination of the colonel's command," in the film's dialogue) does not represent a change in American policy. Instead, this reenactment of the ritual death of the king-god of myth and legend only serves to show that Willard's apotheosis as supplanting redeemer makes him politically equivalent to the father figure he succeeded.[8] In the finale, Willard appears to act on Kurtz's "fatherly" advice—"Drop the Bomb. Exterminate them all."—by calling in the air strike that decimates the Cambodian compound.

Despite these hawkish examples, the film's prowar message is qualified by scenes showing the U.S. foisting its culture on Vietnam: destroying a village so that soldiers can surf, capsizing a peasant fishing boat while waterskiing, disturbing the serenity of native life with blaring radios and tapes, and fencing out the Vietnamese from the USO show. Willard's heavy drinking and breaking of the mirror may represent not only his own suicidal tendencies, but the U.S.'s self-destruction in Indochina as well. But even this view is compromised by chauvinism, because it concentrates on *America*'s suffering and self-doubt, rather than on the destruction wrought on Vietnam and its people. It is as if we were fighting and killing not the Vietnamese, but ourselves.

In many ways, *Apocalypse Now* conjoins eloquence and idiocy as the twin opposites of the Vietnam War. It suggests that the war had a certain amount of power and valor attached to it but that a bunch of "four-star clowns" were running the show. The mission may have been worthy, but the "missionaries" were too lazy, comfortable, and well protected, and they sorely lacked ruthlessness. Thus, blame is displaced from American political leaders and the citizens who voted for them onto the officers. The brass is criticized, not the policy or the populace. Nonetheless, even such a limited protest of the military establishment can have more far-reaching repercussions. A carnivalesque USO show ends in complete chaos, with no one in control. At the Du Long bridge, Willard asks who the commanding officer is and is asked in return, "Ain't you?" The absence of military leadership in these scenes may be likened by extrapolation to the absence of rational political direction in Washington. Even when an authority figure *is* in charge (for example, Kilgore or Kurtz), he is usually unbalanced and thus linked by implication to an insane national policy.

Two subtle cinematic details (both dependent on the sound track) reinforce this point. When Willard first examines Kurtz's top-secret dossier on board the river patrol boat (PBR), the lyrics of the Rolling Stones's song "Satisfaction" are heard off-screen: ". . . some useless information, supposed to drive my imagination." This use of sound-image counterpoint suggests that the military's information gathering is ineffective ("useless information") in defining Kurtz's crimes, even while it inspires Willard to admire his prey ("drive my imagination"). Later, as Willard looks at a stateside newspaper photograph of Charles Manson, acidhead Lance Johnson reads aloud, "Manson ordered the slaughter of all in the home anyway as a symbol of protest." This ironic phraseology applies just as well to Kurtz, Willard, and the top brass, all of whom murder innocents in an insane cause. By subtly linking "back-home" madness (Manson's apocalyptic rampage) with the Vietnam debacle, the film seems to undercut some of the prowar sentiment established in other scenes.

Several other incidents provide equally strong evidence of the film's anti-war stance. The very first scene, a long, static *plan séquence*, shows a primeval jungle that is eventually napalmed into extinction. By first establishing the forest as lush, peaceful, and beautiful, Coppola makes the intrusion of the helicopters and bombers even more hostile than the classical Nature versus Civilization imagery warrants. This shot dissolves to our initial view of Willard, our identification figure (and national representative), who is seen upside-down, a camera angle that implies an abnormal personality and thus an abnormal national purpose.

Willard's blatant murder of the innocent Vietnamese woman on the sampan provokes sympathy for the victim by recalling the My Lai massacre of 1968 and reverses some of the racist portrayals. The woman's death is especially heartwrenching because of the cinematic treatment. First she is wounded by machine-gun fire from the overzealous PBR crew because she made a sudden move to protect her dog. Then the guilt-ridden crew decides to rush her to a medical station. Finally Willard punctuates the sequence with a single shot from his weapon, killing the woman to avoid delaying the mission. This emotional roller-coaster ride is based on a tension-relief-despair structure that is reflected in the sound track (continuous loud machine-gun fire, the calm after the storm, then ultimate finality). Similarly, the quick cut from the noisy helicopter attack to the quiet of a peaceful village filled with schoolchildren belies the heroism of the raid, especially given that the village is destroyed so that Lance (whose real name is L. B. Johnson) can surf. Nonetheless, the "peaceful" village is later shown to be a heavily defended Vietcong stronghold, complete with antiaircraft artillery and women who conceal bombs in their hats. This fact compromises the scene's original antiwar message and partially justifies the crew's wounding of the sampan woman later in the narrative.

This battle scene features Coppola's cameo appearance as a television newsreel cameraman who, rather than record the action that is occurring, directs Willard into giving a performance: "Don't look at the camera. Just go by as if you're fighting." The director's brief walk-on is an obvious self-reflexive in-joke, but it also implies the absurd, gamelike nature of the war. This "war is swell" theme is furthered in scenes such as the sex rioting at the *Playboy*-sponsored USO show, the crew's dancing and smoking pot on the PBR, surfing at "Charlie's Point" ("Tube City," in Lance's Malibu terminology), or "made-for-TV" fighting (complete with musical accompaniment). Coppola's cinematic soldiers cling to their stateside pursuit of pleasure and entertainment amid the combat realities of a jungle war. Again, the film's irony can be understood as vacillating between a generalized antiwar/anti-American commentary and a specific critique of the military higher-ups/ordinary "grunts" ("rock'n'rollers with one foot in their graves," in Willard's voice-over description).

Apocalypse Now is filled with double binds and mixed messages in its attempt to have it both ways. One subtle scene provides evidence to support this idea: as the hatchet-lit general (his face is bisected by harsh light and heavy shadow) gives Willard his mission, he begins to pontificate about human existence: "There is a conflict in every human heart between the rational and the irrational, between good and evil, and good does not always triumph." As he says "rational," he turns his head to the dark side; when he says "irrational," his head turns toward the light. This minute gesture suggests that a tilt to the "dark side"—ruthlessness—might be the rational and efficient way to win the war. At the same time, the general's dialogue is severely critical of Kurtz's "unsound" methods precisely because they are so ruthless.

Ambivalence abounds in the opening scene as well: an image of tranquil Nature destroyed by American technology and firepower is backed by musical lyrics that state—at *exactly* the moment the bombs strike—"This is the End." So the beginning is the end, and vice versa. Maybe the point is that the Vietnam War was over before it began, but more likely this juxtaposition represents an aesthetic circularity, since the final images, the actual *end* of the film, also feature blazing napalm. The ambivalence is conveyed through images of fire and water, a motif (borrowed from the Bible, Jesse Weston's *From Ritual to Romance*, and T. S. Eliot's "The Waste Land") that wends its way throughout the film. Another subtle example of the fire–water dichotomy occurs when Kilgore is about to offer a dying Vietcong suspect a canteen of water.

Apocalypse Now *is filled with double binds and mixed messages, . . . as [when] the hatchet-lit general (his face is bisected by harsh light and heavy shadow) gives Willard his mission.*

Stooping to give the water to his enemy, Kilgore is told that Lance Johnson, the surfer, is now in his unit. Forgetting his humanitarian mission, he tosses the water onto the ground as the pleading Vietcong prisoner reaches for it. Just then, in the background of the shot, there is a huge fireball explosion. Shortly thereafter, during the surfing scene, Kilgore points out to Lance that the waves "break both ways." His precise dialogue—"[They] can break right and left simultaneously"—is illustrative of the film's (and the U.S.'s) divided political rhetoric. Whether seen in isolation or in conjunction, the motifs of fire and water become emblematic of the whole contradictory ideological project of the film.

From a political perspective, the ultimate problematic of *Apocalypse Now* was its conception. Coppola directly stated, "My very first notion . . . of the style of the film—and, of course, *style was going to be the whole movie*—I wanted it to sweep; I wanted it to have grace."[9] By subordinating content to style and foregrounding aesthetic ambiguity and richness, the director secondarized the ideological implications of a deeply political question—the Vietnam War. As such, the filmmaker's ideological message became as murky and subject to random interpretation as the cinematography and characterizations. To make a more forceful statement about the Vietnam conflict, social responsibility needed to be integrated with artistic expression. This is not to say that the film is full of empty stylistic features but rather that the multivalent formal elements of the film are deeply implicated in its social effectivity.

Coppola also said, "Truth has to do with good or evil—life and death—we see these things as opposites, but they are one."[10] This sort of sublation works fine in metaphysical speculation, but it makes for apolitical films on decidedly political subjects. It is tantamount to ethical "fence-sitting" to suggest that the political and combat realities of an illegal and imperialist war can be incorporated into a vague philosophical unity of opposites. Although the film makes several visual and aural allusions to Dante's *Inferno*—most notably in the Du Long bridge scene—Coppola, as a latter-day Dante, seems to equivocate about whom to condemn to his modern Hades.[11] The director forgot that Dante reserved a special spot in Hell for those who refused to take a stand and remained silent in times of moral crisis.[12]

The film's ahistorical tact can be exemplified by this Coppola quote: "I started moving back in time, because I wanted to imply that the issues and themes were timeless. As you went further up river, you went deeper into the origins of human nature."[13] By seeking timeless and universal truths about the Human Condition, the film elided the specificity of its historical moment. In addition, that human condition is defined by means of a false contradiction that used the Vietnamese and Cambodians to represent the primitive "origins of human nature" and the Americans to represent humankind's more "civilized" side. Historically, the National Liberation Front forces did not use aboriginal weapons such as bows and arrows or spears to achieve their independence, although they used them in the film to kill Chief. Here (and elsewhere) dramatic license in the service of universal truth exacerbates the unconscious racism of the film's figurations and its portrayal of the essential otherness of Third World peoples. (The infamous Russian roulette scene in *The Deer Hunter* is another example of a fictional conceit that had no basis in reality in the real Vietnam War.) If *Apocalypse Now* does indeed tell a universal story about the never-ending conflict between Eastern primitivism and Western civilization, then it may unconsciously be fueling American fears of a barbarism and a future war more horrific than anything known in Vietnam. Yet *Apocalypse Now* is not alone in terms of such historical errors of omission and commission. All of the Hollywood Vietnam War movies are told from an American perspective. The ambivalence in *Apocalypse Now* is a product of a conflicted and xenophobic culture, not one filmmaker's murky vision.

Nonetheless, Coppola can be faulted for his aesthetic failure to account for the ideology of form, to historicize the stylistic paradigm, so to speak. The almost constant "hatchet lighting" on all the major characters mirrors their apparent insanity and moral duality. The film's cinematic correlatives for the nation's ambivalence on the war, then, were intercut prowar and antiwar scenes, dualistic lighting, stroboscopic editing of light and dark scenes (the ritual slaughter of an ox intercut with Willard's "termination" of Kurtz), and subtle contrapuntal image-sound articulations.

That Coppola showed up at the Cannes Film Festival with two endings suggests the ambivalence of the film's overall narrative discourse. The "antiwar" ending, used in the film's initial 70 mm. release, showed Willard renouncing Kurtz's brutality and power by dropping his machete to the ground (causing the natives to do likewise) and leading Lance away from Kurtz's compound. This action is followed by a cleansing rain that symbolically puts out the fire of the opening images of napalmed Nature (another use of the fire–water motif). This version had an authentically modernist, unresolved finale in which classical denouement was elided in favor of the penultimate step of dramatic construction, falling action. In other words, the 70 mm. variant eschewed the powerful and cathartic ending of the traditional war movie in favor of a more subdued and thoughtful conclusion. The final image showed the PBR drifting away from shore, with dissolves to a mysterious blue idol superimposed—a rather serene, almost pacifistic, conclusion that showed Willard disavowing Kurtz's insane injunction to "Drop the Bomb. Exterminate them all."

The "prowar" ending conveys just the opposite effect. The conclusion that now accompanies all 35 mm. prints and videocassettes shows the PBR drifting away from Kurtz's compound, but it also has base command making radio contact with Willard ("Calling PBR Streetgang; this is Almighty"). What follows is a spectacular series of fiery explosions, apocalyptic air strikes, that seem to represent, on the diegetic level, Willard's orders to Command to "drop the bomb" and "exterminate them all." Although apparently chosen so as to provide a circular narrative structure, full-fledged emotional catharsis, and dramatic closure to the mass audience, the current ending has ideological consequences. It proves that Willard has learned Kurtz's lessons so well that he *has become him*, and allowed the colonel's last wish to be fulfilled. By providing an ending that better satisfied the genre expectations of mass audiences, Coppola acceded to classical dramatic structure but substituted the least artistic Aristotelian device—spectacle—for the full power of tragedy. In recutting the film, the filmmaker "deambiguated" its ending and provided crucial evidence to support a prowar reading.

The exploding napalm also represents a contemporary correlative for one of the film's mythic substrata, the original Apocalypse, the New Testament's Book of Revelation. There are numerous other references to the final book of the Bible in *Apocalypse Now*. For instance, the juxtaposition of the beginning and the end in the movie's first image-sound articulation recalls the "Alpha and Omega" speech of the Lord in John's final gospel. The bleeding of Willard (and the stigmatalike wounds of Colby), liturgical vocabulary ("for my sins they gave me a mission," "Operation Archangel," "Almighty"), sealed orders (like biblical scrolls), tiger, lamb, multitudes, trumpets of Kilgore's cavalry charge, temple, thunder, and representations of destruction all recall imagery from the kaleidoscopic picture-book text of John's revelations.

Coppola's penchant for allusionism ultimately contributes to a depoliticization of the Vietnam War (a process present in almost all the Hollywood Vietnam films). At one point, the camera glides over three books in Kurtz's compound: the Holy Bible, James Frazer's *The Golden Bough*, and Jesse L. Weston's *From Ritual to Romance*. This shot follows hard on Kurtz's recitation of T. S. Eliot's poem "The Hollow Men," whose epigraph is itself a quotation from *Heart of Darkness*: "Mistuh Kurtz, he dead." These references are not without ideology. Eliot was known for his conservative beliefs, while Weston and Frazer foregrounded a cyclical theory of history that has more affinity with an essentialist view of human nature than with a politically progressive one. The cultural subtext of the film's allusions precludes social transformation. The main character was even consciously conceived as a postmodernist compendium of mythic and literary allusions. According to cowriter Milius: "Willard is Adam, Faust, Dante, Aeneas, Huckleberry Finn, Jesus Christ, the Ancient Mariner, Capt. Ahab, Odysseus, and Oedipus."[14]

This complex reticulation of intertextual references makes for interesting art but ambivalent politics. By plunging us into a vertiginous vortex of mythic citations, the movie displaces interest from the specificity of the combat and political realities of the Indochina conflict onto the ambiguous "quest" of one individual, Captain Willard, and the even more ambiguous accretion of "universal" mythologemic detail. By thus subsuming the Vietnam War under an appeal to the "primitive" within us all, *Apocalypse Now* blames everyone (and hence no one) for the policy decisions that created the conflict. In addition, it suggests that the war was lost because the United States was not willing to "get primitive" enough to exercise its "will to horror" (even though six times the tonnage of bombs used in World War II were dropped on a country the size of New Mexico).

CONCLUSION

As symbolic systems, myths and legends still form the basis of more contemporary social "languages" such as Hollywood films.[15] Neither ancient myths nor modern motion pictures have force and intrinsic meaning as wholly auton-omous entities; rather, they derive and pass on their significance from binary oppositions and contradictions rooted in their cultures. Thus, language speaks, myth thinks, and signs signify within a given social matrix. But in analyzing the products of the culture industry—especially Hollywood's Viet-nam films—it is not enough to say that they "mirror" or "reflect" a bifurcated national mood, in a homological one-to-one correspondence. The concern should also be to investigate the means by which a film like *Apocalypse Now* goes beyond reflecting social realities toward creating national attitudes and political ideologies.

According to Lévi-Strauss, we live in myth and seek refuge from it in history, because history itself is a myth conceived to satisfy our need for sta-bility and order. *Apocalypse Now* and most of the other Hollywood Vietnam films participate in that coded historical mystification by conflating and sub-lating the contradictory social realities that were familiar and important to American society (for example, the war was morally wrong/the war was a noble cause; the officers failed/the foot soldiers failed). The establishment of these false antinomies allowed Americans to shift and displace their own blame as citizens and voters onto politicians and the military. And the mixed messages of the films rewrote that period's history for those who lived through it and for those who will come to know it mainly through its media representations.

All this leads to a theoretical point about the politics of film reception. Al-though much contemporary film theory valorizes the idea of the "open" text, subject to polyvalent readings and interpretations, what is really needed—at least in terms of Vietnam War movies—is a *closed* text, a film that takes an *un*ambiguous stand on the imperialist involvement and illegal conduct of the Vietnam conflict. Only three American films have taken unequivocal positions: the prowar *The Green Berets* (1968) and the antiwar *In the Year of the Pig* (1969) and *Hearts and Minds* (1974). Displacing and abstracting political real-ities onto the universal and ambiguous realm of myth (as was done in *Apocalypse Now*) rewrites history. We live in history, no matter how we write, think, theorize, or mythologize about it. The traditional role of myth has been to give a society an account of its historical past and a prescription for its future, even if those accounts are unverifiable. The nebulous fence-sitting stance of the Hollywood Vietnam War subgenre in general and of *Apocalypse Now* in partic-ular may assist the American public in "putting the war behind us," but such social amnesia does not help Americans understand the history of their Indo-china involvement or prevent future neocolonial incursions. A text without a context is a pretext, a pretext for real historical analysis and a pre-text for wars and war movies to come.

NOTES

1. Claude Lévi-Strauss, *Structural Anthropology*, trans. Claire Jacobson and Brooke Grundfest Schoepf (London: Penguin, 1972), p. 309.

2. Lévi-Strauss, *Le cru et le cruit* (Paris: Plon, 1966), p. 20 (my translation).

3. Lévi-Strauss, *L'homme nu* (Paris: Plon, 1971), p. 590 (my translation).

4. Lévi-Strauss, "On Manipulated Sociological Models," quoted in *The Structuralist Controversy: The Language of Criticism and the Sciences of Man*, ed. R. Macksey and E. Donato (Baltimore, Md.: Johns Hopkins University Press, 1970), p. 232.

5. Bronislaw Malinowski, *Myth in Primitive Psychology* (New York: W. W. Norton, 1926), p. 13.

6. Francis Ford Coppola, quoted in Robert Hatch, "*Apocalypse Now*," *The Nation*, 25 August 1979, p. 154.

7. Gregory R. Pruitt, "War Is Good" (Paper, Ithaca College, 8 May 1984).

8. This myth pattern is most exhaustively analyzed in James Frazer, *The Dying God*, vol. 4 of *The Golden Bough*, 4 vols. (New York: Macmillan, 1935).

9. Greil Marcus, "Journey Up the River: An Interview with Francis Coppola," *Rolling Stone*, 1 November 1979, p. 55.

10. Ibid.

11. The hellish *mise-en-scène* (a messenger sloshes through the boiling, reddish Phlegethon-like river to deliver Willard's mail) and dialogue ("You're in the asshole of the world, Captain") seem like intertextual correlatives from the poet's Twelfth Canto. See Dante Alighieri, "*La divina commedia*," trans. Laurence Binyon, in *The Portable Dante*, ed. Paolo Milano (New York: Viking, 1947), pp. 115–120.

12. Ibid., canto 3, pp. 14–19.

13. Marcus, "Journey," p. 56.

14. Richard Thompson, "Stoked: An Interview with John Milius," *Film Comment* 12 (July-August 1976): 15.

15. This argument is developed in detail in Frank P. Tomasulo, "Mr. Jones Goes to Washington: Myth and Religion in *Raiders of the Lost Ark*," *Quarterly Review of Film Studies* 7 (Spring 1982): 331–340.

9

The Deer Hunter:
The Superman in Vietnam

The superman character made his first appearance in Hollywood Vietnam films in Karel Reisz's *Who'll Stop the Rain?* (1978). Constructed out of a mix of sources—traditional American myth, nineteenth-century European philosophers like Nietzsche, and the literary vision of modern writers like Mailer and Hemingway—the superman was an American soldier or officer who lived beyond conventional values, projecting an aura of almost superhuman courage and power and personal invulnerability.

The creation of the superman character gave Hollywood a vivid, transcendent figure who could help blur the war's connection to specific American political choices and policies. The movie audience could view Vietnam as a horrific, agonizing war, but one fought by men whose psychic lives existed on a more murderous and grandiose plane of reality than those of ordinary men. And a war fought by supermen poses different questions than combat where ordinary grunts are the central figures. Watching a superman figure like *Apocalypse Now*'s Colonel Kurtz (Marlon Brando), with his egregious posturing, and listening to his pretentious philosophic musings about becoming "friends with moral terror" places the audience at a far remove from the historical roots of the war. The death and destruction that the war brought then becomes more a question of the corruption and brutality of the human condition or a tale of one man's assertion of will. And the political and moral questions that American intervention raised (e.g., the moral responsibility of the American public for actively supporting or passively accepting Vietnam) is obliterated in the process.

It is with Michael Cimino's working-class hero, Michael Vronsky (Robert DeNiro), in *The Deer Hunter* (1978) that the superman character begins fully to take shape. Michael is one of three Russian-American steelworkers from a Pennsylvania factory town, Clairton, who, without any hesitation, enlist to fight in Vietnam. They are part of a community that adheres to God and country as its central values, and treats the American flag and the local church as its prime icons. The trio's departure for Vietnam is celebrated at the American Legion Hall by the whole community, with only one dissenting or skeptical word voiced (a specterlike Green Beret who can only respond to their questions about Vietnam by murmuring a despairing "fuck it").

Michael, on one level, is an integral part of that steel town. He is one of the boys, with his hunting prowess, daredevil exploits behind the wheel of a Cadillac Coup de Ville, and profound link to his more easygoing, extroverted roommate, Nicky (Christopher Walken), and friends like the shy, mother-dominated Steven (John Savage). Michael wrestles, guzzles beer, jokes with his friends, and is greeted as Mike or Mikey by many of the people in the town.

However, there are aspects of his character that allow him to be turned into a symbolic figure—part of that American romantic tradition stretching back to James Fenimore Cooper: a mythic figure who carves out his identity in confrontation with nature. Like Cooper's Natty Bumppo in *The Deerslayer* and *The Last of the Mohicans*, Michael is an outsider—chaste, honorable, forbearing, revering the mountains and nature, and given to a purity of purpose embodied in his deer-hunting gospel of the one-shot kill.

. . . a mythic figure who carves out his identity in confrontation with nature.

The hunt is treated almost operatically—a sound track that alternates heav-enly sounding choirs with absolute silence, mountain mists, reflecting pools of clear water (Cooper's Lake Glimmerglass), and infinite, cloud-filled skies—Michael is seen in close-up and silhouetted in Fordian long shot, close to the horizon, silently tracking a stag. Here Michael is alone in the world, a solitary figure, separated from everything around him but the hunt. In this scene and the one where Michael tears off his clothes and makes a naked dash from Steven's wedding, the film conveys a sense of a man yearning for some-thing more than the working-class world he lives in. Michael's silence, self-control, and inarticulate, poetic desires (he reads the sky for signs) place him outside the intellectual and emotional understanding of his friends, who re-spect Michael but also see him as odd. In the wedding sequence and other scenes Michael is often an observer, seen standing in the background at a re-move from his friends, who, except for Nick, he amiably regards as "assholes."

The Deer Hunter treats Michael as both an unusual steelworker and a ro-mantic hero. Cimino's Michael is a man-warrior committed to a code built on loyalty and Hemingway's notion of grace under pressure. He is an indomita-ble, fearless figure who, when Nick and Steven become overcome with terror, is able to confront death calmly. From one angle, he can be viewed, as D. H. Lawrence said of Cooper's heroes, as "hard, isolate, and a killer."[1] The "killer" aspects of his character only emerge fully in Vietnam when Michael wills Steven, Nick, and himself to freedom out of the grasp of their NLF cap-tors and their demonic game of Russian roulette. The scene is shot in tight close-up and reaction shot—rapid and brilliantly manipulative cutting from anguished close-ups of a terrified Nick to close-ups of a defiant Michael shouting out encouragement to him, to close-ups of a malevolent, laughing Vietcong torturer back to Michael's baleful, murderous stare as he pre-emptorily slaughters their captors and frees Nick and Steven. It is also height-ened by the use of red filters and the alternation of the harsh, grating click when the gun fails to go off with earsplitting explosions when it does. Throughout the scene the audience is brought so close to the action that they can't help being affected by it. Michael's controlled, heroic act exhibits the sort of hubris—the overweening sense of national self-confidence and invul-nerability—that brought American troops to Vietnam in the first place. When the film first came out the scene elicited applause and cries from the audience about "getting the Commies." Here Michael becomes the incarnation of the superman (in this case the apotheosis of American courage and daring)—a transcendent figure who seems almost immortal. And although no nihilist—never a man who embraces the murderous for its own sake—he is still able to kill easily, without fear or constraint.

In Cooper's time, the mid-nineteenth century, the eastern frontier had long moved West and been replaced by a more complex and structured society. So for his readers, a solitary and heroic individual like Natty Bumppo could serve as a mythic and nostalgic embodiment of the values of those who lived on the border of the wilderness. For Cimino's audience, Michael's unsurpassed

5191-7581-15A   31

The "killer" aspects of his character only emerge fully in Vietnam.

bravery and loyalty turn the tortured morass of the war into a struggle between a heroic good guy, who like Bumppo embodies the virtues of a purer age, and a group of Vietcong barbarians. For one scene the audience can feel satisfied about a war that could only be perceived as a tragedy or debacle for America, and return to a simpler cinematic past. It could imagine that the Vietnam quagmire has become World War II or the frontier West, with a surrogate John Wayne coolly and inexorably machine-gunning the enemy again and garnering the audience's cheers.

Vronsky, like Stallone's cartoonish, simplistic 1980s Vietnam hero,

Rambo, is linked to Cooper's frontier hero's ability to wrest the land away from the Indians. In the Vietnam films the Vietnamese have become the Indians, and the frontiersman unreflective, working-class heroes who can survive, even triumph, in the war's moral and psychic wilderness. The working class have become the new frontierspeople—a group who can spawn pure, self-reliant, physically courageous heroes. In these films they have become the last Americans—"real Americans"—unspoiled and unselfish men who can act simply and unambiguously out of loyalty to both their country and their friends.

Richard Chase in *The American Novel and Its Tradition* sees Cooper's novels as romances—"fiction with a penchant for the marvelous, the sensational, the legendary, and in general the heightened effect."[2] The novels are permeated with personal and cultural experiences like "marriage, war against man and nature and death," which are given mythic significance "by an emotive appeal to the past, to the traditions of the culture, or to the superhuman powers of heroes."[3] With its superman hero, who is often seen silently brooding in dramatic close-up—distinguishing him from his more mortal friends—and its tendency to ritualize and heighten certain experiences—the hunt and the Russian roulette game (which, for example, has no reality except in Cimino's baroque imagination)—*The Deer Hunter* conforms in a number of ways to Chase's definition of romance.

Still, the film carries a powerful realist component. Cimino has a gift for capturing the shapelessness and incidental detail of daily experience. Much of the dialogue is colloquial—for example, the monosyllabic Axel's (Chuck Aspegren) constant use of "fucking A"—and totally in character—the steelworkers either groping for words or sounding each other out. In the extraordinarily lengthy wedding sequence, the church ceremony and rituals are treated with great care, the camera tilting and panning around the ornate, stained-glass and mosaic-filled Russian Orthodox church and intercutting the church choir singing in full voice. During the wedding party sequence the camera dollies around the participants, who include young children, stocky Slavic housewives, and grizzled older workers, and shooting from floor level evokes the joy, energy, cacophony, and brawling stupidity that characterizes the celebration. Cimino uses long takes, natural sound, a great many nonprofessional actors, and the skilled improvisation of his professional cast to give the wedding the formless texture of real life.

Cimino also animates the communal rituals of Michael and his friends by jaggedly panning around the dark, claustrophobic spaces of John's bar as they relax after work drinking, watching pro football, playing pool, and singing rock songs along with the jukebox. Except for Steven they are men without families (which is almost an imperative for a superman like Michael), and these rituals are the center of their lives. It reminds one of a less painterly, less composed, more kinetic version of the rituals and horseplay that John Ford's heroic (but mortal) cavalry men indulge in. Here, however, the rituals unfold casually, like natural extensions of their daily lives rather than Ford's vision of them as an institutional or religious sacrament.

The film also remains absolutely fixed on male bonding (as in the work of Cooper and Hemingway); the most powerful emotions and commitments are expressed in almost erotic two shots and shot–reverse-shots between Nick and Michael. His love for and loyalty to him is so absolute that Michael is willing to risk death both by entering Saigon during its final collapse and playing Nick one final, deadly game of Russian roulette. The corollary is that the women characters are in the main giggling or supportive adjuncts to the men. Even Meryl Streep's sweet, sensitive, dignified Linda—Michael and Nick's supposed romantic interest—elicits little passion from the two men. In fact, her only function is to look delicate and soulful, sometimes a little too much so for a supermarket cashier in a Pennsylvania steel town.

Despite the realistic detail that Cimino uses to construct his portrait of a working-class community, their working lives are given a sentimental gloss. The "boys" labor wearing silvered, heat-reflective work clothes—sooty, sweating medieval knights. They work with gusto and pleasure without a visible sign of exhaustion or resentment amid intense noise, welder's sparks, and blast furnace flames that vividly contrast with the murderous flames engulfing burning bodies in Vietnam. They love their seedy, industrial town, never expressing a desire to leave it. The wedding party conveys a powerful sense of communal feeling and coherence—with what seems like the whole town joining in the celebration—and the street and bar scenes evoke the feeling of men at ease in an unthreatening and warm world (though it took eight different locations to create a composite of the town, and untroubled steel towns were far from the American norm in the late 1960s). Cimino augments this sympathetic evocation with beautifully composed long shots of a silhouetted factory at dawn—a powerful monolith billowing smoke into an azure sky. Cimino does not quite turn the town into a working-class version of Andy Hardy's hometown, however; there are still solitary men drinking from bottles in doorways, and Linda's father is an angry alcoholic who abuses her.

Cimino's steel town is a world built on a sense of permanence and community where human rather than material values are preeminent. The steelworkers are satisfied working in the factory, acting out their communal rituals, and living in a traditional world untouched by dreams of mobility or an appetite for success— "the whole thing is right here."

This is clearly a romanticized version of factory town reality. In the late 1960s and early 1970s all was not serene in the factories. There were wildcat strikes in auto plants, automation replacing jobs in the steel mills, and a generalized sense of worker discontent. There was a great deal of job turnover, some young workers began to use drugs, others engaged in petty sabotage, and many began to file grievances against their employers.[4] As one auto worker said, " 'Every day I come out of there I feel ripped off. . . . They could always find somebody stupider than me to do the job.' "[5]

Cimino is not interested in providing a complex portrait of the working-class ethos, however. His workers are traditional American heroes, not men frustrated with their work and angry with their employers. The world that Cimino constructs demands celebration, not criticism nor interpretation.

Cimino never stands back and questions the adolescent nature of the male bonding or the origins of the unthinking patriotism that propels his heroes into Vietnam, or what role social class may play in the lives of the steelworkers. This almost Edenic image of Clairton and its people serves to make what follows in Vietnam even more emotionally painful and disruptive to the film's audience.

The film's second half begins with the use of a jaggedly moving handheld camera to give an agonizing emotional immediacy to Michael's perspective of the war. Through his eyes we viscerally feel the danger, terror, and uncontrolled violence and murderousness of Vietnam combat. Vietnam has no limits: everyone—civilians and soldiers, women and children—is blown up, burned alive, or shot.

Cimino's ultimate focus is not the actual fighting in Vietnam, however, but the effects of the war on Michael and his friends and their secure world. Vietnam, which is in the main framed very tightly and claustrophobically, leaves nobody unscathed: a traumatized Nicky drug-addicted and so psychologically destroyed that he becomes a star on Saigon's Russian roulette circuit; Steven a despondent paraplegic who hides away in a veteran's hospital; and Michael, who remains physically whole but returns home disoriented and ill at ease with his friends. Even Michael's code begins to unravel. The hunting has gone sour, and this time around in the mountains, catching a deer within his gun sight, he shoots harmlessly into the air. He even reluctantly gives up his chastity for Linda, for whom it's clear he has always had an unexpressed passion.

Michael may radically alter his code, but he has enough of the romantic hero—loyalty and grace under pressure—left in him to return to face the dangers of a collapsing Saigon and attempt to bring Nick home. Though Nick kills himself, Michael does first break through Nick's disassociated silence by invoking memories of the one-shot kill—the rituals of the hunt and home still sufficiently powerful to provide a tearful catharsis despite all the horror he has endured.

The Deer Hunter's emphasis on Michael's will, heroism, and Bumppo-like purity has the effect of making the Americans innocent and guiltless victims and the Vietnamese the brutal aggressors in the war. It's this ethnocentric identification with the mythic Michael and his world that makes *The Deer Hunter*'s vision of the Vietnamese both invidious and politically dangerous. In close-up the camera makes us see them as "the other"—demonic or decadent variations of "the yellow peril." The grinning and guttural-sounding Vietcong viciously coerce Michael and his friends to play Russian roulette for no other purpose than their sadistic pleasure, and pen them like animals in bamboo cages under water with rats or behind barbed wire while waiting for "the game" to begin. In turn, the Saigon roulette game is run by corrupt, heartless South Vietnamese businessmen, who eat voraciously while they gamble vast sums on Nick and other star-victims of "the game." The South Vietnamese are seen as gross, materialistic, urban capitalists—the antithesis of the severity and rectitude of the American romantic hero.

The city of Saigon itself is depicted as a squalid, ominous, teeming inferno either shot through red filters or saturated in blue-black *film noir*-style darkness. The noise, filth, and decay (a prostitute beckoning to Nick while her child cries in the next bed) contrasts sharply and invidiously with the worn, humane streets of the Pennsylvania steel town. The Saigon images tend to a self-conscious expressionism: a trip with a decadent, cynical Frenchman in a small boat over a river with fires ablaze—one more metaphor of Vietnam as purgatory. And though the Saigon bars contain go-go dancers, wagon wheels, and American names, which should suggest some American responsibility for this urban hell, the thrust of the film turns the insidious Vietnamese into the destroyers of pure American souls and lives.

There are brief, sympathetic images of the Vietnamese—dazed refugees streaming along the road with what's left of their possessions—survivors of a conflict that has plunged their lives into total chaos. However, they are usually seen in long shot, anonymous victims in a film that has no interest in their anguish. And in almost every instance that the camera gets sufficiently close to personalize the Vietnamese, they are savagely caricatured—a war whose murderousness they deserve and seemingly have brought upon themselves.

The Deer Hunter's implicitly racist vision of white Russian-Americans as men of integrity and courage (few black soldiers appear in the film) and the Vietnamese as chillingly malevolent figures has the effect of totally distorting the historical and moral reality of the war. The fact that they are Russian-American both frees them from the ethnic stereotypes and audience expectations other ethnic groups carry in Hollywood films and gives the war an even more racial cast. For now the Cold War aspects of Vietnam get lost, Russians being the good guys here fighting as Americans against the barbarism of the alien, yellow-skinned Vietnamese.

Cimino's depiction of Vietnam is a politically indifferent one, transforming it into a war, where, on one level, three decent, apolitical steelworkers play out existential dramas of courage, fear, and breakdown. On another level, an American archetypal hero—the superman—quietly, bravely, and murderously attempts to keep his friends and world together. Cimino never asks why we were in Vietnam or touches on the fact that the three steelworkers—however personally virtuous—serve in the army of a country who was the aggressor in what was basically a civil and colonial war.

Although it's doubtful that Cimino made the film to affirm American policy in Vietnam, its total identification with Michael and his friends' point of view on the war denies the audience any sort of critical take on Vietnam. Like most Hollywood films, *The Deer Hunter* personalizes history, constructing a Vietnam that is a charnal house where good guys struggle with bad ones to survive, rather than a war determined by social ideology, Cold War politics, and nationalism.[6] There is no hint here that there is anything more to Vietnam than the subjective experience of men like Michael Vronsky or Nick. And the central metaphor of the film, Russian roulette, moves it into still another direction, turning the war into a self-destructive game of chance—probably true for surviving day-to-day combat, but not much of an explanation of the causes of the war.

This American desire to see political conflict in personal and moralistic terms rather than in historical and ideological ones is in line with the American romantic tradition, which defines the world in all-or-nothing terms. In that tradition the ambiguities of human experience, be it a war or the settlement of the frontier, are turned into an abstract moral struggle without much political or psychological shading. Cimino's evocation of a Manichean Vietnam in *The Deer Hunter* fits perfectly into that tradition.

Of course, the power of *The Deer Hunter* does not rest with Cimino's capacity for illuminating the war's political and social context. His strength is his ability to convey, by utilizing a striking variety of images, camera angles, and dazzling camera movements, how the war affected the psyches and lives of American G.I.'s. It achieves this with much more stylistic originality and emotional power than a more liberal, politically sophisticated Vietnam film like *Coming Home* (1978) does. For example, in a searing close up of a mute, anguished Nick confronted by the inane, irrelevant questions of a doctor in an army hospital, surrounded by the mutilated and the dying, coffins and body bags, Cimino incisively evokes the trauma of the war for American soldiers.

The final scene is a perfect illustration of the film's emotional impact, and Cimino's skill for moving us in a scene whose perspective I find politically disturbing. After Nick's funeral, Michael and his friends gather for breakfast and sit in pained silence. Suddenly, John collapses into tears and begins to sing "God Bless America," and then the rest join in tremulous, muted voices. Cimino cuts from one to another of the characters, as they uneasily affirm their belief in America and their desire to reconstruct their own fragmented community. There are, however, no illusions inherent here that they can magically heal the agony and loss that the war has brought.

There is also no sign of directorial irony in the sequence. Cimino never questions or treats satirically the values and rituals of the steelworkers. And Cinemo's *mise-en-scène* and camera setups move us toward total empathy with their feelings. As a result, *The Deer Hunter* leaves us with the indelible image of Vietnam as an abbatoir but then implicitly absolves the U.S. of the responsibility for helping bring it about by creating a working class who are viewed as both the war's heroes and its victims. The portrait is so sympathetic that it allows the late 1970s audience to feel somewhat relieved of its uneasiness and distress about America's role in Vietnam, and with even some hope that the American Dream can be renewed by men like Michael Vronsky.

Cimino's heroic superman is one in a long tradition of literary and cinematic heroes—from Bumppo to Dirty Harry—who live according to an individualist code that has its roots in a mythicized past. The horror of Vietnam was not an analogous experience to Dirty Harry's San Francisco besieged by the psychopathic killer of a genre film. Vietnam was a terrifyingly real war that was too complex and left too much anguish in its wake to be conceived in a historical and social vacuum. And *The Deer Hunter*, despite its formal and emotional power, lacked just that historical and social imagination that would have allowed it to go beyond the superman conceit and evoke the political heart of Vietnam.

NOTES

A different, shorter version of this essay appeared in *How the War Was Remembered: Hollywood and Vietnam*, by Albert Auster and Leonard Quart (New York: Praeger, 1988).

1. D. H. Lawrence, *Studies in Classic American Literature* (Garden City, N.Y.: Doubleday, 1951), p. 73.

2. Richard Chase, *The American Novel and its Tradition* (Garden City, N.Y.: Doubleday, 1957), p. 21.

3. *Ibid.*, p. 53.

4. Andrew Levison, *The Working Class Majority* (New York: Coward, McCann and Geoghegan, 1974), p. 215.

5. Stanley Aronowitz, *False Promises: The Shaping of American Working Class Consciousness* (New York: McGraw Hill, 1974), p. 21.

6. Albert Auster and Leonard Quart, "Hollywood and Vietnam: The Triumph of the Will," *Cineaste* 9, no. 3 (1979):4–9.

PART THREE

OTHER FRAMES
Subtext and Difference

10

The Colonialist Subtext
in *Platoon*

Platoon manages a few significant ruptures with Hollywood's past portrayal of the Vietnam War, fewer yet with its classical hold on American myth and storytelling practices. It bows, however, to familiar limits of discourse in its deployment of black troops.

True to the revisionary trend in black imagery, the blacks in *Platoon* are shifted from the token status of *Apocalypse Now*, from the background where the Vietnamese are either victims of atrocities or vigorously fight back, but short of the foreground, rather under it, off its center. They occupy a second tier, where they are deployed as shadows deepening the moral conflict between Elias and Barnes for Chris Taylor's soul, an archetypal Western male narrative discourse that reverberates *The Man Who Shot Liberty Valance*, *Billy Budd*, and, most classically, *Paradise Lost*. The precepts of Elias and Barnes are echoed on this lower frequency by the examples of two black foot soldiers, King and Junior.

King eases Chris into the tent of the smoke-heads, Elias's perch, where the values of communal, antipatriarchal sharing are celebrated, where head-tightened men dance together to "The Tracks of My Tears." Junior lies miserably in the tent of the whiskey-heads where Barnes hangs out, sour with sadistic, macho male self-testing and Junior's jingoistic rants against whites. Like Elias and Barnes, their names signify: "King" matched with nobility (savage?) and generosity, qualities he shares with his namesake, America's most charismatic moral figure of those times; "Junior" signifies a stage of moral minority and immaturity. It also signifies his derivativeness.

These black shadows register with a difference that relates to their unoriginality and dependence, the reduction of their being to appendages of the moral principals. In Lawrence Kohlberg's five-stage schema of moral development, King and Junior rest at stages stepped down from those of Elias and Barnes. King is actually more of a father figure to Chris than Elias is; but deprived of the moral authority that neither the film nor its primary audience will grant him, his characterization tips toward the familiar role of black male mammy to innocent white youth. A Nigger Jim who protectingly advises, 'Come back to the foxhole, Chuck, Honey.' Where Barnes's negativity is an abstract, militaristic dehumanization, Junior's is a reversion to childhood and primitivism. Where Elias's affirmation is an activist, apocalyptic salvationism, King's is a brotherly accommodationism.

These shadow qualities don't come out of nowhere. King is a convention, a soulful, down-home, church-mothered brother. But the genealogy of Junior's persona, once decoded, is even more classical. He is, on top, the black

King is actually more of a father figure to Chris than Elias is; but deprived of moral author-ity, . . . his characterization tips toward the familiar role of black male mammy to innocent white youth.

nationalist of Hollywood fabrication, most visible in black exploitation mov-ies, negative, petty, whining, unfair, and dramatically ineffectual. The nega-tive stereotyping in *Platoon* that angers black vets is mostly located in Junior. He sleeps on guard, causing casualties, and blaming Chris. Though he shadows Barnes in negativity, the two are not allies, as shown in the battle scene where he malingers until Barnes shouts, "Get up, Nigger, or I'll shoot you!" Minutes later he wheels in fearful flight, smack into a tree, knocking himself out.

These are throwback bits from the Golden Age of Hollywood, the 'humor-ous' reflex actions of grotesques like Stepin Fetchit and Willie Best. The ori-gin in old-time coon stereotypes is masked here (nobody laughed in two audiences) by the violent terror of the battle scenes. Their lineage traverses Hollywood Sambo figures to classical Western portraits of the African as oth-erness, a negation, idolatrous and superstitious in relation to 'real knowl-edge,' which grants whites and their perceptions priority.

Under his contemporary trappings, Junior is an infidel from the evergreen colonialist scenario, literally, lacking faith, outside the faith, displaying in-fidelity or disloyalty to the accepted knowledge and creed that both Barnes and Elias share. His tree-collision is another of those instances in Western cin-ema where the character-destiny of the infidel, his just reward, is death or de-feat by his own self-destructive action, thereby confirming the power and infallibility of the true faith more convincingly than punishment at the hands of the faithful.

A dilemma weakly faced by Stone in dealing with the war's color politics is that actually many more black troops than whites felt they had little real stake in the war, as I discovered while researching *Vietnam and Black America*.[1] They therefore had more complex reasons for taking on less moral responsibility for its conduct than indicated in the portrayals of King and Junior. The film's reference for this complex, anticolonialist rage and anguish, expressed in a black pride movement, symbols of racial identity, Black Panther units, mutinies, officer-fragging and shoot-outs with white units, is the parodistic mask of Junior's antics.

Viewed from the vantage point of this underground black subtext, *Platoon* cannot escape the paradigm of the colonialist warrior narrative. This myth patiently awaits any competitive male drama peopled interracially—cops in the ghetto, basketball—but particularly those texts where white men fight nonwhites with faithful and unfaithful nonwhite helpers. *Platoon*'s unsuccessful confrontations with the limits of this discourse loses ground at two heavily defended positions of its paradigm, the center-focusing of the white hero and the question of political violence.

What kind of rupture would have been made if Chris had been cast as black, subject to the doubts and questions troubling many black troops? We should recall here than even Chris has his black alterego. But instead of occupying the foreground this new recruit cowers behind him until emboldened by Chris's courageous actions. While Chris is medi-vacuated with honorably earned wounds, his black shadow stabs himself in the leg to get off the front line.

But if Chris were black, his blowing away of Barnes would burst the repressive limits of colonialist myth-making, would have challenged the nervousness in American movie culture about black political violence, would have released the unspeakable text of anticolonialist violence. A revealing double standard in this colonialist discourse is made clear by noting what is allowable in *Platoon* compared to *A Soldier's Story* (1984), where all the principals are black. When Chris survives his killing of Barnes both physically and psychologically—Billy Budd killing Claggart—an intriguing break is made with order-must-be-preserved traditions. But when a black infantryman in *A Soldier's Story* kills a black sergeant as fascist as Barnes, the film's text condemns him—another black militant made an example of. The black lieutenant pronounces the approved moral judgment: Who gave you the right to decide who could be black? When the real question, unless black is other than human, might be whether Sarge and his lethal self-hate had a right to survive.

The simplest key to the depiction of blacks in *Platoon*, as in the tradition, is that they are made attractive or repulsive on the strength of their acceptance of Western preeminence and values: the good nigger/bad nigger schema of characterization. As Ngugi points out for colonialist literature, "The reader's sympathies are guided in such a way as to make him identify with Africans collaborating with colonialism and to make him distance himself from those offering political and military resistance to colonialism."[2] Significantly, King and Junior never confront each other, as these types often do in colonialist movies. If they had, what could they fight about except whether to risk their lives for white interests?

The simplest key to the depiction of blacks in Platoon . . . *is that they are made attractive or repulsive on the strength of their acceptance of Western preeminence and values.*

Because it must deal with the colonial complex and its bottom line take on race and power, *Platoon* puts into perspective the current revision of black imagery in American films, reminiscent of the 'Negro interest' phenomenon of 1949–1950. Like most of these revisionist portrayals, it elevates the sympathy and humanity of blacks to a semicolonial limbo, not so far as to break the limits of dependency, but far enough to separate them from Third World people gaining visibility as terrorist baddies. To make this last point, *Platoon* pictures Mannings, a black soldier, mutilated by the Vietnamese.

As an ultimate illumination, "We were at war with ourselves" is an easy, consumable, almost obligatory thematic sentiment to sound on Vietnam, no different from a dozen other Hollywood films or network soliloquies. It sounds an echo as hollow as the suspect moral pronouncement of *A Soldier's Story*. How can Americans find resolution to their war with themselves so long as they continue to repress, through myth, ideological masks, and atavistic stereotypes, their much more violent war upon others that is its projection?

NOTES

1. (Garden City, N.Y.: Doubleday/Anchor, 1973).
2. Ngugi wa Thiongo, *Decolonizing the Mind* (Portsmouth, N.H.: Heinemann, 1986), p. 92.

Night of the Living Dead:
A Horror Film about the
Horrors of the Vietnam Era

> . . . Repression has indeed been the fundamental link between power,
> knowledge, and sexuality.
>
> *Michel Foucault,* The History of Sexuality, *vol. 1*

FILM CRITICISM: TEXT VERSUS CONTEXT

In the 1960s, George A. Romero and Pittsburgh friends, bored with making
commercials and industrial films, formed Image Ten to produce a horror
movie on the assumption that an investment capitalizing on the film industry's
"thirst for the bizarre would be relatively safe." John Russo and Romero
wrote a script based on Richard Matheson's "I Am a Legend," an allegory
about the mass return of dead creatures who feasted on the flesh and blood of
the living. All the filmmakers became involved in the production process and
"took turns loading magazines, gaffing, gathering and making props, shooting, recording [and] editing." Seed cash amounting to $60,000 was raised.
Payment of the balance of the film's cost, which totaled $114,000, was de-
ferred until distribution. Although the filmmakers initially had problems finding a distributor, the Walter Reade Organization released the film as *Night of
the Living Dead* in 1968.[1] At the time, the film was little noticed except to
provoke argument about censoring its grisly scenes. But the *Film Daily*
reviewer commented, "This is a pearl of a horror picture which exhibits all the
earmarks of a sleeper. Accorded the right exploitation, it could make a whale
of a box office showing."[2] Five years later, *Night of the Living Dead* had become the "most profitable horror film ever to be produced outside the walls of
a major studio."[3] A decade after its release, it had grossed more than
$15,000,000 and had been exhibited internationally after being translated into
more than twenty-five foreign languages.[4]

Night of the Living Dead was released in 1968, a year of tumultuous events
such as the Tet offensive, the assassinations of Martin Luther King, Jr., and
Robert Kennedy, and the Chicago police riot that spilled onto the floor of the
Democratic convention. What does a low-budget release that became a classic
in the horror film genre reveal about the era of civil rights and the Vietnam
War? Such a question raises issues about the ways in which film critics analyze the relationship between text and context, if indeed they contextualize
their readings at all. For the most part, poststructuralist critics engage in for-
malist or textual analyses of film to the exclusion of empirical data about production, distribution, and audience reception, and especially about the larger

sociohistoric context. Granted, the contextualization of readings requires an interdisciplinary approach to the study of film, especially a knowledge of history. But since poststructuralists are entrapped in what Fredric Jameson calls the "windless closure of the formalisms,"[5] interdisciplinary study has distinct advantages, as this reading of a well-known horror film will demonstrate.

Since the horror film provides a rich source for readings based on psychoanalytic and semiotic models used by poststructuralists, first let us consider the limitations of the way in which these critics theorize about the spectator. Poststructuralists use the Lacanian psychoanalytic model of the formation of the human subject and Althusserian notions about ideology to explain film reception in terms of spectator positioning, that is, the way cinema and its apparatus position the subject as spectator to receive the dominant ideology. For instance, Laura Mulvey's seminal essay was an analysis of feature film as spectacle constructed for male spectatorship, specifically in relation to the female body as fetishized or devalued on screen. Subsequently, feminist critics raised the issue of gender in delineating the spectator in readings against the grain, especially in response to a dominant cinema constructed for the male gaze. But the female spectator has remained a textual effect or construct and is thus an ahistorical abstraction. Put another way, feminist critics have ignored the social as opposed to the textual construction of gender so that class and ethnic distinctions, for example, are seldom considered. As British cultural critics have pointed out, the interaction of text and subject in the poststructuralist model becomes one in which the text is understood as reproducing the subject isolated from social and historical structures. Consequently, a textual determinism has displaced a sociological one.[6]

Alert to the politically conservative implications of such a model, characterized as "driving its students into monastic cells rather than the streets," Robin Wood declines to use the Lacanian version of psychoanalysis in his well-known study of the horror film. As an alternative, he proposes a model that differentiates between basic repression, which is universal, and surplus repression, which is specific to capitalistic culture. Further, he sees a continuity between *re*pression and *op*pression in that he defines *re*pression of desires not accessible to the conscious mind as "fully internalized oppression" by something "out there." "What escapes *re*pression has to be dealt with by *op*pression." Closely related to this concept of repression and essential for understanding ideological issues is the concept of "the Other": that which the bourgeois mentality cannot recognize or accept but must deal with by annihilating, rejecting, or assimilating. Psychoanalytically, the Other functions "as something external to the culture or to the self, but also as what is repressed (but never destroyed) in the self and projected outwards in order to be hated and disowned." As a result, the Other includes women, children and youth, gays, ethnic groups, the working class, rival political systems and ideologies, and, in horror movies, the monster. Wood concludes that the horror film is a collective nightmare masking repressed desires that are a threat to the existing social order. By employing a non-Lacanian interpretation of Freud, he posits a relationship between the unconscious and societal forms of oppression.[7] As a film critic, however, he focuses on horror films as texts and refers to capitalism as an abstraction rather than relating changes in the genre to specific political and economic developments in the postindustrial society of the 1960s and '70s.

Dominick LaCapra, a historian interested in the uses of literary criticism, has examined the relation between psyche and society from a reverse perspective by raising "the question of the extent to which what is repressed or suppressed historically and socioculturally tends to return as the repressed in psychology." Citing Foucault's *Discipline and Punish*, La Capra points out that "Freud's all-seeing superego is the internalized counterpart of techniques of surveillance and control that were being disseminated in public life. The very opposition between public and private opened the public sphere to regulatory agencies while the private sphere was to be kept inviolate from 'external' control only to be subjected to extremely demanding 'internal' strictures. Civil rights and freedom of speech in public life were thus offset by internal norms and mechanisms which set up 'private' parameters to freedom of 'inner' life and thought." La Capra concludes that Foucault's critique of the "repressive hypothesis" did not go far enough because it only intimates that "a crucial problem in the modern period . . . is the conjunction of extremely 'civilized' if not 'repressive' control and at times 'neobarbaric' excess"[8]—a contrast certainly evidenced by events of the Vietnam era. La Capra's argument enables us to understand the contradictions of the 1960s and '70s as decades during which dissent, though vocal, ultimately gave way to Reaganism,

"A crucial problem . . . is the conjunction of extremely 'civilized' if not 'repressive' control and at times 'neobarbaric' excess."

and revolution in Vietnam, though ending Western imperialism, meant Vietnamese repression of neighboring Cambodia.[9] As a prerequisite for understanding these developments in relation to *Night of the Living Dead*, we need to investigate further the historical context of the film.

RECENT AMERICAN HISTORY: THE SIXTIES AND SEVENTIES

So that readers of this essay may have at least minimal access to relevant historical data, the following is a much abbreviated summary of significant developments concerning the status of blacks and the progress of the war in Vietnam during the 1960s and '70s. Readers are urged to study the timeline (1954–1980s) in the appendix to this anthology.[10]

Despite the landmark Supreme Court decision on school desegregation and the Montgomery, Alabama, bus boycott led by Martin Luther King, the civil rights movement languished until students galvanized resistance by staging the first sit-in in Greensboro, North Carolina, in 1960. During the ensuing decade the American public became familiar with news reports of such passive disobedience tactics as freedom rides, marches, and voter registration drives—civil rights actions that provoked extreme retaliation and violence. The hard-won legislative victories of the 1960s included the Civil Rights Act of 1964, the Voting Rights Bill of 1965, and the Civil Rights Act of 1968.[11]

During the mid 1960s when black protest crossed the Mason-Dixon line, some factions began to espouse militant action as the issue became less one of civil rights and more a question of reallocating economic resources. Also committed to effecting structural change in America was yet another protest movement in which youth were active, the New Left, specifically the Students for a Democratic Society. As the Vietnam War escalated, black activists and student radicals had no choice but to focus on the conflict. Aside from the crucial economic issue of guns versus butter, the question of military service in Vietnam was troubling: more blacks than whites were being drafted, and blacks comprised a greater percentage of combat troops.

Contrary to myth, American involvement in Vietnam was a direct consequence of Cold War politics and a policy of containment. The U.S. had not only financed the French military effort to reestablish colonialism in Indochina but had stepped into the vacuum after the French suffered a spectacular defeat at Dienbienphu in 1954. Contravening the Geneva Accords, the United States opposed national elections that would have meant the reunification of Vietnam under the Marxist-Leninist faction that had overthrown French rule and supported instead successive puppet governments in South Vietnam. Despite massive American aid, South Vietnamese leaders were unable to effect economic reforms to win the support of the peasants. After the Tet offensive in 1968, American opposition to the war escalated so that President Richard Nixon finally negotiated a withdrawal in 1973. President Nguyen Van Thieu remained in control of South Vietnam, but the North Vietnamese and the remnants of the National Liberation Front marched victorious into Saigon in 1975.

Because the Vietnam War was such a painful experience for Americans, it has already generated myths. First, there is the myth that our involvement in the war was a mistake. In fact, American action in Vietnam was the result of deliberate and intentional foreign policy decisions based on our opposition to global communism. From Truman to Nixon, successive postwar administrations adhered to a containment policy. Second, there is the myth that Americans fought the war with one hand tied behind their backs, or that politicians constrained military action. In fact, American forces in Vietnam enjoyed the advantage of the most sophisticated technology ever used in modern warfare. At Khe Sanh, for instance, General William Westmoreland installed an electronic laboratory that transmitted data from seismic sensors to computers in Thailand. During that siege, the American military employed B-52 bombers, an airborne control plane, C-47 transports, rocket-armed helicopter gunships, starlight scopes enabling night vision, people sniffers detecting troop movements, gravel mines, fragmentation shells containing steel darts, napalm, white phosphorus, chemical defoliants and solvents, and marine artillery. Short of using nuclear weapons, a tactic that had in fact been debated, U.S. troops in Vietnam were hardly deprived of firepower.[12]

American defeat in Vietnam, both military and moral, has become so intolerable that it has been repressed in our political unconscious, to use Jameson's phrase. Since the visual media first assumed a pivotal role in the representation and thus the outcome of historical events during the 1960s, film and television have fittingly been instrumental in rewriting the struggle in Vietnam to render it more acceptable to the public. But less obvious forms of repression, if not revisionism, were evident during the height of the war before defeat occurred, as revealed in *Night of the Living Dead*. Although it was the product of an independent, low-budget effort in Pittsburgh, this horror film became a classic that can be viewed as part of the process of cultural production registering both repression and resistance during the sixties.

NIGHT OF THE LIVING DEAD

According to Wood, *Night of the Living Dead* is an apocalyptic example of the evolution of the horror film since 1960 in that sexuality has become "totally perverted from its functions, into sadism, violence, and cannibalism." For Wood, this grotesque development is logical, since "cannibalism represents the ultimate in possessiveness, hence the logical end of human relations under capitalism."[13] (A Leninist corollary would extend this metaphor to include Western consumption and imperialist exploitation of Third World peoples.) *Night of the Living Dead* is indeed a nightmare in which human and nonhuman relations have become indistinguishable, primordial, red in tooth and claw. Cannibalism has become especially horrific because it occurs within what Christopher Lasch has regressively labeled *Haven in a Heartless World*, that is, the patriarchal institution par excellence, the family. A child resurrected as one of the living dead devours her father and brutally kills her mother with a trowel. A brother, also returned from the dead, attacks his blond sister, an assault foreshadowed by his sadistic behavior when he was still alive. A married couple bickers while an unmarried one is devoured by monsters because the woman endangers both herself and her lover.

Alone without familial or emotional ties to the other characters, a black man named Ben, whose relationship to the blond sister has repressed overtones, is desexualized as a technician who invents tactics to resist a siege. Interestingly, his brothers would include Barney in *Mission Impossible*, Mr. T. in *The A-Team*, and T.C. in *Magnum, P.I.*, as well as the computer whiz in *Die Hard*. As Eldridge Cleaver asserts, the black man as "Supermasculine Menial" has been denied a brain but represents a powerful sexual threat. Recent characterizations of black men as technicians illustrate an adroit reversal of this paradigm in that blacks are still in subordinate positions but less disturbingly sensual in being identified with machinery, gadgets, and hardware. Despite this reformulation, blacks still have little space within which to maneuver. In *Night of the Living Dead*, Ben displays ingenuity and leadership, but his destruction should come as no surprise, for assuming the prerogatives of the white "Omnipotent Administrator" (who has access to the "Ultrafeminine" white woman) or possessing the sexual virility of the "Supermasculine Menial" are both offences punishable by death.[14]

What are we to make of this paranoiac scenario within the context of the turbulent 1960s and '70s? According to Wood's interpretation, the living dead who prey upon the living in the film represent the Other in contemporary bourgeois society. Specifically, what threats to the social order are being repressed

Ben displays ingenuity and leadership, but his destruction should come as no surprise.

in *Night of the Living Dead* as the mechanism of surplus repression essential to capitalism momentarily breaks down? Certainly, revolutionary sentiment was being expressed at the time by blacks, whose demands ranged from civil rights and integration to black power and separatism. Further, the upheaval of the 1960s and '70s was fueled by women who challenged the patriarchal structure of the family, by gays who came out of the closet to proclaim their sexual preference, and by counterculturalists who dropped out of mainstream society. Contrary to orthodox Marxism, the working class in postindustrial America had become invested in the status quo and moved right of center, a situation exploited in the blue-collar sitcom *All in the Family*.

From Wood's perspective, events of the 1960s and '70s could be interpreted as a breakdown of surplus repression that ultimately resulted in oppression. As astute commentators pointed out at the time, dissent did not necessarily bring about change but functioned instead to perpetuate the status quo. Protest legitimated essential ideological beliefs such as freedom of speech and enabled dissidents to blow off steam while political, economic, and social structures remained intact.[15] Further, as La Capra suggests, demonstrations in the public sphere were more than offset by internalization of repressive strictures in the private sphere. Put another way, political movements intent on effecting institutional change were thwarted because individuals who had internalized dominant cultural norms were engaged in self-repression.

Although blacks, women, gays, and counterculturalists emerged as a brief threat to white male dominance during the 1960s and '70s, yet another group, the Vietnamese, functioned as the Other. Significantly, Americans came to know these aliens through images telecast during the evening news. Whether American-backed South Vietnamese, the National Liberation Front or the Vietcong (who in fact were South Vietnamese), or North Vietnamese, these distinctions collapsed as there arose images of the yellow peril dating back to treatment historically accorded Chinese and Japanese. Vietnamese were "gooks" or "slopes." As Philip Slater has pointed out, "We attacked North Vietnam in part because we were unwilling to admit we were fighting the people of South Vietnam."[16] Whatever Americans called them, the Vietnamese in their dogged and inspired resistance to France and subsequently to the United States became part of a moral debate about our policies both at home and abroad.

Granted, there are no Vietnamese in *Night of the Living Dead*, but in effect they constitute an absent presence whose significance can be understood if narrative is construed, as Jameson asserts, "as the specific mechanism through which the collective consciousness represses historical contradictions."[17] What is collectively repressed or intolerable is the nightmare of class exploitation as experienced by the oppressed as well as the threat of proletarian revolution for the bourgeoisie, a revolution that fails to occur. Consequently, for Jameson, history is an absent cause in that political upheaval has not taken place, but "what is visible, there for interpretation, is the way the ideological structure registers the strain of having kept it repressed."[18] Specifically, then, with respect to *Night of the Living Dead*, what contradiction is being repressed in the text as the political unconscious? Such a question leads to a consideration of the film as collective discourse: its subtext about class and ethnic conflict can be decoded through an analysis of significant details beginning with the credits.

Night of the Living Dead begins with a bleak credit sequence in which a brother and sister are driving to a cemetery to place a bouquet of flowers on their father's grave. Signifying the nature of events that await them, the music on the sound track is eerie and disturbing. At the end of the credits, Romero's name is superimposed over the American flag waving symbolically in the foreground as the couple finally arrive at the cemetery. Although much of the surrounding landscape appears stark and defoliated, we learn, ironically, that it is Sunday, the first day of Daylight Saving Time. ("April is the cruelest month . . .") Johnny, the brother, is irritable about the long drive necessary to perform an annual ritual that has become meaningless, and he admonishes his sister, Barbra, that "Praying's for church." In contrast, Barbra is a dutiful daughter, frightened by Johnny's sadistic behavior as a bogeyman. Once Johnny has been felled by a ghoul and Barbra takes refuge in a farmhouse with Ben, who arrives moments after her frantic entrance, strangers hidden in the basement reveal themselves; the only connection these characters have with the outside world is through a radio and television set.

According to the media, a sudden state of emergency exists as a result of horrifying events. A television newscaster reports a "wave of murder" and "creatures who feast upon the flesh." The presidential cabinet, the FBI, the joint chiefs of staff, and the CIA have been in conference but have not divulged any information to the public. (Interestingly, the term "credibility gap" was coined with respect to government disclosures about significant events of the 1960s and '70s.) News reporters who manage to interview the so-called experts receive contradictory views as to whether radiation caused by a satellite explosion, a NASA project, has resulted in a deadly mutation of the dead, a plot development recalling 1950s science-fiction horror. Vivian Sobchack has pointed out that the television newscasts are photographed in frontal and symmetrical shots that contrast with the distorted angles of the film; she claims that this formal device stresses the irrelevance of the media to the plight of the besieged.[19] Actually, there is a hand-held interview of Washington officials against the Capitol dome on television that mirrors some of the unstable framing in the film. But Sobchack's emphasis on visual style ignores the audio component of both radio and television as media and thus an important clue about the film's meaning as revealed by the newscaster.

This television newsman, a local broadcaster who wrote his own copy, refers to a "search and destroy operation" against the ghouls to be carried out according to Pentagon instructions, an unmistakable reference to search and destroy missions in Vietnam.[20] An unconscionable aspect of these maneuvers was their deterioration into a My Lai massacre, an incident that occurred in 1968 but was undisclosed for a year or so. Reminiscent of the body counts related by news anchors each night during the reporting of the war, an official interviewed on television says about the ghouls, "We killed nineteen of them in this area." As Frances FitzGerald explains in her prize-winning and controversial work, *Fire in the Lake*, the obsessive body counts reported during the Vietnam conflict, an unprecedented aspect of coverage about a war, had racist overtones, as did our saturation bombing policy that led to tonnage three and a half times that dropped during all of World War II, or the reference of American military men to NLF or Vietcong territory as Indian country.[21] Interestingly, General Custer's massacre of Indians in *Little Big Man*, released a year after the disclosure of the My Lai incident in 1969, has unmistakable search and destroy overtones.

Lastly, the final sequence of the film, whose grainy black-and-white photography aptly recalls newsreels, begins with a shot of a helicopter, that quintessential symbol of the Vietnam War, as it descends from the sky during the concluding search and destroy mission against the ghouls.[22] By this time the lone survivor in the farmhouse is Ben, the black man, who has taken refuge in the cellar, contrary to his initial strategy. Fittingly, law enforcement authorities are shown with attack dogs such as those used during search and destroy missions in Vietnam and seen in nationally televised footage of civil rights events, such as the protest led by Martin Luther King in Birmingham, Alabama, in 1963. In fact, there is a cut from the police dogs to a medium close-up of Ben, hiding in the cellar and alerted by the barking of the animals

Law enforcement authorities are shown with attack dogs such as those used during search and destroy missions in Vietnam and seen in nationally televised footage of civil rights events. [Night of the Living Dead]

that rescue may be at hand. From Ben, there is a cut back to barking attack dogs straining at the leash. Symbolically, when Ben goes upstairs to peer through the window, he is shot between the eyes. During the final moments of the film, now in grainy still shots, his body is dragged with meat hooks to a burning pyre as the chopper is heard on the soundtrack. We need hardly be reminded that black men were lynched and burned in our recent past. Nor need we be reminded that the burning bodies of Buddhist monks and nuns were part of the sensational and horrifying aspect of news coverage of the protest of South Vietnamese against the American-backed Catholic Diem regime during the Kennedy years. Diem's arrogant sister-in-law, Madame Nhu, whom the press stereotypically labeled the Dragon Lady, dismissed these acts of self-immolation as barbecues. Americans, too, failed to understand the symbolic significance of these acts as geographical insularity and status as a world power created the illusion that they need not comprehend foreign cultures.

Film theorists have yet to delineate the ways in which social and historical factors are related to the unconscious as opposed to constructing a spectator based on (Lacanian) psychoanalytic models. But if horror films are a collective nightmare rendered intelligible by a shared ideology, as Wood asserts, a source of the images of that nightmare during the 1960s and '70s was coverage of the Vietnam War. Still imprinted in our minds, for instance, is the photograph of the naked Vietnamese girl running down a road after being seared by napalm, or the Vietcong captive being shot point-blank in the head by a South Vietnamese officer. Significantly, the Walter Reade Organization, which distributed *Night of the Living Dead*, refused to subscribe to the MPAA code as the film raised the threshold of screen violence to such an extent that the *Variety* critic labeled it an "unrelieved orgy of sadism" and expressed doubts about the "integrity and social responsibility of its Pittsburgh-based makers."[23] Although the shocking imagery associated with media reports of the Vietnam War has surfaced in films as diverse as *Persona* (1966) and *Manhattan* (1979), it seems especially apt for a horror film such as *Night of the Living Dead* in which the role of television is pivotal. What are we to think of the televised images of war that became part of the vocabulary of a horror film that set a precedent for grisly scenes? Was American innocence corrupted by the Vietnamese experience, as Oliver Stone implies in *Platoon* (1986)? Or did it never exist, as Stanley Kubrick implies in *Full Metal Jacket* (1987)? Was Vietnam an aberration that resulted in a moral crisis prompting antiwar protesters to demonstrate against the Pentagon? Or was it the latest and most publicized development in the history of American capitalism and imperialism?

Since the hero of *Night of the Living Dead*, if indeed there is one, happens to be a black man mistaken in the end for a ghoul and shot by law enforcement agents, the subtext of the film as class discourse involves more than controversy about our actions in Vietnam. Despite Romero's assertion that Duane Jones was cast in the role of Ben because he auditioned well, not because he was black, the hero's color provides the film with strong political overtones.[24] Jones's presence reminds us that Americans had engaged in racist and genocidal policies long before Vietnam. Specifically, the pursuit of Manifest Destiny meant the extermination and relocation of native Americans to facilitate the growth of an internal market. We are reminded, too, of racial exploitation as evidenced by a plantation economy built by black slaves and a labor market that has historically been subject to ethnic stratification and tensions. Significantly, black leaders in the mid 1960s had come to view their cause as one of reallocating the nation's economic resources. As Andrew Kopkind observed, "To 'revolutionize' the role of blacks would require commitments of resources, sacrifices of status and the drastic reallocation of priorities which politics as currently constituted is unable to make. 'Socialism' would perhaps be a beginning, but only that."[25] Predictably, the enormous cost of the Vietnam War, which surpassed $20 billion a year in 1967, became a critical issue. For the New Left, debate about guns versus butter had preceded escalation of the Vietnam conflict. As stressed by leftist dissident Tom Hayden, author of the Port Huron Statement, member of the Chicago Seven, and future husband of "Hanoi Jane," government spending was related to the preservation of a "permanent war economy."[26] Lyndon Johnson himself recognized that his ambitious domestic program, "the woman I really loved," would be subverted by expenditures for "that bitch of a war on the other side of the world."[27]

Further clarification of the subtext of *Night of the Living Dead* requires that the film be read in relation to the significance of the history of both the Vietnam War and the protest movements. Although Jameson characterizes history as an absent cause in that revolution has failed to occur, events in Vietnam did in fact prove to be revolutionary, though questions have been raised about the nature of that revolution. As FitzGerald has stressed, the Vietnamese struggle was simultaneously a national war for liberation against Western powers *and* a class struggle in the Marxist-Leninist sense. American-backed South Vietnamese governments consistently failed to win popular support, or, as our officials put it, "the hearts and minds" of the peasants, by accomplishing economic reforms. For the American public the turning point of the conflict was the Tet offensive, a bold and massive assault that caught General Westmoreland off guard.[28] Politicians like Robert Kennedy began to question whether the war was "winnable." If the war could not be won because the conflict was ultimately political and not military, a subtlety most American political and military personnel failed to grasp, indeed the nature of the war as revolution was repressed.

As for the relationship between events abroad and events at home, revolution failed to occur within our own boundaries: the 1960s prominence of the New Left was short-lived. Although the Port Huron Statement called for a participatory grass-roots democracy that would result in real structural change, the New Left could not overcome factionalism within its own ranks.[29] Counterculturalists like Timothy Leary and Ken Kesey's Merry Pranksters, who shared the New Left's antiestablishment sentiment, eschewed politics in favor of mind-expanding drugs to alter human consciousness. As the Beatles sang in their song about revolution, "We all want to change your head." Ultimately, neither the New Left nor the counterculture could effect changes to end individual powerlessness in a postindustrial society. Americans remained impotent and frustrated. Philip Slater has observed that both institutional *and* psychological changes would have been necessary to revolutionize American society.[30] But LaCapra's argument that public and private spheres alike are subject to repressive control leads to rather bleak conclusions about the possibilities for change.

After the turmoil of the Vietnam years, Americans returned to status quo ante as the cooption of the term "revolution" by Reaganites in a yuppie era would indicate. Perhaps the most appealing aspect of dissidence during the 1960s and '70s, including the naive attempt of flower children to set up communes, had been a sense of shared purpose absent in a society characterized by excessive individualism and atomization. As a mirror that reflected American traits to ourselves, not just with respect to our conduct of war or foreign policy but to our way of life insofar as it frustrated our need for community, revolution in Vietnam was necessarily repressed in our political unconscious. Long before the appearance of such revisionist films as *Uncommon Valor* (1983) and the comic-book style *Rambo* series (starting in 1982), the Vietnam War as revolution proved so disturbing that it invited repression. *Night of the Living Dead* is proof. Significantly, George Romero has claimed that he was not aware of the politics of the film and that critics read too much into "the creations they are studying."[31] Indeed, by contextualizing a classic horror film with reference to a revolution that failed at home and only partially succeeded in Vietnam, we as critics can read a great deal.

NOTES

I wish to thank my husband and colleague, Robert J. Smith, for editorial suggestions and my colleague, Kenneth O'Brien, for encouraging me to teach a course about recent American history.

1. See George A. Romero's preface to John Russo's *The Complete Night of the Living Dead Filmbook* (Pittsburgh: Imagine Inc., 1985), pp. 6–7.

2. *Night of the Living Dead* Clipping File, Margaret Herrick Library, Academy of Motion Picture Arts and Sciences, Beverly Hills, Ca.; hereafter cited as AMPAS.

3. Paul McCullough, "A Pittsburgh Horror Story," *Take One* 4, no. 6 (July-August 1973):8.

4. *Night of the Living Dead* Clipping Files, AMPAS and Library and Museum of the Performing Arts, Lincoln Center, New York.

5. Fredric Jameson, *The Political Unconscious* (Ithaca: Cornell University Press, 1981), p. 42.

6. Dave Morley, "Texts, Readers, Subjects," in *Culture, Media, Language,* ed. Stuart Hall et al. (London: Hutchinson, 1980), p. 163. See also Christine Gledhill, "Recent Developments in Feminist Criticism," *Quarterly Review of Film Studies* 3, no. 4 (Fall 1978): 457–493; reprinted in *Film Theory and Criticism*, 3rd ed., ed. Gerald Mast and Marshall Cohen (New York: Oxford University Press, 1985) and in *Re-Vision*, ed. Mary Ann Doane, Patricia Mellencamp, and Linda Williams (Frederick, Md.: University Publications of America, 1984). Since

there is ample literature on women and horror films, I have not stressed gender in my reading of *Night of the Living Dead*.

7. Robin Wood, "An Introduction to the American Horror Film," in *Movies and Methods II*, ed. Bill Nichols (Los Angeles and Berkeley: University of California Press, 1985), pp. 196–197; 200, 203. An earlier version was published as "Return of the Repressed," *Film Comment* 14 (July-August 1978): 27–32. See also James B. Twitchell, *Dreadful Pleasures: An Anatomy of Modern Horror* (New York: Oxford University Press, 1985), pp. 267–271. As a historian I have reservations about the way film scholars use the concept of the Other, a practice I experimented with here, because it is a convenient category that is historically nonspecific. See Sumiko Higashi, "Ethnicity, Class and Gender in Film: DeMille's *The Cheat*," forthcoming in *Unspeakable Images: Ethnicity and the American Cinema*, ed. Lester Friedman (Champaign-Urbana: University of Illinois Press).

8. Dominick LaCapra, "History and Psychoanalysis," *Critical Inquiry* 13, no. 2 (Winter 1987): 243–246.

9. American foreign policy with respect to Cambodia was even more reprehensible than our treatment of Vietnam, as we destabilized a neutral country whose inhabitants were peaceful and relatively prosperous. When the Khmer Rouge came to power, it decimated at least a million people, one seventh of the population. See Arnold R. Isaacs, *Without Honor: Defeat in Vietnam and Cambodia* (Baltimore: Johns Hopkins University Press, 1983).

10. Several texts about recent American history are available in paperback, including William Leuchtenburg, *A Troubled Feast: American Society since 1945* (Boston: Little Brown, 1979); James Gilbert, *Another Chance: Postwar America, 1945–1985*, 2nd ed. (Chicago: Dorsey Press, 1986); William H. Chafe, *The Unfinished Journey: America Since World War II* (New York: Oxford University Press, 1986); Dewey W. Grantham, *Recent America: The United States since 1945* (Arlington Heights: Harlan Davidson, 1987); Norman L. Rosenberg and Emily S. Rosenberg, *In Our Times: America since World War II*, 3rd ed. (Englewood Cliffs, N.J.: Prentice-Hall, 1987).

11. *Mississippi Burning* rewrites the civil rights movement as a Ramboistic struggle between the KKK using terrorist tactics and FBI men resorting to the same. Distortions in the film include the portrayal of the FBI, since neither black nor white civil rights workers could rely on them for protection. As the civil rights equivalent of Rambo films about Vietnam, the film glorifies white, macho heroics and represses and denies black activism.

12. Peter Carroll, "Khe Sanh, Tet, and The War at Home" (Paper delivered at State University of New York College at Brockport, September 1988).

13. Wood, "American Horror Film," p. 213.

14. Eldridge Cleaver, *Soul on Ice* (New York: Dell, 1968), part 4. According to Romero, background information about the Duane Jones character was cut. See Tony Scott, "An Interview with the Director of *Night of the Living Dead*," *Cinefantastique* 2, no. 3 (Winter 1973): 12. I am indebted to Ron Gottesman for characterizing the asexual nature of Ben as a technician. For a dicussion of the significance of Ben's color, see Richard Dyer, "White," *Screen* 29, no. 4 (August 1988):59–63. Dyer cautions that political readings "may not be easy 'to integrate' with the fantasies of physical degradation and vulnerability characteristic of the contemporary horror film."

15. Philip Slater, *The Pursuit of Loneliness: American Culture at the Breaking Point*, rev. ed.(Boston: Beacon Press, 1976), p. 46.

16. Andrew Kopkind, "Protest and the Illusion of Change," in *The Discontented Society*, ed. LeRoy Ashby and Bruce Stave (Chicago: Rand McNally, 1972), pp. 5–9.

17. William C. Dowling, *Jameson, Althusser, Marx: An Introduction to the Political Unconscious* (Ithaca: Cornell University Press, 1984), p. 115.

18. Ibid., p. 117; Jameson, *Political Unconscious*, p. 81.

19. Vivian Sobchack, *Screening Space: The American Science Fiction Film* (New York: Ungar, 1984), pp. 188–190.

20. "Filming *Night of the Living Dead*: An Interview with George Romero by Alex B. Block," *Filmmakers Newsletter* 19 (January 1972):20.

21. Frances FitzGerald, *Fire In the Lake: The Vietnamese and the United States in Vietnam* (New York: Vintage Books, 1973; first published by Random House in 1972), pp. 491–502. Interestingly, FitzGerald reviewed DePalma's *Casualties of War* and labeled it sadomasochistic pornography. See her "Casualties of Cinema," *The Village Voice*, 22 August 1989, p. 45. For a widely used text about the war, see George C. Herring's *America's Longest War: The United States and Vietnam 1950–1975*, 2nd ed. (New York: Knopf, 1986). Also well known is Michael J. Arlen's coverage of television reporting, *Living-Room War* (New York: Viking, 1969).

22. In *The Living and the Undead* (Urbana: University of Illinois Press, 1986), Gregory A. Waller writes a very lengthy analysis of Romero's film in which he mentions both the chopper and the search and destroy mission, but fails to relate these aspects of the film to the Vietnam War. Stuart Samuels writes in detail about *Night of the Living Dead* within the context of 1960s politics in *Midnight Movies* (New York: Collier Books, 1983), pp. 66–67. Samuels quotes J. Hoberman, whose review appeared in *The Village Voice*, 13–19 January 1982, and Joseph Lewis, who wrote that had Lyndon Johnson seen the film, he might "never have permitted the napalming of the Vietnamese." R. W. H. Dillard briefly discusses the film in relation to the war but asserts that its real horror cannot adequately be explained thereby. See his "Night of the Living Dead: 'It's Not Just a Wind That's Passing Through,' " in *Horror Films* (New York: Simon and Schuster, 1976), pp. 58–59. Reprinted in *American Horrors*, ed. Gregory A. Waller (Urbana and Chicago: University of Illinois Press, 1987). See also Dyer, "White." Although horror films readily lend themselves to different readings, downgrading political ones contributes to repression in the political unconscious.

23. *Variety* film review, 15 October 68, in *Night of the Living Dead* clipping file, AMPAS.

24. Romero in Russo, *Living Dead Filmbook*, p. 7.

25. Kopkind, "Protest and Change," p. 7.

26. "The Port Huron Statement," in *America Since 1945*, 3rd ed., ed. Robert D. Marcus and David Burner (New York: St. Martin's Press, 1985), pp. 187–204. The document was principally authored by Tom Hayden. See also Irwin Unger, *The Movement: A History of the American New Left 1959–1972* (New York: Dodd, Mead, 1975).

27. Doris Kearns, *Lyndon Johnson and the American Dream* (New York: Harper & Row, 1976), p. 251.

28. FitzGerald, *Fire in the Lake*, p. 296.

29. "The Port Huron Statement," pp. 199–204; Unger, *The Movement*, chaps. 6, 7.

30. Slater, *Pursuit of Loneliness*, chaps. 5, 6.

31. Scott, "Interview," p. 10; Russo, *Living Dead Filmbook*, p. 115.

Boys Will Be Men:
Oedipal Drama in *Coming Home*

In the United States, the production of antiwar films has been beset with a myriad of political and economic problems, from government intervention to a production system hesitant to become embroiled in controversy.[1] When a film critical of war is produced, liberal filmmakers and critics are quick to join in praising both the film and the political courage of the filmmakers, frequently disregarding the limited ideological parameters in which these films often still operate. The following argument will focus on these limited ideological parameters in the Hollywood antiwar film, especially as they are evident in the film *Coming Home* (1978).

Like most of Hollywood's output, antiwar films rarely if ever focus on the specific social and historical forces underlying the conflicts. In the case of Hollywood's antiwar films, the economic causes of war are fundamentally ignored, and imperialist and nationalist ideologies remain unexamined. Instead, war becomes a personal battle, with combat's impact on individuals the primary constituent of the film's critique. As a consequence, the Hollywood films that have a reputation for antiwar sentiments are significantly ahistorical; they focus on neither the specific historical causes nor the specific outcome of the war being represented. The contemporary social and cultural milieu may be prominent, as it certainly is in *Coming Home*'s sound track and iconography, or in the by now cliché use of sixties rock music in almost any film about Vietnam; but this is backdrop to a narrative pattern that overshadows the historical and social dimension of the events depicted. History in these films amounts to little more than the music, clothes, and hairstyles of the period, negating the significance of economics, social class, and gender to the real events represented by the film, as well as their representation *in* the film. What passes for an indictment of war in general, or any specific war, is an imprecise representation of a particular environment, the battlefield (where "life is cheap"), or the war's aftermath, with men who are physically and psychologically crippled.[2] In these films, a nearsighted humanism laments the loss of American (male) lives and, sometimes, their innocence. The visual and narrative distinctions between ally and enemy are generally no different than in the conventional war film. No matter who the "enemy" is in the film's particular war, s/he remains an Other, strange or exotic, generally exhibiting behavior and belief repugnant to the film's representation of American sensibilities.

This narrative reorganization of the actual events of the war might be compared to the psychoanalytic patient reexperiencing a traumatic moment, subordinating that moment to conventional linguistic and/or narrative patterns. In the films that follow a particular war and narrate that war as a "traumatic moment" (as opposed to the patriotic tenor of the great majority of Hollywood films about World War II), the events of war are commonly subordinated to a conventional Oedipal narration, one that displaces a radical social critique of economic, social, and historical forces while focusing on the development of a male subject-hero. This narrative reorganization follows a pattern typical of most Hollywood films. The presentation of male desire as the story's driving force creates an identification between the viewer and the heroic male subject that eliminates the potential for outlining the historical specificity of the war in any fashion that doesn't confine itself to the trials and tribulations of the male subject-hero. As Raymond Bellour has said, "The American cinema . . . finds itself enacting . . . the most classic paradigms elaborated for the subject of Western culture by Freudian psychoanalysis. *Its massive attempt to socio-historical representation is basically shaped* by the type of subjectivity, whose logic was first recognized and imposed by psychoanalysis . . . *a classic Oedipal scenario*" (emphasis added).[3]

This connection between narrative, desire, and Oedipal pleasure is a recurrent theme in recent narrative theory, one that scholars have recognized as an indication of "the inherent maleness of all narrative."[4] As Teresa de Lauretis argues, the defining distinction that all narrative establishes is one of sexual difference, "predicated on the *single* figure of the hero who crosses the boundary and penetrates the other space. In so doing the hero, the mythical subject, is constructed as human being and as male."[5]

In her essay "Desire in Narrative," de Lauretis cites the work of Jurij Lotman, who reduced the "number and functions of what Propp called the *dramatis persona* to the two involved in the primary conflict of hero and antagonist (obstacle)."[6] As a result of this mythical view of narrative, no matter how "varied the conditions of presence of the narrative form in fictional genres, rituals, or social discourses, its movement seems to be that of a passage, a transformation predicated on the figure of a hero . . . an actively experienced transformation of the human being into—man. This is the sense in which all change, all social and personal—even physical—transformation is understood."[7] In many Hollywood antiwar films, this "passage" is generally given geographic concreteness. In films like *The Big Parade* (1925), *All Quiet on the Western Front* (1930), *A Walk in the Sun* (1945), and *Platoon* (1986), the male hero-subject traverses an unknown and threatening landscape over which he ultimately gains control, indicating his "transformation into man."

In films about returning veterans, like *The Best Years of Our Lives* (1946), *The Men* (1950), and *Coming Home*, this geography is usually absent, an aspect of the character's past that preexists the narrative's representation. Thus, the passage to manhood must be completed on a terrain that, unlike the battlefield, does not offer a spectacular visual and narrative "obstacle" to that passage, an "obstacle" that must often then be filled by another character. Usually this other character is a woman, the male subject's wife or lover, as is the case in these films. De Lauretis's work notes the similarity between this landscape and woman, as the passage of the male hero involves "entry into a closed space . . . interpreted as 'a cave,' 'the grave,' 'a house,' 'woman' . . . whatever its personification [as] morphologically female."[8]

This scenario's relationship to any film or story that is ostensibly a work of social criticism, as are Hollywood's antiwar films, is problematic, since an Oedipal narration functions to construct "subjects who fit smoothly into the existing social order."[9] Thus, the films' antiwar sentiments will stand in an inevitable contradiction to their Oedipal narration, which both narratively and visually represents the male subject taking his place in a traditional social role.

Set after a war, *Coming Home*'s narrative emphasizes the Vietnam conflict's psychological damage, represented by physical crippling, a narrative reminiscent of melodramas like *The Best Years of Our Lives* and *The Men*. In all of these films, individual characters provide the vehicle through which not only conventional figures of identification but also the consequences of war are delineated for the viewer. *Coming Home* attempts to criticize American fighting in Vietnam by emphasizing the emotional and physical price American men paid for that involvement. The viewer is encouraged, at least initially, to extrapolate from the individual case to the nation as a whole, and further to reflect back on a misplaced sense of patriotism underlying our role in Vietnam. Not atypically, the film holds "to the pattern of emphasizing American perceptions of American experience," with no apparent concern for the impact of U.S. involvement on the Vietnamese.[10] Americans are both the subjects of the Vietnam "war" *and* its victims, a perspective that can only limit the film's ability to mount a historically specific critique of the causes of the conflict.[11] As a result of the film's Oedipal reorganization of the political issues of the Vietnam conflict, the film's representation of war and its aftermath serves less as the substance of social criticism than as an extraordinary and especially challenging backdrop for the construction of a male subject-hero. In *Coming Home*, as in many Hollywood antiwar films, war is not viewed as the result of a nationalist and imperialist worldview, nor as the result of economic doctrine; instead, it is a monument to male Oedipal crisis and resolution.

Coming Home, however, seems different from conventional Hollywood antiwar films. The first scene presents the sounds and images of actual hospitalized Vietnam veterans discussing their attitudes about the war and their disabilities, all presented in a cinéma-vérité style. The hand-held camera and the overlapping dialogue privilege no particular individual, providing no specific figure of identification. The statements of actual disabled veterans and the documentary-like presentation appear to initiate a historically specific and critical treatment of the conflict in Vietnam. Yet the final movement in this opening scene is a slow zoom into the face of Jon Voight, lying disabled on a gurney. As a recognizable "star" of fiction films, and one whom the viewer knows is not disabled, Voight's introduction initiates a tension between reality and fiction, history and narrative that echoes throughout the film. The subsequent introduction of Bruce Dern's character, Bob Hyde, and the presentation of the credits, prolongs this tension for the moment by cross-cutting between Dern jogging and the disabled veterans in the hospital. By the end of the credits, the parallel edits contrast only Bruce Dern's Bob Hyde and John Voight's character, Luke Martin, seemingly closing off the film from reality by initiating a melodramatic narrative pattern, one that emphasizes social conflict as played out among opposing characters. Yet such a closing off, such a diminution of tension between reality and fiction, is short-lived.

Jane Fonda's character provides the most troubling source of tension between the reality, or more specifically, the images of reality that surround the film and the film's story. The film's Oedipal trajectory is in fact premised on the suppression of both Fonda's public image and her character as the film's

The history of Fonda's image is virtually reconstructed . . . from Fonda as a sexual subject . . .

. . . to Fonda as the subject of her own antiwar activities.

subject, as well as the transposition of antiwar activity to Luke, the film's final subject-hero. The history of Fonda's image is virtually reconstructed by the film's narrative progression, from Fonda as sexual subject—an image initiated by her role in *Barbarella*'s camp science fiction evocation of a "revolution" in sexual mores—to Fonda as the subject of her own antiwar activities. The symbolic role she played during the war, as a celebrity who could be used by the media to focus antiwar sentiment and as a focus for a hawkish backlash, is still prominent— in the fictionalized portrayal of her in *Hanoi Hilton* (1987), for example, as well as in the "Nuke Fonda" bumper stickers.

Also troubling to *Coming Home*'s Oedipalized narrative and visual text is the central role her character plays. Not unlike a great many Hollywood films, the action of this film begins with the absence of the Father, in this case Bob Hyde, husband and commissioned officer whose ideological stance regarding Vietnam mirrors the government's. Even before he leaves for Vietnam, however, the power conventionally exercised by this figure is undermined in several ways. First, by its earlier presentation of disabled veterans and their more complex attitudes about the war, the film has already distanced the viewer from the naive and jingoistic mentality he expresses. Second, in the opening scenes of Bob and Sally, Sally appears to be the subject of the film's action. This is most evident in the film's representation of Bob's inability to bring Sally to orgasm his final night at home. The viewer watches a close-up of Sally's face, her lack of satisfaction evident, as she waits for her husband to have his orgasm. The scene mirrors a similar one in *Klute*, in which Jane Fonda's prostitute character looks at her watch as she waits for the john to come.

By its virtual repetition of this scene from *Klute*, the film extends the sense that Fonda's image as a sexual subject is somehow incomplete. A troubling echo of earlier representations of Fonda's sexuality is imbricated in the text, focusing the viewer's interest in Fonda's characterization on the resolution of this persistent problem.

When Bob departs the following day, the film opens the possibility for Sally to fill the void he leaves. As in many other "women's pictures"—*Mildred Pierce* (1945), *Reckless* (1935), *Alice Doesn't Live Here Anymore* (1975), or *An Unmarried Woman* (1978), for example—the absence of a husband or father raises the question of whether the female character can "rule" the household and the family. In more structural terms, the question is whether the female character can maintain her role as the subject of the film, with her desire "ruling" the narrative.

By virtue of its strong concern with Sally Hyde, the film seems to offer something different from previous films that have dealt with the problems of returning veterans. The best-known examples, *The Best Years of Our Lives* and *The Men*, as well as the potentially exploitive versions following Vietnam (for example, *Taxi Driver*, *Who'll Stop the Rain?*, and *Rolling Thunder* [1977]), have female characters who are unproblematically situated in an Oedipal narration of either successful or failed male social integration. In contrast, Fonda's character functions as the innocent who receives a political education on the Vietnam conflict, even if it is an education based on the physical horrors of the conflict and not on its political or social dimensions. Of equal significance, Fonda's character serves as a surrogate for the viewer, initially a figure of identification that slants the film's address to a "feminized" spectator, whether female or male. In the context of the history of Hollywood cinema, the film's strong concern with Sally's social reintegration following the absence of her husband has more in common with films marketed to a female audience than with the conventional antiwar film. However, its melodramatic preoccupation with social integration is represented partly as a domestication of violence, potently evident in the film's climax when Luke conversationally disarms Bob Hyde in the latter's living room. More significantly, the film's Oedipal trajectory is premised on the domestication of the character of Sally, initiated by her later narrative and visual subordination to Luke, and finalized by her returning to her husband, even when such a narrative resolution seems unsatisfactory.

The film's early concern with the satisfaction of female desire and the construction of a female subject is indicative of the "feminizing" of *Coming Home*'s narrative and the viewer's engagement in that narrative. The early scenes in the film focus on Sally's dissatisfaction with her life as a "base" wife and her desire for change. Initially, one option is identified with another woman, her friend Vy, who represents by dress, mannerism, and domestic space a sixties alternative lifestyle. As such, the film provides narrative exposition that offers the opportunity to fulfill that desire through a relationship between women. This opportunity is subsequently suppressed by the shift to Luke's development and Sally's role in it. The film's feminist pretensions are evident in the exchange between Vy and Sally on her not being allowed to remain in the officers' quarters, with Vy telling her, "You're the hole in the donut, and when there's no donut there's no hole." Later, after her initial encounter with Luke at the hospital, she and Vy are perusing Sally's old high school yearbook, noting Sally's response to the question, "What's the one thing you would want on a desert island?" Sally's answer at the time: "A husband." Her response today is a sarcastic "I was so ambitious." Yet the sense of some newfound independence is quickly displaced as their attention shifts to Luke's picture, prefiguring the ultimate focus of her desires.

Thus, the film's emphasis on female independence and on the education of Sally Hyde begins to appear as something of a sham. As indicated by her attention to Luke's picture, the narrative will limit her process of political education by ultimately defining it in strictly sexual terms as a choice between male lovers, reiterating a narrative model from the "women's pictures" of the thirties and forties. *Coming Home* further undermines the construction of a female subject by balancing the portrayal of Sally's desires with the simultaneous exposition of Luke's inability to accept his paralysis and once again become an integral part of society. Sally's dissatisfaction and Luke's are not unrelated, though. Sally pursues an alternative to her life as a "base wife" by volunteering her work in the veteran's hospital, defying her absent husband/Father. Her first encounters with Luke are marked by her control over him (and her denials of that control) and by his humiliation and angry resistance to her. Luke lies face down on his gurney, his mobility impaired except when Sally attends to him, his powerlessness represented by the loss of control in the lower regions of his body. The film's representation of his humiliation and vulnerability comes in his very first meeting with Sally. She accidently bumps into him, bursting his urine bag, signifying his lack of phallic control. He responds by lashing out angrily at the hospital staff, wildly swinging the phalluslike canes he uses to propel himself through the hall of the hospital.

This initial inversion in the conventional narrative relations of power between male and female is represented in a visual fashion as well. Luke's position face down impedes not only his movement but also his vision. His humiliation is aggravated by his vulnerability to Sally's gaze—her look, like her ignorance, serving as a surrogate for the spectator. In these early scenes, the film engages the viewer's curiosity about the disabled, displacing the conventional Hollywood voyeurism, which turns on controlling the image of women through an erotic male gaze.[12] As a consequence, the gaze the viewer now shares with Sally becomes tainted by its unconventional and seemingly perverse nature, expressed by Sally averting her eyes and denying her control over Luke.

Simultaneously, the film's emphasis on her desires and on her visual perspective is further undercut by the focus on her adulterous involvement with Luke and by Luke's growing independence, with the film eventually displacing the issues of Sally's developing political consciousness in favor of Luke's Oedipal transformation. For example, when Sally's increased political awareness results in a failed attempt to get the women who work on the base newspaper to print a story on disabled veterans, she attempts to share her failure and disappointment with Luke and the other hospitalized veterans as she helps them off a bus. Even though the men treat her condescendingly because of their sense of her naiveté, her expression of anger is directed at the other women, only one indication of the film's betrayal of its earlier emphasis on female relationships.[13] In its stead is the developing relationship between Sally and Luke, summarized in the concluding moments of this scene, as Luke gazes at Sally framed in the door of the bus (shot from his point of view), and tells her that she's "beautiful when she's excited." Similarly, in a later scene following dinner at Sally's, Luke tells her that "People . . . don't see who I am," to which Sally replies that people only see her as as a "captain's wife." More significantly, even as she confides in him that sometimes she "feels she's becoming what people see," she is cut short by Luke's confession (again, shot from his point of view) that he spends "ninety-five percent of [his] time . . . thinking of making love to you."

The remainder of the film's narrative works to operationalize this shift from Sally's desires to Luke's, a narrative movement marked by delays generated by the "return of the Father," Sally's husband, Bob.[14] When Sally goes to meet Bob on leave, the film begins to finalize its shift from an interest in Sally's developing political consciousness to a conventional melodramatic interest in her choice of lovers.[15] Even more significantly, her estrangement from Luke does not preclude the narrative's continuing enactment of his growing sense of power. When Sally goes to tell Luke she's meeting Bob in Hong Kong, he tells her that he is leaving the hospital. Thus, the film's representation of Luke is no longer mediated by Sally's perspective. As Luke moves from gurney to wheelchair to automobile, and from veteran's hospital to apartment, his newfound mobility extends the film's representation of the shift from Sally's point of view to Luke's as the predominant perspective on the film's events.

The suppression of Sally's subjectivity in favor of Luke's is further represented by the displacement of Sally's growing political consciousness in favor of Luke's growing political commitment. Paralleling Luke's newfound lifestyle, Sally moves, buys a new car, and changes her hairstyle, these changes now having displaced her earlier more substantive growing political consciousness, and as a consequence, possibly *our* interest in the politics of the Vietnam War. Luke's political commitment is engendered by the suicide of Vy's brother. His potential heroic stature is indicated by his attempted "last-minute" rescue, the failure of which is followed by him chaining himself to a Marine Corps "recruit depot." The film's representation of this event also works to undermine Sally's perspective. Not only does the viewer's awareness of Luke's actions precede Sally's, but as she watches Luke's arrest on television news, her vision is now mediated and impotent.

The film's empowering of Luke and its undermining of Sally's subjectivity are significantly related. In the film's narrative and visual development, the power Sally exercises over Luke in early scenes, and her initial resistance to his sexual interest, structurally come to serve the role of "obstacle" noted earlier in de Lauretis's analysis of Oedipal narration. Again, as de Lauretis argues, the "obstacle" is not necessarily a woman, but it is necessarily ("morphologically") "female." As such, "female is what is not susceptible to transformation . . . ; she (it) is an element of plot-space . . . a resistance."[16] Even though the film's Oedipal narration is not so clear-cut, as Sally is "susceptible to transformation," that transformation is arrested by the narrative in favor of her function as the "obstacle" to Luke's development.

This contradiction between the film's feminist pretensions and its increasingly Oedipal textual mechanics is nowhere more evident than in the scene of Luke and Sally making love. Echoing this split is the conventional objectification of Jane Fonda's body even as the scene emphasizes her sexual satisfaction. The (male?) viewer's interest is focused in two seemingly contradictory directions in this scene, both distastefully voyeuristic, curious about Jane Fonda's body and curious about sex among the disabled.[17] The conjunction of these narrative forces allows the film to maintain to some extent its feminist pretensions in its presentation of the nonphallic sexual satisfaction of Sally. Yet in a further contradiction, it is her sexual satisfaction that sums up the film's only real interest in her as a subject in the actions and events of the narrative, finally domesticating the troubling echo of both Sally's earlier sexual dissatisfaction and Fonda's extratextual screen image as a sexual subject.

This scene most obviously appeals to the cinema's conventional voyeuristic emphasis on sexual acts, but more significantly it also marks the point at which, in the film's terms, Luke proves himself a man. That Luke's manhood and Sally's orgasm are gotten orally rather than phallically maintains the pretense of a "feminist" sensibility, which was marked most obviously in the text in Sally's earlier subjectivity and the maintenance of some semblance of that subjectivity in this scene. The distinction between their lovemaking in this scene and Luke's earlier confession that in high school Sally was known as "Sally bend her over" denies the aggressiveness (in de Lauretis's words, "the inherent maleness") of the film's Oedipal structuration. The fact that Luke's manhood and Sally's orgasm are gotten orally rather than phallically, then, is only significant as it disguises the film's Oedipal textuality. In *The Pornography of Representation*, Susan Kappeler notes the continuance of male subjectivity and domination in the historically specific, supposedly liberated sexual ideology of the sixties:

> Culturally, ideologically, the supreme subject does not want to acknowledge his responsibility for his relations with the Other. In the modern age, where the Other is theoretically considered to have become a subject as well, he wants to convince himself that his position of power and supremacy and his acts of domination and oppression, are the will of the newly enfranchised subject. Her willingness is his need, a justification for his unchanged supremacy, his continued domination.

Kappeler also notes that

> throughout the "sexual liberation" this pattern persists, for it is not the liberation of women, but the liberation of the female sex-object, which is now expected to orgasm.[18]

Tellingly, this is the last scene in which Sally's subjectivity is in any way significant. When Bob returns to the States, his presence does not resolve the film's actions, as the "return of the Father" might. He also has been marred by the war, as he hobbles off the plane, cane in hand. His impaired mobility reverberates with what now, following the fact of Sally's orgasm, becomes an earlier sign of his impotence, his failure to satisfy Sally sexually. Bob's inability to maintain the role of the Father on his return is further elaborated by his false heroism and the sham ceremony where he accepts the Purple Heart. After the FBI discloses to Bob their surveillance of Luke and Sally, Bob informs Luke of the FBI's actions. The film continues to mask the emphasis on Luke's Oedipal development by having the two men conclude that "the rest is up to Sally"—a decidedly false indication of whose desires are of concern here and who exactly has the power to resolve the film's issues.

Bob's final attempt to salvage his manhood involves physically threatening Sally, holding her at bay with his M-16. Luke arrives to affect a "last-minute rescue," disarming Bob with an ethnocentric appeal to their common humanity ("I'm not the enemy"). The conventional male camaraderie that is the focus of many antiwar films—creating an opposition between the "brotherhood of man" and military conflict—resurfaces here.[19] More significant to the film's Oedipal narration, what has become Sally's limited role in the plot, nursing Luke back to mental health and manhood, is emphasized by Luke telling Bob to "Give her a chance; she can help you." Finally, in the context of *Coming Home*'s individualized Oedipal drama, Luke exits alone, heroically the film's subject, separated from Sally and Bob not only by the film's continued commitment to heterosexual monogamy and the filmic conventions of individualized male heroism, but also by his visual separation from the couple, who appear together in reverse two-shots.

Despite the resolution of conflict in this scene, the film's concluding moments do not provide satisfactory closure for all three characters. In the final scenes, each character is separate, connected only by the film's pattern of cross-cutting. Bob runs naked into the surf, either to cleanse himself or to kill himself, while Sally, reunited with Vy, goes to the supermarket to shop for steaks for an outdoor barbecue. Only Luke's story comes to any sense of resolution, continuing its heroic trajectory, as he lectures high school students on the "bullshit" they are being told concerning war, heroism, and Vietnam.

The lack of closure for all but Luke's character may be a consequence of the film's Oedipal scenario. Bob awash in the surf is possibly a fitting image of the Father's loss of power, but only in this metaphorical and textual sense does it provide a viable sense of resolution. Sally comes full circle, returned to the family and domesticity. Her character has become, in de Lauretis's words, "an element of plot-space," a projection of the male subject's desires, an "obstacle" overcome in his heroic transformation. As Raymond Bellour puts it, "the American cinema is entirely dependent . . . on a system of representations in which the woman occupies a central place only to the extent that it's a place assigned to her by the logic of masculine desire."[20]

Undoubtedly, the displacement of the narrative's early emphasis on Sally's independence and developing political consciousness causes some of the trouble with this final return to domesticity. But what makes this rather conventional melodramatic conclusion even more troubling is the "place assigned" to Jane Fonda within this story of male Oedipal development. Bruce Gilbert, one of the film's producers, is recorded as saying that *Coming Home* "would attempt to re-define what manhood and patriotism meant, and to get it financed we knew Jane needed to play a pivotal character caught between two people [men]."[21] As a "bankable" star, Fonda's role had to be a prominent one in order to lure backers. In and of itself, this necessity to give her character a "central place" would make it difficult to relegate her finally to a less significant role, both narratively and ideologically. Even more difficult to subordinate to the film's Oedipal narrative, though, is the public image of Jane Fonda as a highly visible celebrity opposed to U.S. intervention in Vietnam. Like the issues of her sexuality, the film's initial focus on her political consciousness reverberates beyond the confines of this particular narrative, making her return to domesticity that much less credible.

The displacement of Sally's subjectivity in the film's narrative and visual pattern is matched by the displacement of the film's "feminized" address. Again, Gilbert's comments are telling: *Coming Home* "would attempt to re-define what manhood and patriotism meant." In a number of ways that redefinition is premised on creating a "feminized" hero. Luke not only lacks the phallic wholeness of more conventional male hero-subjects, he also defines a "feminized" heroics in more historically specific terms. We know that Luke has been to Vietnam, but what we see is a fairly conventional image of a war protestor. Luke wears long hair, he's nonviolent (even in performing a "last-minute rescue"), and he chains himself to a recruitment center. As a consequence, the film's address seems to focus on those who stayed "home," not those "coming home," those whose appearance (long hair) and demeanor (nonviolent) were imaged publicly in a fashion that called into question their "manhood." *Coming Home* thus not only uses the "feminine" as an "obstacle" to male subjectivity, but also exploits the "feminine" to visually and narratively create heroic male subjects of those who stood in opposition to the war in Vietnam and thus to the conventional image of male heroism.

Of course, the film's "feminized" address, like its suppression of Fonda's public image and her character's subjectivity, is at best partial. As with other Hollywood antiwar films, *Coming Home*'s real concern is with the construction of male subjects who regain their humanity, a transformation that makes the film's critique of U.S. involvement in Vietnam subject to an Oedipal narration. The horrors of combat in Vietnam, even as they are visually if not narratively absent from the film, form the spectacular backdrop against which men prove themselves to be men, in a fashion undistinguished from other Hollywood antiwar films. Luke's disability, like the horrors of combat, presents only a superficial critique of U.S. intervention in Southeast Asia, representing this war not in the light of nationalist sensibilities and economic policy but as Hollywood films view all wars, as a challenging proving ground for American manhood. *Coming Home*'s "feminized" address pretends to an enlightened sensibility about the U.S. role in Vietnam, but in fact it only recreates an Oedipal drama in this context. Like Hollywood antiwar films that preceded it, and many that follow, the limited critique presented by *Coming Home* is a result of a narrative problem that is not limited to the antiwar film; in fact, it is the very problem of narrative itself and the specific mechanism of its progression, a function of the operation and projection of male desire.

NOTES

1. I will use the term *antiwar film* to designate films that have been viewed as critical of war in general or critical of a particular war as such a view is indicated by writings in the popular press, which may represent some sort of cultural consensus, or in film scholarship. As should be apparent, since I am highly critical of the contradictory ideological stance of these films, the use of the term is a convenience and should not be construed to imply some specific and bounded set of films that unproblematically represents antiwar sentiments.

2. In the first category, we could put films like *The Big Parade* (1925), *All Quiet on the Western Front* (1930), *A Walk in the Sun* (1945), *Platoon* (1986), and *Full Metal Jacket* (1987). In the second category, we could put *The Best Years of Our Lives* (1945) and *The Men* (1950), as well as films following the Vietnam War that represent the psychological damage of Vietnam service in a character's sociopathic relationship to life in the United States, as in *Who'll Stop the Rain?* (1978), *Taxi Driver* (1976), *Heroes* (1977), and the latter half of *The Deer Hunter* (1978).

3. Janet Bergstrom, "Alternation, Segmentation, Hypnosis: An Interview with Raymond Bellour," *Camera Obscura* 3–4 (1979):93.

4. Teresa de Lauretis, *Alice Doesn't: Feminism, Semiotics, Cinema* (Bloomington: Indiana University Press, 1984), p. 108.

5. Ibid., p. 119.

6. Ibid., p. 118.

7. Ibid., pp. 113, 121–122.

8. Ibid., pp. 118–119.

9. Kaja Silverman, *The Subject of Semiotics* (New York: Oxford University Press, 1983), p. 73. Silverman focuses on the Oedipal scenario's construction of male subject positions. A similar view is given by Deleuze and Guattari, who emphasize the manner in which an Oedipal scenario constructs subjects who "fit" an advanced capitalist social order. Gilles Deleuze and Felix Guattari, *Anti-Oedipus: Capitalism and Schizophrenia*, trans. Robert Hurley, Mark Seem, and Helen R. Lane (New York: Viking Press, 1977).

10. Peter McInerney, "Apocalypse Then: Hollywood Looks Back at Vietnam," *Film Quarterly* 2 (Winter 1979–80):29.

11. Gilbert Adair criticizes this ethnocentrism directly, even if parenthetically: "(. . . it's a disconcerting feature of almost all Vietnam cinema . . . that the war's 'victims'

are generally understood to be maimed or traumatized *American* soldiery and only incidentally the Vietnamese people.)" *Vietnam on Film: From the Green Berets to Apocalypse Now* (New York: Proteus, 1981), p. 109.

12. The literature on the controlling male gaze in Hollywood visual representation is quite extensive. See, for example, Laura Mulvey, "Visual Pleasure and Narrative Cinema," *Screen* 16, no. 3 (Autumn 1975): 6–18; Mulvey, "Afterthoughts on 'Visual Pleasure and Narrative Cinema' Inspired by *Duel in the Sun*," *Framework* 15/16/17 (1981): 12–15; E. Ann Kaplan, *Women and Film: Both Sides of the Camera* (New York: Methuen, 1983); Annette Kuhn, *Women's Pictures: Feminism and Cinema* (London: Routledge and Kegan Paul, 1982); also see de Lauretis, *Alice Doesn't*, and Silverman, *Subject of Semiotics*.

13. The film's betrayal of its feminist pretensions, and one might argue its fundamental misogyny, is especially evident in two moments involving minor female characters, both of whom are offensively insensitive to the plight of the disabled veterans. The first is in the scene of the meeting of the base newspaper staff, where one of the officer's wives responds to Sally working in the hospital with the following exceptional logic: "When I was on my diet, I didn't want candy lying about the house." The other scene is later, when Luke is shopping for groceries and a "housewife" (conventionally unattractive by Hollywood standards, replete with curlers and housedress) ignores his courteous request to move her cart from his path.

14. For a brief discussion of narrative "delays," see Roland Barthes, *S/Z: An Essay*, trans. Richard Miller (New York: Hill and Wang, 1974); pp. 75–76: "The dynamics of the text (since it implies a truth to be deciphered) is thus paradoxical . . . the problem is to *maintain* the enigma in the initial void of its answer; whereas the sentences quicken the story's 'unfolding' and cannot help but move the story along, the hermeneutic code performs an opposite action: it must set up *delays* (obstacles, stoppages, deviations) in the flow of the discourse . . . between question and answer there is a whole dilatory area whose emblem might be named 'reticence' . . . To narrate (in the classic fashion) is to raise the question as if it were a subject which one delays predicating . . ."

15. One might compare the other well-known feature film produced by Indochina Peace Campaign films, *China Syndrome* (1979), where Jack Lemmon plays the innocent surrogate for the viewer who is educated in the politically correct position on nuclear power, without sidetracking the issues into questions of his romantic and sexual satisfaction.

16. De Lauretis, *Alice Doesn't*, pp. 118–119.

17. In a *New York Times* article, "The Five-Year Struggle to Make *Coming Home*" (February 19, 1978), Kirk Honeycutt gives some significant space to the issue of representing sex by a disabled soldier. According to the article, the film's makers felt that it was necessary to "confront this," and to do so, they did extensive research into the "sexual disabilities of the disabled," involving the director of the Sexual Dysfunction Clinic at UCLA, and his wife, a sex therapist, as well as "access to many patients and therapists." As the article also states, "Mr. Voight, however, received a more colorful education in these matters. 'Five hundred guys were telling me how they did it. Every time I turned around somebody would say, 'You know what I do?' or, 'Want to make it really terrific?' " The *New York Times* article goes on to mention in the next paragraph that "Miss Fonda was extremely reluctant to play the love scene nude, fearful audiences would not see the character but Jane Fonda up there naked on the scene [sic]." Ultimately, a "body double" was used. In any case, the article's concern with this issue, and the connection it establishes between the sexuality of the disabled and the presentation of Fonda nude, attests to the duality of spectator interests in this scene.

18. Susan Kappeler, *The Pornography of Representation* (Minneapolis: University of Minnesota Press, 1986): pp. 165, 160.

19. This camaraderie is evident in numerous films, including *The Big Parade, Grand*

Illusion, The Best Years Of Our Lives, The Men, and Vietnam films *Platoon, Good Morning Vietnam, Full Metal Jacket,* and most significantly *The Deer Hunter.* It is at the level of the use of male camaraderie as a signifier of humanity that we can see the close affinity between the antiwar film and its prowar counterpart, which uses the same signifier to indicate a sense of resolution, in the ultimate cohesion of the fighting unit in World War II films, for example.

20. Bergstrom, "Alternation, Segmentation, Hypnosis," p. 93.
21. Honeycutt, "Five-Year Struggle," p. 13.

13

SUSAN JEFFORDS

Reproducing Fathers:
Gender and the Vietnam War
in U.S. Culture

It is a key theme of U.S. films, novels, essays, and personal accounts of the
Vietnam War that women are associated with life and men with death. John
Wheeler, former army captain and West Point graduate, states this gendered
thesis most clearly: "I consider my commitment [to the military and his coun-
try] as a statement that there are things worth dying for. It is a masculine statement. I think it is *the* masculine statement. This is why war has tended to be
viewed as a masculine enterprise. . . . Woman expresses the idea that there
are things worth living for."[1] These associations with life and death are most
often articulated in Vietnam narratives through the images of birth and death,
with reproduction and birth standing as the antitheses of the death of war. For
William Broyles, Jr., Vietnam veteran and former editor of *Newsweek*, "War
was an initiation into the power of life and death. Women touch that power at
the moment of birth; men on the edge of death."[2] But the philosophy of
William Eastlake's *The Bamboo Bed* is clearest: "[E]very soldier hears death
ticking off inside him. . . . Not only every soldier . . . but every male human
being. Not every female human being. They don't hear death ticking off inside them because they feel life ticking inside them. . . . A female would
rather fuck than fight." Women, Eastlake's main character suggests, "don't
have to go to war to prove something."[3]

War is, as Broyles declares, "for men, at some terrible level the closest
thing to what childbirth is for women: the initiation into the power of life and
death." Following this logic, men who don't go to war "now have a sort of
nostalgic longing for something they missed, some classic male experience,
the way some women who didn't have children worry they missed something
basic about being a woman."[4] Broyles's view is indicative of a more comprehensive logic at work in recent accounts of the Vietnam War in which war is
described as a biological (and thus "natural") necessity for the human male
while reproduction is portrayed as a requisite for the *social* well-being of the
human female, something she feels a nostalgia for having "missed." Nicole-
Claude Mathieu's discussion of maternity as a biological role and paternity as
a social one contradicts this view and reveals its motivation.[5] Most
importantly, her opposing view cautions that once reproduction is defined as a
social and not a biological activity, it becomes possible for the masculine to
appropriate this role to itself, to encompass the feminine position of reproduction within its own sphere of control.[6] On the other hand, to the extent that
women are limited in their roles by their biologically ascribed status, they will

be unable to incorporate a masculine role. This blurring of the social and the biological in Vietnam representation takes place predominantly through discussions of reproduction. It is just such confusions that enable the appropriation of gender by the masculine, and the derogation of women in warfare to a biologically limited status.

Some of the reasoning behind this paradigm is explained by Judith Hicks Stiehm: "Were women to enter combat, men would lose a crucial identity—warrior. *This is the only role now exclusively theirs,* the one that is as male-defining as child-bearing is female-defining" (emphasis added).[7] As Nancy Hartsock points out in her description of the birth of the *polis* or city-state as an extension of the warrior-role, the exclusion and socialization of reproduction are linked not simply locally but also historically to the role of the male warrior.[8] For this to be masculinity's only exclusively remaining space for identification in modern times marks the reason for the insistent resurgence in Vietnam narratives of confrontations between reproduction and masculinity, confrontations that end with the exclusion of the woman/mother and the appropriation of the tasks of reproduction by the masculine.

In this essay, I want to explore in some detail how that appropriation takes place, particularly how the masculine character assumes to itself the province of reproduction—not biological reproduction, but social, familial, and historical reproduction—principally by claiming for itself the tasks of "birthing" and self-sufficient parenting.[9] Vietnam narratives here provide some of the primary material for a larger cultural argument that is at work throughout current U.S. dominant representational productions. The fathers, both biological and social, of television programs like *My Two Dads, Full House, Who's the Boss?,* and *Paradise,* and the fathering figures of programs such as *The Equalizer* or *J. J. Starbuck* are only the most straightforward examples of a pattern of gender relations that pervades dominant culture representations in the contemporary United States. Fathers or father figures are being shown as taking over and surpassing women in their roles as mothers or maternal models; at the same time, they are maintaining previous masculine qualities and characteristics, that is, maintaining the power affiliated with masculinity in the United States. Further, family sitcom fathers are emblematic of the reappearance of strong paternal images throughout society, most obviously in the political realm, but less obviously in corporate relations, law, advertising, and international affairs. In all of these cases, the masculine appropriation of reproduction works to show not only male characters that have regained control of gender definitions but also a masculinity that is able to "reproduce" itself, apart from challenges by femininity, feminism, or women.

The most logical arena within which to display this control is that over which men in the United States have exclusive domain—combat and warfare. The firmest basis for these arguments in recent years is found in depictions of the Vietnam veteran. As the television miniseries *Amerika* stated most clearly, it is only the Vietnam veteran who retains the values, strength, and will to stand as a fathering figure, not simply within a nuclear family too dominated by women, but for the culture at large, as the hero (Kris Kristofferson) becomes a symbol for culture-wide rebellion against a Soviet system. Recent films present Vietnam veterans as marginal figures—imprisoned (as in *Amerika*, or Rambo [Sylvester Stallone] in *Rambo: First Blood Part II* [1985], or Colonel Braddock [Chuck Norris] as a POW in *Missing in Action* [1984]); living in a mobile home on a beach (Riggs [Mel Gibson] in *Lethal Weapon* [1987]); holed up in a sculpting studio (Wilkes [Fred Ward] in *Uncommon Valor* [1983]); or hospitalized (Luke [John Voight] in *Coming Home* [1978]). Isolated from American culture and saved from its deterioration and feminization, veterans are characterized as able to revitalize a U.S. society that has lost or corrupted its own.

In such terms, the appropriation of reproduction that is narrated in Vietnam films, novels, television, and nonfiction marks the first and most significant step in furthering arguments that reestablish previous relations of difference, especially as they affect gender, race, class, and sexual preference. Because this operation takes place primarily through the incorporation of reproduction into the masculine character, I am focusing here upon the difference of gender; as I will argue, it is principally through the oppositional relations of gender that contemporary dominant U.S. culture is redefining and reinscribing itself.

Reproduction is *the* repressed recognition of Vietnam representation, the topic whose eruption orients the identification of women as the mothers/whores whose appearance requires such violence to control, whose entrance into combat and the masculine collective demands death and silence. Vietnam representation meets this demand in two ways, each an image of the other: first, by identifying the feminine with reproduction and subsequently rejecting and replacing it with the masculine; second, by abstracting and technologizing reproduction as a prelude to its appropriation by the masculine. A reading of three of Vietnam representation's most popular and debated narratives, Michael Cimino's *The Deer Hunter* (1978), Oliver Stone's *Platoon* (1986), and Francis Ford Coppola's *Gardens of Stone* (1987), will illuminate this exclusion and appropriation of reproduction, showing three phases of gendered representations of warfare in recent years: first, the exclusion of women from warfare in favor of the masculine bond; second, the appropriation by the masculine of the feminine role in reproduction, enabling the self-sufficient (re)production of masculinity and the reinstallation of the paternal family; and third, the promotion of a revitalized patriarchal voice that can act as a stabilizing center for a reformation of U.S. society.

THE REPRESSION OF REPRODUCTION IN *THE DEER HUNTER*

Framed by the imagery of masculinity and structured by its bonds, the narrative of *The Deer Hunter* tells the story not of the war in Vietnam but of gender. The feminine scenes of the wedding are explored in such detail in order to have them rejected so thoroughly by the scenes of masculine bonding that dominate later sequences in Vietnam. The first half of the film revolves

The feminine scenes of the wedding are explored in such detail in order to have them rejected so thoroughly by the scenes of masculine bonding.

around the promise of reproduction—the child that Angela is carrying and whose identity is so crucial to the narrative's progress. The second half revolves around that which denies reproduction, the promise of the masculine bond. The structure of the film rotates around the one figure—Nick (Christopher Walken)—who links the two experiences of reproduction and warfare, of feminine and masculine bonding.

Nick's graphically violent death is an indication of the stance *The Deer Hunter* takes toward men who attempt to balance these two worlds. His is the point at which gender is made manifest because he is part of both the masculine and the feminine promise, having made a pact with Michael (Robert DeNiro) to "not leave me over there" as well as a proposal of marriage to Linda (Meryl Streep). His own sexuality mimics the ambivalence of his position. He is, on the one hand, fulfilling the demands of masculinity by going to fight in a war, yet, on the other, linking himself to the feminine through Linda and Angela.[10] In addition, while heterosexually defined through his link to Linda, Nick is also the most "feminine" of the male friends. His dancing in the bar is a type of erotic display in male company, in which he becomes the "feminine" object of Michael's stationary gaze, as Michael sits and watches from his bar stool.

Nick's position in relation to the oppositional structure of the masculine and feminine in *The Deer Hunter* might seem at first to be a deconstruction of that polarity offered by the film. Resting in neither the masculine nor feminine worlds, Nick's character and function in the narrative appear to take on the quality of what Jacques Derrida calls the "sexual otherwise," the point at which gender distinctions no longer determine meaning.[11] But the overt presentation and punishment of Nick in the film suggest that such androgynous positions are not only destructive but must themselves be destroyed. Rather than deconstructing or in any way challenging gender oppositions, Nick's ambivalence and death assure their continuation.

Nick's feminine position in relation to Michael is so pronounced that it prompted Robin Wood to propose a reading of *The Deer Hunter* in which the tension of the film is not that of reproduction but of homosexuality. In his reading, "Nick both is *and knows himself to be* in love with Mike and Mike reciprocates that love but can't admit it, even to himself."[12] Wood closes his reading with a plea for a resolution of the tension between the masculine and feminine that takes on an almost transcendental tone: "The problem [of the repression of bisexuality and the oppression of women] . . . can only be resolved when the boundaries of gender construction become so blurred that men can move with ease, and without inhibition, into identification with a female position."[13] But I would suggest that Nick's ambivalent relation to the promises of masculinity and femininity does not constitute a moving beyond the categories of gender, but merely a blurring of them, a maneuver to avoid—both filmically and critically—the threat of reproduction.

The flaw in Wood's "solution" lies at the heart of his overreading of *The Deer Hunter*; more importantly, it is the nexus for Vietnam narrative's response to reproduction. Most important both for Wood's reading and for a study of Vietnam narratives is that Wood depicts this desired change in gender structures *from the point of view of the masculine*. It is because Wood does not interrogate this point of view that he accepts unquestioningly the male-male relationship as the center of meaning in *The Deer Hunter*.[14] He, like the films and narratives of Vietnam, represses the matrix of reproduction in favor of the masculine bond. Wood's desire to "blur" the lines of gender is the hidden secret of Vietnam narratives: to confuse the categories of gender by asserting the masculine colonization of the territory of reproduction.

FATHERS, NOT MOTHERS—*PLATOON*

Platoon takes up where *The Deer Hunter* left off, beginning with and assuming the establishment of the masculine bond. *Platoon* then posits out of this bond the production of the masculine subject as "the child of two fathers," thereby bringing the narration of reproduction to the point where women are not only repressed but replaced as parents. With women effectively eliminated from the arena of warfare and the masculine bond confirmed as the new "family," reproduction can now be taken over by men as the province of the self-sufficient father. This is "Viet Nam, the way it really was."[15]

Platoon . . . posits out of this [masculine] bond the production of the masculine subject as "the child of two fathers."

Like so many other Vietnam narratives, *Platoon* depends upon the eradication of difference through the institution of the masculine bond during wartime, what Broyles calls "brotherly love," a "love" that "transcends race and personality and education."[16] But while *Platoon* disrupts barriers between blacks and whites, lower and upper classes, Southerners, New Yorkers, and Californians, the film establishes other lines of difference, ones that do not depend upon social structures from the "World" but upon a "new" set of values belonging to the "Nam," values defined along lines of gender difference.

Chris Taylor's introduction to the "underworld" of the bunker is cross-cut with scenes of the "outerworld" populated by other soldiers. Those in the underworld smoke dope, laugh, dance together, and seem to share a common vision of the war and its significance. Their closeness and shared activity make their bond not only indiscriminate but erotic as well, with the men's bodies framed by the small bunker that surrounds them. The leader of this world is Sergeant Elias, whose approach to Taylor in the underworld is laden with erotic connotations. After Taylor takes his first toke, Elias appears out of the haze and asks, "First time?" He then holds a rifle up to Taylor, saying "Put you mouth on this," after which Elias blows smoke through the rifle barrel into Taylor's mouth. In spite of *Time* phrasing this a "fraternal toke,"[17] this act signals Taylor's virgin initiation into an underworld defined by homoerotic masculine bonds.

In contrast to the underworld, race is a source only of tension in the outerworld, where Junior calls Bunny's music "honky shit" but will not enter the underworld to hear Motown with other blacks. The erotic as well is handled differently here. Bunny is biting pieces out of beer cans, while delivering comments on the relative desirability of women: "Ain't nothing like a piece of pussy, 'cept maybe the Indy 500." In this heterosexual eroticism, differences that separate men are emphasized rather than overcome. There is no body contact, no intimacy; there is only violence (when asked to join a card game, Lieutenant Wolfe replies, "Wouldn't want to get raped by you guys"). The voice of authority in this world is not the seductive Elias but the death-decreeing Barnes, the alternate figure in the battle for Taylor's soul.

Time tries to analyze this battle in the frame of good and evil and comes up empty: "Has [Taylor] become Barnes in order to kill him? . . . A good man, and a murderer? It is . . . a mark of Stone's complexity that he can argue either side and believe both."[18] Stone and his film seem to maintain *both* good and evil in Taylor's character, making it unclear who really "wins" the battle for his soul. And surrounding this confusion over the central tension of the film is its overall meaning, whether it should be interpreted as pro- or antiwar, for or against violence, as justifying and supporting American involvement in Vietnam or condemning it.[19]

Reading *Platoon* through a gendered perspective produces an interpretation of the film that cuts through these confusions to a more systematic and coherent thematic it shares with other Vietnam representations. If, as the film's early scenes of difference suggest, the battle between Elias and Barnes—between what is called good and evil in the film—is a confrontation of the feminine and the masculine, then Barnes's murder of Elias is a direct attempt to eliminate these feminine qualities from the arena of Vietnam. Taylor's subsequent murder of Barnes would seem then to be a clear reinstatement of the feminine over and against the masculine, with Taylor assuming Elias's role in this struggle. But Taylor's final soliloquy denies such a simplistic reading, as he says, "Elias is in me and so is Barnes. . . . I felt like a child born of two fathers." By killing Barnes, Taylor ends the film, not in the position of the masculine *or* the feminine, but in both. Can't this be seen as a rejection of the limitations of masculinity and femininity and a move toward an alternate gender formation?

I think not. The answer lies in the fact that while Taylor incorporates Elias's femininity and attitude toward the war into his final character, he uses Barnes's methods to do so. Where Elias stood passively when Barnes held the rifle to kill him, Taylor acts as Barnes did to murder Barnes himself. He must become Barnes—the masculine—in order to successfully create a space in which he can be "born" as the masculine/feminine child. In Rhah's words, "Only Barnes can kill Barnes." But more significantly, Taylor's character is not androgynous because Stone presents in *Platoon* the same kind of structure offered by Wood, one that enables men to occupy "with ease, and without inhibition" the position of the feminine. This movement is seen in *Platoon*, as in Wood, only from a masculine point of view, one that allows the masculine to incorporate the feminine into itself, not to become the feminine, but to ingest it, as a means of (re)producing its own character.

Taylor's confession that "he felt like a child born of two fathers" stands metaphorically in *Platoon*'s dialogue, but its literal meaning is equally accurate and indicative of the gendered frame promoted by this and other Vietnam films. He has no mother in the film, but only two fathers, is (re)produced by two men. He goes to war to be "like grandpa in World War I and dad in World War II." Films like *Platoon* work out representationally what Gena Corea identifies as technologies whereby "fathers can be, or appear to be, the sole parent," scenarios in which men can be the "child of two fathers," and women and the feminine are eliminated or absorbed into the positions of masculine or of father.[20]

Because both Elias and Barnes are incorporated into Taylor's character through the masculine point of view, the good and evil they represent are finally not challenges to masculinity itself but a reaffirmation of its powers to appropriate difference into its own character. In such terms, the possibility for a "good" that is defined outside the frame of the masculine being presented in this film is very remote. At the same time, because of its expansive plot structure and its far-reaching themes, *Platoon* presents itself as addressing issues not only of war but of life itself. What this film suggests then is that these issues can finally be resolved only through a masculine frame, a resolution born, like Chris Taylor, "of two fathers."

The "misunderstanding" that Corliss sees as the interpretive product of *Platoon*, so that antithetical meanings seem to be simultaneously and appropriately produced, is not so much a misunderstanding as a misdirection, in which blurred categories prevent us from recognizing the film's basis of meaning. Out of this sea of "misunderstanding," Stone sends forth the veterans of this war, who "have an obligation to teach others what we know." But what Stone's veterans teach is not truth, not justice, not good, not even how to win a war, but that "meaning to this life," Taylor's final desire, is to be found only within the frame of men, inside the platoon.

PATERNALISM IN *GARDENS OF STONE*

The final stage in this strategy of masculine (re)production is best seen in Francis Ford Coppola's *Gardens of Stone* (1987), a film that shows not the "birth" of the father in combat but the "duty" of the father at home. Though set during the time of the Vietnam War, *Gardens of Stone* shows no combat, taking place entirely within and around Washington, D.C., as decorated Vietnam veteran Clel Hazard (James Caan) uses his assignment to the Old Guard Regiment at Arlington National Cemetery to prepare young men for what they will see in the war. These preparations find them battling not the Vietcong but the bureaucracy and inefficiency of the military and political systems. Clearly, in the language of this film, the young men Clel Hazard oversees are being prepared not for the war but for the battles that take place back in the "World."

Clel's position as father in this film is specified not in relation to his own daughter, who is grown and separated from him, as is his divorced wife now in a mental institution, but in relation to his troops, particularly the young Jack

Clell's position as father . . . is specified . . . in relation to his troops.

Willow, a new recruit who is on his way to Vietnam. Hazard, a friend of Willow's father, becomes Jack's sole parenting figure when Willow, Senior, dies early in the film of a heart attack.[21] Emblematic of Hazard's fathering role with other young soldiers, Willow's growing idolization and emulation of Hazard marks this as the key relationship of the film.

In contrast, the significance of male-female relations in *Gardens of Stone* lies in their reference to reproduction. None of the women in the film has children: Clel's fiancée, Sam Davies, is sterile; and Willow's new bride, Rachel, widowed when Jack dies in war, will have no children by him. Even Betty Rae Williams, wife of Clel's closest friend, Sergeant Major Homer "Goody" Williams (James Earl Jones), is metaphorically denied reproductive possibility through a crude joke recited in the film's opening scenes. During an inspection of the barracks, Goody asks recruits sexually explicit questions to embarrass them. When Goody asks Willow, "How do worms copulate? Willow replies, "Asexual reproduction." Goody continues, "Who first came up with that idea?" and Willow answers, "Your wife, sir?"[22]

The film places women's relations to reproduction only in the realms of sterility and asexuality. Negating women's reproductive capacities, the close of the film leaves the territory of reproduction entirely to men, who seem to have the only functional relations to (re)producing children. Though Clel's daughter is not seen, he writes to her; the mother is, presumably, unable to communicate with her daughter due to her mental imbalance (only a crazy woman would have left this man). And Willow, whose father dies during the film and is replaced by Hazard, has no mother alive during the film; she died much earlier. Only men in this film actually have relations to children; women have been shown unable to have them; and the clearly significant relations in the film—Hazard–Willow, Hazard–Goody—are all between men.

What we have here and in all of these films is an arena in which the family is composed either exclusively or significantly of fathers, not mothers, and relations between fathers and sons, not daughters. Fathers are shown in each case to be not only the key parenting figures for the nuclear family but the primary examples of parenting for the social family. Their position is, like that of Clel Hazard, to "teach others what we know," to reshape a sterile and insane family that had been dominated by women into a firm and stable family guided by men.

THE PRODUCTION OF FATHERS

The appropriation of reproduction by the masculine, according to Gena Corea, is generated by the life-death boundary tension foregrounded in war narrative: to conquer the barrier of death through the creation of immortality by continuous self-production. Epitomized in projects like cloning and artificial wombs is what Corea describes as "the patriarchal urge to give birth to onself, to be one's own mother, and to live forever," so that "the desire to control birth through the reproductive technologies, then, is also a desire to control death."[23]

By inserting themselves into the birth process, Vietnam's narrators endeavor to gain control over the moment of reproduction through technology and thereby to control death. In doing so, they must eliminate women from the birth process—and from war—altogether. This battle with death is thus not a cooperative but a competitive one, one that, as Robyn Rowland suggests, centers on power itself: "with the possibilities offered by technology [men] are storming the last bastion [of women's power] and taking control of conception, foetal development, and birth."[24] In such terms, the foregrounding of technology in Vietnam narration marks the cultural force of these representations—to respond to the anxieties of the boundary between life and death by repressing and repossessing those who have been traditionally assigned the social, cultural, and biological power over that realm—women and the femininity that has come to be associated with them.[25] In Vietnam narratives, the masculine gives birth to itself as a technologized body in which the individual is an extension of the equipment he carries (Sylvester Stallone says of Rambo that "he's a perfect killing machine"), a body that not only defies death but incorporates—*embodies*—the very means by which death itself is to be conquered.

Vietnam narration interposes itself at the point of (re)production, generating the birth of the masculine subject, apart from the mother, *self-delivered*. It is far more significant to the (re)production of the masculine that its character can be produced during war, so that the arena of the masculine and the masculine character can be joined together and not separated as they might be if that character were to continue to be associated only with "home" or "career" or "fraternity." The bonds of other masculinities are drawn together and redefined to encompass these diverse personalities so that in Vietnam representation, the masculine subject *as subject* is (re)produced.

It is to this end that Vietnam representation narrates the appropriation of reproduction by the masculine character, not simply to negate a traditional role of social power for women, or to create a "feminized" male hero, but to establish a masculine character who can incorporate into a revitalized figure of masculine consciousness the capacities to (re)produce itself, a figure that has been salvaged from feminism by the socially isolated Vietnam veteran. Through this role, gender positions are being restructured and restabilized in such a way as to reassert the primacy of the masculine point of view in determining definitions of difference.

While space does not permit a full discussion of the consequences of such developments in the United States, I would like to suggest briefly a few ways in which these narratives are relevant to an understanding of some of the operations of contemporary U.S. culture. Films like *Lethal Weapon* (1987) and *Rambo III* (1988) display this new Vietnam veteran as not only stronger than his old image but more active as well. It is no accident that the regeneration of the Vietnam veteran as father figure coincides with a resurgence of violent action films in recent years, many with the Vietnam veteran at their center. A major sector of dominant cinema is currently presenting images of masculinity that are equated with the ability to act, and this most often violently. In most cases, such abilities are posed as counter to the narrative's institutional strengths—often represented by women—as the ability to repress action or the inability to decide how or when to act. Examples include *The Big Easy*, *Lethal Weapon*, *Rambo III*, *Robocop*, *Die Hard*, and numerous others.

Such narratives of action intertwine with narratives of fathers not only by reinforcing images of decisive and active father figures who are able to protect and reunite a frayed domestic scenario, but by infantilizing viewers as well, putting us all in the position of regarding these strong and thriving men as our own ideal social fathers. Feeling unable to accomplish such "missions" themselves, concerned about not protecting their own domestic arena, and sensing the alienation from consequential action that is a thesis of postmodern cultural production, viewers of these films are positioned to look up to these men as hopeful reconstructions of the failed fathers of their own domestic scenarios.

While feminist film theorists would counter that such positioning is at best ambivalent for female viewers who would have a different relation to such narration,[26] I would argue here that contemporary dominant cinema is constructing an alternate subject position that, through infantilization, may be more gender neutral[27] than and would fix historically the male gaze identified by Laura Mulvey in dominant cinema of the 1950s and '60s.[28] The idolizing and idealizing gaze of the camera as it watches Rambo is quite distinct from the male gaze of the camera identified by Mulvey that objectifies women in classic filmic narrative.[29] This gaze does not fix Rambo by viewing him *from* a position of power and control—from a male viewpoint—but by gazing at him as if he *were* the source of power and control himself (as Rambo's Afghan guide explains of a woman's gaze at Rambo, "They're not used to seeing men like him"). Through infantilization, the viewer is made to feel the helplessness of the child in the face of the dominant father,[30] a paradigm essential to the reproduction of patriarchal social constructions.[31]

In such terms, the ending of *Lethal Weapon* becomes paradigmatic of this new phase of Vietnam films.[32] After protecting the daughter and family of his partner from violent criminals, Riggs, formerly viewed in his isolated mobile home, is invited to his partner's home for dinner. The film closes upon a shot of Riggs and his partner walking up the sidewalk to the front door of a middle-class suburban home. These narratives thus record that the Vietnam veteran has finally "come home," not as a soldier of a distant war but as the savior of the American family he has "come home" to protect. And we, positioned as the children anxious for the return of his protection, are to invite him in.

NOTES

1. John Wheeler, *Touched with Fire: The Future of the Vietnam Generation* (New York: Avon, 1984), pp. 140–141.

2. William Broyles, Jr., *Brothers in Arms: A Journey from War to Peace* (New York: Knopf, 1986), p. 201.

3. William Eastlake, *The Bamboo Bed* (New York: Avon, 1969), pp. 249, 85.

4. Broyles, *Brothers in Arms*, pp. 61, 56. There are numerous cases of men who did not fight in combat in the Vietnam War—whether through draft deferral, draft avoidance, or having a noncombat position in the military—who state that they regret this condition. See Christopher Buckley, "Viet Guilt," *Esquire*, August 1983, pp. 68–72, or James Fallows, "What Did You Do in the Class War, Daddy?", in Grace Jevy, ed., *The American Experience in Vietnam: A Reader* (Norman: Okla.: Oklahoma University Press, 1989), along with Fallows's comments in Myra MacPherson, *Long Time Passing: Vietnam and the Haunted Generation* (New York: Signet, 1984), p. 180. On the other side, there are some feminist writers whose assertions about the significance of childbirth for women sound remarkably like the claims Broyles wishes to make for warfare and men. Sheila Kitzinger says, for example, in *The Experience of Childbirth*, that "The experience of bearing a child is central to a woman's life. . . . It is unlikely that any experience in a man's life is comparably vivid" (Harmondsworth, England: Penguin, 1974), p. 17.

5. Nicole-Claude Mathieu, "Biological Paternity, Social Maternity," *Feminist Issues* 4, no. 1 (Spring 1984): 63–72.

6. I will distinguish throughout this essay between "men" and the "masculine." Clearly, there are qualities of masculinity as it is socially defined in the United States that are not shared by all men, and individual men may choose to reject or feel ambivalent about many of those qualities, and/or may choose to adopt what are generally recognized as "feminine" characteristics.

7. Judith Hicks Stiehm, *Bring Me Men and Women: Mandated Change at the U.S. Air Force Academy* (Berkeley and Los Angeles: University of California Press, 1981), p. 296.

8. Nancy Hartsock, *Money, Sex, and Power: Toward a Feminist Historical Materialism* (Boston: Northeastern University Press, 1983). While Hartsock interprets this appropriation in terms of the masculine control of creativity and rhetoric (p. 197), I am emphasizing here the much more literal appropriation of reproduction itself.

9. Though such an appropriation would seem impossible, recent cultural narrations have been presenting it as more and more plausible. In *Enemy Mine* (1985), a film about an "androgynous" lizardlike alien creature, the actor who portrays the alien, Lou Gossett, Jr., has such a deeply "male" voice that his subsequent admission that he is pregnant seems less a sign of androgyny than of a pregnant male. That the baby is delivered by caesarean is in keeping with any possible male reproduction. In the premier episode of *St. Elsewhere*'s 1987 season, a Vietnam veteran not only believed he was pregnant but convinced some of the young doctors of it as well. In an acted-out "birthing," he "delivers" a memory of killing a child in Vietnam. Neatly, his wife becomes pregnant at the same time, as if to carry out "his" pregnancy.

10. In *The Remasculinization of America: Gender and the Vietnam War* (Bloomington: Indiana University Press, 1989), I have argued that Nick is the father of Angela's child. See specifically chapter 3 for further discussions of reproduction and the Vietnam War.

11. Jacques Derrida, "Choreographies," *Diacritics* 12, no. 2 (1982):76.

12. Robin Wood, *Hollywood From Vietnam to Reagan* (New York: Columbia University Press, 1986), p. 294.

13. Ibid., p. 291.

14. Linda Dittmar points out an interesting irony here, that the intended argument of Wood's book—to challenge singly heterosexual definitions of masculinity and to uncover homosexual and bisexual subtexts—is compromised by his failure to question a masculine point of view within which his alternate readings take place.

15. Richard Corliss, "*Platoon*: Viet Nam, The Way it Really Was, On Film," *Time*, 26 January 1987, pp. 54–61.

16. Broyles, *Brothers in Arms*, p. 58.

17. Corliss, "*Platoon*," p. 57.

18. Ibid., p. 59.

19. Richard Sklar's collection of critical responses to *Platoon* reveals similar ambivalences ("*Platoon* on Inspection: A Critical Symposium," *Cineaste* 15, no. 4 [1987]: 4–9).

20. Gena Corea, *The Mother Machine: Reproductive Technologies from Artificial Insemination to Artificial Wombs* (New York: Harper and Row, 1985), pp. 292–293.

21. This displacement of the father marks an important distinction between World War II combat films and films of the post-Vietnam era. As Jeanine Basinger says of *Sands of Iwo Jima* (1949), where Sergeant Stryker (John Wayne) becomes a father figure to a young private (played by John Agar), "Wayne then becomes the father that Agar needs to become a man. This does not constitute displacement of the real father, since Wayne himself was created by that same father in military terms [Agar's father was Stryker's commanding officer], if not biological ones" (*The World War II Combat Film: Anatomy of a Genre* [New York: Columbia University Press, 1986], p. 165).

22. It is important to note that this exchange, in the context of reproduction, must be read as a joke. The threat of a female power, especially black female power, as independent reproduction—asexual and therefore without males—would be too great to assert in any other context.

23. Corea, *The Mother Machine*, pp. 262–263.

24. Robyn Rowland, "Reproductive Technologies: The Final Solution to the Woman Question?," in Rita Arditti, Renate Klein, and Sally Minden, eds., *Test-Tube Women: What Future for Motherhood?* (Boston: Pandora, 1984), p. 363.

25. The many popular discussions of male disposability in the reproductive process as a result of technologization (metaphorized in *Rambo* as "expendability") are merely the flip side of this logic, not an alternative to it.

26. See, for example, Teresa de Lauretis, *Alice Doesn't* (Bloomington: Indiana University Press, 1984), especially chapter 5.

27. I want to distinguish this argument from E. Ann Kaplan's *Rocking Around the Clock* (New York: Methuen, 1987), in which she suggests that there are certain MTV videos that present what she calls a "maternal gaze," a gaze that is pre-Oedipal and therefore not gender-identified. Her argument is limited to the televisual and may not be transferrable to large-screen cinema. By gender neutral I do not mean that the process of infantilization in fact operates identically upon male and female viewers, but that the viewer is positioned as nongendered rather than male.

28. See Laura Mulvey, "Visual Pleasure and Narrative Cinema," *Screen* 16, no. 3 (Autumn 1975); 6–18.

29. The idolizing gaze directed toward the male hero is not to be confused with the "male" gaze of the camera directed at such figures as Nick in *The Deer Hunter*, where Nick's body is objectified in the bar scene as if he were female.

30. I am speaking here of the socially constructed relations between child and father in dominant U.S. culture, For a further discussion of the father/son dynamic in U.S. culture, see Jeffords, "Masculinity as Excess in Vietnam Films: The Father/Son Dynamic of American Culture," *Genre* 21, no. 4 (Winter 1988): 487–517.

31. These discussions of fathers, reproduction, and dominant cultural representation of the domestic are appropriate only to a dominant white culture in the United States. Cultural interpretations of domestic relations are shaped in significant ways by issues of race as well as gender and would produce differently specific analyses than those offered here. For a discussion of these issues, see Hortense Spillers, "Mama's Baby, Papa's Maybe: An American Grammar Hilen," *Diacritics* 17, no. 4 (Summer 1987): 65–81.

32. For an excellent discussion of the intersections of race and gender in this film, see Robyn Weigman, "Negotiating AMERICA: Gender, Race and the Ideology of the Interracial Male Bond," *Cultural Critique* (forthcoming).

14

MARTIN F. NORDEN

Portrait of a Disabled Vietnam
Veteran: Alex Cutter
of Cutter's Way

One of the most engaging aspects of *Cutter's Way* (1981) is its refusal to be obvious about its concerns. The film revolves around a disabled Vietnam veteran but pays only minimal attention to his rehabilitative process and the Vietnam War per se. Its surface story exhibits the trappings of a murder mystery, but the identity of the killer remains unresolved by film's end. It embodies sexist views (most notably, that men are the decision-makers and action-takers while women are the powerless victims) yet poses a critique of those views. It features the time-honored convention of a hero fighting against social injustice but confounds that tradition by employing a highly unconventional protagonist with questionable motives and maintaining a deliberate vagueness about the nature of the injustice. These ambiguities, which haunted the film during its production and initial distribution history, contribute directly to one of the film's greatest strengths: its evocation of the conflicting senses of deep-seated cynicism, noncommittal complacency, and moral uncertainty that characterized the post-Vietnam American landscape.[1] The process by which *Cutter's Way* reveals these qualities is complex, however, and continues to pose a challenge for audiences and critics alike.

Since so much of *Cutter's Way* rotates around Alex Cutter and his "way" of making sense of—and acting upon—the morally murky world around him, I propose to devote the majority of this essay to an analysis of his character. Two long-standing Hollywood stereotypes of physically disabled people define his character to some degree, but, as we shall see, the whole of Alex is considerably greater than the sum of several clichéd character types. My hope is that this investigation of stereotypes and the combination of attributes and contexts that ultimately sets Alex apart from the stereotypes will provide a better understanding of a film just as quirky and elusive as the disabled Vietnam veteran at its center.

Written by Jeffrey Alan Fiskin (who based his script on Newton Thornburg's critically lauded novel *Cutter and Bone*) and directed by Ivan Passer, *Cutter's Way* tells the story of two unlikely friends who live in Santa Barbara: Alex Cutter III (John Heard) and Rich Bone (Jeff Bridges). Alex, who lost an eye, an arm, and a leg in Vietnam, is alternately witty and foul-mouthed. He is self-destructive, as evidenced by his constant smoking, heavy drinking, and quickness to antagonize everyone around him. He thinks nothing of insulting several blacks in a bar early in the film, for example. When they back off after his able-bodied friend Rich intervenes by mentioning that Alex was in the war, Alex in turn directs his hostility toward his would-be defender, an athletic "golden boy" and part-time gigolo who sells pleasure boats for a living. Indeed, Alex berates Rich throughout the movie. For instance, Alex tells Rich not to lecture him on morality by pointing out that he was getting shot up in Vietnam while Rich was getting laid in the Ivy League. The bland, non-committal Rich and the sardonic, passionate Alex make a fascinating study in contrasts. When they eventually work together to unravel a murder mystery in their hometown it is as if two sides of a single personality have united.

The basis for Alex and Rich's friendship is one of the film's several ambiguities. The movie never reveals any shared history other than the fact that George Swanson (Arthur Rosenberg), who grew up with Alex, happens to be Rich's boss at the pleasure boat company, and that Alex's depressed wife, Mo (Lisa Eichhorn), knows Rich very well. Apart from their social marginality within the Santa Barbara milieu, the characters appear to have little in common.

As a disabled Vietnam veteran, Alex shares an obvious similarity with two other movie vets: Luke of *Coming Home* (1978) and Stevie of *The Deer Hunter* (1978). A sense of differing agendas begins to emerge, however, after examining the ways that the three disabled vets respond to civilian life. In what may be a yearning for the moral simplicity of World War II, the makers of *The Deer Hunter* simply and quietly reintegrate Stevie into his western Pennsylvania society after he has overcome initial adjustment problems, none of which concerned his sense of the morality of the war. *Coming Home* shows Luke seething with rage and eventually channeling that rage to a larger purpose: protesting the war through symbolic acts and speeches. Alex exhibits the same kind of anger and frustration, but, unlike Luke, he does not expressly protest the war. He comes off as restless, bored, and rudderless. As initially portrayed in *Cutter's Way*, Alex is all passion and no purpose.

A way of finding a context for these conflicting images of disabled Vietnam veterans is to compare them with a Hollywood stereotype that achieved prominence thirty years before: the Noble Warrior. During the final years of World War II and throughout the decade following the conflict, Hollywood produced a mini-genre of films that dealt with the plight of returning veterans and was very much a part of Hollywood's great age of social consciousness.[2] These films frequently featured disabled vets as main or supporting characters, including *Pride of the Marines* (1945), *The Best Years of Our Lives* (1946), *Till the End of Time* (1946), *Home of the Brave* (1949), *The Men* (1951), *Bright Victory* (1951), *Bad Day at Black Rock* (1954), and *The Eternal Sea* (1955). The portions of these films that deal with the disabled veterans focus mainly on the vets' psychological conflicts, readjustment problems, and ultimate rehabilitation leading up to their successful reentry into civilian life. As an example, *The Best Years of Our Lives* presents a vet who lost both hands in the war (Harold Russell) as one of three ex-military men who find the road to readjustment a bit rocky although, with the support of family and friends, ultimately maneuverable. *Best Years* and the other films of its vintage spend considerable time studying the processes by which their Noble Warriors

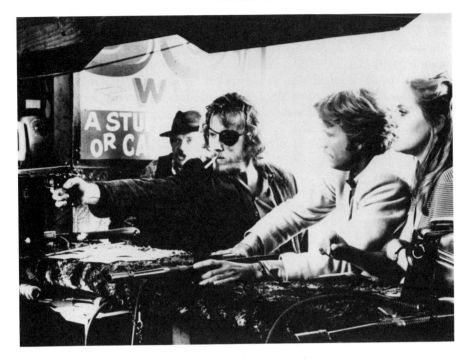

As initially portrayed in Cutter's Way, *Alex is all passion and no purpose.*

eventually overcome difficulties before getting on with their new day-to-day lives.

These World War II–era "problem pictures" differ from *Cutter's Way* and other films featuring veterans disabled by the Vietnam War in a number of respects, all which revolve around the notion of heroism. Hollywood filmmakers of the day predicated the Noble Warrior stereotype on the belief that World War II veterans were heroes and should be rewarded for their sacrifices and struggles. These ex-soldiers automatically wore a mantle of heroism as a result of having participated in a "good" and "just" war, and the movies, in their eagerness to prove that the vets' heroic status was no fluke, show the vets demonstrating their mettle by triumphing over readjustment problems and helping family and friends overcome any misgivings they might have about being around a person with a physical disability. After the vets score these final victories, the movies conclude with the implication that the good life in America awaits them.

Unlike their World War II peers, whose heroic status was never in doubt, the veterans of Vietnam returned home to experience something far different than a hero's welcome; they were greeted instead with alternating rounds of hostility and indifference. Harold Russell, the disabled World War II serviceman who won an Academy Award for his performance in *The Best Years of Our Lives*, echoed this observation in relation to society's tolerance of people with disabilities: "Unlike past wars—Vietnam and Korea—World

War II veterans came home as heroes. So it's a strange thing; while a disability was not [normally] acceptable in the minds of American people, the fact that you were a disabled veteran made you acceptable."[3] The Vietnam films presenting disabled vets eschew the World War II heroic portrayals in favor of characterizing the vets either as ordinary people quietly integrated into a society that barely acknowledges their service in Vietnam or as social misfits who exude moral indignation. Stevie, who comes the closest of the disabled Vietnam vets to matching the Noble Warrior stereotype, merely dissolves into his circle of friends; Luke goes on to become a hero of a different sort by marshaling his energies to protest the war. Alex shares Luke's passion but not his purpose, and his portrayal is finally at odds with that of other disabled vets, regardless of the war in which they fought.

The point at which Fiskin and Passer decided to begin their story provides a key to understanding their regard for their decidedly different vet and the world he inhabits. Unlike the Noble Warrior films as well as *Coming Home* and *The Deer Hunter*, *Cutter's Way* begins after its disabled veteran has been released from the VA hospital and after he and the people around him have come to terms with his new life as a disabled person. The lateness of this point of attack suggests that the filmmakers had something else on their minds besides wanting to explore their character's ability to cope with new day-to-day challenges. Though the movie frequently reminds us that Alex is indeed a physically disabled person (film critic Stanley Kauffmann described him as "a hobbling, hot-mouthed, ever-present reminder of past American sins"),[4] the heroic struggle to overcome quotidian problems so much at the heart of the Noble Warrior films is curiously incidental in *Cutter's Way*.

By starting the film after the disabled vet has already begun his post-rehabilitative life, the makers of *Cutter's Way* are in a better position to pursue another agenda: exposing society's shift in attitudes toward its disabled veterans. What they reveal is unsettling, to say the least; the promise of the "good life" that concludes so many of the Noble Warrior films is nothing more than a cruel hoax in the post-Vietnam era. The film shows Alex as a cynic and an alcoholic who tries to mask his bitterness by turning everything into a joke and, as Leonard Quart and Albert Auster have noted, manages to make his way through an uncaring world by using his wounds to manipulate others.[5]

Alex eventually finds a purpose toward which he can divert his pent-up energy and rage, and it forms the main focus of the film's surface story: solving the brutal murder of a sodomized high school cheerleader, whose body the filmmakers visualized along the lines of a classic Hitchcockian fetish-object: a pair of high-heel-shod feet sticking up out of a back-alley trash can near Rich's parked car. Rich reluctantly becomes involved in the murder investigation by telling the police that he had seen a shadowy figure wearing sunglasses dumping what turned out to be the woman's body in the trash can that midnight. Alex becomes fascinated with the case and starts working with Rich and Valerie Duran (Ann Dusenberry), the dead woman's sister, to put the pieces together. Alex's interest becomes acute when Rich later sees a horseback rider in a local parade and says, "That looks like the guy I saw at the trash can." Ironically, it is Alex and not Rich who immediately identifies the imperious man on horseback: J. J. Cord (Stephen Elliott), a multimillionaire oilman whose corporation owns the boat company that employs Rich.

Rich and Valerie's reasons for wanting to solve the murder are simple and straightforward; Rich wants to get out from under the thumb of the police and return to his casual lifestyle, while Valerie wants to see justice served. Alex's reasons are more complex, however, and are really at the heart of the movie.

First, Alex wants to be a hero, a status that mainstream America never bestowed on him following his return from Vietnam. He makes his position clear as he explains his desire to get involved:

> ALEX: The world lacks heroes, Rich.
> RICH: I don't want to be one.
> ALEX: (*As he removes his shirt, revealing his severed arm*) It's got nothing to do with you. You never wanted to be one.

True to his service background, Alex sees his heroic quest to ensnare Cord in terms of a military campaign. As he, Rich, and Valerie make plans to enter Cord's corporate headquarters to deliver a blackmail note, Alex talks of being "on point" and venturing into "Purple Heart land." Lest any viewer miss the point, the filmmakers have Rich affirm Alex's desire to George: "He feels the world's short of heroes. He's trying to fill the gap."

In addition, the perspective that Alex takes is considerably broader than Rich or Valerie's. He wants to do something about the immorality of people in high positions of power, particularly the way they manipulate and then toss aside vulnerable people like so much litter. Alex insists that Cord is not just responsible for the young woman's death; instead, he and other corporate bigwigs are responsible for the world's problems—problems that affect countless numbers of disadvantaged people but never the powermongers themselves. Alex does not specifically mention Vietnam in this context, but the implication is clear.

Alex's deeply felt desire to be a hero leads us to the other—and considerably darker—Hollywood stereotype that informs his character to some extent. It is not nearly as well known to modern audiences as the Noble Warrior, but its similarities to Alex are too conspicuous to be ignored: the Obsessive Avenger. A dominant movie image of physically disabled people made popular by actor Lon Chaney and director Tod Browning during the 1920s and early 1930s, the Obsessive Avenger is an egomaniacal sort who does not rest until he has had revenge on those he holds responsible for disabling him and/or violating his moral code in some other way. Frequently, his vengeful actions are misdirected; by the end of the film, he and the audience often learn that he has targeted his wrath at an innocent person. Lest the Obsessive Avenger escape their own moral code unscathed, the filmmakers almost inevitably show him perishing as a result of his error in judgment.[6]

Since the Obsessive Avenger and the focus of his anger are almost always male, we can perhaps read the Avenger's disability in terms of a symbolic castration; a prominent, older male has disempowered the main character, and in a distinctly Oedipal act of hostility—and one absolutely reeking of machismo—the Obsessive Avenger seeks to reclaim his manhood by relentlessly pursuing the person presumed to have committed the disabling act with the intent of exacting revenge.

In spite of the obvious fact that the Obsessive Avenger lacks the political context of the Vietnam experience, Alex matches the stereotype in a number of important respects. He holds the oilman responsible for numerous acts that violated his moral code: the deaths of the teenager and his own wife, Mo (the former dies from a cracked skull and crushed trachea after being sexually abused, while the latter is charred to a cinder in a suspicious blaze that burns the Cutter house to the ground), as well as the exploitation and abuse of relatively powerless people such as himself. In a manner similar to his filmic predecessors, Alex's desire to bring down the patriarchal figure escalates into a full-blown obsession. The machismo with which Alex pursues Cord is so strong that it occasionally lapses into misogyny; for example, when Rich and Valerie decide to go sailing instead of helping Alex with his quest to get Cord, Alex pointedly calls after them, "Have fun, girls," implying that "girls" run away from responsibility while "men" face up to it. Finally, Alex may well have directed his vengeful actions toward the wrong person—the film never provides substantive proof of Cord's culpability—and he does die as a result of his quest. (Indeed, Alex is one of Hollywood's exceedingly few disabled war veterans—perhaps the only one—who dies from something other than war-related injuries.)

An important literary antecedent for Hollywood's Obsessive Avenger is Captain Ahab of *Moby Dick*, and the makers of *Cutter's Way* were quite conscious of the Melville novel and the famous obsession that drives it.[7] Alex's utterance of "Thar she blows!" on seeing Cord's corporate headquarters is one of the film's several references to *Moby Dick*, as critic Richard Jameson has observed: "Alex Cutter entered the film making a barbed joke about his unscarred buddy as an Ishmael who carries 'Moby Dick,' an exotic social disease; and more than Alex's poetically apt wounds qualify him to be a contemporary Ahab. Cord is Cutter's Leviathan, and the way Fiskin and Passer present him, he partakes of something akin to the whiteness of Melville's whale: he is a blank on which any idea can be projected."[8]

Cord's "blankness" suggests a close kinship between Alex and the Obsessive Avenger of years past in that Alex may have ascribed a crime to an innocent person. As the film portrays him, Cord is more icon than human; he is usually photographed at a distance, on horseback, all sunglasses and regal bearing. He does not speak until the end of the film, and when he does he sounds eminently reasonable, even telling Rich in private that he himself is a war veteran and knows what war can do to some people. Beneath the almost caricatured trappings of wealth and power, Cord is essentially a neutral figure. Significantly, the film provides no evidence that Cord is guilty of any crime; there are no last-minute confession scenes or flashbacks of him committing evil deeds, and Passer himself has suggested that Cord "probably isn't guilty" of the crimes that Alex attributes to him.[9]

Alex's relatively close conformity to the Obsessive Avenger stereotype forces us to reconsider not only his version of the murder but also the veracity of an expository tale that he told Rich concerning George's parents and Cord. According to Alex, George's father owned most of the Santa Barbara marina during the 1930s and turned down Cord's repeated requests to sell him the property. George's mother died under mysterious circumstances, and his father, believing Cord responsible, went after him in a rage. George's father died from injuries inflicted by Cord's security men, whereupon Cord took an undue interest in young George—he took care of him, paid his way through school, and so on—and George reciprocated by becoming one of Cord's most loyal employees. Apart from George's simple statement that Alex's mother raised him like a second son, no one offers any corroboration of this story. It is possible that it and the current scenario involving Cord and the murdered teenager are entirely the products of Alex's imagination.

What are we to make of all this? Passer, a Czech émigré who survived not only World War II but also the Soviet suppression of the 1968 Prague Spring, has indicated that a major consideration that attracted him to the *Cutter's Way* project was the chance to explore the mental workings of a person debilitated by war:

> I was very familiar with this kind of disillusionment. I've seen quite a few people who, in one way or another, were victims of violent experience, or products of violence. After the war, people were put in prisons in thousands for no reason whatsoever and some of them would come out damaged psychologically. And because of that I said, "Yeah, I can do this movie better than most people."[10]

With the implication that Vietnam veterans, through no fault of their own, found themselves in a postwar society just as psychologically scarring as a prison, *Cutter's Way* suggests that such an experience can sharply alter the way they view life. In Alex's way of making sense of the world, the people in his life work as representations of the Vietnam experience. From a perspective that harkens back to the classic populist cinema of Frank Capra, Alex sees in Cord a link between Big Business and Big Government (that is, Big Militarism) in a world where bigness clearly equals badness. Though he may have had nothing directly to do with Vietnam, Cord represents for Alex the Vietnam policy-setters who demanded unquestioning loyalty. George represents that stratum of American society whose support for government policy in Vietnam was unwavering even when it meant that loved ones were dying because of it. George's mother, the murdered teenager, and Mo represent the "grunts" who died as a result of power politics and also suggest the powerlessness and victimization experienced by women living in a patriarchal society, while Rich symbolizes America's uncommitted populace who eventually turn against the war. Finally, Alex sees himself and George's father as those early activists who protested America's involvement in Vietnam.

Despite Alex's many affinities with the Obsessive Avenger, several important differences have bearing on what this film is finally about. First, there is the ethical dimension of Alex's quest, made considerably ambiguous by the hazy post-Vietnam morality of the film's setting. The Obsessive Avenger films of the 1920s and 1930s make it absolutely clear that their protagonists were wrongheaded in their vengeful efforts, but no such certainty exists in *Cutter's Way*. Though the film provides only scant evidence, it is possible that Alex is right on the mark in his belief that Cord is the murderer. Since the filmmakers elected not to give clear-cut evidence of Cord's guilt or innocence, we are led to believe that it is not the main point of the film.

The main point of *Cutter's Way* is connected to the other major difference between the Obsessive Avenger and Alex: unlike the former character who usually does his scheming alone and ultimately fails in his quest, Alex has an able-bodied peer in the form of Rich who helps him finish his heroic deed. The film suggests that Alex is incomplete physically while Rich is incomplete morally. They do come together at the end of the film, however, when Rich sheds his fuzzy morality and acts on his newfound beliefs.

Consider the way *Cutter's Way* ends. Dressed in suits and ties, Alex and Rich crash a sedate outdoor party held by Cord. Rich uses the alias of "Alexander Richard," suggesting a symbolic merging of their identities, but he quickly finds himself apprehended by Cord's security guards. As Cord questions Rich, Alex steals one of Cord's horses (a white one, no less, which recalls Mo's earlier remark about waiting for a Prince Charming to whisk her away on his white charger) and rides it at a full gallop through the window of the room where Cord had been holding Rich. He aims a pistol at Cord but dies from his new wounds before he can fire. The "merger" of Alex and Rich becomes complete—and Alex's heroic quest fulfilled—when Rich fires the pistol, still held by Alex, at Cord.

Despite its importance as a cultural document, *Cutter's Way* is more than an examination of the life of a disabled Vietnam vet or a treatise on America's moral malaise during and after the Vietnam era; it is ultimately about the wholeness that people can gain for themselves when they break out of their self-centeredness and work together to achieve moral and political goals. The film suggests that people by themselves are incomplete and their actions ineffective; working together, however, they can achieve a measure of completeness that enables them to move beyond personal concerns and work for social change. Alex almost failed in his quest to halt a powerful authority but did triumph after another joined his struggle. Though such a message is not new, it is hardly stale. As film critic Lawrence O'Toole suggested of *Cutter's Way*, "The movie's ultimate statement—that people must be responsible for something other than themselves—may seem an outdated message, but remains worth saying."[11] That the film uses an ironic means to create this message—Alex is, after all, exceedingly solipsistic in the way he makes sense of his world—only adds to the richness of this paradoxical film.

NOTES

1. In its original incarnation as *Cutter and Bone*, *Cutter's Way* almost died a premature death after reviewers for *Variety* and *The New York Times* came down hard on the film. Still smarting from the critical and financial drubbing it had taken only months before on *Heaven's*

Gate, United Artists yanked *Cutter and Bone* from theaters only four days after it premiered. Highly favorable reviews began appearing almost immediately after UA withdrew the film, however, and they provided the key to the film's survival and eventual triumph. As the film's director, Ivan Passer, noted of UA executives: "They took a baby that was just born and threw it on the street in cold weather, and the critics picked it up and warmed it, and it's alive!" United Artists Classics, UA's "art film" division, took over the handling of the film, renamed it *Cutter's Way*, and began submitting the movie to international film festivals. The tactic bore fruit within weeks; at the 1981 Houston International Film Festival, *Cutter's Way* won the awards for best feature film, best director, best scriptwriter, and best actor (John Heard). For more information on the film's troubled production and distribution history, see Joe Leydon, "Ivan Passer and Jeffrey Alan Fiskin interviewed by Joe Leydon," *Film Comment* (July-August 1981): 21–23; and Chris Chase, "At the Movies," *New York Times*, 29 May 1981.

2. The plight of returning vets, racism, alcoholism, anti-Semitism, and malignant social institutions were among the many social issues explored when Hollywood filmmakers combined postwar liberal sentiments with the realization that such topics were, for the time, hot box-office material.

3. Interview on *Good Morning America*, ABC-TV, 11 February 1983.

4. Stanley Kauffmann, "Sons of Riches," *New Republic*, 15 August 1981, p. 26.

5. Leonard Quart and Albert Auster, "The Wounded Vet in Postwar Film," *Social Policy* (Fall 1982):30–31.

6. Together or separately, Chaney and Browning accounted for more than a dozen films during the late silent and early sound eras of film that featured the Obsessive Avenger and the tragedies that resulted from his quest. Two examples should suffice. In *The Penalty* (1920), directed by Wallace Worsley, Chaney essayed the role of Blizzard, a San Francisco underworld czar who lost both legs as a result of surgery performed on him as a child. The film implies that his corrupt and bitter nature stems largely from his long-standing belief that society, as represented by the surgeon, needlessly victimized him. Blaming the surgeon for his disability, Blizzard carries out a bizarre revenge scheme; he holds the doctor's daughter hostage and demands that he graft the legs of the woman's fiancé onto his stumps. During the operation, however, the doctor performs surgery on the legless man's brain and somehow restores his moral equilibrium. Although Blizzard is now cured of his evil ways, he must still pay the penalty; a former crony bumps him off to end the film. Chaney also starred in *West of Zanzibar* (1928), a similar tale of revenge directed by Tod Browning. Here Chaney played Phroso, a professional magician who becomes paralyzed from the waist down after his wife's lover pushes him off a balcony. His desire to seek revenge on the lover is heightened after he finds his wife dead alongside a little girl. Thinking that his rival is the girl's father, Phroso (now called "Dead Legs" in the film) abducts and raises her and over a period of eighteen years devises a most sinister form of revenge: he plans to have the young woman murdered while her father watches. The plan backfires after "Dead Legs" learns that the young woman is his own daughter, however, and he dies after saving her from his hired killers.

7. The preeminence of the 1956 movie based on *Moby Dick* obscures the fact that several film versions of the Melville novel appeared during the age of Hollywood's Obsessive Avenger noted in the text: *The Sea Beast* (1926) and *Moby Dick* (1930), both starring John Barrymore as Ahab.

8. Richard T. Jameson, "Passer's Way," *Film Comment* (July-August 1981):19.

9. Quoted in ibid., p. 21.

10. Quoted in "Dialogue on Film: Ivan Passer," *American Film* (November 1988):16.

11. Lawrence O'Toole, "Looking Out for Number One, and Two, and Three," *Maclean's*, 12 October 1981, p. 60.

"Strange Hells":
Hollywood in Search of
America's Lost War

Ivor Gurney's poem "Strange Hells" is, on the surface, a fairly straightforward account of one particular action involving Gurney's Gloucester Regiment during the Great War. In an almost casual and anecdotal fashion it details the events of one particular bombardment and charge across No Man's Land. The heavy bombardment and subsequent charge over the trenches are not, however, the hell to which the poem refers; ironically, through their actions, the Gloucester soldiers are able "to quite put out" this hell. It is the "strange hell" of memory, of "Hells within the minds War made," the strange, distant and unapproachable subject of the poem, which befuddles the poet and the veterans of this action in the end.

Gurney's poem touches a subject that was to become a common one for poets of the First World War and other wars in the twentieth century: the psychological costs of war and the individual soldier's travails of memory. With World War I, the emergence of armies comprised of citizen soldiers, of conscript armies made up of individuals who have fought their countries' wars neither as zealots nor as professionals, had profound implications. For the first time, the issues of the social and psychological readjustment of veterans extended beyond the military establishment. Since World War I common soldiers have returned to their homes carrying their memories of combat with them. As a group they carried with them the demand that their experience, their hell, be validated and vindicated through benefits, privileges, or other cultural sanctions, such as parades, by the society that enlisted them. Such sanctions reunited veterans as civilians on the homefront and effectively diminished the distance between veterans and their civilian counterparts. Experience has shown that the absence of such sanctions can create deep antagonisms and divisions within societies as well as within the psyches of returning veterans. In London in the spring of 1919 angry members of the National Association of Discharged Soldiers and Sailors had marched on Parliament demanding jobs, throwing wooden blocks and crutches at civilians along the way. Later, on Victory Day, July 19, they had rioted in Glasgow, Epsom, Coventry, and Luton. Similarly, in the United States, Walter Waters's Bonus Expeditionary Force of World War I veterans set off from Portland, Oregon, demanding jobs and bonus payments and arrived in Washington, D.C., over forty thousand strong. U.S. troops under Douglas MacArthur were called in to disperse the bonus army. Memories of these ugly moments led to the development of more elaborate benefit programs, including tuition payments, housing subsidies, and training programs under the G.I. Bill of Rights for World War II veterans.

More than fifteen years after the war in Vietnam ended, America's returning soldiers still have found few sanctions for their participation in combat and have received inadequate benefits as compared to veteran of others wars. Moreover, their future health and economic and emotional stability have been jeopardized by the questions presented by issues such as Agent Orange and Post-traumatic Stress Disorder. Still, in the aftermath of Vietnam, American society has begun the struggle to come to terms with the experience of that war. On many fronts, and recently with increased urgency, the effort to come to terms with the war has been carried forward. The problem any such effort faces can be reducible to a question: Can we come to terms with this experience without providing a "full accounting," an accounting that includes an examination of the social, cultural, and political dimensions of our involvement in Vietnam and also an accounting of the veteran's experience?

Coming to terms with the war must mean coming to terms with the soldiers who fought it. This has not been an easy task so far, either for the soldiers themselves who must do their own interior searching or for the society that sent them. Efforts at understanding have in fact been very fragmented, taking place in various venues—classrooms, libraries, vet centers, even government offices. For the public at large, however, the most visible locus of this effort at understanding has been in Vietnam War films.

These films are often quite different from the large-scale dramas of World War II, which were set against the the vast panoramas of the Pacific and Europe, where almost everyone in the audience could be counted on to know the battles and the generals' names and bear common images from newspapers and newsreel footage screened in cinemas. The films about Vietnam expect no such knowledge from the audience; their scale is small, focusing at the level of the squad and the individual soldier. The subject of these films is not the simple human drama within the war as in World War II films. With at most the fragmented frame of television coverage as a common backdrop, each action within the drama bears the weight of creating or re-creating its own frame. The metaphorical and allegorical passages and moments of personal illumination of the soldier-hero carry the weight of leading the general audience to a greater understanding of the war's meaning. For veterans this has been a source of considerable confusion.

This confusion emerges at several levels and for several reasons, the most dangerous being the trivialization of actual experience. The small dramas of life, which in composite make up the collective experiences of soldiers who fought the war, are subsumed within these films into a larger, more important drama. It is this larger drama that the films demand we understand. Richard Rush places this dilemma squarely at the center of his film *The Stunt Man* (1980). Though not ostensibly a Vietnam film (the plot involves the shooting of a World War I film) *The Stunt Man* has a lot to say about the experience of veterans and the demands of filmmaking. In choosing for his naive hero the character of a Vietnam veteran who wanders onto a the set of a war film, mistaking the film sequence for an actual battle, Rush underlines the paradox of response. As the confused veteran rushes in to save the dying soldiers and old woman on the beach, his action can be viewed from the standpoint of heroism, pathos, or Olympian detachment and humor, depending on the viewers distance, his or her frame. Yet the director discovers he needs this veteran to carry forward the tension of reality his war film requires. Rush develops a tension and sexual rivalry between the veteran and the director, including intimations that the successful completion of this realistic portrayal of war will involve killing off the veteran in a chase scene where his car skips over a bridge and into the waters below. He will die, escape, or emerge from the waters released and reborn according to the viewer's perspective, a fact underscored by the director hovering above in a helicopter.

In an important sense, *The Stunt Man* points forward to the ways the dynamic of the Vietnam War film exactly replicates what many veterans feel their experience has been during and since the war. The ambivalent responses many veterans have to these films begins with initial elation at the prospect of recognition and at last an adequate representation of their experiences, but in the end there is deflation and a sense of somehow once again having been used.

The nature of these films as public events has also fed this confusion. The Vietnam War film, unlike films from previous wars, is often advertised as a social statement, an engaged piece of filmmaking, and invites our reaction and interpretation. We have a good idea of what World War II movies will be about; their context is set and their advertisements are framed against the great recruitment posters and images of that war. In the case of Vietnam, there were no recruitments posters, contexts remain debatable, and the images of the war were horrific. To entice us, then, the promotional frame for the film is often that of a statement or experience requiring our thoughtful response. Private and personal deliberations about their power, meaning, and impact are carried out in a public dialogue in which veterans, whether they are comfortable with their role or not, are forced to play a part. Each new release brings requests for veterans to appear on talk shows to discuss the issues.

This secondary drama, which takes place outside the confines of the theater, is in an important sense the true but displaced subject matter of these films. Within their narrative structures, they seek a missing key to closure on our understanding of the war. Yet, this key to understanding is often placed in the philosophical or ethical spheres, rendering the empirical folds of experience, the war, as only its dark shadow.

This situation and the problems it engenders for veterans may be best understood by reviewing the particulars of some of the most popular of these films. Granted, Hollywood's first attempts to locate the experience of the Vietnam War took little serious heed of the combat experience of veterans. These early films fell into two general categories. In one category were the seemingly simple action films starring, respectively, Chuck Norris and Sylvester Stallone, *Missing in Action* (1984) and *Rambo: First Blood Part II* (1985). In another category there were the more serious and provocative efforts such as *Apocalypse Now* (1979) and *The Deer Hunter* (1978). The Rambo group was based on tired but appealing formulas, pitting the forces of good against those of evil. The soldier, or veteran, appeared as a stunt man. Given little in the way of dialogue, and less in the area of self-consciousness, the heroes of these films, through an arcane knowledge of primitive and sophisticated methods of violence, seemed to seek to blow a hole through to the past and undo it. More often than not, they were on return voyages, not of self-discovery, but of efforts to recapture the moment of betrayal where victory turned to defeat.

Rambo, *Missing in Action*, and other films of this genre are adolescent in their appeal and sometimes too easy to dismiss. They offer a cartoon version of history, and like cartoons they eschew complex argument in favor of direct action to reach their desires ends. In their portrayal of the scarred veteran, however, they evoke a very profound sense of the trauma of loss. Here, it is more than the war that has been lost. The fate of the POWs in these films, tortured by sadistic Vietnamese and betrayed by their own government, is always emblematic of the fate of the films' veteran heroes, who are portrayed as being equally scarred, betrayed, and tortured. The "full accounting" their political message demands refers literally to the accounting and repatriation of live POWs and MIAs in Vietnam, but at a deeper level it refers to the veterans of the war who remain prisoners, missing, and as yet not fully repatriated since the war in their extended experience within American society.

What is most objectionable about such films is that with some cunning they make a direct association between the marginalized status of veterans and a war lost due to a failure of will in America brought about by liberals, radicals, and self-serving government officials. These films exploit the marginal positioning of veterans and the anger it causes to serve a particular conservative political view. They represent no serious attempt to come to terms with the complex experience of the war and the postwar period, their goal being a simple-minded, income-producing revisionism that feeds on the pain of veterans and makes dangerous overtures to a new heroic image. Veterans have expressed their revulsion at this exploitive marketing strategy by picketing theaters and selling miniature plastic body bags outside stores in malls where Rambo dolls are sold. In Boston, local veterans gathered in the rain outside Harvard's Hasty Pudding Club to confront Sylvester Stallone as he arrived to receive their "Man of the Year" award following the release of *Rambo: First Blood Part II*. Held back by police lines, the veterans were accosted and told to "go home" by a group of teenagers waiting to get Stallone's autograph. Stallone, the teenagers screamed, was "a real veteran." In a scene worthy of the ironies of *The Stunt Man*, Stallone, meanwhile, slipped into the reception through the back door.

The second group of films approach the subject of Vietnam with more complex and literary pretensions. However, like their one-dimensional counterparts, *Apocalypse Now* and *The Deer Hunter* seek the same "full accounting." Rather than offering heroes who are opaque, heroes who are weapons driving toward their inevitable conclusions, these films offer a view

In Boston, local veterans gathered . . . to confront Sylvester Stallone . . . following the release of Rambo: First Blood Part II *. . . and [were] told to "go home" by a group of teenagers. . . . Stallone, the teenagers screamed, was "a real veteran."*

of the world as seen through the eyes of heroes whose visions are troubled and through whom we see Vietnam as a landscape alive with allegory, metaphor, and allusion.

These films suggest a content beyond the military subject matter of the war, their true subject being the psychic conflicts that precipitated our involvement and remain after. Here, Vietnam is a background against which larger questions are projected. Vietnam is not much more than landscape against which the cultural myths that dictated our downfall are played out. When all is said and done, the painted landscapes of the mist-covered mountains and the world of the failing mills of Pennsylvania are as contrived as Kurtz's dialogue. The veteran in these films inhabits a world marked by totems and is the sacrificial agent for the enactment of certain cultural and heroic myths. The veteran protagonist struggles to interpret and understand what Vietnam has come to represent, struggles to interpret its mystery, and America perhaps more than Vietnam is the landscape against which the cost of his failure of interpretation is indelibly etched.

Despite their differences, *Rambo*, *Missing in Action*, *The Deer Hunter*, and *Apocalypse Now* remain locked in the same thematic dead end as older American quest films, owing more to the legacy of John Ford than to the legacy of Ho Chi Minh. Their precedents are to be found in films like *The Searchers* (1956) rather than *Hearts and Minds*. *Rambo* and *Missing in Action* are ostensibly about the quest to redeem lost honor and rescue American POWs. In a sense, so are *The Deer Hunter* and *Apocalypse Now*. Kurtz, the darker counterpart of *Apocalypse*'s hero, Willard, and Michael, Nick's counterpart in *The Deer Hunter*, are literally both MIAs; they are both lost in their individual struggles with horror, veterans who have gone back upriver struggling with what has already become a "strange hell." They represent the "best" of America, lost, gone amok somewhere in the morass of Vietnam. Their fate, as much as the fate of Rambo's MIAs, must be accounted for; they must be saved or silenced.

All these films seek to discover and redeem what has been "lost" in America's lost war. For *Rambo* and *Missing in Action* the answers are dangerously and simplistically suggested beneath the script: we lost the war because of a lack of will, moral fiber, and that is exactly what is "lost" in America today and must be rediscovered. For *The Deer Hunter* and *Apocalypse* the answers are different: we lost the war because we were already lost, a morally and spiritually confused power. In these films what is lost cannot be retrieved because the image of an integrated and functioning family, philosophy, or psyche is presented as an illusion.

Again, despite their apparent differences, all of these films insist on the image of the outcast veteran and have thus reinforced the image of veterans as being somehow lost. For *Apocalypse* and *Deer Hunter* the ultimate image is one of inarticulate and existential suffering in a morally ambiguous universe. It is no mistake that the Green Beret intruder in the wedding scene of *The Deer Hunter* can only down shots of whiskey while muttering "fuck it," and that Kurtz when found is reduced to uttering poetic babble. For *Rambo* and

The ultimate image is one of inarticulate and existential suffering in a morally ambiguous universe. [Apocalypse Now]

Missing in Action the image is different and perhaps more frightening, but again inarticulate; the image is one of a power restrained waiting to be unleashed.

The distance upriver, the distance back up into the mountains and jungles of Vietnam in these films expresses a sense of a space difficult if not impossible to bridge, the final unbridgeable distance between Rush's stuntman and his director, heroic, pathetic, and laughable at once. Through the metaphors and images, these films also express the sense of an incommunicable distance between the nation and its veterans, who have become the symbolic repositories of all the horrific details it would rather not know.

When *Platoon* appeared in 1986, a film made by a Vietnam veteran that placed the grunt experience at center stage, it was no wonder veterans rushed to embrace it. *Platoon,* however, is difficult to assess. The film still lingers with us as no previous Vietnam film ever could. Dedicated to those who fought and died in Vietnam, it was heralded as not just a film but a major statement about the "true" nature of war. This was the grunts' story, a critical, profound, and missing element in our understanding of our experience in Vietnam. Unrealistically perhaps, we hoped *Platoon* would capture some truth all the other films were seeking and missing. In it we hoped to rediscover our lost veterans. For the media, the scene of veterans coming to view the film to find and validate what was missing became a story in itself. News footage of veterans emerging from the darkened theater to testify to their harrowing ordeal of rediscovery seemed to mock the entire genre of previous Vietnam war films. They had come to see a film where the stuntman had emerged finally as the director. Veterans entering the darkened cinema were "going back" on a personal mission of rediscovery and redemption, a rescue mission whose object was not the discovery of lost honor but of lost friends. The resonance of this scenario remains intact today. In Boston, three years after the opening of *Platoon*, a local station still promotes its arts and entertainment reviewer by showing her sitting in a darkened theater surrounded by uneasy veterans in camouflage fatigues watching *Platoon*.

A mystique enshrouded the film from the beginning, suggesting it would provide important answers, and the press was quick to try to show that it did. But did it? *Platoon* is undoubtedly an important film that goes about the business of demystifying much of the heroic nonsense handed down through other films. But as much as it seeks to debunk the old clichés, it remains bound by new ones. The truth of Oliver Stone's film is the truth of our passions, and the power of the film is in its passionate telling. Stone offers the audience the world of the war as immediately perceived through the searching eye of his hero. The inner realms of friendship, hatred, loneliness, love, and fear as well as the outer realms of insects, rain, night, and all our hidebound existence are conveyed in detail as tactile living sensations to be shared by the audience.

A mystique enshrouded the film from the beginning, suggesting it would provide important answers. [Platoon]

This passionate desire to evoke the details of Vietnam as a lived experience through the representative force of film suggest an effort to bring the repressed memory of the G.I.'s experience of Vietnam back to consciousness. Ironically, as the hero's letters tell us, this quest to discover the truth of the war is what has first brought him to the war; like those in the audience he has come because he needs to see it to understand it. This quest brings the veteran filmmaker back as well.

What we see in *Platoon*, what Stone shows us and what the hero Taylor discovers, is that Vietnam is not a noble mission. It is a place, physically and spiritually, where no one wants to be, a place where everyone knows something drastically wrong is happening but from which there is no escape. The lessons Taylor learns are lessons the blacks in the platoon already know: the poor and disenfranchised are merely fodder for the fantasies and illusions of the powerful. There is nothing noble in all this. Even the death of the "good" sergeant, Elias, which is depicted with all the Christological symbolism of World War I poetry, is somehow irrelevant. Elias's efforts to redeem this world, as a "good" Rambo figure, are ineffectual. As the final message of the film states, all that is left is to find some goodness and meaning in the "strange hell" that remains beyond the hell of Vietnam. The possibility of finding this meaning and goodness, however, remains the privilege of the film's hero. The other survivors of the platoon might not fare as well. George, Taylor's black counterpart, has his stretcher carried off in another direction; the powerful Hispanic squad leader remains a lasting image standing his ground in the hell of Vietnam.

Platoon points to an important dilemma for veterans. In the last scene, as Taylor leaves Vietnam, he leaves behind his comrades. Like the war itself, like the images of the film, they will dissolve, emerge, and dissolve again into memories. The scene points to the most enduring psychological legacy of Vietnam, survivor guilt, but here it is a guilt that comes from a knowledge that the lines of class and race separate the characters as much as their own tenuous struggle for individual survival. This is the knowledge veterans have taken home from Vietnam, and *Platoon* evokes a deep sense of loss because it resurrects that knowledge. Herein lies the power of Stone's film for veterans, a power that resides not in the accuracy of its portrayal of fighting and jungles, but in the accuracy of its evocation of conflict and loss, which endure long after the war is over.

The genius of Stone's film is that it seeks to evoke feeling, not knowledge. Stone's quest is not a quest for lost meanings or redemption; it is a quest to rediscover the origins of our feelings of loss. To grasp and understand these feelings and their source is to embrace and know ourselves again. The crushing emotional weight of the film attempts to diminish the distance between the veteran and nonveteran audience for a time. This is the greatest strength of *Platoon*, but it is also a potential limitation. There is more than this to know, and the evocation of the conflicting emotions that surround the trauma of loss must move forward toward other articulations.

Veterans have often been faulted because they have not been able to convey what Vietnam was like. But Vietnam was not "like" anything. It had its own reality, a reality transformed by memory into yet another complex set of powers and forces. It is this transformation in the mind, in memory, that Stone's film gets at, the Vietnam that is always there and yet is not, for each and every one of us. Stone's film frees us for the first time from Vietnam so that we may begin to speak of what truly ails us, what we truly need to know. Whether film can accomplish this or not is questionable. What we truly need to know and remember is the enormity of the destruction of the war and the cost it exacted on the poor and the minorities of this country and the Vietnamese. What ails us is an inability to absorb spiritually or psychologically the dimensions of pain this ordeal has incurred for many, Vietnamese and veterans especially. Yet, if we as a society cannot absorb this, cannot accept this knowledge and the persons who embody it, if we opt for a mythology that claims this knowledge and those who embody it are lost, inarticulate, we shall pay the price in the "strange hells" such secondary violence to truth commands. The final quatrain of Gurney's poem describes part of this price.

> Where are they now on State-doles, or showing shop patterns
> Or walking town to town sore in borrowed tatterns
> Or begged. Some civic routine one never learns.
> The heart burns—but has to keep out of face how heart burns.

Unfortunately, like many veterans of World War I, Ivor Gurney lost his struggle with the hell of memory. *Wars Embers*, in which "Strange Hells" appeared, was followed by a breakdown. In 1922 Gurney was committed to the City of London Mental Hospital where he lived until he died in 1937, still writing war poetry, still believing the war had never ended. Sixty-five thousand British soldiers shared this same fate. Since the end of the Vietnam war it is estimated that a like number of Vietnam veterans have been lost to suicide and other unnatural causes.

PART FOUR

OTHER FORMS
DOCUMENTING THE VIETNAM WAR

Documenting the Vietnam War

> The document, then, is no longer for history an inert material through
> which it tries to reconstitute what men have done or said, the events of
> which only the trace remains; history is now trying to define within the
> documentary material itself unities, totalities, series, relations.
> *Michel Foucault*[1]

> One day at the battalion aid station in Hue a Marine with minor shrapnel
> wounds in his legs was waiting to get on a helicopter. . . . "I *hate* this
> movie," he said, and I thought, "Why not?"
> *Michael Herr*[2]

For the last half of the decade the war in Vietnam was the largest single
determinant of other economic, social, and cultural developments in the
United States, eventually becoming the master metaphor by which they were
understood. As the imperial state declared itself in the ghettos, in the streets of
Chicago, and on the campuses of the rest of the country, albeit with less ferocity than in the villages of Vietnam, Blacks and war protesters came to feel
themselves to be fighting alongside the Vietnamese people in the same war of
liberation. When Black Power's equation of the struggles of domestic minorities with that of the Vietnamese expanded to include other marginalized
groups, then the notion of a unified Third World could stand in place of the
largely absent class analysis, and acts of resistance against the state, especially as they became more violent in the Weatherman period, could be
thought of as parallel to the Vietnamese resistance rather than simply ancillary
or subordinate to it. The Progressive Labor Party's attack on North Vietnam's
participation in the Paris peace talks as a betrayal of world revolution marks
the extent to which the initially hegemonic confrontation in Asia could be re-
contained in the political developments it engendered. Until this point, however, the operations in the Asian theater were the parent actions from which
the "two, three, many Vietnams" of Che Guevara's injunction were
spawned. Each of the special interest groups—students, G.I.'s, the Vietnamese themselves, and indeed everyone conscious of the way his or her experience of capitalism, even at the psychic level of alienation from oneself,
recapitulated the situation of Third World people—had thus a "Vietnam" of
his or her own, a lived experience of imperialism.

This pandemic dispersal of the Vietnam War is the context for the specific
issues faced by filmmaking that sought to intervene in it, either directly, by
attempting to propagandize against it, or indirectly, but no less importantly, by
confronting the establishment media's complicity in the social consensus that
allowed the administration to fight the war on its own terms. Consideration of
the way in which even the most dissident filmmaking was incriminated,

on some level or other, in the international political system of which the Vietnamese decolonization struggle was the rupture eventually produced meta-cinematic reflections that argued themselves as the only politically valid film-making. As their only means of negating mass media representations which, however situated ideologically, only profited from the war, they refused to allow any unmediated image of Vietnam or any film practice engaged in its purview to pass without saturating it with the evidence of its own contradictions. Carried to their logical conclusions, such meditations would call into question the possibility of even making film, and so would open the road to a refusal that could authenticate itself only by espousing silence or self-destruction, or by totally recasting the practices under which cinema could be pursued. The filmic form of appearance of these cinematic issues is the tension between image and discourse in the documentation of the war. The inflection of general problems of representation by the specific question of representing the war imposed semiological crises upon the political crises involved in the dissemination of images and in the relation between such images and the institutions producing them. Contestation of the establishment definition of the war, of what constituted "Vietnam," thus inevitably involved contestation of the methods of representing it, of the agencies of representation, and hence of the relationship between media institutions and the other institutions of state power.

That the photograph manifests a stronger existential bond with reality than do most other forms of representation is accepted even by those semiologists who are most careful to insist that ostensibly transparent referentiality is in fact produced by means of the codes of visual language.[3] And so while Brecht's remark that by itself a photograph of the Krupp ironworks does not say very much may be true, one thing it does say is that the photographer has been there. In the case of motion pictures, this "*having-been-there*" of the still photograph "gives way before a *being-there* of the thing,"[4] but in both instances the assertion of one or another kind of presence is fundamental both to the rhetorical power of the higher levels of signification articulated by the image itself through the codes of its legibility and to the other languages with which it is contiguous. In most 1960s documentary war films, the resonances of the cinematic codes of World War II feature films that depend on this illusion of presence are amplified and directed by accompanying verbal languages—indirect speech, titles, direct speech, voice-of-God narration[5]—in which the image is encased. But even when such discursivity is not explicit, in genres like cinéma vérité that claim the aural and visual reproduction of nature as it is, the apparent iconicity only frames an intrinsic exposition. Thus presence and meaning—object and interpretation, denotation and connotation, representation and discourse—are the terms between which sequences of images argue a point of view while maintaining the semblance that their mediation is neutral, merely the articulation of what is implicit in the evidence they make present.

Bridging the pacific distance that kept the war in Asia from its production in the United States, the Vietnam War documentary exploits and compounds at two points especially the polemical assumptions of the documentary model in general: at the point where to use Bazin's inaugurating image, a photographic "impression"[6] is taken from the war by light and at the point where it is delivered to the public. The transactions involved at both points were scrutinized in the period in reflexive assaults on the theory of representational documentary, but in most Vietnam War documentaries, the precariousness of these moments when reality was transformed into film and when reality was recovered from it was typically supplied by a compensating excess of affirmation, so that the vehemence with which such and such film was offered as proof or disproof of the war's justification depended upon corresponding assumptions that the derivation of its images from situations of danger and horror empowered them with a more than ordinary authority. To invoke a metaphor used in one of the most rank exploitations of the war, those images secured from the heart of darkness were held to be simultaneously beyond language and the most eloquent. It is entirely appropriate that, as if in recognition of the centrality of this model of authority in the discourse of the Vietnam War as a whole, even Hollywood, in its only contemporary attempt to deal directly with the war rather than allegorizing it or displacing it into one of its adjacent issues, recognized that the politics of the Vietnam War were inseparable from the politics of its representation.[7]

Though a fictional feature, John Wayne's *The Green Berets* (1968), made when public opinion was already swinging against American presence in Vietnam, directly addressed the obligation of the press to produce domestic consensus. It dramatized the education of a skeptical journalist who is invited by a marine captain played by Wayne himself to go to Vietnam and share the day-to-day life of the Green Berets. The journalist becomes convinced of the necessity and indeed virtue of the U.S. defense of the south from Communist aggression, not through argument of the historical process or explanation of the sequence of colonial penetrations that have produced the war, but by being brought face to face with National Liberation Front (NLF) atrocities. The wrenching visceral encounters he experiences—the sight of a murdered Montagnard chief, a G.I. horribly killed by a bamboo skewer booby trap, and finally the NLF attack on Fort Dodge—bring the war into focus for him as an altruistic response to a worldwide Communist threat that only has been obfuscated by the cant of a liberal press. Though Wayne continuously interprets this evidence to ensure that the correct implications are construed, the journalist is essentially convinced by the nature of the atrocities themselves; they are, as it were, self-explanatory, conjuring a history and an ethics out of their own material presence. Like Eric Sevareid in 1966, like Morley Safer in 1967, he goes to Vietnam *to see for himself*, and he returns to the United States determined to report the truths that firsthand observation has made plain to him. He thus enacts the model role of the documentary filmmaker, even as intradiegetically he has enacted the role of the ideal audience for such a documentary.

Like *The Green Berets*, the typical Vietnam War documentary re-creates a trip to the front; its transformation of the movie theater into the theater of war depends on the effectiveness with which the audience can be made to experience phenomenally the textures and terrors of battle. The crucial nexus is the G.I., and, just as in the war itself he is our surrogate, so in the film he is intermediary between us and Vietnam.[8] His experience of the war, always weightier and more authoritative than ours and circumscribing any experience we can have, is proposed as the moment of authenticity and knowledge—of authenticity as knowledge—upon which the war can be evaluated and validated, just as his sacrifice is the war's justification, the proof of its virtue. Television specials like CBS's *Christmas in Vietnam* (1965) and films like Pierre Schoendorffer's *The Anderson Platoon* (1966–67) and Eugene Jones's *A Face of War* (shot in 1966 but not released until 1968) are representative of such documentaries that propose the G.I. as the site of exemplary understanding.

For three months in 1966, Jones and his crew lived with a company of the Marine Corps that was unsuccessfully resisting the NLF's liberation of a small village. With as many as three cameras simultaneously, all equipped with radio microphones, the filmmakers followed the soldiers through all their activities. By virtue of the closeness of this surveillance and the crew's readiness to follow the soldiers into action, *A Face of War* does succeed in making available what is probably the most densely textured version of the G.I.'s experience of the Vietnam War and of the day-to-day conditions under which it was fought. Jones does not fall into the obvious formal and ideological trap of structuring his presentation dramatically upon the experience of a single hero and subordinating the remainder of the company in a hierarchy around him (and to this extent the concern of the film remains the generalized experience of the G.I.'s almost as a historically representative class); still, some of them become sufficiently familiar that the remoteness of their civilian lives from the Asian front emphasizes both the poignancy of their attempts to make sense of Vietnam and the political mediation that lies between the G.I.'s as individuals and the G.I.'s as agents of an imperialism of which they have no understanding or real knowledge.

Inevitably the film's highlights are the points when these contradictions are greatest; in the combat scenes the cameramen's defensive reaction to enemy attack causes the coherence of the visual and aural fields to fall apart into the energized cacophony of the recording apparatus's own contact with violence, reproducing in the enunciation the chaotic violence of the exchange of fire and the cries of pain of the wounded. The film's overall structure exploits the tension between tortuous and fearful silence and these sudden eruptions of filmic and profilmic violence, with collision montage used to juxtapose the terror and destruction of battle with the soldiers' attempts to befriend the peasants. The most powerful of these rapid shifts comes in a sequence showing the GIs providing medical care to the villagers when a truck is suddenly blown up by a land mine and a number of young soldiers are killed. In the jarring unpredictability of these alternations—the suddenness with which a silent march through empty paddies can be transformed into a miasma of destruction— Jones locates the essence of the G.I.'s experience. And by following the soldiers into the heart of battle and by so fully subjecting himself to their risks that he was twice wounded—shooting so assiduously that he himself was shot—he appropriates for his film the authenticity of their extreme jeopardy.

While this most crucial assertion of Barthes's *"having-been-there"* does have its value, not the least of which is its unspoken but unmistakable conclusion that the G.I.'s are as much victims as heroes, still the fallacies of the cinéma vérité model expose its naiveté. Its suppositious faith in the capacity of reality to reveal itself, the basis of its humanist pathos, is discredited by the clearly staged nature of many sequences, and especially by the self-consciously plangent, high-art photography of scenes such as that of soldiers on watch at dusk silhouetted by flares against coils of barbed wire, or of old women weeping as these same soldiers burn their homes. This implicit pleading on behalf of the military that finally only recapitulates the most egregious of the war's justifications comes to a head in the covert appropriation of World War II as a master metaphor. Most of the motifs *A Face of War* employs—the man on point listening to the jungle and waving his troop on, the chaplain's prebattle address giving the imminent self-sacrifice a divine sanction, the football game in the mud, the communal bath in a natural pool, the smiles and gratitude of the natives, and even the birth of a baby—are recruited from Hollywood features; their silent intent is to rewrite imperialist invasion as the anti-fascist liberation of Asia from the Japanese, or of Europe from the Nazis.

As World War II supplied the model for understanding the Vietnam War, so

Cinéma vérité's . . . suppositious faith in the capacity of reality to reveal itself, the basis of its humanist pathos, is discredited by the clearly staged nature of many sequences. [A Face of War]

Hollywood war movies provided the vocabulary for conducting it. Michael Herr's *Dispatches*, an attempt to write the soldiers' stories that was preempted by an artificiality that made the war for them already a movie,[9] is only the most perceptive account of the war as a totally media-ted event, itself made over into the conventions of art. Such a Wildean mimetic inversion presents a particular problem for a would-be objective documentarist, for further trans-formations into language of an already aestheticized reality merely multiply the layers of reflexivity. What saves Herr himself from capitulation to total subjectivity and gives substance to his torrent of psychedelic flotsam is not appeal to the adequacy of any one story or to the actuality of events, for these are more bizarre than any trip; rather, it is the establishment of self-con-sciousness of the medium between events and any representation of them—the attention to language itself in the face of its attrition—that makes a place for understanding.[10]

Elsewhere that attrition, the dissolution of meaning into labyrinthine ironic jargon, facilitated the army's and the administration's use of the public media to present the war as non-ideological, as an apolitical, humane response to ideologically motivated aggression. Thus Jones, and in fact the establishment media at large, would have it that the intensity of the Vietnam experience was not only its own justification, it was also its own explanation. The affirmation of presence in the film image supposes a parallel aesthetic of empiricism, a repression of knowledge that can be countered only by an engagement with what it must suppress: history. As the war grew, the need for explanations of it was in no way lessened by the currency that television gave to hard-core imag-ery of its atrocities. Whatever value same-day footage of the bombardment of Khe Sanh or the fighting in Hue had in legitimizing the war or in authorizing an account of it became eroded by familiarity, but also by the disparity be-tween the visceral overload and its lack of meaning. Films like *A Face of War*, which privilege the G.I.'s trauma as the explanation of the war, were collusive with the tragedy they lamented. Suspended across the absent explanations of the historical events which produced the war, and by virtue of those absences contributing to public mendacity; they were collusive with the White House, which was able to prosecute the war for so long precisely by misrepresenting its causes.

The most important of the official apologies for the war was *Why Vietnam?* (1965), an extension of the Pentagon's World War II *Why We Fight* series. Scripted by the State Department to garner support for President Johnson's bombing of the north, its point of departure was a speech made by the Presi-dent in July 1965 in which he cited a letter from "a woman in the Midwest" who wanted to know why her son was in Vietnam. The answer, articulated both in Johnson's own words and in the extrapolation and commentary of a narrator, described a drama of aggression and appeasement: in the tradition of Hitler and Mussolini, Ho Chi Minh had invaded South Vietnam in a Commu-nist offensive aimed initially at the rice and the mineral industry, but with long-term ambitions stretching as far as East Pakistan. Blatantly misrepre-senting history, Johnson argued in the film that Vietnam was a defensive war;

the United States was simply "helping a free people to defend their sovereignty" against Ho and his plans for "a reign of terror." But his claims—Dien Ben Phieu had been a battle between Communist and non-Communist Vietnamese; at Geneva, Vietnam was divided into two in the pattern of Korea; there had been free elections in the south; the United States destroyers in the Gulf of Tonkin had been fired upon without provocation—are all apparently supported by documentary evidence. There is enough footage of fleeing peasants to prove the repressiveness of Ho's regime; shells with Chinese markings justify the assertion that the invasion is part of a global Communist offensive; and though the enemy is as invisible in this film as he was reputed to be in the jungles of Vietnam, still the evidence of his presence is borne upon the bodies of the wounded American soldiers. Substituting for the indirect address of cinéma vérité the direct address of the narrator, and incorporating Johnson's discourse into its own even as it appropriates presidential authority, the mendacious history on the sound track closes the visual text and encloses the plenitude of meaning it is supposed to contain. In the ten thousand prints circulated throughout the country and shown to all G.I.'s before departure to Vietnam, *Why Vietnam?* epitomizes the conjunction of a system of representation and a system of distribution—a film and a cinema—that together form the object radical film would have to contest. In that contestation, the representations of the Vietnamese and their methods of representation had a privileged role, one which may best be approached *via* their ideological and material absence from most Vietnam films.[11]

In *Fire in the Lake*, Frances FitzGerald's perception that the war was a Vietnamese rather than simply an American event enabled her to collate the strategic crisis with the crisis in American misconception of the Third World in general. She suggested that the American command's absolute failure to understand the Vietnamese was matched by the soldiers' inability even to perceive their adversaries. Ignorant of the role of the village as the pivot of Vietnamese social life, the G.I. was incapable of knowing how the NLF had used that role to confound the distinction between combatant and noncombatant, drawing entire sectors of South Vietnam into its ranks and redefining the conditions under which the war could be fought. "In raiding the NLF villages, the American soldiers had actually walked over the political and economic design of the Vietnamese revolution. They had looked at it, but they could not see it, for it was doubly invisible: invisible within the ground and then again invisible within their own perspective as Americans."[12] Running like leitmotif through both the films and the other accounts of the war, the invisibility of the Vietnamese allowed them to be everywhere but also to be everywhere absent. It was a fact not only of the military experience but also of the media activity that reenacted it; and ironically so, since the privileged role of the Vietnamese as the verminous enemy or as the vanguard of the revolutionary resistance to imperialism endowed their images—representations of them and their representations of the war—with a peculiar authority.

Such images did have several kinds of use for the administration and the army, and in fact one of the most interesting of all the films produced by the war is *Know Your Enemy—The Viet Cong* (AFIF 172), the U.S. Army's representation of captured NLF footage of its own combat operations and non-military and propaganda work. In this film the army narrator, who is shown reviewing the footage, continually attempts to discredit scenes of NLF activity, for example, women and children transporting weapons on modified bicycles, casualties being met by doctors and nurses and assigned to underground hospitals, and the production of liberation newspapers—all scenes in which they appear to be proficient soldiers and fully human people—by warning the audience to remember that what they are seeing is "the Viet Cong as the Viet Cong would like to see themselves."

By and large, however, the White House and the corporate interests behind the war preferred to repress the Vietnamese's view of themselves and of the war and so reproduce in the domestic theaters that invisibility which was so devastating in Asia. Whose interests were finally served by the media's decision to follow the military in conceptualizing the Vietnamese people only as body counts is difficult to tell. The dinner-time saturation of the American psyche with what became known as "'bang bang' coverage"[13] was by definition and structure piecemeal, and unable to deal in anything that could not be reduced to visual sensationalism; it probably did the administration as much harm as good, but certainly the media attempted to follow the official line. The networks regularly aired documentaries that parroted the government rationales, often under immediate direct pressure from sponsors and the White House,[14] and they refused to show the many available documentaries that presented an opposite point of view.[15] Felix Greene's *Inside North Vietnam* is a case in point; although CBS sponsored it and supplied Greene with stock and laboratory services in return for an option, it deemed the film unshowable.[16] Even Walter Cronkite's celebrated expression of reservations about the war on his visit to Vietnam in February 1968 merely reflected the shift in majority opinion that had happened eight months before.

With American and world support necessary for the continuation of the war, the media became as much the site of the war as the place where it was depicted, forcing the antiwar movement to adopt tactics whose decentralization, infiltration, and other strategies had a good deal in common with the NLF. Since access to images of the NLF was always a function of social power, a mark of a position in respect to the war mediated through specific relations with the army, with the State Department, and with the media institutions, and since wherever the Vietnamese people's struggle was supported or reenacted such images were most highly prized, the way they were handled was intrinsically so important that the contest of representation was inseparable from the contestation not only of the agencies of representation, but also of the modes of representation.

In this guerrilla war these multiple interdeterminations demanded a new relation between image and exposition, between sight and sense, such as had, in fact, been developed by the NLF. "The Viet Cong do use films, but not widely. However, they use filmstrips quite widely. All the Viet Cong films I've seen—captured propaganda films used in South Vietnam by the Viet

Cong—are *silent*. These films are *accompanied by a narration delivered by a man during the projection*. It's as if this was an illustrated lecture. In that way he can *suit his content to the current local situation*."[17]

This extreme revision of cinema must have been substantially determined by material conditions, by the logistics of jungle warfare, by technological exigency, and by a limited cine-literacy on the part of the audience (and in any case it is not generalizable to all NLF films, some of which were extremely sophisticated). Still, it must be understood as a decisive and programmatic reorientation of the use of the apparatus. Indeed, it is in precisely such terms—and almost certainly drawing on the Vietnamese as a model—that the concept of a "Third Cinema" was formulated. In domestic attempts to reproduce this guerrilla cinema, supplantation of spectacle and consumption by the "film act," "A MEETING—an act of anti-imperialist unity . . . [in which the] film is the pretext for dialogue, for the seeking and finding of wills,"[18] together with other revisions of the social relations of film, is crucial. In their integration of cinema into the liberation struggle, the Vietnamese made concomitant modifications in the filmic.

The discovery that films "offer an effective pretext for gathering an audience, in addition to the ideological message they contain," and that "the capacity for synthesis and penetration of the film image . . . makes the film far more effective than any other tool of communication"[19] meant that formal codes had to be reconstructed accordingly. Interposing himself like the *benshi* between the film and its audience, the NLF spokesperson inserted his discourse between the image and its self-articulation. In doing so he contained its presence inside his present-ation of it, inaugurating the possibility of a reading of the film and dispelling the unity of the diegesis into "a field of signs"[20] capable of further amplification and specification. Supplanting mimesis by the more fully articulate and situationally flexible verbal discourse, and retaining images only as subordinated illustration within that discourse, the NLF's rejection of theatricality in the reconstruction of cinema as an interactive educational and suasive process within a larger struggle against capitalism necessitated the destruction of the signifying procedures developed by capitalist cinema. The analogous American domestic guerrilla cinema developed by the Newsreels may be introduced by reference to the two most interesting attempts to engage the conditions of the discourse of liberation inside the largely unified hegemonic film text of Vietnam: Émile de Antonio's *In the Year of the Pig* (1969) and Nick Macdonald's *The Liberal War* (1972).

An intervention against the media's collusion in the administration's misrepresentation of the war, *In the Year of the Pig* differs from even establishment recognitions (like *Why Vietnam?*) that Vietnam had a history by emphasizing that history as the site of competing discourses rather than as a single unified text, a fact. The film is an assemblage of archival footage culled from East Germany, Hanoi, and the NLF offices in Prague, as well as from American companies such as ABC, UPI, and Paramount news, together with interviews with and speeches by over eighty politicians, and soldiers including Ho Chi Minh, Nguyen Huu Tho, Daniel Berrigan, Senators Wayne Morse and Everett Dirksen, Lyndon Johnson, Robert McNamara, and Generals LeMay and Westmoreland, as well as interviews with scholars like Paul Mus, David Halberstam, and Jean Lacouture. In its presentation of a history of the texts of Vietnam, the film contains scenes of colonial days followed by information on the life of Ho, on the Japanese occupation, on the expulsion of the French, and finally on the stages of American involvement.

Throughout, filmic documentation is not an authoritative showing forth of the truth so much as the occasion for interpretation. Eschewing the continuity of a single narrative voice, it replaces both the self-articulation of reality and the unified text of history with a collage in which visual information destabilizes and contradicts the verbal interpretations. For example, while Hubert Humphrey claims that prisoners are not being ill-treated, we see a Vietnamese beaten and kicked, and scenes of the self-immolation of Buddhist monks are juxtaposed with Madam Nu suggesting that it is a media event, not to be taken too seriously. The apologists for the war are betrayed by their own excess—General Patton's glee that his men are a "damn good bunch of killers," for example, or Curtis LeMay and General Mark Clark talking about the soldiers as "precious commodities." Other accounts are discredited by contradictory juxtapositions. *Why Vietnam?* presented the Gulf of Tonkin incident by means of a unified narrative consisting of footage of Johnson's speech, footage of American planes strafing and bombing, and a press conference in which, according to the omniscient voice-over that synthesized all these, "Secretary McNamara sets the record straight" by reiterating North Vietnamese provocation. In *In the Year of the Pig*, however, McNamara's flat assertion that the U.S. ships were reacting defensively to attacks on them is ruptured by testimony from a sailor from the Maddox who denies that these attacks ever took place. Setting one discourse against another, de Antonio calls into question all institutional versions of the war, especially discrediting the naive use of putative attacks on American soldiers to justify the administration's offensive. Consequently, the television network battle footage he eventually incorporates as his account moves into the present can no longer unequivocally manifest the war's propriety. His reconstruction of the history of Vietnamese liberation struggles and the competing ideological interests within them reveals the sacrifice of the GIs as a consequence of political maneuvering rather than of the innate perfidy of the NLF.

Nick Macdonald's homemade film *The Liberal War* (1972) abandons all pretense at realism and objectivity and, supplanting iconicity with symbolism, shifts presence away from the image to the voice of a narrator, who claims only that his account of the invasion of Vietnam and the genocide committed upon its peoples is "my own view, the way I see it." That narrational exposition is an account of the origin of the war during the Kennedy administration, in which it appears not as a mistake blundered into, but as the direct result and indeed logical implication of liberal policies. In illustration of the successive stages of the U.S. invasion, Macdonald supplies not scenes of soldiers or refugees, but models made out of toy soldiers and weapons, newspapers, and household bric-a-brac.

Events and conditions are illustrated diagrammatically, often by literalizing the para-metaphoric language of the war's discourses: Diem's puppet regime is represented by a hand puppet with his face stuck on it; the difficulty of extricating American troops, by toy soldiers trapped in a narrow-necked bottle; the imprisonment of peasants in the concentration camp–like strategic hamlets, by plastic figures entombed in bricks; Kennedy's repression of the press, by cutting up *The New York Times*; the domino theory, by actual dominoes; and American financial interests, by coins on the map of Vietnam. When photographic images of the war do occur, it is their material nature as cultural signifiers that is stressed rather than the plangency of the represented scene; in illustration of napalm, it is a photograph rather than actual peasants that we see burning.

In its use of footage commonly available, *The Liberal War* exposes the social implications of de Antonio's archival footage and interviews almost as much as it does those of the "bang bang" aesthetic of the networks. It thus makes possible a critique of almost all use of front-line imagery as the trace of collusion with the institutional powers that control access to Vietnam. This is not pursued or made explicit by the film, but the domestic political implications of its own artisanal minimization of the cinematic apparatus are suggested by the film's fictional setting. While clues suggest that the narrative voice is Macdonald's own, his account is displaced hundreds of years into the future, so that it appears as a historical reconstruction made in an anarchist

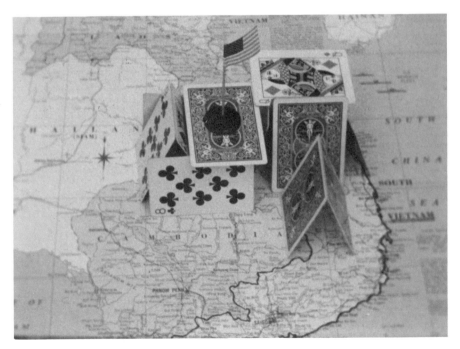

Events and conditions are illustrated diagrammatically, often literalizing the para-metaphoric language of the war's discourses. [The Liberal War]

community that has transcended Kennedy's liberalism and authoritarian centralism in general. Imaged, in shots that open and close the film, as a natural paradise cleansed of technology, this utopian future is clearly a projection of sixties ruralism and carries with it all the contradictions of such idealisms. But although the intense rationality and social systematization of the Confucian bases of rural Vietnamese society would have no place in this Walden of the future, it is also in some sense Vietnam; the hostility to the city and to the instrumentalizing of social relations, the emphasis on self-discipline and decentralization, with a *bricoleur*'s resourcefulness that can fabricate the model of the massive financial and technical complexity of the war from the odds and ends lying around the house, recapitulate the resourcefulness of the Vietnamese themselves—their ability to take apart American bombs and tanks and make such technological spillage over for their own purposes.

In Macdonald's refusal to represent the war iconically and his abstinence from imagery drenched in the presence of the military experience, a critique of the war becomes a critique of the media's use of it. The technical simplicity of his film, its articulation of its partisanship and subjectivity, its insistence on the discursiveness of historical interpretation, and its inevitable foregrounding of its own enunciation all reject the liberal languages of the war, as well as the liberal war itself. Though *The Liberal War* is not as explicit about the war's utility for the media as is *In the Year of the Pig*, in which, for example,

[In] In the Year of the Pig, . . . *the clear visibility of ABC microphones in interviews with soldiers lays bare the superimposition of station advertising upon ostensibly objective documentation.*

the clear visibility of ABC microphones in interviews with soldiers lays bare the superimposition of station advertising upon ostensibly objective documentation, Macdonald's rejection of the technological resources and the language of the media industry allows him to project a *cinematic* alternative, displaced equally from hegemonic processes of cultural signification and from hegemonic cultural production.

Though implicit in both films' difference from the media practices that surround them, attention to their own mode of production or social location is not overt in either's critique of the communications industries. Confident and unselfconscious in their own formal mode, neither questions or even alludes to its own cinematic situation, though both were components in an alternative cinema and were used against the war. *In the Year of the Pig*, for instance, was "used as a tool by the Moratorium; it was a benefit for the Chicago Seven at the opening of their trial; the Australian antiwar movement used it as its primary film weapon."[21] Nevertheless, the films do not themselves articulate the issues of the alternative cinema. The remainder of this chapter is concerned with production that does manifest consciousness of itself as cinema and that confronts either intradiegetically or as practices of cinema not only institutional filmic codes, but also the hegemonic modes of cinematic production, consumption, and distribution. A summary of the issues of radical documentary film and a definition of the conditions under which a radical cinema could be established may be found in one of the most precise statements of the limits of the modern cinema, Jean-Luc Godard's section in Chris Marker's compilation film, *Far From Vietnam* (1967).

Far From Vietnam is compiled from several different kinds of representation of the war: Joris Ivens's footage of North Vietnam, a history of the war from the resistance to the French through the U.S. subversion of the Geneva agreements; a modified television address by General Westmoreland; interviews with the family of Norman Morrison, a Quaker who immolated himself on the steps of the Capitol; collages of television and magazine journalism; and documentation of protest activities in both Europe and the United States. This displacement of the war into its repercussions throughout the world is reciprocated in the displacement of the illusionist documentary mode into varying degrees of abstraction, discursivity, and reflexiveness. The questions of where the war is and of what an appropriate cinematic response to it is do come together, however, in Godard's section, which is a pivotal and seminal moment in modern film because it articulates a termination for modern cinema.

Introduced as "Camera Eye," the segment details a situation that is, in fact, exactly antithetical to Vertov's, for where Vertov's reflexivity flowers from his confidence in the role of the filmmaker in socialist society, Godard is paralyzed by the realization that in his society the impossibility of making a film about the Vietnam War means that film in general may be no longer possible. The newsreel footage, which Godard reproduces even as he admits that it is all he would have come up with had he been a cameraman for ABC in New York or for Soviet television, is only indirectly available to him, since the North

Vietnamese correctly recognized that his ideology was "a bit vague" and refused him an entry visa. Obliged to remain in Paris, he realizes that the best thing we can do for Vietnam is to let Vietnam invade us and find out what part it plays in our everyday lives. The practical implementation of such a scrutiny would be for Godard to make films for and about the French working class—from whom he is as estranged as he is from the Vietnamese. The only film he can make—this one—comprises shots of the Mitchell studio camera, interspersed with fragments of newsreel footage and of his previous attempts to deal with Vietnam (the scenes from *La Chinoise* in which Juliet Berto as a Vietnamese peasant is attacked by U.S. planes). But the industrial camera is itself the site of contradictions, and scrutiny of it summarizes the contradictions faced by the film as a whole. A beautiful object, almost erotic in its responsiveness to his manipulations, the Mitchell is typical of the American technology with which the war is fought. But its instrumentality in the war goes beyond the analogy between the precision of its gear, the accuracy of its movements, and those of the war machine; as the means of production of American and French commercial film, it is the means by which U.S. cultural imperialism has stifled Third World cinema.

A function of his previous career in the industry and of his inability at that time to imagine a feasible alternative to it, Godard's impasse did make clear the need for an alternative cinema by which mass media collusion in imperialism could be contested, even though Godard was not himself capable of inaugurating it. The same imperatives define radical American film, which in its best instances produced a revolutionary, anti-industrial cinema that decolonized production and distribution, both participating in and enacting collective political action.

NOTES

This essay is reprinted from *Allegories of Cinema: American Films of the Sixties* (Princeton: Princeton University Press, 1989); reflecting the concerns of that book, it deals only with the documentaries produced during the period of the war.

1. Michel Foucault, *The Archaeology of Knowledge*, trans. A. M. Sheridan Smith (New York: Harper and Row, 1972), p. 7.

2. Michael Herr, *Dispatches* (New York: Avon, 1978), pp. 188–189.

3. On this debate, see especially Umberto Eco's demonstrations of the limitations in the Peirceian concept of iconicity (Eco, "Articulations of the Cinematic Code," in *Movies and Methods*, ed. Bill Nichols [Berkeley and Los Angeles: University of California Press, 1976], pp. 593–596) to refute Metz's assertion that, in its "perceptual literalness," the film image "reproduces the signified spectacle; and thus it becomes what it shows to the extent that it does not have to *signify* it" (Christian Metz, *Film Language* [New York: Oxford University Press, 1974], pp. 75–76).

4. Roland Barthes, *Image-Music-Text*, trans. Stephen Heath (New York: Hill and Wang, 1977), p. 45.

5. The term was coined by Paul Rotha, but I take it from Bill Nichols's taxonomy of documentary forms. Nichols, *Ideology and the Image: Social Representation in the Cinema and Other Media* (Bloomington: Indiana University Press, 1981), pp. 170–208.

6. André Bazin, *What is Cinema?*, trans. Hugh Gray (Berkeley and Los Angeles: University of California Press, 1967), p. 12.

7. Although Hollywood's avoidance of the Vietnam War—by 1975 only four combat films had been set there (Julian Smith, *Looking Away: Hollywood and Vietnam* [New York: Scribners, 1975], p. 3)—was indeed a function of the political complexities, the failure to represent accurately the Vietnamese and their position was a cinematic as well as an ideological problem that arose from the inapplicability of the anti-imperialist model of World War II movies. Thus, while it is an oversimplification, Julian Smith's witty summary, "Vietnam did not generate a great many films but it may have been America's first film-generated war, the first . . . war to grow out of attitudes supported, perhaps even created, by a generation of movies depicting America's military omnipotence" (ibid., p. 4), correctly points to the fact that representation was only half of Hollywood's role in the war. Writing after the rush of big-budget Vietnam films of the late seventies, Gilbert Adair is able to address some of the conditions that made them so amenable to revisionist histories of the war, refurbishing for the Cold War revival the imperialist rhetoric of the sixties (Adair, *Vietnam on Film: From* The Green Berets *to* Apocalypse Now [New York: Proteus, 1981]).

8. Like representations of the G.I. in general, films about the G.I.'s experience of the war reproduce his military instrumentality in his instrumentality in the political functions of the cinemas in which he is contained; hence his own extreme disenfranchisement, his exclusion from production. On the one hand, the films made by the army for Vietnam soldiers, the Armed Forces Information Film series, and The Big Picture series (many of which are still available) and, on the other, the various films made about or on behalf of veterans opposed to the war, such as Joseph Strick's *Interviews with My Lai Veterans* or the various documentations of the Winter Soldier hearings, and films made to counter the Army's own recruiting publicity, such as Newsreel's *Army*, are necessary adjuncts to the present discussion, especially in the way they fail to deal with the ambivalent location of the G.I. as simultaneously the agent and the victim of imperialism. The army indoctrination/training films are an especially interesting case of the politics of representation, in which the categorical servitude of the common soldier is reproduced in his absolute cinematic disenfranchisement.

9. Herr, *Dispatches*, pp. 188, 206.

10. Since by and large only those filmmakers who were favorably disposed to the administration's idea of the war either chose or were allowed to go to South Vietnam, there is no equivalent in film of Herr's awareness of the effect of the penetration and presence of the recording apparatus. The reflexive moment did not occur in American film until the object of documentation became the war at home.

11. Cf. "From *Saigon* to *The Green Berets*, American films set in Vietnam always emphasized American characters and did not create a single important Vietnamese who is not defined through his or her relationship to Americans" (Smith, *Looking Away*, p. 111).

12. Frances FitzGerald, *Fire in the Lake: The Vietnamese and the Americans in Vietnam* (New York: Vintage, 1972), p. 192.

13. Michael Arlen, *Living Room War* (New York: Viking, 1969), p. 112.

14. For the Nixon White House's attempt to determine media coverage of the war, see also Todd Gitlin, *The Whole World Is Watching: Mass Media in the Making and Unmaking of the New Left* (Berkeley and Los Angeles: University of California Press, 1980), pp. 277–279.

15. Films from the NLF and North Vietnam that were available in the United States were listed in "Films in Vietnam" (*Film Comment* 2 [Spring 1969]:46–88), and also in the various Newsreel catalogues. Four had been described by Peter Gessner in *The Nation* three years earlier (Gessner, "Films from the Vietcong," *The Nation* 202, no. 4 [24 January 1966]: 110–111). Documentation of the North had been begun in 1954 with the Soviet Union's Roman Karmen's *Vietnam* (1955). Later, escalation documentaries were available from both the NLF and North

Vietnam, from Cuba (Santiago Alvarez's *Hanoi, Martes Trece* and *79 Primaveras* [*79 Spring-times*]), from East Germany, and from Japan. Most were suppressed in the United States. For Vietnam documentaries, see especially Erik Barnouw (Barnouw, *Documentary: A History of Non-Fiction Film* [New York: Oxford University Press, 1974], pp. 262–287). Television coverage of the war is summarized by Charles Montgomery Hammond, Jr. (Hammond, *The Image Decade: Television Documentary, 1965–75* [New York: Hastings House, 1981], pp. 194–221). Because many of the films shot in North Vietnam, such as Newsreel's *People's War* (1969), Felix Greene's *Inside North Vietnam* (1968), and Santiago Alvarez's *Hanoi, Martes Trece* (1967), tended to recapitulate the aesthetics of presence, substituting the effects of U.S. bombing—the devastation of hospitals, the rebuilding of roads and bridges by peasants, individual bomb shelters, and burying the dead—for the village patrols, the booby traps, and the NLF dead show in the establishment documentaries, they remain empirical and subjective; Greene's, for instance, subtitled *A Personal Report*, is emphatically his presentation of the North's position.

16. Barnouw, *Documentary*, p. 281.

17. The informant here was a United States Information Service (USIS) filmmaker who worked for two years in South Vietnam. He also noted that the improvisational quality of NLF films, their inevitable crudeness, gave the "impression of being the films of a revolutionary force" ("Films in Vietnam," p. 58). Consciously imitated for the same reason by radical filmmakers in the United States, such crudeness was ideologically loaded when assimilated with a war that culminated in a great victory over capitalist technology per se. In this respect the NLF's film *Young Puppeteers of Vietnam* is especially interesting. Showing how teenagers in liberated areas of Vietnam make puppets from bits of a downed U.S. plane and travel through the country putting on puppet shows that illustrate their resistance to the United States, the film is important in documenting the reconversion of the enemy's technology to instruments of liberation and also in documenting an art form largely supplanted by film in "advanced" societies.

18. Fernando Solanas and Octavio Gettino, "Towards a Third Cinema," in *Movies and Methods*, ed. Nichols, p. 62.

19 Ibid, p. 53.

20. Cf. "We may, in fact, consider the *benshi*'s entire discourse as a *reading* of the diegesis which was thereby designated as such and which thereby ceased to function as diegesis and became what it had in fact never ceased to be, *a field of signs*" (Noel Burch, *To the Distant Observer: Form and Meaning in the Japanese Cinema* [Berkeley and Los Angeles: University of California Press, 1979], p. 79).

21. Émile de Antonio, "*Year of the Pig*: Marxist Film," *Jump Cut* 19 (n.d.):37.

MICHAEL RENOV

Imaging the Other:
Representations
of Vietnam in Sixties
Political Documentary

> And when we desire the Other himself, on what is our desire focused if
> not on this little possible world that it expressed, that the Other was
> wrong to envelop in himself, instead of allowing it to be free to float and
> fly above the world, developed as a glorious double?
> *Gilles Deleuze, "Michel Tournier and the World Without Others"* [1]

> When we discover that there are several cultures instead of just one and
> consequently, at the time when we acknowledge the end of a sort of
> cultural monopoly, be it illusory or real, we are threatened with the
> destruction of our own discovery. Suddenly it becomes possible that there
> are just *others*, that we ourselves are an 'other' among others. All
> meaning and every goal having disappeared, it becomes possible to
> wander through civilization as if through vestiges and ruins. The whole
> of mankind becomes in imaginary museum. . .
> *Paul Ricoeur, "Universal Civilization and National Cultures"* [2]

Following upon Ricoeur's vision of what, from the above quotation, might
be termed postmodern ethnography, I propose to take a stroll through the
imaginary museum, along the corridor marked "Vietnam: 1969–1971." The
metaphor is an apt one, as we shall see, for indeed the study of the representations of the Other—the ways cultures have invented other cultures—must of
necessity involve consideration of psychic processes, of the imaginary line
drawn between self and Other through which the illusion of absolute difference is maintained. This line of demarcation is both necessary (to the construction of the self) and dynamic (ever capable of realignment). For if the
domain of the Other is constitutive for the subject (the self produced through
difference), it is also equivocal, the repository of images of things we fear or
glorify. Homi K. Bhabha, in theorizing Otherness within the field of representation, writes of the productive ambivalence at the very core of the stereotype
of colonial discourse whose object is always the site of both desire and deri-
sion.[3] Sander L. Gilman has explored the psychopathology of stereotyping;
his insistence upon the bipolarity of psychic projections helps to situate the
present discussion and its exploration of positive idealizations of the Other.

> The Other is invested with all of the qualities of the "bad" or the "good."
> The "bad" self, with its repressed sadistic impulses, becomes the "bad"

Other; the "good" self/object, with its infallible correctness, becomes the antithesis to the flawed image of the self, the self out of control. The "bad" Other becomes the negative stereotype; the "good" Other becomes the positive stereotype. The former is that which we fear to become; the latter, that which we fear we cannot achieve.[4]

It is, for the most part, the "good" Other that will occupy our attention here, for the subject of this essay is a selection of films produced in the late sixties in the U.S. by filmmakers working in solidarity with the people of the Democratic Republic of Vietnam under the leadership of Ho Chi Minh and with the National Liberation Front struggling to free itself from foreign domination. The Other as represented in these pieces inhabits the domain of idealization, Ego-Ideal and thus introjection rather than that of projection—the expulsion of negative, frequently racially stereotyped traits familiar from mainstream depictions of the enemy in war films the world over. The examination of representational strategies in three films—two from the radical documentary collective Newsreel: *The People's War* (1969) and *Only the Beginning* (1971); one by Emile de Antonio: *In the Year of the Pig* (1969)—is also an interrogation of the notion of solidarity in the field of representation and its relationship to the Imaginary.

Such a study remains alert to current developments in the theory and practice of ethnography and the questions raised regarding power and privilege, for indeed these films speak in the place of the Other, producing at best a kind of cultural ventriloquism, at worst, yet another variant of colonized speech. As Trinh T. Minh-ha has suggested, "One cannot really 'give voice' to the others without unlearning one's privilege as speaking/making subject."[5] The films under consideration here are, however, less ethnography than agitation and propaganda produced from clearly defined political positions with the support of the North Vietnamese Committee for Cultural Relations with Foreign Countries. One might well argue that such cultural exchange under these conditions constitutes "willed appropriation." Even so, there is much to be gained from exploring the means by which the Vietnam *represented* becomes the Vietnam *constructed*—more in the image of the subject of the enunciation than of its object. Such a study offers a further yield for its insights into the nature of documentary discourse more generally, the ways in which objects of nonfiction are produced and conditioned through the agencies of fantasy and imagination.

For the past two decades, an energetic and rather polemicized debate has raged in the West around questions of representation and the Third World. Despite the global transformations of the sixties that announced the decline of colonial rule based upon territorial possessions, struggles for self-determination at the level of representation have accelerated. Herbert Schiller, among others, has written of the information commodity that remains in the hands of the few; notions of core and periphery, metropolis and colonial outpost can now also be understood as issues of media access. One need not be a citizen of an African, Asian, or Latin American nation to experience exclusion from the means of representation. This attention to the centralization of the electronic information flow as global threat ought not to obscure, however, the lingering and very material effects of what has been termed colonial discourse, that system of representation that articulates difference as racially determined, positing the colonized "as a fixed reality which is at once an 'other' and yet entirely knowable and visible."[6]

Edward W. Said has traced the history of colonial discourse about the East to many sources, including Karl Marx, whose statement "they cannot represent themselves; they must be represented" serves to inaugurate Said's *Orientalism*. In Said's persuasive argument, the meaning of the Orient has been *contained* and *represented* by dominating frameworks produced by Europeans and North Americans; Orientalism becomes that body of images, fantasies, myths, and obsessions which "has less to do with the Orient than it does with 'our' world."[7] A succession of philosophers has theorized the Other as a kind of social category external to the self through which a differential identity is produced (for example, Sartre's notion of the Other as an object under my gaze capable of returning the look and transforming me into an object as well). But Said's version of Orientalism insists on the ontological and epistemological hierarchy that the scholarly and artistic tradition installs in its study of the East through a Western optic. "A certain freedom of intercourse has always been the Westerner's privilege," argues Said, "because his was the stronger culture, he could penetrate, he could wrestle with, he could give shape and meaning to the great Asiatic mystery, as Disraeli once called it."[8] While the precise contours of that "imaginative geography" which is the West's collective daydream of the Orient may vacillate, embracing visions of Edenic purity as well as depravity and irrationality, Orientalism is ultimately an exercise of cultural power. Furthermore, Said is careful to link Orientalism's political component—Europe's will to govern—to the psychosocial dimension—the *projection* of stereotypical characteristics, of strangeness, silence, and mystery upon an exoticized Other.

The notion of projection requires further examination. Defined in the psychoanalytic literature as that "operation whereby qualities, feelings, wishes or even 'objects,' which the subject refuses to recognize or rejects in himself, are expelled from the self and located in another person or thing," projection is at the root of the Other as representation.[9] And yet it is important to recall, despite the stereotypical, often dehumanizing imaging of the enemy in the war film—the casting of Otherness as threat to order and control—the essentially bipolar nature of all projective processes discussed previously. The Other, a kind of surrogate or underground self, is always the site of a marked ambivalence capable of encompassing projections of good and evil.

CULTURAL CODES IN THE SERVICE OF STEREOTYPE

The Oriental as bad object in American popular culture, particularly demonstrable in the Hollywood film of the World War II period, has its roots in centuries of exploitation of the Chinese and Japanese as a cheap labor supply not easily assimilable to the nativist, Eurocentric tradition. In a series of award-winning war posters displayed on the walls of the Museum of Modern Art in the autumn of 1942 and in the pages of *Life* magazine's 21 December 1942 issue, the distinction between the European and Oriental enemy is dramatically inscribed. The two hundred posters were part of a campaign planned by a group called "Artists for Victory" in which war slogans—many of them inspired by Roosevelt's 1942 State of the Union speech—were to be vividly dramatized. One group of posters bearing the legend "This Is the Enemy" illustrates the contrast between the stereotyping of Japanese and German. While the European nemesis may be figured as a defiler of the sacred, engaged in ripping up an American flag or smashing a stained-glass church window with a blood-stained dagger, the Japanese is Othered with far greater vehemence. In one poster, a Japanese soldier, swarthy and simian of posture, stands half erect, with a naked woman slung over his shoulder; the alabaster of her exposed skin contrasts hyperbolically with that of her captor. In yet another instance, a dagger-wielding Japanese soldier, his yellow face drawn wide in a snarl, reaches for a horror-stricken white woman fleeing from the lower left edge of the frame. The grotesquerie of the image results from two excessive elements: the teeth and nails (now fangs and claws) of the Asian man are hyperbolized in the direction of the bestial while a low-key, low-angle lighting effect transforms the painted image into nightmare. While the threat of the Other is in all cases figured as the brutalization of the woman, the most fundamental assault within the patriarchal order because it annihilates the medium of exchange and reproduction, the savagery and bestiality of the Asian is crucially foregrounded.

The 29 April 1944 cover of *Liberty* magazine is equally explicit in its projection of animality upon the Japanese. Three uniformed soldiers of the Empire—one bedecked in medals, all buck-toothed and bespectacled—are shown perched upon a fallen tree trunk as bombs rain down from behind and above. The gestured pose of this figure group—hands placed over ears, eyes, and mouth respectively—enact the "hear no evil, see no evil, speak no evil" adage. But the cover illustrates far more than a hackneyed moral injunction, for once again these enemy soldiers are imaged as apelike, their dark, fur-covered hands and feet inhumanly outsized and grasping. Such dehumanizing representations can, in the end, be said to have a cumulative effect. The atomic resolution to the war could now be faced without remorse by a society assured of the enemy's subhumanity.

In films such as *The Purple Heart* (1944) and *Guadalcanal Diary* (1943), visual as well as cultural codes were mobilized in the service of stereotype. In the latter film, the enemy was depicted in camouflage, capable of merging with the jungle flora, much as the Vietnamese were in *Platoon* (1986). This is clearly not a Rousseauian reference; the enemy is *of nature* to be sure, but in a manner suggestive of the simian reference of the *Liberty* cover. When, in *Guadalcanal Diary*, a patrol discovers an enemy encampment only recently abandoned, one soldier cannot conceal his distaste for the alien look and smell of the Other's cuisine. His face a mask of disgust, the G.I. sniffs gingerly at what look to be the remnants of a rice cake and some raw fish, foods now much in demand by Western sophisticates. In *The Purple Heart*, Japanese linguistic characters are described as "chicken scratch"; the enemy's most elemental powers of symbolization are devalued at the same moment that the figure of animality recurs. Low-angle placement of camera and light source reinforces the sense of threat and grotesquerie established by stereotypical casting and costuming; the Japanese were inevitably imaged as leering, bucktoothed aggressors.

STEREOTYPE IN THE SERVICE OF SOLIDARITY

When I went to Vietnam and I saw the way that the Vietnamese dealt with us . . . the very self-conscious but collectively self-conscious way that they would work out what they were going to say to us . . . it presented me with an image of the way they were organized. When you're carrying a camera around, I was carrying a camera, I didn't know what to point it at, didn't know what I was trying to photograph because often what I was trying for was the inside of my head and I couldn't find that out there.
Voice-over narration from Summer '68 *(Newsreel, 1969)*

More than years separate the stereotyping of the Japanese in Hollywood films of the forties from the depictions of the Vietnamese in the films under consideration here. The distinction to be drawn is not so much ontological as psychoanalytic, insofar as the Other here becomes a site of idealization and introjection rather than its expulsive counterpart, projection. Several crucial circumstances deserve mention. As I have argued elsewhere, philosophers such as Herbert Marcuse had by the late 1960s written convincingly of the emergence of a new Reality Principle that would invalidate the historic oppositions between imagination and reason, higher and lower faculties, poetic and scientific thought.[10] In the streets of Paris during May 1968, students, passionately engaged, "dared to dream." The new historical subjects of the Great Refusal felt themselves to be entering a new phase of history as described by Marcuse: "Under these circumstances, radical change in consciousness is the beginning, the first step in changing social existence: emergence of the new Subject."[11]

The New Left sensibility, wellspring of such organizations as the Students for a Democratic Society (SDS) and the radical Newsreel film collective, gathered inspiration from sources oppositional to the established order—from the militant minorities, the urban underclasses, and the revolutionary zealots of other cultures. Posters of Malcolm X, Ho Chi Minh, and Che Guevara, the flag of the NLF—these were the icons of choice for disenchanted young Americans. The films made by Newsreel that touched upon the Vietnam War were typically event-oriented. Indeed, one of the first Newsreel films, *No Game*, was shot at the march on the Pentagon in October 1967; its focus was the confrontation between the military and the assembled antiwar protesters.

The idealized other, imaged in its several incarnations—warrior, artist, and intellectual

Virtually no film could be made in this period without reference to the war, primarily because the analysis shared by the Newsreel collectives nationwide was that all social ills were rooted in an exploitive capitalist system whose international face was imperialism. The Vietnamese people were seen as the shock troops of the very same revolution being waged in the streets of every major city in the United States. Che Guevara himself had issued the manifesto in slogan form long before his death in a Bolivian rain forest: "Two, three, many Vietnams." World revolution was the master narrative of the militant Left.

What is pertinent to this discussion, however, are the effects that this principle generated at the level of filmic representation. In each of the instances under analysis, the desire to link the struggles in the streets of Chicago or Watts with the "heroic efforts" of the Vietnamese people contributed to a kind of palliation or disavowal of racial, national, and cultural difference. The will to solidarity, to the forging of a shared identity, resulted in the construction of a Vietnam of radical imagination, capable of functioning as a screen for desire. Like the French author Alphonse de Lamartine, author of *Voyage en Orient*, for these filmmakers a trip to Vietnam was an imaginary odyssey; they might well have echoed Lamartine's pronouncement: "un voyage en Orient [etait] comme un grand acte de ma vie interieure."[12]

We thus find ourselves making an ironic return to the realm of Said's Orientalism, with the crucial difference that here the Asiatic is rendered as the good object, idealized rather than vilified. Through the construction of stereotype and a complex play of projection/introjection, it can be said that the Vietnam of these films deserves Said's diagnosis: "In the system of knowledge about the Orient, the Orient is less a place than a *topos,* a set of references, a congeries of characteristics."[13] It now remains for us to trace out the contours of that imaginary Vietnam, that topos of radical desire.

IN THE YEAR OF THE PIG: THE APPEAL TO RATIONALITY

The thing that I think we fail to recognize is that Ho Chi Minh,
Communist or what-not, is considered by the people of Vietnam . . . as
the George Washington of his country.
        Sen. Thruston B. Morton (R-Ky.), In the Year of the Pig

Emile de Antonio has said that what interests him most about the films he has made is their structure. And, without doubt, such works as *Point of Order* (1963), *In the Year of the Pig* (1969), and *Millhouse: A White Comedy* (1971) are among the most carefully constructed of American documentary films. With special attention to the capacity of edited images to be imbued with newfound, frequently ironic layers of meaning, de Antonio has undertaken a project of historiography through a two-stroke process that places in tension "present tense" interview material and archival footage scavenged from diverse sources. Visual documents from past and present are thus allowed to interrogate one another, the recycled "action footage" (in *In the Year of the Pig*, images of the French occupation as well as battle footage from American and Vietnamese sources) offering contrast with the reflections and analyses of interview subjects. The sound track offers yet another interpretive layer through its counterpointing of image and unexpected sound elements. One striking example of this strategy in *In the Year of the Pig* occurs at the close of the sequence chronicling the defeat of the French at Dien Bien Phu; "La Marsaillaise" is plaintively rendered by a Vietnamese stringed instrument over images of the triumphant Viet Minh. Thomas Waugh has drawn attention to de Antonio's unique working methods in his excellent essay, "Beyond Vérité: Emile de Antonio and the New Documentary of the Seventies," labeling the hybrid result "collage essay" for its coupling of a collagist aesthetic ("I do everything at once . . . so the process was always one of collage") with the development of a didactic line, uninterrupted by external narration.[14]

But de Antonio's Vietnam is unabashedly his own. In responding to a remark from interviewer Alan Rosenthal ("in *Year of the Pig*, Ho Chi Minh and North Vietnam always come out like God and Kingdom Come"), the filmmaker replied that while the film was never intended as an objective statement, neither was it an outright falsehood. "There are no lies in the film," says de Antonio, "there are prejudices in the film. I wanted the Vietnamese to defeat the United States, and the Vietnamese did defeat the United States."[15] His statements remind us of the efficacy of Bill Nichols's analysis of discursivity in the documentary film in his seminal discussion of "The Voice of Documentary." There Nichols makes the crucial distinction between the agency of voiced narration and the *effects* of textual voice or point of view achieved through the multiplicity of codes "orchestrated into a single controlling pattern." "We may think we hear history or reality speaking to us through a film, but what we actually hear is the voice of the text, even when that voice tries to efface itself."[16]

The particular element of the film's textual voice to be considered here is, of course, its representation of Vietnam and the Vietnamese. While the three films under discussion can be said to share a significant and global strategy in their representation of the Other (mobilizing stereotype in the service of solidarity), each instance textualizes this impetus in specific and distinguishable ways. *In the Year of the Pig* is notable for its appeal to a rationality that is identifiably American. Trained as a philosopher, influenced by his friends the abstract expressionists, de Antonio pursues an inevitable if circuitous logic in his work that places footage in relief, producing commentary through juxtaposition.

De Antonio's didacticism is linked to his unrelenting search for causation in the topics he addresses. The blunders and horrors committed by a McCarthy, Nixon, or Westmoreland are brought to public attention in his films; but, more than that, the historical and thus ideological conditions that made these individual actions possible are elucidated as their necessary social matrix. It is thus not at all surprising that *In the Year of the Pig* is a film more about the United States than about Vietnam. Senator Morton's labeling of Ho Chi Minh as the George Washington of his country strikes the appropriate chord early on, as does the American Civil War iconography of the credit sequence. Vietnam is, to a degree, domesticated, made familiar.

The authorities interviewed in the course of the film are much on the order of Said's Orientalists, the "experts" who, as scholars, journalists, political and military leaders, set the agenda for policy decisions and establish the limits of public debate. Pauline Kael's charge that Ho Chi Minh was the hero of de Antonio's Oscar-nominated film ignores the weight of expert testimony, which produces that heroism in absentia. From Yale professor Paul Mus to David Halberstam, to Harrison Salisbury, to former State Department specialist Roger Hillsman—these are the unimpeachable sources capable of rethinking the history of American intervention. The counterweight to this present-tense testimony is not the thought or action of the Vietnamese offered as proof so much as the public pronouncements of Charles Wilson, John Foster Dulles, Curtis Le May, Mark Clark, and George Patton, Jr., recycled from the past. These historical figures are revealed in their arrogance and chilling indifference to human suffering with Patton's grinning praise of his soldiers ("they're damn good killers") the graphic prototype.

De Antonio, unlike the other filmmakers considered, never went to Vietnam, nor did his project require it. The formal and rhetorical logic of the film's unfolding is profoundly American, its object a reflection upon a national blindness rooted in a lengthy and complex history. The nativist character of *In the Year of the Pig* results in part from its attention to American diplomats, journalists, and military men whose testimony slowly, meticulously builds a mosaic and in so doing charts one nation's collision course with a fateful intervention. The film is conspicuously American in another way as well: it is one part the rationalist discourse of a philosopher trained in the American, analytical tradition (de Antonio did indeed once teach philosophy), one part the creative tapestry of a New York-based artist influenced by his contemporaries, the Abstract Expressionists. In this instance, the Other is a topos defined less by Vietnamese geography or custom (though these concerns are addressed in numerous interviews) than by the outer limits of the American imperial mind projected abroad with fateful consequence.

ONLY THE BEGINNING: A BROTHERHOOD OF VICTIMS; *THE PEOPLE'S WAR*: THE APPEAL TO POPULISM

[Identification is the] psychological process whereby the subject assimilates an aspect, property or attribute of the other and is transformed, wholly or partially, after the model the other provides. It is by means of a series of identifications that the personality is constituted and specified.
        Laplanche and Pontalis, The Language of Psycho-analysis[17]

The Newsreel collective, founded by an assortment of politically engaged filmmakers and political activists in December of 1967, was dedicated to offering an alternative vision of the political storm brewing worldwide.

Newsreel was, and remains in its current incarnations, an outgrowth of the Movement, that loosely defined coalition of forces that, by the late sixties, had established a sense of itself through a succession of struggles from Berkeley to Selma, Alabama, to Chicago. The maze of constituencies to which the Movement responded (student radicals, blacks, Puerto Ricans, early feminists, trade unionists, draft resistance organizers) was an amalgam of those who, like the first generation SDS leadership, were resisting privilege (sharing the struggles of the underclasses), those fighting for a piece of the American Dream, and those devoted to challenging and disrupting the system in its entirety. Little wonder that such an uneasy mix, on the verge of irreparable fracture, attempting to define itself outside the hostility or indifference of the mass media, became enmeshed in what has been called "identity politics." The imperative of the day was indeed the forging of an identity for the New Left, one that could bind together disparate elements in conscious coalition. But identity formation, as we know from French psychoanalyst Jacques Lacan, is a process rooted in the Imaginary, founded upon misrecognition. In the mirror stage which Lacan has elucidated, the subject assumes an image, a fantasy that "extends from a fragmented body-image to a form of its totality"; in such a formulation, the agency of the ego is situated "in a fictional direction."[18] As an image of the (collective) self, political identity is equally shaped by a dynamic process that allows idealizations to be internalized. For a troubled New Left, deeply fractured, revolutionary forces abroad could function as an ideal-I, as a "form of its totality." Across a broad range of films focusing on specific events (campus occupations, strikes, demonstrations) or sectors of cultural resistance (guerrilla theater, the G.I. coffeehouse movement, the underground press), Newsreel was in the business of identity-construction, offering up to the Movement viable versions of itself.

The films inscribe the pluralism of their audience in several ways—through a collective authorship that submerged creative individualism and through their trademark usage of multiple voice-overs offering a broad dispersal of cinematic authority. Much of the Newsreel oeuvre can fairly be described as radical cheerleading; the best of the films, however, to borrow Colin Mac-Cabe's pronouncement on Godard's video work of the seventies, raise questions that silence answers. One film, *Summer '68* (1969), addresses the politics of identity with a combination of formal virtuosity and studied self-awareness. It concludes its presentation of the events of those tumultuous months of 1968 in the streets of Chicago with a voice-over issuing from filmmaker Norman Fruchter:

> Once the troops were called out, we thought we'd won. But won what? All we'd managed was a disruption. But we'd fought for days and so many people had joined us that we felt much more than ourselves. For once, we thougt we *were* the people. When we left Chicago to go back to our own communities, our sense of triumph quickly became a memory. What we went back to was the tough, day-to-day work of building a revolutionary movement. And what Chicago finally came to, for us, was the feeling of what it might be like after making that revolution, when anyone could say: "We *are* the people!"

Only the Beginning and *The People's War* raise the question of identity only implicitly. Yet it is the issue that dominates both films. In the former, the focus of the piece appears to be disenchanted Vietnam vets engaged in a counter-ritual on the periphery of the White House. One after another, these ex-G.I.'s take their turn at the microphone, expressing, by turns, denunciation and radical advocacy. As is so often the case with early Newsreel, the focus of the film spirals out from its point of origin, cutting across space and time with little regard for precise coordinates or the labeling of sources. This aesthetic choice is also an ideological one in its suggestion that "the struggle is one." The cutaways from the Washington event to the testimony of radicalized vets at home or overseas provide a double suture: geographic distance as well as racial difference is bridged. It is the most disenfranchised that are awarded greatest access: the Indian, the black, the Chicano, and—notably—the handicapped, for in the figure of the handicapped vet are condensed all the wounds—psychic, emotional, and spiritual as well as corporeal—that were the legacy of combat.

It is precisely this notion of injury that provides the linkage to the Vietnamese people who are the film's third nodal point. From the militancy of the vets to the incipient insurgency of the soldiers in the field to the victimization of the indigenous population—this is the metonymy of sympathy or resemblance that structures the film. Damaged warriors of East and West are graphically united through a sequence that documents the brutal dispersal of an organized protest by disabled South Vietnamese soldiers, the tear gas haze the sign of repression at home or abroad. Only a slight focal shift is then required for a consideration of the effects of Agent Orange upon the unborn children of Vietnam. The fusion or cross-cultural identification of the war's victims is reinforced in hindsight through this reference to the pathology of chemical defoliants whose full range of long-term effects upon Americans is only now being discovered. The prognosis for the child exposed to thalidomide in utero, born with Down Syndrome, posits a "being against nature," a figure pertinent to all the victims as well as to those in solidarity whose resistance and sympathy appeared, at times, so futile as to halt the powers of speech. For, of the child disabled by chemical exposure we are told: "When she cries she chokes, because her tear ducts run back down her nose to her mouth, instead of out to her eyes."

Sympathy is aroused early on in *The People's War*, a forty-minute piece coauthored by three first-generation Newsreelers—Robert Machover, Robert Kramer, and Norm Fruchter. But it is the warp and woof of life in the People's Democratic Republic of Vietnam that occupies center stage in this film, shot over a two-month period one year after the debacle of the Chicago Democratic Convention. If collective identity for the Movement had been problematic that summer of '68, how much farther removed was a viable and shared sense of purpose after the disintegration of a unified Left, in those "Days of Rage"? For veterans of nearly a decade of organizing efforts and planned actions in the neighborhoods of America (an earlier film, *Troublemakers* [1966], co-directed by Fruchter and Machover, featured Kramer, Tom Hayden, and other SDS activists organizing in Newark's black ghetto), disenfranchised violence of the sort practiced by the Weather Underground was an unacceptable alternative. While *The People's War* was no doubt motivated by the desire to show the heroic struggle of an embattled people in their own terms, it also offered a model of ongoing revolutionary activity, responsive to community needs, that contrasted favorably with terrorism. *The People's War* is the clearest instance of the "voyage en Orient" structure; it is a romance of collectivism, a fantasy of populism. It is, perhaps, a vision closer to Frank Capra than to Dziga Vertov.

The film's title is a slight misnomer in that war is suborned to the texture of everyday life. In keeping with the overarching motif of populism, the film takes as its object an elemental communalism, powerful in its simplicity: "What we want is simple," says a peasant woman translated in voice-over, "a better life for all our people." In this wished-for Vietnam, every breach common to industrial society is annulled by the salve of collective action: work and play, city and country ("Hanoi is the capital city. But it must never be apart from our villages."), male and female. Each of these potential disjunctures becomes instead a site of popular unity. The struggle to live and fight together is documented in the factories, where the women without families volunteer for the night shift, and in the village marketplace, where scientific methods safeguard public health, in the fields and at the dikes and rice paddies that dot the landscape.

In this realm of revolutionary romanticism, knowledge is applied rather than abstract; research for its own sake is a luxury reserved for peacetime. Work is to remain concrete and task-oriented until every citizen has equal access to leisure. The words of a young chemist trained at the polytechnic are spoken in translation by filmmaker Fruchter: "All of us feel the same excitement here as we begin to work with the tools we need. Yes, we know that our work is practical and applied when compared to scientific research in the West. But all our tasks are concrete and practical until the entire country is no longer underdeveloped."

The vigilance of the citizenry is equaled by a necessary resourcefulness. The looms in the factory survive from the days of the French occupation and must suffice. But the deeper meaning of the ingenuity so poetically rendered in Santiago Alvarez's *Hanoi, Martes 13* (1967), as in all the films of solidarity, is tied to the notion of bricolage, that process whereby the inhabitant of the Third World appropriates the forms of the modern capitalist West and fragments then intersperses them with indigenous ones in a reflexive, critical montage of synthetic contradictions.[19] According to one social witness in *The People's War*, "We constructed or invented all our tools." Just as the bicycles of the farmers hauling their rice to market can be transformed into trucks, so too is the society as a whole rendered capable of performing the most elemental transmutation. "We transform hatred into energy." Used as a leitmotif in *Hanoi, Martes 13*, the slogan and its first-person-plural grammatical construction effectively weld the filmmaker's process to that of his subject. Revolutionary society and the art that promotes it are the sublimate of this social alchemy.

The People's War comes to rest at its populist base, the village cooperative whose frequent meetings are a forum for constructive criticism and the formulation of strategies to increase production. The group process depicted in the film becomes the "good object" counterpart to the divisive and self-destructive dynamic endemic to the American New Left during the same period. The final words belong to Ho Chi Minh, a figure all but absent from the film otherwise. This exclusion, offering stark contrast to Alvarez's *Seventy-nine Springtimes* (1969), a virtuosic encomium to Ho produced the same year, is altogether in keeping with the film's attachment to the grass roots. This is, after all, the same constituency to which Fruchter, Kramer, and Machover devoted themselves in the mid-sixties through their involvement with the Newark Community Union Project—the SDS organizing effort—and the film *Troublemakers*, which documented that lengthy process. Ho's benediction sounds all the notes of the celestial scale of revolution: "My ultimate wish is that our whole party and people, united in struggle, build a peaceful, unified, independent, democratic and prosperous Vietnam and make a worthy contribution to the world revolution."

But it is the physical setting of the film's conclusion that most dramatically enforces this romance of identity. In a protracted sequence quite beautiful for its evocation of labor process as silent communion among equals, a small-scale shipbuilding operation comes to signify the harmony and quiet strength of the Vietnamese worker/soldier. The style of the sequence is that of cinéma vérité; the desire to capture the ineffable rhythms of daily life is only partially contained. The gentle pulse of movement in the carefully defined space is shown through the performance of a final transformative act, the conversion of trees into transportation. Here, in this final representation of collective labor, work and art are made to coalesce—the populist utopia is achieved.

Recent work on representations of the Other has tended to privilege one psychic mechanism—projection—at the expense of other terms within this complex discursive formation. While the attention to the construction of the bad object, the negative stereotype, the appropriated other within colonial discourse is strategically correct, too little attention has been paid to the "productive ambivalence" that characterizes the dynamic exchange between self and object. For this ambivalence is literal. Through the paired forces of projection and introjection, self and other engage in a constructive dialectic that is mutually defining. That dynamic is also equivocal with regard to its moral valence; the good and bad Other are linked by a principle of inversion that Freud assures us (in the context of dream interpretation) is simply a permutation of identity. While it may be descriptively sound to claim that the Other in Western thought has typically been thematized as the "threat to be reduced, as a potential same-to-be, a yet-not-same," rarely has the introjective reflex been accorded its place within this dynamic.[20] For with the construction of the good object or ego ideal, the threat to be reduced originates not in the external world but in the fear of the self's inadequacy. The idealization effected speaks a solidarity that is psychic in origin, building a bridge between the subject and the wished-for object that unseats that fear. If the American Left of the late 1960s found itself inadequate to the task of broad-based social change through a democratic group process, it could look outside itself for a heroic mirror. In the example of Vietnam such a mirror was found. I have here attempted to test the representational limits of this complex process in three films of the period, to explore the concrete ways in which the Left's collective daydream, the Democratic Republic of Vietnam as imaged, enabled Marcuse's "new Subject" to proclaim: "We have met *their* enemy, and they are *us*."

NOTES

1. Gilles Deleuze, "Michel Tournier and the World Without Others," *Economy and Society* 13 no. 1 (1984):63.

2. Paul Ricoeur, "Universal Civilization and National Cultures," in *History and Truth*, trans. Charles A. Kelbley (Evanston: Northwestern University Press, 1965), p. 278.

3. Homi K. Bhabha, "The Other Question: The Stereotype and Colonial Discourse," *Screen* 24, no. 6 (November-December 1983):19.

4. Sander L. Gilman, *Difference and Pathology: Stereotypes of Sexuality, Race, and Madness* (Ithaca, N.Y.: Cornell University Press, 1985), p. 18.

5. Trinh T. Minh-ha, "Introduction," *Discourse* 8 (Fall-Winter 1986–87):6.

6. Bhabha, "The Other Question," p. 23

7. Edward W. Said, *Orientalism* (New York: Vintage Books, 1978), p. 12.

8. Ibid., p. 44.

9. J. Laplanche and J.-B. Pontalis, "Projection," in *The Language of Psycho-analysis* (New York: W. W. Norton, 1973), p. 349.

10. Michael Renov, "Early Newsreel: The Construction of a Political Imaginary for the New Left, *Afterimage* 14, no. 7 (February 1987):12–15.

11. Herbert Marcuse, *An Essay On Liberation* (Boston: Beacon Press, 1969), p. 53.

12. Quoted in Said, *Orientalism*, p. 177.

13. Ibid.

14. Thomas Waugh, "Beyond Vérité: Emile de Antonio and the New Documentary of the Seventies," in *Movies and Methods*, vol. 2, ed. Bill Nichols (Berkeley and Los Angeles: University of California Press, 1985), pp. 233–258.

15. Alan Rosenthal, *The Documentary Conscience: A Casebook in Film Making* (Berkeley and Los Angeles: University of California Press, 1980), p. 216.

16. Bill Nichols, "The Voice of Documentary," in *Movies and Methods*, vol. 2, ed. Nichols, p. 262.

17. Laplanche and Pontalis, "Identification," in *The Language of Psycho-analysis*, p. 205.

18. Jacques Lacan, "The Mirror Stage as Formative of the Function of the I," in *Ecrits: A Selection*, trans. Alan Sheridan (New York: W. W. Norton, 1977), pp. 4, 2.

19. Hal Foster, *Recodings: Art, Spectacle, Cultural Politics* (Port Townsend, Wash.: Bay Press, 1985), p. 201.

20. Wlad Godzich, "Foreword" to Michel de Certeau, *Heterologies: Discourse on the Other*, trans. Brian Massumi (Minneapolis: University of Minneapolis Press, 1986), p. xiii.

"We Aren't on the Wrong Side, We Are the Wrong Side": Peter Davis Targets (American) Hearts and Minds

The first image we see is a horse-drawn cart, meandering down a dirt track through a small village. Even if we didn't know what *Hearts and Minds* (1974) was about, we're tipped off by the characteristic saucer hats worn by everyone the cart passes and by the strange "Asian" song on the sound track, different from what we expect as music, yet peaceful, not jarring. Children, carrying what look like schoolbags, frolic in the fields while adults go about their business, agricultural tasks of some kind. Unobtrusively, an American soldier passes by. The people appear to take no notice as they rest under the shade of a tree. More soldiers pass along the dirt embankments that separate the flooded rice paddies from each other. Why are they there? What do the Vietnamese think about them? At this point, we don't know, the film has not said. Yet the opening image is one of calm and peace, a nonthreatening image of Vietnam. We will not see that again in this movie.

Director Peter Davis structured this opening to show us a different Vietnam from the one we were used to seeing. "The idea of the opening of the film is to bring you into a different world . . . to suspend the world you are normally familiar with and learn about something else . . . to initiate audiences into the reality of Vietnam."[1] Davis focuses on the Vietnamese; they are the center. The Americans appear, still subtly, perhaps even benignly at this point, but coming from off camera as outsiders, perhaps invaders. Throughout the film, Davis continually comes back to this reversed perspective. Unlike most Americans and virtually everyone in the mainstream media, Davis asks, "What did we do to Vietnam?" not "What did the Vietnamese do to us?" In his answer he paints a picture of the U.S. as strong militarily but sick and soulless culturally. American war-making in Vietnam was technologically sophisticated but barbarous—grinding up the lives of both Vietnamese and Americans in an almost casual way. Anticommunism, machismo, and self-satisfied indifference on the part of the U.S. population drove the war on. "We aren't *on* the wrong side," Daniel Ellsberg says in the film, "we *are* the wrong side."

Davis has made a powerful indictment of the U.S. war. Yet the indictment has weaknesses—weaknesses characteristic of the beliefs, organizing styles, and social position of the antiwar movement at the time. More than anything else, the successes of the antiwar movement made it possible for *Hearts and Minds*, an explicitly antiwar documentary, to receive the studio backing and wide exposure that it did. However, *Hearts and Minds* also shares the antiwar movement's lack of clarity about the ultimate responsibility that the average American citizen bore for the actions of their government in Indochina.

By 1972, when Davis began work on the film, the antiwar movement had fought the Nixon administration to a standstill. A majority of Americans wanted an end to U.S. involvement and favored some form of U.S. disengagement. Many members of the intelligentsia, including Hollywood insiders, opposed the war vigorously and identified with the antiwar movement. Bert Schneider, whose production company had made *Easy Rider* (1969), *Five Easy Pieces* (1970), and *The Monkees* TV show, wanted to produce an antiwar documentary focusing on government lying and the Pentagon Papers trials. He hired Davis to direct the documentary, on the strength of his exposé of the Defense Department's public relations activities, *The Selling of the Pentagon* (1971). It was an exemplary document of the antiwar mood among TV industry professionals, about as hard-hitting as TV ever got on the subject of the war.[2]

Despite its successes, the antiwar movement in the early seventies was in a desperate mood. The majority of Americans opposed the war on pragmatic grounds—more out of war weariness than principle. In other words, they didn't oppose U.S. intervention because it was wrong (the position of most antiwar movement activists) but because it was too costly to America in lives and money, or because it was dragging on and U.S. goals no longer seemed clear or attainable. Nixon and his advisors devised the Vietnamization strategy to defuse popular alienation from U.S. war policy by giving the impression that the U.S. was disengaging from the war, but avoiding (in reality postponing) the trauma of defeat. Thus, Nixon claimed he was for peace, but "peace with honor." For the antiwar movement, however, Vietnamization changed nothing of importance about why they opposed the war, but the policy's success as a public relations tactic did throw the movement into some disarray. Although U.S. casualties declined, the Nixon administration, through material support of its South Vietnamese client and intensified bombing that relied on U.S. personnel, ensured that the war would continue. Many activists despaired over their inability to end the war even after years of organizing and protest. Some, like the Weathermen, wrote off the mass of Americans as the enemy and embarked on a politically suicidal program of confrontation for its own sake. Others simply withdrew from political activity.

Davis seems to have shared this despair. He told an interviewer, "By the early seventies, we were destroying Indochina as a reflex action; most people didn't even want the war anymore but felt no great pangs about its continuation." Thus, Davis set out "to understand the psychological bases and needs for this war," but also to document that destruction.[3] We can see Davis's statements as part of a strategy to force apathetic, uninformed Americans to confront the reality of what the U.S. had done to Vietnam. Davis told Newsweek that he was particularly pleased with the way people with no well-developed point of view on the war responded to *Hearts and Minds*:

They come away with serious questions and they do more thinking as a result of seeing the film. It's this audience that gives me both pleasure as a filmmaker and hope as an American. These are the people I want the film to reach: those people who may not have thought very much about the war but who have that particularly healthy American trait of doubt.[4]

Gilliatt relates an anecdote that shows what Davis was hoping for:

[A] woman of about sixty-five came alone into the theatre. . . . She stood stock still beside me for a few minutes looking at the screen with festering surprise. Obviously when I thought about it, the title had misled her: . . . she expected . . . a love story; instead of that, there was a screen showing wounded Vietnamese, wounded GI's, assured United States pol- icymakers in office spouting upholstered bombast, confused and skeletal Vietnamese sorrowfully quitting the debris of their American bombed homes. . . . I glanced at her now and then. She took in everything, looked startled, cried. At the end, she went on sitting in her place with her eyes still on the now blank screen, and said to me, without turning round, "I didn't know we'd done that." Pause. "I like what the American wom- an said about a mature person's being able to make a mistake so why can't a government."[5]

Davis structured *Hearts and Minds* to produce such a strong reaction to the brutality and arrogance of U.S. war-making. His technique can be usefully contrasted to the ways that the mainstream news organizations reported the war. Davis turned the mainstream's conventions on their head to make his antiwar point. However, he took a contradictory position on who bore respon- sibility for the U.S. war effort which partially undermined the empathy he felt for the average American and jeopardized the effectiveness of his message.

Daniel Hallin's careful content analysis of Vietnam coverage in *The New York Times* from 1961 through mid-1965, and on network evening news from August 1965 until January 1973, convincingly refutes the widely held belief that the news media were significantly responsible for U.S. defeat in Indo- china.[6] Overall, Hallin finds the media almost totally accepting of U.S. war aims throughout. The mainstream media never questioned the Cold War polit- ical rationale for American policy. They never challenged the idea that the U.S. was responding to, in the words of *Times* writer Hanson Baldwin (16 September 1962), "centrally directed Communist aggression," in "an un- declared war against the proxy armies of Soviet Russia—the North and South Vietnamese querilas." Similarly, the news organizations virtually always framed their reports with an assumption that U.S. policy stemmed from "good will" and "desire to help."[7] When reporting from the field appeared to contradict the assumptions of American benevolence, as in Morley Safer's critical account of a search and destroy mission in August 1965, network ex- ecutives deliberated extensively about whether to run the report at all. Safer's report showed G.I.'s burning peasant huts with their cigarette lighters and focused on civilian casualties of the operation. Safer's bosses were extremely concerned about negative political fallout from the story, even though they eventually gave the story approval. Yet as Hallin notes, they routinely approved the airing of stories framed around U.S. battlefield victories, combat heroism, or the atrocities of the "enemy." Stories that shared the administration's assumptions were routine; stories that contradicted the government's frame were deviant. The frames used by TV news in the period 1962–1967 survived the collapse of the U.S. consensus around war aims after the 1968 Tet offensive. TV news still stayed solidly within accepted political discourse about U.S. foreign policy.[8]

Day-to-day TV news practices are structured by what Hallin calls the "ideology of objective journalism."[9] Three key concepts make up this ideology. Journalists should be *independent* of political commitments and outside pressures. Journalists should be *objective,* presenting the facts with opinion and judgment clearly demarcated and recognizable as such. Coverage should be *balanced,* fairly and equally representing all sides of a story.

In practice, however, the conventions of day-to-day journalistic practice undermine these lofty goals. Journalists give predominant coverage to official government sources. Often stories simply consist of what the government spokespeople announce. The tendency is particularly marked when the president is involved. Mainstream journalists let the government create the frame by reporting whatever officials say as fact, without comment or interpretation. In addition, journalists focus almost exclusively on immediate events. As a result, historical context, which always carries with it an evaluative dimension, gets short shrift. The historical context, then, becomes whatever the newsmakers choose to "remember." The president denouncing North Vietnamese infiltration into South Vietnam is news. U.S. responsibility for the creation of two Vietnams by subverting the 1954 Geneva Accords remains unmentioned.

Turning to *Hearts and Minds*, we can see that Davis and company take the TV news frame and the canons of "objective journalism" and turn them inside out—reverse the meanings they give in order to subvert support for U.S. war policy.

Where "objective journalists" enshrine government spokespeople as the authorities and only sometimes provide a balancing speaker, *Hearts and Minds* ridicules the officials and substitutes war opponents as the "authorities." Walt Rostow, former advisor to Kennedy and Johnson, was so outraged by his portrayal that he sued (ultimately unsuccessfully) to enjoin the producers from using interview footage of him in the film. Davis shows Rostow as arrogant and vindictive, unwilling to admit that the policy he helped formulate has failed. First we see Rostow saying, pompously, that he knew of no analysis, "Communist or non-Communist," that claimed that the majority of South Vietnamese supported the Communists. In one of the few times he allows the audience to hear his interview questions, Davis asks from off camera "Why did they need us, then?" Rostow starts to answer, "Because they were subjected to hostile military action from outside." Then he bristles,

"Are you really asking me this goddamn silly question? . . . It's pretty pedestrian stuff at this late stage of the game." Davis then remarks barely audibly, "There's a lot of disagreement . . ." and Rostow cuts him off, "No, there's not!" Then condescendingly, "I didn't really expect to go back to this sophomoric stuff, but I'll do it." Rostow then launches into his lecture on the origins of the war, but Davis ends the scene there. Davis does not give us Rostow's explanation, he shows us the contempt Rostow feels for others who question his competence.

Hearts and Minds portrays General William Westmoreland, commander of U.S. forces in Vietnam as a dull, dim man, the personification of Hannah Arendt's "banality of evil." In one of the most shocking and controversial sequences from the film, we see a funeral for an ARVN soldier; family members cry, a small boy stares intently at a framed photograph, presumably of the deceased, a sobbing woman tries to climb into the grave after the coffin is lowered, and several men restrain her. Then Westmoreland, in civilian dress, filmed in a garden, explains softly, blandly, "Well, the Oriental does not put the same high value on human life as does the westerner. Life is plentiful, life is cheap in the Orient; and uh, as the philosophy of the Orient, uh, expresses it, life is not important." A screaming U.S. jet and napalm exploding across a road follows, then the famous footage of a naked Vietnamese girl, burned by napalm, running down the road toward the camera. Many people I've talked with picked out this sequence as the most memorable of the whole movie, several recalling it after ten years. The graveside scenes make Westmoreland's views seem shockingly callous, and the sequence that follows underlines the genocidal conclusions that his beliefs would lead to.

In *Hearts and Minds*, Davis does not use a voice-over narrator to explain to the viewer what points they should be getting. As noted above, except in two cases, he does not allow the audience to hear the interview questions he asks. Davis also eschews any kind of chronological ordering of his material, and the absence of historical narrative gives the film a chaotic, formless quality. In her *New Yorker* review, Penelope Gilliatt went so far as to claim, "If all the sequences . . . were thrown up in the air and put together again in random order, the meaning of the film would still be the same."[10] This does not mean, however, that Davis hasn't carefully crafted *Hearts and Minds* to put forward a point of view. Davis carefully combined footage from diverse sources, specially filmed interviews and American scenes, network battle footage, scenes from North Vietnamese sources, historical footage of U.S. leaders, and clips from U.S. war movies. He arranged this material in sequences and used particular editing techniques to communicate his overall meaning to the audience.

In his treatment of Westmoreland, Davis juxtaposes other material to contradict him and undermine his credibility and, as a result, the viewer's identification with the U.S. war effort. By confronting Westmoreland's pronouncements about Vietnamese complacency about death with the specially filmed funeral scenes that show just the opposite, then using the famous napalm footage to show the tremendous destructive capacity of American firepower,

Davis places Westmoreland in a highly unsympathetic light. Davis ultimately suggests that it is the Americans who are complacent about death—as long as the deaths are Vietnamese. The racist underpinnings of the war come through far more powerfully than simply by showing Westmoreland making prejudicial assumptions about "Orientals." Davis used Westmoreland to show that the U.S. leaders have so little regard for Vietnam that they are literally willing, in the famous phrase, to destroy the country in order to save it.

Davis uses the same technique to savage President Nixon. As Hallin notes, the mainstream press usually reports presidential actions as straight news without commentary. Davis, however, shows the deadly consequences of presidential posturing. We see a festive banquet for returned U.S. POWs, as Nixon tells the adoring crowd that his "most difficult decision as President was on December 18." He's referring to the resumption of American bombing raids against North Vietnam—the "Christmas bombing" of 1972. The crowd, most of whom had witnessed the bombing from their POW camps, goes wild with appreciation. Nixon then triumphantly calls for "a round of applause for those brave men who took their B-52's in and did the job!" While he talks about the "tough decision" he made to order the bombing, we see planes being readied and then shots of B-52 bombers taking off. After a series of bombing scenes, abruptly, footage of Bach Mai Hospital, destroyed in the bombing appears. In almost total silence, except for the sound of wind whistling, the camera pans through the wreckage.

The consequences of Nixon's actions are now clear. A Vietnamese woman kneels, weeping, and the camera then shows us two dead children laid out on mats, in a formal pose—eyes closed and hands folded across their chests. From this silent picture of grief, Davis escalates the tension. A distraught father shows us the ruins of his farmhouse where his eight-year-old daughter and three-year-old son were killed in the bombing. "Here is her beautiful shirt," he says, showing us a bloody rag. "Here is where she died," and the camera shows the remnants of walls and cooking gear. "They say they bomb military targets, no targets here." Camera pans over empty fields. "Nixon, murderer of civilians! Take this shirt back to the U.S.—throw it in Nixon's face! Tell him she was only a little schoolgirl." So much for the "brave men who did the job."

In the sequence just described, Davis refuses to extend the deferential treatment that the media usually accord the President. Instead he shows the consequences of Nixon's orders: the unsettling scenes of battle; massive destruction, with Bach Mai Hospital suggesting that civilian targets were bombed routinely; and finally the deaths of civilians, including children, shown explicitly. The result is a delegitimizing of American leadership and, Davis hopes, a decline in deference shown by the American people toward their leaders' explanations of U.S. policy goals. Ellsberg, at one point in the film, begins a litany with "Truman lied about French plans for colonial reconquest of Vietnam," and then goes down the list from Eisenhower to Nixon "who lied and lied and lied," and *Hearts and Minds* shows them doing it.

Davis offers new authorities to the audience to replace the U.S. leaders he

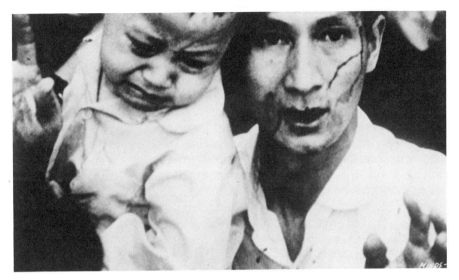

Hearts and Minds: *Demanding that we take the feelings of the Vietnamese into account.*

has discredited. Just as he holds U.S. leaders up to ridicule, he sympathetically portrays those whom he wants the audience to believe. Recall his desire to make Americans confront what the war was doing to Vietnam. Key in the Nixon sequence is the film's demand that we take the feelings of the Vietnamese into account. As Hallin notes, less than 10 percent of TV Vietnam war coverage concerned South Vietnamese politics, government, and economy.[11] The feelings and beliefs of the average Vietnamese received an infinitesimal part of total coverage. By contrast, "representative" Vietnamese are key sources of information in *Hearts and Minds*. In particular, they, like the man who wanted the film crew to throw his daughter's bloodstained shirt in Nixon's face, talk of the disastrous impact of the war on their lives. Davis chooses to highlight this aspect of the war, in sharp contrast to the mainstream media's decision to ignore how the Vietnamese civilians feel about the U.S. role in the war.

Davis tries to decrease cultural and emotional distance between Americans and Vietnamese by showing how Vietnamese feel about the U.S. war. In one powerful sequence he intercuts the recollections of two former American flyers with the feelings of Vietnamese bombing victims. The flyers recall bombing as an exciting exercise in technical mastery. As they talk about the sheer pleasure of doing a highly complex job like flying, Davis cuts away to the same village of the opening scene, but this time, instead of a sense of peace, we see a girl hurrying along the road glancing over her shoulder apprehensively. Shots of the flyers are intercut with film of planes, falling bombs, and explosions.

Two old women follow. Their seventy-eight-year-old sister has been killed and their house reduced to rubble. We see one lighting candles in what looks like a memorial ceremony. She wipes away tears: "I'm so unhappy." One of the U.S. flyers says, "You never see any blood from up there, never hear any screams. . . . I was just a technician." Cut away to the old woman entering a ruined building as he finishes talking; she compares herself to a bird without a nest. The point is clear: what we regard as the technology of fighting, good strategy for winning the war, or even simply an exciting career, means tragedy for the Vietnamese.

While the old women express their grief, Davis keeps them on camera for a long time in comparison with the normal length of a TV image, despite the fact that they do not say anything. He uses this technique often when a character is undergoing an extremely emotional experience, or when a scene of violence is on the screen. It forces the viewer to confront the feelings of the people on the screen. Time seems to stand still, no other image comes to the rescue by diverting the viewer's attention from what has gone before. *Hearts and Minds* tries to break down the viewers' emotional distance from the brutality of the war in order to allow people to be horrified by it. The film tries particularly hard to build empathy between the viewer and the Vietnamese. Davis asks the viewer to imagine how they might feel had their liberators bombed their homes. By keeping them on camera Davis invites the viewer to fill what might be dead time by imagining what they are feeling.[12]

In the following sequence, Davis suggests what the Vietnamese really think, away from the intrusive pressures of the camera. We see two men inspect the ruins of a small building. The shot is from a medium distance, so that while we can hear them speak, they talk to each other, not the camera, and the scene has the quality of eavesdropping on a private conversation. Noticing the camera and camera operator, one says (with disgust, in the rendering of the voice-over translation), "Look, they're focusing on us now. First they bomb as much as they please, then they film." Clearly they regard the Americans not as saviors but as intruders, privileged by their technological superiority, especially in their capacity to make war.

Finally, dissident G.I.'s are a powerful set of antiwar "authorities" in the film. Hallin notes that TV news reporting from Vietnam "was structured by a set of assumptions about the values of war—not so much as a political instrument, but as an arena of human action, of individual and national self-expression."[13] Network reporting focused on the actions of soldiers in the field and framed them with the propositions that war is a manly American tradition, and that American strategy was rational because the U.S. was winning. Even after Tet, network news never questioned the political assumptions under which the U.S. fought, but began to portray the war as a meaningless stalemate and to focus on American efforts to disengage. *Hearts and Minds* uses G.I.'s to assert credibly that the war was not simply a tragedy or stalemate but a waste of American lives that accomplished nothing except the devastation of Vietnam.[14]

Hearts and Minds features former Marine Robert Muller and ex-pilot Randy Floyd. Each appears more than once, continuing a story that describes their growing disillusionment with the war. Muller appears three times, telling the story of how he received the wounds that cost him the use of his legs. He

Veteran Robert Muller: Losing the love of one's country "hurts most." [Hearts and Minds]

enlisted in the Marine Corps out of patriotism and a desire to serve, but sums up the experience by saying that what "hurts most" is the loss of love for his country that he feels.

Immediately after his statement, the film shows footage of U.S. brutality. Soldiers burn peasant huts with flame throwers, and spill grain on the ground. The sound track plays "Over There," the patriotic World War I song. The irony is savage. We see a Vietnamese, presumably an NLF suspect, gasp for air as his head is pulled out of water. He is being tortured, and American soldiers are doing it. He stands up and the hand of his unseen interrogator slaps him in the face. The effect of brutality administered casually or perhaps routinely is horrifying. Now we *know* why Muller can no longer feel the same love for the U.S. that he once did.

Former pilot Randy Floyd focuses explicitly on what he did to the Vietnamese, not what the war did to him. Davis plays him in counterpoint to Navy Lieutenant George Coker, a returned POW. Coker suffers no doubts about his role in the war or the legitimacy of U.S. policy. He blandly asserts that the U.S. won the war, asserts his readiness to go to war again, and tells a school assembly that Vietnam is a beautiful country but that the people who live there are "backward" and "mess everything up." (These statements from Coker always elicit gasps from students when I show *Hearts and Minds* in my class on the 1960s. They see him as a buffoon, exactly as Davis intended.) Floyd, in contrast to Coker, appears in the film to be haunted by the realization that the bombs he was dropping hit innocent people.

Davis edited the footage so that Floyd's regret comes across more strongly as the film progresses. He notes that the antipersonnel bombs he dropped are designed to wound, not kill, forcing the "enemy" to allocate valuable personnel to nurse the wounded. He speaks of his lack of comprehension, that he could not understand at the time that the bombs he dropped killed and maimed real people. "We as Americans have never experienced devastation of any kind; I never saw a child burned by napalm." The gravity of what he did overcomes him. "I look at my children now. What would I think if someone napalmed them?" he asks, and then bows his head weeping. Here again, Davis holds the camera on him for an extended period to induce reflection in the audience. It is this kind of identification that Davis is striving for—asking the audience to imagine themselves experiencing the kind of destruction the U.S. had brought to Vietnam. In this way Davis hoped to bring the war home to Americans, by trying to get his audience to share Floyd's feeling of responsibility for the U.S. destruction in Vietnam.

Davis is extraordinarily empathetic toward the Vietnamese and antiwar G.I.'s, those who have been hurt by the war and understand its true nature. He communicates that to the audience hoping that it will first create sympathetic identification with the war's victims that might light the spark of antiwar consciousness in the minds of apathetic viewers. By contrast, Davis displays no such sympathy in looking at those Americans who support or are indifferent to the war.

The antiwar movement was bedeviled by its inability to attract the support of many Americans even when a majority opposed the war.[15] Particularly vexing was the movement's inability to transcend its base on the campuses and among liberal professionals by reaching out to the poor, blue-collar workers, and members of racial minorities. Politically and socially isolated from much of the population, members of the movement were torn about how much to blame ordinary Americans as a whole for the war. Did the war stem from elite manipulation of the mass or was the average American as much to blame as the elite? Davis certainly skewers the elite, Nixon, Rostow, Westmoreland, for responsibility in causing the war, but he is muddled on the question of mass responsibility. In assessing responsibility for the war, Davis suggests that there is something malignant, racist, and warlike in American culture that infected the population as a whole and ultimately "caused" the war.

Davis shows us rank-and-file military men who present chilling pictures of evil. Recall Lieutenant Coker's racist attitude against the Vietnamese, which prevented him from feeling any remorse for the damage he had inflicted in Indochina. Elsewhere in the film, George Patton III solemnly describes a memorial service held for three men in his unit. After describing the reverent air of the men, his face brightens. "They're still a bloody good bunch of killers!" he says with a broad grin. An anonymous G.I. tells an interviewer, "Some guys kill because it's a job and some do it because they like it." "Which kind are you?" the interviewer asks. He smiles mischievously, "I like it." These people aren't simply doing their duty, muddling through a tough situation. Davis seems to be saying, "They are sick, they like to kill. They need to dominate others."

Davis shows that a significant section of the American people embraced these killers as heroes. Lieutenant Coker gets a welcoming parade when he returns to his hometown after being released from POW camp in Vietnam, and the film closes with shots of a "Victory in Vietnam" parade in New York City. Davis selects images drawn from popular culture to suggest that Americans are driven to support the war by a violent, competitive, racist culture. He uses clips from movies, which portray Asians as barbaric killers and show World War II G.I.'s getting righteous revenge against the Japs. Davis uses footage of a high school football game most extensively to indict American culture as a whole. In one particularly powerful scene, a coach ends his half-time pep talk by hysterically flailing away at his players until they also start to scream in a violent frenzy as they charge out onto the field. Davis also shows us clips of the crowd screaming, players lying injured, and a minister telling the players that their loyalty to their team is "God's work." The implication is clear: social sanctions for violent behavior in our culture lead to violent behavior overseas.

This part of the film doesn't work, and no working-class person could be blamed for finding it insulting, and perhaps concluding that Davis was an elitist who deserved no hearing at all. Davis doesn't listen to his football crowd in the same way he does to the antiwar G.I.'s. He plays on liberal stereotypes of violent hardhats to suggest that there is an organic connection between football and the war.[16] We don't know what the football crowd thinks about the war or even what they think they're doing at the game, because Davis does not ask them. And Davis does not show us whether they have had to endure disappointment or grief from the war. Maybe they see this as a harmless outlet that helps keep aggressive impulses from intruding on other aspects of their lives. Davis depends on the audience's visceral reaction against football for the effect here. Only a specific type of middle-class audience can be expected to have that kind of reaction. Violent as the game is, it's very different from the Vietnam violence he shows. The two sides are relatively even in strength and there are rules governing behavior. Moreover, both sides have chosen to play. It's just a game; no one is likely to be killed.

Politically, Davis equates the actions of average working-class Americans with the those of the elite. As Peter Biskind puts it, "American rulers, monstrous as they appear in the film, become less authors of a genocidal culture than its agent, no better or worse than the people they rule."[17] He lets the war planners off the hook by not attributing any more responsibility for the war to them than to any other American.[18] Davis ignores the way prowar Americans were shaped by culture just as surely as the antiwar ones, even if the former have not freed themselves of the mental blinders that afflict them. "For this," according to Biskind, "they [war supporters] deserve . . . compassion. . . . They did not make their culture, they were born into it. They were conscripted into a war not their own and made to like it."[19] As Ellsberg concludes after mentioning some of the lies told by successive presidents about the war: "It's a tribute to the American people that our leaders thought it necessary to lie to us; it's no tribute that we were so easy to fool." Ultimately *Hearts and Minds* only seizes on one side of that insight—that the American people are easy to fool.

As a result, *Hearts and Minds* does not really ask in whose interest the war was fought. It says the war was a crime, but it does not lay greater guilt at the hands of the generals and presidents who planned it than on the foot soldiers who had to obey their orders. It suggests that nothing could be done to end the war, because there was no incentive for any of the morally obtuse Middle Americans to oppose it. "The film accuses us. . . . As an audience we feel . . . impotent to change the monster we have all created."[20] As Biskind says,

> On the one hand, it indulges in an orgy of liberal guilt which cannot but leave a sympathetic audience paralyzed and sick. On the other, by dividing the world into good guys and bad guys, into those who opposed the war and those who supported it, the film allows the former to dissociate itself from American war crimes ("that's not us") and the latter to turn off—in anger at its contemptuous treatment of middle America.[21]

Such moralism and condescension were characteristic of a significant section of the antiwar movement at the time and helped perpetuate the movement's isolation from large segments of the population. Thus, they perpetuated the very isolation that fueled the condescension in the first place.

The contradictions of *Hearts and Minds*, then, are the same contradictions that afflicted the antiwar movement. This should not surprise us, since the movement created the national climate that permitted the film to be made and released into mass distribution. At its best, it forcefully put forward an antiwar position that had the power to move the uninitiated. *Hearts and Minds'* strength lies in the way it reversed the frame of reference that Americans were accustomed to using in looking at the war. It forced Americans to empathize with the Vietnamese and U.S. victims of the war. It led people to ask what we did to Vietnam and to care about the destruction that they discover. It indicted U.S. leaders as criminals who ordered the devastation of Vietnamese society. As such it is a powerful antiwar vehicle.

Yet, as we have seen, it also shared the moralism, condescension, and despair that afflicted the antiwar movement. These political weaknesses led to a very ambivalent analysis, laying the blame for the war on American culture as a whole, not on the elite war planners specifically. Nevertheless, *Hearts and Minds* is a stunning portrayal of the horrors of the Vietnam War, and it reached a wide audience. And if my students are at all typical, it has the power to move people today.

NOTES

1. Bruce Berman, "The Making of *Hearts and Minds*," *Filmmakers Newsletter* (April 1975):24.

2. For more details about the making of *Hearts and Minds*, see ibid.; Penelope Gilliatt, "The Current Cinema," *The New Yorker*, 28 April 1975, pp. 120–126; "First an Undeclared War, Now an Unseen Film," *New York Times*, 17 November 1974; "Film Unit to Cut Rostow Sequence," *New York Times*, 4 January 1975; "The False Art of the Propaganda Film," *New York Times*, 23 March 1975; "The Man Who Brought Us Greetings From the Vietcong," New York Times, 4 May 1975; "Faces of War," *Newsweek*, 3 March 1975, pp. 67, 70, "War Torn," *Time*, 17 March 1975, p. 4.

3. Berman, "Making of Hearts and Minds," p. 21.

4. "Faces of War."

5. Gilliatt, "Current Cinema," p. 120.

6. All material in this section is based on Daniel Hallin, *The Uncensored War* (New York: Oxford University Press, 1986), unless otherwise noted.

7. The term I will use for TV's constructed presentation of reality is *frame*. Gitlin describes a frame as follows: "persistent patterns of cognition, interpretation and presentation, of selection emphasis and exclusion, by which symbol-handlers routinely organize discourse, whether verbal or visual": Todd Gitlin, "News as Ideology and Contested Area; Toward a Theory of Hegemony, Crisis and Opposition," *Socialist Review* 9, no. 6 (November/December 1979):12.

8. Hallin, *Uncensored War*, p. 133. For discussion of the pervasiveness of Cold War analysis in the U.S. mass media, see two works coauthored by Noam Chomsky and Edward Herman, *After the Cataclysm* (Boston: South End, 1979), and *The Manufacture of Consent* (New York: Pantheon, 1988).

9. Hallin *Uncensored War*, pp. 64–70.

10. Gilliatt "Current Cinema," p. 124

11. Hallin *Uncensored War*, p. 210.

12. Empathy, emotional identification with others, was key in building the antiwar mentality. Seeing the Vietnamese as real people with the same capacity to feel as Americans is crucial. Recollections from antiwar G.I.'s point to a moment when something snapped, and they saw what they were doing to the Vietnamese in a new light. After that they could not participate in the war effort anymore. See James Gibson *The Perfect War* (New York: Pantheon, 1988), pp. 204–206, for examples.

13. Hallin, *Uncensored War*, p. 145.

14. Davis's use of veterans as antiwar spokesmen parallels the emergence of an antiwar movement among G.I.'s after 1968. As average Americans who had seen the war firsthand, the rest of the movement hoped that active-duty G.I.'s and veterans would have the credibility with the public and news media that protesters from other backgrounds lacked.

15. Jim O'Brien notes that "a poll taken in 1968 . . . showed that among all those people who favored complete withdrawal from Vietnam a *majority* held a negative view of war protesters." "The Anti-War Movement and the War," *Radical America* 8, no. 3 (May–June 1974):57 (emphasis in original).

16. In contrast to Davis's stereotypes, 1968 poll data shows that a larger percentage of people of low "social position" favored withdrawal from Vietnam than those at an intermediate or high position (O'Brien, "Anti-War Movement, p. 58.).

17. Peter Biskind, "*Hearts and Minds*," *Cinéaste* 7, 1 (1975): 31.

18. Ironically, this analysis of the causes of the war is similar to an influential liberal

analysis that Paul Joseph terms "The System Worked" perspective. This view, associated with Leslie Gelb and Richard Betts, *The Irony of Vietnam: the System Worked* (Washington: Brookings Institution, 1979), is analyzed in Joseph, *Cracks in the Empire* (Boston: South End, 1981), pp. 29–33. As Joseph notes, Gelb and Betts suggest that the force that drove the U.S. deeper into involvement in Vietnam was the militantly anti-Communist political culture of the country, over which the elite had little control.

19. Biskind, "Hearts and Minds," p. 32.

20. Saul Landau, "'Hearts and Minds': An American Film Trial," *Jump Cut,* August/ September 1975, p. 5.

21. Biskind, *"Hearts and Minds,"* p. 32.

Dear America: Transparency, Authority, and Interpretation in a Vietnam War Documentary

Dear America: Letters Home from Vietnam, a ninety-minute documentary produced for the Home Box Office (HBO) cable network and later released to theaters and through home video outlets, is a hybrid text, difficult to place along the fiction/nonfiction axis. In amalgamating documentary fragments—letters written by G.I.'s in Vietnam and read by actors, excerpts from news reports, footage from news and the Department of Defense archives, home movies, still photographs, and popular music—director Bill Couturie and his associates have created a highly constructed, heterogeneous, and complexly coded work.

Couturie aptly described *Dear America*, built out of an amalgamation of sources into a chronological framework, as having the structure of a scrapbook: "You make it like a scrapbook, a time capsule. . . . Everything is from the period. Not us editorializing from now."[1] Like a scrapbook or photo album, *Dear America* is constructed of powerful, memory-laden fragments, culled from a large selection of potential pieces, and structured by a chronological narrative of the war. No identifiable conventional narrator takes a viewer through its pages, but the sound track of letters read aloud, superimposed captions introducing the film, identifying place, time, and individuals, and providing other forms of commentary, and the film's musical accompaniment act together to guide our experience with and interpretation of the film, just as a friend or relative might guide one through their personal scrapbook. Although the filmmakers purposively selected fragments from the vast body of archival material available, the fragments' status as bits of "actuality" tend to elide the filmmakers's work in constructing the whole and allow the makers to frame the film within a position of authority and self-effacement.

Dear America can be situated within the subgenre of compilation films, a style of documentary whose history begins with the early cinema and includes newsreels, work by Dziga Vertov, and, later, filmmakers such as Santiago Alvarez, Emile de Antonio, and Peter Davis (*Hearts and Minds*). Almost by definition historical, and often a vehicle for war documentaries, the compilation film has traditionally been employed by political filmmakers on both the left and right. Historical material, when used in combination with contemporary narration or interviews, has a malleability and potential for credibility and authority available to a range of polemic strategies in both content and aesthetic structure. The compilation documentary is a form well suited for overtly political documentaries.

Hear
The Music
Through
Their Ears.

See
The Pain
Through
Their Eyes.

Live
The War
Through
Their Words.

★ DEAR ★
AMERICA

LETTERS
HOME
FROM
VIETNAM

Vietnam Like It's Never Been Told Before.

Home Box Office presents Dear America a co-production of The Couturié Company and The Vietnam Veterans Ensemble Theatre Company
Based on the book "Dear America: Letters Home from Vietnam" edited by Bernard Edelman for The New York Vietnam Veterans Memorial Commission
Screenplay by Richard Dewhurst & Bill Couturié Produced by Bill Couturié and Thomas Bird Directed by Bill Couturié

HB☉

©1996 HBO. All Rights Reserved. Design: Crawffalkrieh Associates, NY/The GBA Group.

HBO's promotional poster for Dear America: Letters Home from Vietnam.

Although a compilation film, *Dear America* does not fit within this genre's political tradition. It seeks to operate, instead, as an experiential and emotive work, assuming a pretense of neutrality and attempting to suppress any overt political stance in its representation of the Vietnam War. As I will argue, the film occupies a conservative political position in its avoidance of these issues and in its drive toward textual transparency. In this sense, *Dear America* fits squarely within the conventional forms of the Vietnam documentary and narrative film, as David James described it: "Like *The Green Berets*, the dominant form of Vietnam documentary recreates a trip to the front; its transformation of the movie theater into the theater of war depends on the effectiveness with which the audience can be made to experience the textures and terrors of the phenomenal experience of battle."[2] *Dear America* aspires to re-create and memorialize the experience of G.I.'s in Vietnam through their letters home, and to have the audience identify with their experiences. In doing so, it seeks a position of innocence and an abstention from the difficult issues surrounding the Vietnam War.

By considering the construction of *Dear America* on its own and then in relation to two contexts of its reception—newspaper reviews and comments by Vietnam veterans—I will indicate ways in which the filmmakers' obscure the noticeably constructed, mediated nature of this documentary.[3] Audience responses I elicited indicate that the film encourages viewers to receive *Dear America* as an unauthored, unmediated, raw text. This disparity between filmmaking practice and audience interpretation raises instructive questions about documentary production and reception, particularly with regard to documentaries about Vietnam.

Documentary has a complex and problematic relationship to social reality. It is now widely held that the production of documentary film involves the same degree (although a different process) of constructive, manipulative, and interpretive work as does the production of fiction films. In Michael Renov's phrase, there is "a range of mediating instances, viewed here as sites of meaning construction" in documentary, as there is in fictional cinema, though documentary employs different codes of representation, different structural conventions, and works through different sites of mediation.[4] Grierson's vague, oft-quoted definition of documentary as "the creative treatment of actuality" points to this basic problem in that it does little to distinguish between fictional and nonfictional frames of production and reception.[5] We understand that documentary films are constructed, manipulated, authored works, yet under certain circumstances (involving context of viewing, the nature of the work itself, and the viewer's relationship to the subject matter), many audience members interpret documentaries within a framework that takes their relationship to reality as somehow more direct than that of fictional cinema.

Research into viewer reception of documentary film (and media forms in general) is new and still exploratory. John Corner and Kay Richardson have proposed several categories of interpretive readings of documentaries, two of which are valuable in discussing this case of documentary reception— "mediation" reading and "transparency" reading: "Our general term for interpretations that are intention/motivation-conscious is *mediation reading*; as against *transparency reading* where comments are made about the depicted world as if it had been directly perceived reality."[6] Their research indicates that viewers work through a tension between these readings, pointing to the complexity of documentary reception. In the case of *Dear America*, the frameworks of reception are complicated by the historical importance of the Vietnam War, by viewers' previous encounters with the dense history of its representations, and by the ways in which *Dear America* is situated within that field of conventional representations of Vietnam. What emerges from the reception of the film is that certain of its audiences, particularly veterans themselves, rely much more heavily on a transparency than on a mediational reading of the text, making interpretive comments based mainly on the events depicted in the film and their relationship to other experiences, and less on the text's construction.

Although *Dear America* draws material from a multiplicity of sources, letters from soldiers fighting in Vietnam, taken from the book published in 1985 under the same title, provided the primary material for the creation of the screenplay. Bill Couturie, the director, coproducer, and coscreenwriter, was a somewhat reluctant author of the film. He had previously produced the ABC documentary *Vietnam Requiem: Vets in Prison* (1982) and might have been hesitant to work on another project about the Vietnam War. After being approached on several occasions by Home Box Office chairman Michael Fuchs to direct a documentary that would give a positive image of Vietnam veterans, Couturie and writing partner Richard Dewhurst wrote a screenplay for *Dear America* using letters from the book and were contracted by Home Box Office to produce the film. Bernard Edelman, editor of the book, gathered many of the still photographs used in *Dear America*, and Tom Bird, the artistic director of the Vietnam Veterans Ensemble Theater Company, was the film's coproducer and was also responsible for securing the participation of many of the actors who read letters in the film. A team of researchers assembled the stock footage, home movies, and music that made up the film. The film's institutional formation—a major cable station sponsoring a program produced by an experienced documentary producer, working along with a team of people who had been previously involved with representations of Vietnam, and enlisting the participation of actors, many of whom had played parts in movies about Vietnam—positioned the work from its origin within a field of convention and potential conservatism.

Out of 208 pieces (mostly letters, along with a few poems and diary entries) written by 125 people for the book *Dear America*, 33 were excerpted for the film. The versions of letters that wound up in the film were edited from their original length and sequence; only on occasion do they identify their writers. They are read by a long list of actors (each of whom reads the letter of only one writer), some nationally known film and television celebrities, others theater actors. The actors' only relationship to the letters are in rough correspondence of race, gender, and age. Couturie described the choice of actors for a given letter as based on performance: "We cast the letters the same way a fictional film maker would cast a role, and we didn't do it just for big names. We tried to identify the letter with the personality of the actor we asked to do it."[7] It is clear that interpretive, evaluative choices are made in selecting, editing, and rearranging the letters, the assignment of letters to the actors who read them, and the directing of those performances. Although Couturie seems to be arguing that the movie and television stars who read letters were chosen mainly for their abilities ("we didn't do it *just* for the big names"), it is also true that their names draw attention to the film (the list includes stars such as Robert DeNiro, Michael J. Fox, and Kathleen Turner). Judging from newspaper reviews and comments that veterans made regarding the use of actors, viewers tend, after the opening credits, to disregard the fact that well-known actors read some of the letters, recognizing only one or two of the readers and not attending to the others' identities.[8]

Still, the directorial choices surrounding the selection and performance of the letters represent one important level of mediation; a different set of choices (that is, having the letter writers themselves, when available, or their family members, read the letters) would have had markedly different consequences. As read by the actors, the letters are performed seamlessly, without the unpolished, imperfect aspects of unrehearsed speech, lending the film a marked level of slickness and "production value" and evoking a degree of omniscience and authority difficult for an unidentified speaker to attain.[9] Although not entirely atypical in documentary, this degree of refinement is more characteristic of fictional cinema and of the form and style of documentaries of the 1940s and 1950s, and uncharacteristic of documentaries (influenced by cinéma vérité) made during and after the Vietnam War. This aesthetic approach is indicative of the filmmakers' avowed authorial intention—to present a dramatic, emotional, but ideologically neutral portrait. The film's opening title crawl states their position:

> This film is about young men in war.
> It is their own story, in their own words.
> Words they wrote home in letters from Vietnam.
> Every scene, every shot in the film is real—nothing has been re-enacted.
> The producers wish to thank the following actors for bringing these letters to life.

This opening statement could have a significant (and as I will argue misleading) impact on the interpretive framework through which a viewer would experience and interpret the material in *Dear America*.

A comparison between the letters as they appear in the book and the spoken performances of these same letters in the film reveals patterned ways in which letters were edited, excerpted, and rearranged, and also reveals something of the filmmakers' ideological stance in relation to this work. The more minimal form of editing involved rearranging sentences, allowing pauses, and omitting sections to fulfill what is essentially a narrative function, facilitating the use of letters in close correspondence to footage depicting what the letter writer speaks, and working within the ninety-minute film format.

The editing of letters, though, serves another, more manipulative purpose, the avoidance of topics and statements that might seem uncomplimentary to the letter writers and to the military establishment. For instance, a letter home from PFC George Williams reflects on the beauty of Vietnam, its natural landscape and wildlife, and the orphaned children he observes:

> There are a few kids who hang around, some with no parents. I feel so sorry for them. I do things to make them laugh. And they call me "dinky dow" (which means crazy). I hope that's one reason why we are here, to secure a future for them.
>
> Your son,
> George[10]

The version of the letter spoken on the sound track omits a telling sentence between the last paragraph and signature: "It seems to be the only justification I can think of for the things I have done!"[11] The letter writer's intent, to reflect on the irony of his kindness to orphan children in light of some unnamed injustice done to the country or its people, is simplified into an optimistic, hopeful statement.

Another letter, this one from a female staff member at an Army Special Services club, discussing the glee expressed by the 1st Cavalry on returning to base from the front lines, purposefully omits all the references to "the club" that were in the written version. Perhaps the filmmakers wanted to steer clear of the issues of uneven distribution of privilege and disparities in responsibilities, inequalities that some soldiers resented. A letter to the editor of a small-town newspaper deplores the attention given to war protesters at home, particularly the students killed at Kent State, in lieu of respect for "the 40-plus thousand red-blooded Americans and brave, fearless, loyal men who have given their lives in Vietnam."[12] The letter writer's anger at the protesters is clear, but the film version omits phrases like "young, worthless radicals," "the vile and disease-ridden SDS," whose "feeble and deteriorating and filthy degenerate minds . . . have forced and caused these men to die for nothing."[13] Here, as in other examples, the filmmakers omit some powerful and revealing language and thereby evade political conflict.

Letters gathered for the book have been selected, rearranged, carefully edited, and performed by actors interpreting the text; the performances were most likely edited again by the filmmakers as they were carefully worked into the text of the film; the result is Grierson's "actuality" several times removed. A submerged ideological position that the filmmakers take in relation to this material emerges through the analysis of this work of mediation; difficult, politicized, and potentially polarizing issues concerning the war are avoided, allowing the film to operate on an emotional, personal level and skate over conflict and contradiction. This position was well stated by one newspaper reviewer:

> The director and co-writer, Bill Couturie, tries to limit himself to a non-political, non-revisionist perspective that doesn't always work. . . .

But if you've seen "Platoon," "Hamburger Hill," or "Good Morning, Vietnam," you're already familiar with the point of view this documentary supports. As good as *Dear America* is, it's time for a more confrontive, ambitious film that deals with the reasons behind American involvement in Vietnam.[14]

The filmmakers' authorial position, explained by the stated intention of memorializing Vietnam veterans, raises questions about *Dear America*'s self-presentation that are echoed in the film's construction.

Dear America's narrative structure is propelled not by the letters themselves but by a compressed, simplified chronology of the war, which binds together the scrapbook of film fragments and popular musical accompaniment. In the book *Dear America*, the letters were thematically rather than chronologically organized. The filmmakers abandon this organization in favor of an historical structure, supported by the excerpted news reports, which serve as a time line for the events of the war. The letters operate more as affective narration than as structural support, rooting the footage and sound by offering the viewer entry into a mode of first-person identification with the readers/writers. Short excerpts from television news reports represent the Gulf of Tonkin incident, President Johnson's escalation of the war and later decision not to run for a second term, the shooting at Kent State, and a few other historical incidents, and provide thematic punctuation for the film's topical development. Intertitles and captions furnish contextual information about events, biographical information about individuals (noting, at times, whether a letter writer died during the war), and other historical details, and do the work of a narrational voice in a documentary that has no conventional omniscient narration, although with an apparent transparency that would have been jeopardized by a speaking omniscient narrator.

The historical markers allow the filmmakers to present the war in the familiar cinematic condensation—early involvement was minimal, innocent, and relatively light-hearted; escalation and lack of military success and progress led to a souring of spirits, and an increased sense of confusion, purposelessness, and despair that soon led to misery; the Tet offensive represented a turning point in the American support of the war (a subtitle in the film says just this); and the soldiers were soon coming home. This conventional narrative of the Vietnam War keeps the viewer chronologically oriented; the filmmakers provide a simplified narrative time chart but avoid any detailed explanations about the events themselves. This avoidance is most blatant and problematic with the Gulf of Tonkin resolution, which is depicted through a newspaper headline superimposed over a battleship, followed by short excerpts from a news report and from President Johnson's announcement. The film avoids any questioning of the veracity of government reports about the incident and in that way urges belief in the government's portrayal and, by omission, support for its policies. Historical simplification of this type recurs throughout *Dear America*.

Edited combinations of sound and picture bring about a coalescence of elements in which disparate images and sounds take on a connected relationship, surprising given the relative lack of synch-sound footage and the variety of sources the film draws upon for material. The imagery itself comes from amateur "home" movies shot by G.I.'s, news footage, the newly opened NBC archives, excerpted news reports, and still photographs from news sources and private collections. On a few occasions the filmmakers were able to obtain photographs of specific letter writers to use in combination with the spoken voice (of an actor) reading those individuals' letters, allowing an identification with an otherwise anonymous letter writer. Most often, though, footage of people and events unrelated to the letter writer is used to illustrate descriptions in the text of a letter; the viewer tends to associate and weave the two disparate elements together, regarding the speaker as the character observed in the footage. The effect is that the film produces a heightened illusion of specificity and realism, for the footage seems to be cast as emotionally charged bits of personal memory rather than anonymous fragments.

For example, there is a letter early in the film from Sergeant Allen Paul to his wife describing the first enemy attack he experienced. As the text of the letter unfolds, it closely matches stock film footage of a battle, and it comes to seem as if Paul's letter is narrating the combat that the footage presents—an extremely unlikely proposition. We see and hear a wounded man writhing in pain while an actor reads, "A mortar landed about 30 feet from me and I was lucky enough to have my head down, but the sergeant next to me wasn't and he lost an eye."[15] As Paul describes carrying away the wounded, we see footage of a wounded man lifted onto a helicopter, and so on, through the end of the letter. Lieutenant Colonel Matthew Henn's letter describing his "baptism" in the Saigon bars edited with footage of G.I.'s watching a Vietnamese singer in a nightclub and Second Lieutenant Don Jacques's description of life waiting in siege at Khe Sanh, combined with shots of G.I.'s playing cards in a bunker, are two other such examples.

Such correspondences occur quite frequently in *Dear America* and represent a principle of editing structure in the film. They require careful construction to achieve literal descriptive coincidence between sound and picture, often necessitating the rearrangement of the original text of a letter and the parallel pacing of the letter as read to match the edited footage. In a sense, the letter readers function as a composite narrator, not the omniscient narrator of the expository documentary, but the first-person narrator of the fictional and personal cinema, the guide taking us through a scrapbook. This illusive structure grounds the letters in observable vérité illustration, casting the actuality footage as fragments of first-person experiential memory and subordinating the individual letter writers to the construction of a seemingly raw, unmediated, and unified narrative.

The letters are backed by a constant, almost continuous, musical sound track, comprised mostly of popular music from the late 1960s and early 1970s, along with recurrent original background music. Excerpts from television news reports, speeches, press conferences, or events from the period are occasionally added in, with accompanying imagery of correspondents, politicians, and news footage. These newscasts represent the only synchronous image and sound footage, since we are never shown the images of readers speaking the letters, nor does the film use any contemporary interviews or scenes added to found material. The newscasts are presented as credible, authoritative slices of factual, contextual information. By excerpting these segments without editorial manipulation, they serve to valorize the official, government perspective on the war.[16]

The juxtapositions of selections of popular music and footage are also based on carefully constructed correspondences; the Four Seasons' recording of "Walk Like a Man" fading out over a shot of a G.I. gingerly patrolling through elephant grass, a sequence of soldiers partying in Saigon to Smokey Robinson's "Going to a Go-Go," and Dylan's "A Hard Rain's Gonna Fall" over close-ups of soldiers in a rainstorm. The juxtapositions range from the revealing to the clichéd. The important point is that the two tracks are rarely independent of each other; they often work through close, literal connotation and association, furthering the film's seamless, polished, dramatic presentation, while providing the filmmakers another avenue of editorial commentary.

The sound track's pacing is carefully constructed. Single letters are read or edited with long pauses between sentences to allow either for a thought to sink in, some background sound or musical verse to project through, or a telling synchrony to unfold between sound and picture. At several points the mix of sounds gradually decreases in volume to a quiet musical ambience, setting the viewer up for a shocking barrage of mortar fire, or, in one instance, the fading in of distant strains of "Silent Night."

Sections of *Dear America* take on the structure of music videos, with news footage or home movies edited in close correspondence with a popular music sound track. "A Grunt's Primer," a section during the first third of the film, is an example of this form. With the Rolling Stones' "Gimme Shelter" providing backbeat, a glossary of special terminology from the war flashes in text on the screen, matched to footage defining the terms— "Huey" over the image of the helicopter, "V.C.," "Victor Charlie," "Chuck" and "Mr. Charles" over a series of shots of the enemy, and so on. Other sections of battle footage under hard-driving music (for instance, Creedence Clearwater Revival's "Fortunate Son"), without the presence on the sound track of letters being read, have the same sort of rhythmic feel, placing those sequences within a poetic mode found in many compilation documentaries. Music is also used as literal, often ironic commentary. For instance, a segment representing the escalation of the war consists of shots of the factory construction of helmets, munitions, and jeeps, accompanied by Sonny and Cher's "The Beat Goes On," and later, Stephen Stills's "For What It's Worth" ("Stop, hey, what's that sound . . .") is combined with news footage of the Paris peace meetings.

These examples illustrate how, throughout the film, sound and picture are married together into a text that is highly structured and makes conscious and deliberate use of dramatic codes, engaging the viewer in the affective, un-evaluating, transparent mode of character identification characteristic of fictional cinema, albeit not completely foreign to documentary. Yet Couturie, his colleagues, and many of the film's reviewers position themselves within what

Richardson and Corner would term a transparency reading of the film. They discuss the work as essentially unauthored, driven by the film's content, the letters and the series of events themselves. From the opening credit crawl stating that all of the scenes in the film actually occurred, the filmmakers position the work as transparent reportage, a difficult position to defend given the performances of the letters themselves, the constructive editing of picture and sound, the excerpting of journalistic reports, and the use of popular music of the period. In a sense, everything was reconstructed for the film, not composed anew as a fictional work is, but constructed through the work of selection and juxtaposition.

Couturie, at least in newspaper quotations, essentially denies the constructed nature of the film by invoking what Bill Nichols would call documentary film's indexical relation to its referent, the events of the war.[17] "This is a case," Mr. Couturie said in a recent interview, "where the documentary is more powerful than a fictional film could be. Even if you could have written all these words, shot all these scenes, it can't equal the power of knowing the blood you see is real, not ketchup. The reality is the power."[18] In drawing the analogy of a scrapbook, he suppresses his own constructive role and denies editorializing. "You make it like a scrapbook, a time capsule. . . . Everything is from the period. Not us editorializing from now."[19]

But a scrapbook editorializes, aligning elements in an evocative sequence, selecting bits that represent what its author chooses, eliminating that which the author wishes not to represent, stressing some aspects of history and neglecting others. A scrapbook is the artifact of a point of view, although here an intentionally suppressed one. The work of the documentary filmmaker using found materials is much the same, only more selective and more committed to the work of editorializing. An apt description of this sort of constructed realism was posed as an explanation of authorial voice in ethnographic writing by anthropologists: "The idea is to allow multiple sets of voices to speak for themselves, with my own author's voice muted and marginalized as commentary. While it remains true that I stage these voices, the reader is directed to the originals; the text is not hermetically sealed, but points beyond itself."[20] The multiple voices in *Dear America* are those of the Vietnam veterans writing letters home, yet these voices (and the other documentary fragments) are, as Fischer says, staged—highly orchestrated, arranged, editorialized. With the addition of all the other material in the film, *Dear America* is a decisively authored work.

A survey of forty newspaper reviews revealed a strongly positive reaction to *Dear America*, accompanied by a few dissenting opinions. The sympathies of one reviewer represent a general reaction amongst the whole: "As moving in its way as *Platoon* was about the Vietnam War, *Dear America: Letters Home From Vietnam* is the cinematic equivalent of the Vietnam Memorial in Washington, D.C."[21] Comparisons made in reviews between recent fictional films on Vietnam (such as *Platoon* and *Full Metal Jacket*) and the documentary *Dear America* favored the latter's "realism" and dramatic impact. The authenticity of the documentary material in the film was, generally speaking, unquestioned; reviewer's readings fit into the "transparency" mode I have discussed earlier. "Couturie, who made this film for HBO, illustrates the soldier's words with newsreel footage from the war (some of it unpublished), home movies and old photos. As a result, the quality of images is sometimes poor, but it adds to the film's reality."[22]

There were also several cases where the reviewer attempted to place the film in relation to local concerns, the experience of veterans from the area: "Two of the 42 letter writers have Texas connections. Peter Elliot of Dallas survived. He's a former sportswriter who now runs his own construction company. Joseph K. Bush, Jr., whose home was in Temple, Texas, was killed in Vietnam on Feb. 10, 1969. His widow, Carol Bush Hunt, teaches first grade at Corey Elementary in Arlington."[23] This last review goes on to mention which actors read these Texans' letters. A review in the *Austin American-Statesman* mentions that none of the letters in the film were from Austin veterans, but discusses how for a group of local veterans present at a screening of the film at the local Vietnam Veterans of America meeting, the experience of watching the film resonated with their own war experiences.[24] These reviewers reacted in a similar fashion to the veterans who saw the film in that rather than questioning structural, rhetorical, or political dimensions of the film itself, they sought resonances with local experience. The mood of these reviewers is commemorative rather than confrontational.

Still, there were some critical, negative reactions to *Dear America*, reactions that fit into Richardson and Corner's category of mediation readings. The most critical review was in the *San Francisco Examiner*:

> As a movie, it's too swift and slick for its own good; powerful moments either get pushed too hard, or go by too quickly. Unlike the book, the film doesn't present a panoply of personalities—it's more like a group portrait of the Vietnam Vet.
>
> As read in voice-over by an impressive cast, . . . the letters act as an aural scrim, putting you at emotional remove from the action.
>
> You might expect stars this distinctive to be too noticeable; the bigger problem is that they're noticeable not as star personalities but as actors, desperately trying to expand these readings into full-scale performances with throbbing voices and overly intense inflections. With a few exceptions, they ruin the casual forcefulness of the letters.[25]

These last excerpts indicate a concern with authorial intention that was in the minority of responses by critics and the veterans group I held a screening with.

Veterans of the Vietnam War were as positively disposed toward *Dear America* as most of the critics were. The screening session I conducted with twelve veterans was transformed from a discussion about the film itself into an engaging story-trading event. It was difficult to steer the veterans away from recounting their own experiences during the war in relation to events depicted in the film and back to talking critically and analytically about the film itself. Again, the readings tended to be transparent rather than mediational: there were few critical comments about the credibility, point of view, or degree of manipulation of the work itself, and more questions about the representativeness of the events and experiences presented.

Dear America served as a provocation for the veterans' own remembrances, encouraging them to place themselves in relation to the people and events depicted in the program, rather than to receive the work in an issues-oriented perspective. For instance, one veteran discussed his reaction, after returning home, to seeing reports of his own unit fighting:

> I also remember when I did finally come home, I was sitting in a room drinking a glass of beer and watching the news—Walter Cronkite, or whoever it was at the time—talking about how we were now in Laos or how we were humpin' around the boonies . . . I had been there two weeks earlier, when I was in . . . I was doing that, what they were showing you was our unit . . . I was sitting in the tap room watching it on TV, and it was my unit they were filming over there you know . . .[26]

Most of the discussion after the screening involved stories of incidents that these veterans had gone through that were brought to mind by those shown in the film. In general, the veterans felt that *Dear America* was more realistic, that it resonated more closely with their experiences in Vietnam, than any fictional works about the war. "I had good reactions to it. . . . I liked it. I've seen every Vietnam flick that's been made so far, at least once, and I think that portrays things more closer to the mark of what the average feeling of the average guy was when they were over there."[27]

Although this was only a small group of veterans, other informal discussions with veterans about *Dear America* indicate that this group's response is not unrepresentative. It seems fair to say that the scrapbook mode that the film is structured in, its composition as a memorial to the veterans who fought in the war, in conjunction with the proximity of veterans' experiences with those depicted in the film, would have this effect for this audience. But the effect emerges from the way in which *Dear America* coalesces actuality and artifice, innocence and authority in the service of transparency.

SUMMARY

In his analysis of oral narratives from the Vietnam War, Patrick Hagopian has situated these narratives within a "therapeutic discourse about the war in which recovery from the effects of the war is discussed as 'healing the war's wounds' and in which a medical terminology has emerged to discuss the war's traumas at both the personal and societal level."[28] He demonstrates the ways in which oral narratives from the war aspire to a mode of transparency and personalized authority analogous to that found in *Dear America*, and discusses how this approach seeks to avoid reexamination of the war's traumatic issues:

In response to a crisis of rhetorical authority undermining the ability of politicians and others to construct a consensual interpretation of the meaning of the war, the oral narratives offer the authority of personal witness and the appearance of ideological innocence. They allow the Vietnam War to be remembered from a perspective of personal experience that obviates and perhaps precludes a critical engagement with controversial historical questions of politics, strategy and ideology.[29]

The interpretive comments regarding the documentary *Dear America* reveal a tension between seeing the work as authentic, raw, and unmediated, and pointing to aspects of its construction as a made, authored text. By provoking this range of interpretive responses, the film questions the possibility of "a consensual interpretation of the meaning of the war." In a sense, one could roughly map a viewer's relationship to the film's subject matter along a continuum of consciousness of the mediated nature of the text; the closer one was to the war in Vietnam, the more likely one is to interpret this film in a transparent mode, to see it as authentic and unauthored. This supposition is admittedly only suggestive and would need support beyond the anecdotal evidence gathered for this paper, but it indicates an interesting variance in interpretive framework for documentary reception, and, perhaps, in the range of frameworks of reception for any film.

Stephen Neale has theorized the importance of addressing the social context of interpretation: "What has to be identified is the use to which a particular text is put, its function within a particular conjuncture, in particular institutional spaces, and in relation to particular audiences."[30] Viewers' positions in relation to the subject matter of a film, as well as their social identity, have great bearing on these issues of interpretation and reception. Couturie and his associates set out to memorialize the veterans who served in Vietnam, "to make the definitive film on Vietnam from an emotional level."[31] In doing so, they fashioned a text whose function is to acknowledge, appreciate, and render in dramatic, emotive fashion the experiences of the G.I.'s themselves. This text is not oppositional to the government that sponsored the war; it clearly has a special relationship to an audience of veterans and might serve the therapeutic function Hagopian proffers.

Outside of these functions, *Dear America* offers little in the way of suggestions for oppositional readings of the events portrayed, and its mode of construction raises questions about the filmmakers' style of presentation. The comparison one newspaper reviewer made with the Vietnam Memorial in Washington, D.C., is instructive. That memorial was controversial and its reception politically charged because of its design. The Wall's nonconventional form eschewed the usual representational quality of war memorials and thereby raised reflexive issues about its own existence as a work of art. It is just this type of questioning that *Dear America* avoids.

Dear America concludes with a decidedly patriotic and stylized ending at the Vietnam War Memorial in Washington, D.C. Actress Ellen Burstyn's dramatic reading of a mother's letter to her dead son, placed on the Memorial in

Washington, begins over an image of the American flag. The shot slowly pans to a close-up of the Memorial, revealing the name William R. Stocks, the son to whom the letters are ostensibly addressed. The image slowly zooms out from the names engraved in the wall, revealing more and more names. Formal still portraits of soldiers are then superimposed over the slow zoom out, the faces growing larger as the names shrink in size, then dissolving to a zoom in of what we take to be the photo of Stocks taped to the wall. The highly emotional letter ends, the background music swells, and a title fades up stating, "58,132 Americans were lost in the Vietnam War and nearly 3 million came home." The subsequent shot tilts down from an American flag to a veterans' parade ending at the Memorial in Washington, as Bruce Springsteen's "Born in the U.S.A." fades up on the sound track.

Dear America, in the end, belies its claim to ideological innocence, emerging as a politically and formally conservative text. It works within the conventions of transparent dramatic documentary form, operating effectively, for some audiences, on an experiential, affective level, but occupying a conservative authorial position that avoids critical political issues.

NOTES

1. Quoted in *New York Times*, 3 April 1988.
2. David James, "Presence of Discourse/Discourse of Presence: Representing Vietnam," *Wide Angle* 7, no. 4 (1985):41–51.
3. The Northeast Chapter of the Vietnam Veterans Association in Philadelphia was kind enough to participate in a screening and discussion about *Dear America* for this study. I thank them for their receptiveness and thoughtful comments.
4. Michael Renov, "Re-thinking Documentary; Toward a Taxonomy of Mediation," *Wide Angle* 8, nos. 3 and 4 (1986):71–77.
5. John Grierson, *Grierson on Documentary*, ed. Forsyth Hardy (London: Faber and Faber, 1966).
6. John Corner and Kay Richardson, "Documentary Meanings and the Discourse of Interpretation," in John Corner, ed., *Documentary and the Mass Media* (London: Edward Arnold, 1988), pp. 140–160.
7. Bill Couterie, quoted in *Norfolk Virginian-Pilot*, 2 April 1988.
8. This disregard might be attributable to the filmmakers' ability to wed picture and sound into the illusion of realism, but might also be related to the nature of the disembodied voice.
9. The effect of the transformation of written text into spoken performance, often with quite markedly expressive dimensions, was not raised by the director and was disregarded in almost all of the responses I encountered.
10. Bernard Edelman, ed., *Dear America: Letters Home From Vietnam* (New York: Pocket Books, 1985), p. 89.
11. Ibid., p. 89.
12. Ibid., p. 241.
13. Ibid.
14. John Harti, *Seattle Times*, 16 September 1988.
15. Edelman, *Dear America*, p. 24.

16. A comparison with the use of newscasts in films such as *Hearts and Minds* and *In The Year of the Pig* is instructive. These films attack the verity of news reports through juxtaposition with interviews, speeches, and footage that contradict their presentation.

17. Nichols writes:

Unlike an iconic sign, such as a cartoon drawing, and its relation of resemblance to its referent, or the arbitrary sign, such as a word, and its relation of non-resemblance to the object or quality referred to, the indexical sign—e.g., a photograph, sundial, or medical symptom—enjoys an existential bond between itself and that to which it refers. In some manner and to some degree its appearance is determined via specific correspondences with its referent as the photographic image is via the physics of lenses and light. (Bill Nichols, *Ideology and the Image* (Bloomington: Indiana University Press, 1981), p. 239.

18. *New York Times*, 3 April 1988.

19. Ibid.

20. M. J. Fischer, "Ethnicity and the Post-Modern Arts of Memory," in James Clifford and George Marcus, eds., *Writing Culture: The Poetics and Politics of Ethnography* (Berkeley and Los Angeles: University of California Press, 1986), pp. 194–234.

21. Richard Freedman, *Newark* (N.J.) *Star Ledger*, 9 September 1988.

22. Hal Mattern, *Arizona Republic*, 17 September 1988.

23. Ed Bark, *Dallas Morning News*, 2 April 1988.

24. Joe Vargo, *Austin-American Statesman*, 28 March 1988.

25. Michael Sragow, *San Francisco Examiner*, 16 September 1988.

26. Paul Holmstrup, North East Chapter of Vietnam Veterans of America, Philadelphia, during discussion after screening of *Dear America*.

27. Dennis Best, North East Chapter of Vietnam Veterans of America, Philadelphia.

28. Patrick Hagopian, "Oral Narratives and the Memory of Vietnam" (Paper for seminar in American history, Johns Hopkins University, 1988), p. 2.

29. Ibid.

30. Stephen Neale, "Propaganda," *Screen* 18, no. 3 (1977):39–40.

31. Couterie in *New York Times*, 3 April 1988.

APPENDIX A

Chronology: The United States, Vietnam, and American Film

The following chronology spotlights, year by year, salient events occurring in the U.S., Vietnam, and other areas around the world as the context for the production of American films (fiction and documentary) dealing overtly with the topic of war and its effects. Starting out with the assumption that history and representation are in constant dialogue with one another, this chronology aims to stimulate further thought, research, and analysis. As the preceding essays show, to date filmic representations of the Vietnam War have had an uneasy relationship with the history they represent. In particular, these essays emphasize ways in which representations that lay claim to historical accuracy can mask facts, policy, and values. To counter this masking, the chronology foregrounds a historic reading of the Vietnam War and its films. The contextual information it brings to bear on this body of films aims to clarify the effects of representation on the American public's evolving relation to Vietnam before, during, and after the United States's military intervention in its civil war. Of course, historical representations are always incomplete, and the same goes for this chronology. We make no claims that the information provided here is all-encompassing; rather, we wish to make known our criteria for including certain events, so that the reader can approach this outline aware of the priorities that account for its final form.

First, in keeping with the overall subject of this anthology, the emphasis here is on American history and filmic discourse during and after the Vietnam War era, highlighting key domestic and foreign events that shaped American political attitudes and cultural production. We chose to begin with 1954 because in that year the French effort to recolonize Vietnam collapsed with the defeat of French forces at Dien Bien Phu. The United States had largely funded and supplied the latter stages of France's failed attempt to reinsert itself in Vietnam; by 1954, the U.S. was paying 78 percent of the cost of this effort. Faced with France's withdrawal from the region, American attempts to control events in Vietnam became ever more overt and aggressive, and decisions made then set the U.S. on the road to military involvement in Southeast Asia. And 1954 was also an important year domestically, most notably in regard to the civil rights movement and American anticommunism—issues that would continue to play a significant part in the unfolding events of the Vietnam era.

Second, the chronology's organization encourages attention to the interrelations among events listed annually in each of its four categories ("The United States," "Vietnam," "Other Global Events," and "American Film"). The United States section highlights both foreign policy decisions and domestic events in the areas of civil rights, labor, gender issues, the antiwar movement, and the internal effects of the Cold War. That women's history and events pertinent to the gay rights movement are not more fully recorded here reflects that the fact that much of this activity has occurred outside the high-visibility political, economic, and legal arenas that chronologies such as this highlight. Although not the exclusive focus of this section, of special concern is the relationship between domestic developments and the country's escalating involvement in Vietnam and other Third World countries. The Vietnam section supplements this intent by emphasizing events unfolding in Vietnam as they affected or were affected by U.S. foreign policy decisions. Additionally, the chronology lists other significant events around the world during this period, since neither U.S. nor Vietnamese history exist in isolation. As a full and detailed recapitulation of the world's history since 1954 is beyond the scope of this anthology, we focus on information that links the United States involvement in Vietnam to the aftermath of Western colonialism in other countries. The general movement toward autonomy of nations in Africa, Asia, the Caribbean, and the Middle East in the post–World War II period produced a long series of coups and countercoups, authentically democratic and fraudulent elections, temporary alliances, and lengthy border wars that resist simple documentation and are often further complicated by the role external power relations played in any particular nation's history. The chronology cannot cover all of this in detail. Rather, it highlights representative events of national, regional, and global significance. The chronology also does not emphasize the United States's well-documented relationships with the countries of Europe or with the U.S.S.R., though it does include references to certain key events that give an overall sense of the direction of these relations. Partly in response to our contributors and partly out of our own sense of what too often gets repressed in American representations of national and global history, we have tended to emphasize those events that affected the less powerful and the less prominent.

Similar thinking also guided our selection of films. We have listed those films produced in the United States that relate to war and its effects precisely because such films always contain explicit or implicit messages about the nature of the American national character and its enemies, about the short- or long-term effects on human beings who live under the conditions wars produce, about what we fight for and against. Although the chronology does not suggest direct correspondence between events of a given year and the films produced immediately before or after these events, it does suggest reciprocation. Most notable is Hollywood's near silence about the Vietnam war while the United States was deeply involved in it. Other noteworthy correlations include a growing narrative interest in vengeance and heroic rescue following the United States defeat in Vietnam, which in turn interacts with the increasing debate over U.S. intervention in Latin America and the Caribbean. Overall, such contextualization shows that even when films are masked as retrospective historic narratives, they embody values that prove influential in current and subsequent political debate. The inclusion here of both documentary and fiction films highlights the different roles each played in relation to the Vietnam War and the different audiences each aimed to reach. Although the content, form, appeal, and modes of distribution for fiction and documentary films usually differ greatly, each played a part in shaping public opinion. Time and space permitting, we have given brief descriptions of films that have particular relevance to their historical context; many of these are films that have been overlooked because they lack or have been denied access to the promotional mechanisms of the mainstream American film industry.

1954 / HISTORICAL EVENTS

UNITED STATES

Domestic
Military budget requests 68 percent of total government budget draft; Eisenhower proposes relaxation of union protections under the Taft-Hartley Act; House Un-American Activities Committee recommends that U.S. mailing privileges be denied to "subversive organizations" and that membership in the Communist party be considered proof of conspiracy to overthrow the U.S. government; U.S. continues nuclear testing; Army-McCarthy hearings televised; in *Brown v. Board of Education*, Supreme Court rules public school segregation unconstitutional; Congressional committee considers censuring of Senator McCarthy; government dismisses almost 7,000 employees, branding them "security risks"; arrests of suspected Communist party members continues across the U.S. under the provisos of the 1948 Smith Act.

Foreign
Eisenhower pledges to continue aid to French in Indochina, later promises that the U.S. will not invade Indochina without congressional approval; Secretary of State Dulles declares U.S. will block communist conquest of S.E. Asia; CIA backs overthrow of Mossedegh government in Iran, and Arbenz government in Guatemala; U.S. signs S.E. Asia defense pact with Britain, France, Australia, New Zealand, the Philippines, and Thailand; FBI chief Hoover vows to end "communist conspiracy" in Puerto Rico.

VIETNAM

French fortress at Dien Bien Phu falls to Vietminh, 6,000 French troops killed or wounded, 10,000 captured; negotiations begin in Geneva to end conflict in S.E. Asia; Bao Dai, head of the French colonialist government, appoints Ngo Dinh Diem as his prime minister; the Geneva Conference results in agreements signaling the end of foreign rule in Indochina: to facilitate disengagement of armed factions, Vietnam is temporarily divided into two sections (north and south) until outcome of nationwide elections to be held in 1956 determines who will rule a united Vietnam.

OTHER GLOBAL EVENTS

Nasser becomes Egyptian premier; Mau Mau revolt against British rule in Kenya; Peronists reelected in Argentina; Haile Selassie gives U.S. rights to Ethiopian military bases for 99 years; years; assassination of government leaders results in crackdown on nationalist movement in Puerto Rico; striking workers in Honduras and Guatemala win contracts and pay raises from Standard Fruit and United Fruit companies; Britain withdraws from the Suez Canal, U.S. gives aid to Egypt; Algerians revolt against French rule; Iranian minister sentenced to death and 650 others arrested for anti-Shah activities.

1955 / HISTORICAL EVENTS

UNITED STATES

Domestic
Eisenhower urges extension of military draft system; Supreme Court refuses NAACP request to set deadline for implementation of school desegregation plans; Georgia institutes "lifetime

AMERICAN FILM / 1954

FICTION

The Bridges at Toko-Ri—Lawyer is recalled to active duty as Navy jet pilot during the Korean War.

The Bamboo Prison—U.S. POWs resist brainwashing tactics of their Korean captors.

The Caine Mutiny—U.S. naval officers face court martial for relieving psychotic captain of ship's command.

Prisoner of War—American infiltrator investigates the torture of U.S. POWs by Russian and North Korean officers.

Men of the Fighting Lady—Life aboard a U.S. aircraft carrier during the Korean War.

Night People—U.S. military personnel in Germany after World War II attempt to retrieve an American soldier from East Berlin.

Beachhead—Four U.S. Marines undertake a dangerous mission in the World War II South Pacific.

Betrayed—Dutch resistance group undermines Nazi control in World War II Holland.

Hell and High Water—Crew of U.S. submarine attempt to foil Communist plot to start World War III.

The Shanghai Story—Americans in China attempt to leave the country after Communists come to power.

Paratrooper—Man disturbed by previous military experience joins special forces unit.

DOCUMENTARY

Report on Senator McCarthy—CBS compilation film tracing McCarthy's rise to prominence as an anti-Communist crusader.

Victory at Sea—Feature version of popular television documentary series based on Allied naval exploits during World War II.

Take 'er Down—U.S. Department of Defense film traces the history of submarines in the navy from the turn of the century through the development of nuclear-powered submarines in the 1950s.

AMERICAN FILM / 1955

FICTION

Bad Day at Black Rock—Disabled Army veteran uncovers racism and murder in the post-World War II American Southwest.

Jump Into Hell—French paratroopers join the battle at Dien Bein Phu.

ban" against any teacher who instructs a racially mixed classroom; nuclear tests continue at Yucca Flats; local and federal government agencies investigate communist influence in New York theater and summer camp communities; Maryland implements desegregation plan; civil rights activists begin bus boycott in Montgomery, Alabama; AFL merges with the CIO.

Foreign
U.S. begins giving $100 million in aid to Saigon government and assumes training of South Vietnamese military; Congress authorizes use of force to defend Formosa; Vice-President Nixon visits Cuba, awards medal to dictator Batista, and calls for more private investment in Caribbean nations; Secretary of State Dulles and Spanish dictator Franco reach "mutual understanding."

VIETNAM

With U.S. backing, Diem ousts Bao Dai and refuses to participate in Vietnamese general elections called for by the Geneva Accords; after an uncontested local election, Diem announces the formation of the Republic of Vietnam, with himself as president.

OTHER GLOBAL EVENTS

President of Panama assassinated; 60,000 South Africans protest forced removal from Johannesburg; Puerto Rican nationalists convicted of sedition; Conference of Non-Aligned Nations meets in Indonesia; anti-French elements revolt in Morocco and Algeria; France grants Tunisia full internal autonomy; Egypt-U.S.S.R. sign arms pact; Baghdad Pact formed by Iraq, Turkey, Iran, Pakistan, and Britain; military coup ousts Peron in Argentina.

1956 / HISTORICAL EVENTS

UNITED STATES

Domestic
100 southern congressmen pledge to reverse 1954 desegregation ruling; Martin Luther King, Jr. indicted for participation in Montgomery bus boycott; IRS seizes Communist Party and *Daily Worker* offices in New York, Philadelphia, and Chicago; National Guard called up in Tennessee and Kentucky to quell anti-integration violence; Eisenhower defeats Stevenson and begins second term of office; federal court orders end of segregation of buses in Montgomery.

Foreign
U.S. halts arms shipments to Israel; denounces U.S.S.R. intervention in Middle East, pressures England, France, and Israel to withdraw from the Sinai and the Suez Canal.

VIETNAM

Diem supporters win seats in first National Assembly elections in South Vietnam; Diem begins repression of dissident factions.

OTHER GLOBAL EVENTS

Morocco and Sudan gain independence; Egypt nationalizes the Suez Canal, England, France, and Israel attack Egypt; Soviets crush Hungarian revolt.

Mister Roberts—In the World War II South Pacific, crew of Navy supply ship undermines tyrannical captain.

Blood Alley—American aids villagers attempting to escape from Communist China.

The Left Hand of God—American poses as cleric to outwit Chinese warlord.

Battle Taxi—U.S. helicopter crew undertakes dangerous rescue missions during Korean War.

To Hell and Back—Biography of Audie Murphy, the most decorated U.S. soldier of World War II, who later became a movie star.

Strategic Air Command—Baseball player is recalled to active duty with the U.S. Air Force.

The Sea Chase—German ship captain attempts to elude Allied pursuit at the outbreak of World War II.

Other Fiction Films:

Air Strike
Battle Cry
Hell's Horizon
Three Stripes in the Sun
The Court-Martial of Billy Mitchell
The Eternal Sea
Hill 24 Doesn't Answer
The Long Gray Line
The McConnell Story

AMERICAN FILM / 1956

FICTION

Attack!—Cowardly Army officer with homefront political connections causes deaths of enlisted men in World War II.

The Rack—Former POW faces court martial for statements made while being tortured by Koreans.

D-Day, the Sixth of June—Allies prepare for Normandy invasion in World War II England.

Battle Shock—Veteran traumatized by war experience becomes chief suspect in murder case.

The Bold and the Brave—Pacifist soldier finds himself in the midst of combat in World War II Europe.

Other Fiction Films

Battle Hymn
Battle Stations
Between Heaven and Hell
The Teahouse of the August Moon
Away All Boats
Hold Back the Night
Screaming Eagles
The Man Who Never Was
The Lieutenant Wore Skirts
Navy Wife

1957 / HISTORICAL EVENTS

UNITED STATES

Domestic
Arkansas Governor Faubus orders National Guard to prevent black students from entering Little Rock Central High School, Eisenhower sends in federal troops to enforce desegregation; Nashville school bombed as desegregation begins; Martin Luther King, Jr. and southern ministers organize Southern Christian Leadership Conference.

Foreign
Diem visits the U.S., Eisenhower pledges continued support; Saudi Arabia renews leases for U.S. air bases; "Eisenhower Doctrine" announced for Middle East; Nehru's appeal to end nuclear testing rejected.

VIETNAM

Diem consolidates his power, creating a police state in South Vietnam; bomb explodes near U.S. officers' quarters.

OTHER GLOBAL EVENTS

Peronists arrested in Argentina, some escape to Chile; Ghana gains independence; Columbian junta ousts dictator; Egypt bars Israel from Suez Canal; Britain crushes Mau Mau rebellion in Kenya; Cuban leader Battista suspends constitutional rights, Cuban Navy members join Castro's forces; Duvalier imposes martial law in Haiti; first space satellite, Sputnik, is launched by the U.S.S.R.

1958 / HISTORICAL EVENTS

UNITED STATES

Domestic
Eisenhower urges U.S. consumers to help end recession by purchasing more goods; southern states resist implementation of desegregation plans; Virginia and Arkansas move to fund private schools to avoid integration; synagogues bombed in Atlanta, Georgia, and Peoria, Illinois; more southern schools bombed; 13 schools close in Little Rock; first U.S. satellite launched.

Foreign
Crowds demonstrate against U.S. during Vice-President Nixon's multinational tour of Latin American; U.S. denounces new Iraqi government; U.S. warns China not to invade Quemoy and Matsu islands in the Formosa Straits; U.S. Marines sent to Beirut to quell Lebanese civil war.

VIETNAM

Increased repression by Diem regime nearly destroys remnants of the Vietminh organization in the South.

AMERICAN FILM / 1957

FICTION

Paths of Glory—French commanders choose three enlisted men for execution after failed military operation during World War I.

China Gate—A group of mercenaries under French command infiltrate North Vietnam to blow up Communist ammunition depot.

The D.I.—Marine sergeant molds young recruits into real fighting men at Parris Island training camp.

Monkey on My Back—Biography of boxer Barney Ross, who became addicted to narcotics as a result of wounds suffered in World War II.

Other Fiction Films:

The Bridge on the River Kwai
Bombers B-52
Don't Go Near the Water
The Enemy Below
Sayonara
Heaven Knows, Mr. Allison
Men in War
Time Limit
Hellcats of the Navy
Hell Squad
Bitter Victory
Joe Butterfly
Operation Mad Ball

AMERICAN FILM / 1958

FICTION

The Quiet American—An American comes to Vietnam to carry out his own anti-Communist crusade.

Kings Go Forth—In World War II France, American soldier rejects woman he has fallen in love with when he learns she is black.

Torpedo Run—U.S. submarine captain is ordered to sink Japanese ship on which his family is held captive.

Run Silent, Run Deep—Submarine crew questions abilities of new captain as they patrol the World War II Pacific.

The Deep Six—Naval officer grapples with his religious convictions while serving during World War II.

A Time to Love and a Time to Die—A young German soldier home on leave falls in love.

Other Fiction Films

The Hunters
The Young Lions

OTHER GLOBAL EVENTS

Egypt and Syria form United Arab Republic; antiroyalist revolution in Iraq, Iran and Jordan form Arab Union; Guinea gains independence; Indonesian government suppresses anti-Communist revolt; Batista invokes antistrike measures in Cuba, rebels seize Havana radio stations; Pan-African Congress convenes in Ghana; Socialist Salvador Allende nearly wins Chilean presidential election; Argentinian government declares state of siege to combat oil workers' strike.

1959 / HISTORICAL EVENTS

UNITED STATES

Domestic
Alaska and Hawaii gain statehood; four southern cities placed under court order to desegregate schools; FBI chief Hoover calls for sterner treatment of juvenile offenders; first ballistic missile launched; Little Rock opens integrated schools; Civil Rights Commission reports voter registration violations; TV quiz show fraud exposed, FCC powers expanded to prevent corruption; American Legion expels local chapter for ban on nonwhite members.

Foreign
West Berlin mayor visits U.S.; CIA plot to overthrow neutralist government of Cambodia uncovered; Castro warmly received on first visit to the U.S.; U.S. pledges aid to Burma; Nixon visits Russia; Khrushchev visits U.S.; U.S.-Philippines sign military base treaty; Eisenhower embarks on an extensive tour of Europe, the Middle East, Asia, and Africa.

VIETNAM

Hanoi begins initial supply efforts to South Vietnamese rebels as armed resistance to Diem increases.

OTHER GLOBAL EVENTS

Cuban rebel forces led by Castro take Havana as Battista flees; anti-U.S. demonstrations in Bolivia; Britain sells arms to new Iraqi government; land redistribution begins in Cuba; Israel agrees to United Nations' Suez Canal compromise; United Nations denounces South African apartheid; Paraguay rebellion put down.

1960 / HISTORICAL EVENTS

UNITED STATES

Domestic
Sit-in of segregated lunch counters begins in Greensboro, North Carolina, spreads to 15 other cities; Student Non-Violent Coordinating Committee (SNCC) is organized; government re-

The Last Blitzkrieg
South Pacific
Lafayette Escadrille
Suicide Battalion
Tarawa Beachhead
The Naked and the Dead
Darby's Rangers
Imitation General
The Inn of Sixth Happiness
The Key
Me and the Colonel

AMERICAN FILM / 1959

FICTION

On the Beach—People in Australia find themselves facing death from radioactive fallout after nuclear warfare.
Five Gates to Hell— American nurses are tortured by their Chinese captors.
Blood and Steel— Native woman aids U.S. naval troops on a South Pacific island under Japanese control.
Battle Flame—Wounded soldier is reunited with the woman he once loved, now an Army nurse, during the Korean War.
Battle of the Coral Sea—U.S. submarine captain on Japanese-held island attempts to send vital information to naval fleet.

Other Fiction Films
The Diary of Anne Frank
Operation Petticoat
Surrender—Hell!
Never So Few
Up Periscope
Don't Push, I'll Charge When I'm Ready
Pork Chop Hill
Don't Give Up the Ship
Operation Dames
Verboten!
Ten Seconds to Hell

AMERICAN FILM / 1960

FICTION

G.I. Blues—A young American Army sergeant (Elvis Presley) stationed in Germany pursues a night club dancer.
All the Young Men—Racial discord disrupts Army unit during Korean War.

ports that 94% of southern schools are still segregated; Civil Rights Bill invoked for first time in voting rights investigation; Federal Drug Administration approves use of birth control pill; first televised debate between presidential candidates Kennedy and Nixon; Kennedy defeats Nixon in presidential election.

Foreign

U.S.-Japan sign treaty for mutual cooperation and security; Eisenhower orders seizure of U.S. arms shipments to Cuba; Khrushchev accuses U.S. of spying, cancels proposed summit; Eisenhower cuts Cuban sugar imports, proposes more aid to Latin America; Cuban delegation to United Nations refuses free accommodations, moves into Harlem hotel; U.S. recalls ambassador to Cuba; U.S. sends navy to protect Guatemala and Nicaragua; U.S. warns against intervention in South Vietnam by North Vietnamese and Chinese Communists.

VIETNAM

Urban revolts in South Vietnam; National Liberation Front ("Vietcong") is formed in South Vietnam.

OTHER GLOBAL EVENTS

Cuba and Russia sign pact; Nigeria and Mali gain independence; pro-West Premier Nu takes control in Burma; Sharpeville massacre in South Africa; Cuba nationalizes U.S. assets; South Korean President Rhee resigns after fraudulent election practices are exposed; Pan-African People's Conference convenes; military coup in Turkey; Cuba and China sign economic pact; civil war in Laos.

1961 / HISTORICAL EVENTS

UNITED STATES

Domestic

University of Georgia admits two black students; Kennedy bans aid to private schools, bars discrimination in federal employment; Congress of Racial Equality (CORE) organizes freedom rides in South, arrests and violence ensue; with bipartisan support, Kennedy calls up 250,000 reservists to bolster armed forces; thousands of women across the U.S. protest nuclear tests in the atmosphere.

Foreign

U.S. severs diplomatic relations with Cuba; U.S. 7th Fleet moves within striking distance of Laos; Peace Corps established; Bay of Pigs invasion fails as Cubans forces defeat CIA-backed assault, Kennedy initially denies U.S. involvement, later orders closed-door review of CIA's anti-Cuban activities; Kennedy sends more aid and more military advisors to South Vietnam; Vice-President Johnson and General Maxwell Taylor visit South Vietnam; U.S. voices support for anti-Communist military dictatorship established in South Korea; Kennedy and Khrushchev meet; Kennedy visits Latin America.

Hell to Eternity—White American raised by Japanese family becomes hero in World War II.
Under Ten Flags—Nazi ship attempts to evade British pursuit during World War II.
The Gallant Hours—Biography of World War II U.S. Navy Admiral Bull Halsey.
The Mountain Road—U.S. demolitions squad attempts to delay Japanese advance in World War II China.
The Wackiest Ship in the Army—Naval misfits are assigned to sailboat in the World War II South Pacific.
Five Branded Women—Women find themselves shunned by members of their community for consorting with Nazi troops during the Second World War.

DOCUMENTARY

Korea: The Final Phase, 1950-1953—U.S. Air Force film depicts tactical use of fighter planes during the Korean War.
The Truth About Communism—U.S. government film, narrated by Ronald Reagan, depicts the rise of Communism.

AMERICAN FILM / 1961

FICTION

Brushfire—Plantations in Vietnam come under Communist attack.
Judgment at Nuremberg—American jurist tries to understand the nature of fascism during Nazi war crime trials.
The Outsider—Biography of Ira Hayes, Native American World War II veteran who died of alcoholism.
Marines, Let's Go—U.S. G.I.'s frolic on leave in Tokyo before returning to the battlefields of Korea.
A Bridge to the Sun—American woman married to a Japanese diplomat arouses suspicion of the government in World War II Japan.

Other Fiction Films:

The Battle at Bloody Beach
The Guns of Navarone
Operation Bottleneck
Sniper's Ridge

VIETNAM

NLF begins to consolidate liberated territory in South Vietnam; two U.S. helicopter companies assigned to South Vietnam.

OTHER GLOBAL EVENTS

Soviet astronaut first to orbit the earth; Tanganyika gains independence; cease-fire in Laos; East Germany puts up Berlin Wall, closes border to West Germany; Syria dissolves United Arab Republic; Sino-Soviet rift increases.

1962 / HISTORICAL EVENTS

UNITED STATES

Domestic
First U.S. astronaut makes orbit; U.S. Communist party leaders indicted for failing to register party as subversive organization, later convicted; students demonstrate against resumption of nuclear tests; Teamster leader Jimmy Hoffa indicted for making pay-offs; Supreme Court rules school prayer unconstitutional; Students for a Democratic Society (SDS) convention issues the Port Huron Statement, authored by Tom Hayden; U.S. farmers stage boycott; federal government enforces James Meredith's admission to University of Mississippi; labor disputes shut down newspapers in New York City, Cleveland.

Foreign
Kennedy begins Cuban trade embargo; Shah of Iran visits U.S.; U.S. sends troops to Thailand; U.S. recognizes military junta in Peru; U.S. withdraws military forces from Laotian area to meet United Nations deadline; missile installations in Cuba leads to U.S./U.S.S.R. confrontation.

VIETNAM

Military Assistance Command (MACV) created in South Vietnam; Diem's palace bombed by dissident South Vietnamese pilots; helicopter warfare checks NLF movement; number of U.S. military advisors reaches 12,000; strategic hamlet program begins in South Vietnam.

OTHER GLOBAL EVENTS

Lebanon crushes right-wing coup attempt; state of emergency declared in Dominican Republic; Guatemalan students and labor organizations strike to protest election fraud; Uganda gains independence; Peronists win votes in Argentinian election, Peronist supporters in military stage coup; Soviets withdraw troops and abolish command post in East Germany; military coup in Yemen leads to civil war; Sino-Indian border war continues; Algeria votes for independence; coalition government formed in Laos.

Operation Eichmann
Seven Women from Hell
The Steel Claw
Armored Command

DOCUMENTARY

Eyewitness: Diem's War-or Ours?—CBS documentary examines growing American commitment to unpopular South Vietnamese government.
Angola: Journey to a War—NBC film about Portuguese attempt to put down African rebellion.
Mein Kampf—Film documents Nazi rise to power in Germany.

AMERICAN FILM / 1962

FICTION

The Manchurian Candidate—Communists plot to subvert U.S. politics by brainwashing a group of Korean War veterans.
Captain Newman, M.D.—An Army psychiatrist treats soldiers and fights bureaucracy during World War II.
War Hunt—An American soldier becomes obsessed with killing during the Korean War.
Hell Is for Heroes—U.S. Army squad prepares for assault on German lines in World War II.
The Longest Day—Allies invade the Nazi-occupied beaches of France.
Merrill's Marauders—U.S. troops fight the Japanese in Burma during World War II.
Panic in the Year Zero—Family struggles to survive after nuclear attack on U.S.

Other Fiction Films:

The War Lover
The Horizontal Lieutenant
The Counterfeit Traitor
The Pigeon That Took Rome
Red Nightmare

DOCUMENTARY

End of an Empire—CBS film about the French occupation of Indochina and their defeat at the hands of the Vietnamese.

OTHER DOCUMENTARY FILMS:

The Village That Wouldn't Die
Eyewitness: Our War in Vietnam
Eyewitness: Yanks in Vietnam

1963 / HISTORICAL EVENTS

UNITED STATES

Domestic
Desegregation drive in Birmingham, Alabama, results in 400 arrests, Kennedy orders troops into Birmingham, Governor Wallace tries but fails to block integration of University of Alabama; Kennedy calls for new civil rights bill; civil rights activist Medgar Evers is assassinated; 250,000 people attend civil rights march in Washington; 9 Alabama schools integrated; 4 black girls die in Birmingham church bombing; Kennedy is assassinated, suspected assassin Oswald is killed in Dallas, Johnson succeeds to presidency; women win the Equal Pay Act; Malcolm X breaks with Black Muslims; Betty Friedan's *Feminine Mystique* becomes a best-seller.

Foreign
Cuban missile crisis ends as U.S.-U.S.S.R. come to agreement without Cuban participation, Soviets agree to remove missiles in exchange for U.S. promise not to invade Cuba; U.S. recalls government dependents from Haiti because of unrest; U.S.-U.S.S.R. agree to nuclear test ban treaty; Kennedy criticizes repressive measures of South Vietnamese government but refuses to reduce aid; U.S. suspends relations with Dominican Republic after government overthrown; U.S. withholds aid from Indonesia after government seizes all British-owned property.

VIETNAM

South Vietnamese troops lose battle of Ap Bac to NLF forces; South Vietnamese troops fire on Buddhist dissidents; anti-Diem government protests increase, mass arrests follow, U.S. newsmen beaten by South Vietnamese forces; Diem killed in U.S.-backed coup by South Vietnamese army generals.

OTHER GLOBAL EVENTS

Sukarno proclaimed "president for life" by the Indonesian congress he appointed; Duvalier suspends individual rights in Haiti; Park elected South Korean president; Kenya gains independence; Cambodia renounces U.S. aid, demands withdrawal of U.S. and French troops, orders U.S. and British embassy personnel to leave.

1964 / HISTORICAL EVENTS

UNITED STATES

Domestic
Civil Rights Act of 1964 passes, making sex and race discrimination in employment unlawful; Johnson declares "war on poverty"; blacks boycott Cleveland and New York City schools to protest segregation; bodies of 3 civil rights workers found in Mississippi during Freedom Summer; whites attack civil rights marchers in Florida; Mississippi Democratic Freedom Party organized as an alternative political party in the south; urban rioting in Philadelphia, Chicago, and cities in New York and New Jersey; whites boycott New York City schools to protest integration plan; Johnson defeats Goldwater in presidential elections; Free Speech Movement takes place at the University of California at Berkeley.

AMERICAN FILM / 1963

FICTION

The Ugly American—U.S. ambassador to Southeast Asian country attempts to thwart pro-Communist forces.

55 Days at Peking—International settlement is attacked by Chinese rebels.

The Hook—Retreating U.S. soldiers receive orders to kill their North Korean captive.

War Is Hell—American soldier's attempts at heroism during the Korean War places lives of his comrades in jeopardy.

The Victors—Episodic account of American soldiers in World War II Europe.

The Great Escape— Captured Allied troops undertake massive escape from World War II Nazi prison camp.

PT 109—The story of future President John F. Kennedy's naval exploits in the South Pacific during World War II.

A Gathering of Eagles—Authoritarian officer in charge of peacetime U.S. Strategic Air Command base faces difficulties on duty and at home.

Operation Bikini—American troops attempt to keep sunken treasure out of enemy hands during World War II.

Soldier in the Rain—Seriocomic version of life in the U.S. Army during peacetime.

DOCUMENTARY

Crossover—U.S. Department of Defense film follows the U.S. Air Force's 'Thunderbirds' airial drill team on a goodwill tour of South America.

AMERICAN FILM / 1964

FICTION

Dr. Strangelove—Insane U.S. general triggers nuclear holocaust.

Seven Days in May—Members of U.S. military plot overthrow of American government.

The Train—French resistance fighters attempt to foil Nazi plan to steal French art treasures during the final days of World War II.

A Yank in Viet-Nam—U.S. marine pilot, shot down in the Mekong Delta, joins guerrillas to attack Vietcong.

The Americanization of Emily—Navy public relations team plans coverage of the Allied invasion of Normandy.

Back Door to Hell—Americans undertake secret reconnaissance mission on Japanese-held Philippine Islands during World War II.

Foreign

U.S. troops clash with Panamanians protesting presence of U.S. flag over Canal Zone, two dozen Panamanians killed, 300 injured; U.S. cuts aid to 5 nations who trade with Cuba; after visiting South Vietnam, Secretary of Defense McNamara calls for more aid; Gulf of Tonkin resolution, giving President unlimited power in the conduct of the Vietnam conflict, passes in Congress; U.S. increases aid to Vietnam; Johnson refuses Hanoi offer to begin peace talks.

VIETNAM

General Nguyen Kahn takes control in Saigon; NLF makes significant gains in countryside; U.S. planes bomb North Vietnam; South Vietnamese students and Buddhists riot to protest Kahn government; dissident South Vietnamese army officers seize Saigon radio station, but attempted coup fails; Kahn promises new constitution; U.S. military bases attacked; civilian government installed in Saigon, but overthrown by military elements loyal to Kahn.

OTHER GLOBAL EVENTS

Progressive Brazilian president deposed by U.S.-backed military coup, which remains in power for 15 years; Indian Prime Minister Nehru dies; Tanganyika and Zanzibar join Tanzania in the newly formed Organization of African States; Laos government deposed in right-wing coup; martial law declared in South Korea; Bolivian president overthrown.

1965 / HISTORICAL EVENTS

UNITED STATES

Domestic

Johnson pledges to build "the Great Society"; Malcolm X assassinated; mass arrests in Selma, Alabama voter registration demonstrations; Mississippi judge dismisses 17 of 18 indictments in murders of civil rights workers; white civil rights activist shot in Alabama; over 3,000 people participate in Freedom March from Selma to Montgomery; U.S. Commissioner of Education announces Fall, 1967 deadline for school integration; Voting Act of 1965 is passed; Chicago demonstrations protest lag in implementation of school desegregation plan; number of military draftees increases; rioting in Watts area of Los Angeles, 5 people killed; 25,000 join in anti-war protest in Washington, antiwar demonstrations spread to other cities.

Foreign

Johnson orders U.S. combat troops into South Vietnam, pledges increases in aid, troops, and air strikes; fearing another Cuba, Johnson orders 25,000 U.S. troops into the Dominican Republic to counter leftist movement, later joined by small contingents of troops sent from other Latin American countries at U.S. urging.

VIETNAM

General Kahn reinstated in Saigon, later abdicates; first U.S. combat troops arrive; air war in South Vietnam intensifies; U.S. embassy in Saigon bombed; General Nguyen Cao Ky becomes prime minister in Saigon; sustained bombing of North Vietnam begins; U.S. troops clash with North Vietnamese Army regulars for the first time; Ho Chi Minh demands withdrawal of U.S. forces as precondition to peace talks.

Fail Safe—U.S. plane is mistakenly ordered to drop nuclear bombs on the Soviet Union.

The Thin Red Line—Experienced sergeant attempts to train undisciplined young soldier in the ways of combat in the World War II South Pacific.

Ensign Pulver—Sequel to *Mr. Roberts*, as ship's crew continues to undermine military authority.

The Seventh Dawn—American in Malaya attempts to negotiate with pro-Communist forces who are attacking plantations.

The Secret Invasion—Allied commandos join partisans behind Nazi lines in Eastern Europe during World War II.

Other Fiction Films:

The Walls of Hell
Guerillas in Pink Lace

DOCUMENTARY

The Guns of August—Based on the book by Barbara Tuchman, film explores the roots of World War I.

Vietnam: The Deadly Decision—CBS film examines increasing U.S. involvement in Vietnam.

AMERICAN FILM / 1965

FICTION

Operation CIA—U.S. agent sent to Saigon becomes involved in an assassination plot.

The Bedford Incident—U.S. Navy destroyer commanded by obsessive officer chases a Russian submarine in the North Atlantic.

Battle of the Bulge—Nazis break through American lines in the closing days of World War II.

Other Fiction Films:

Von Ryan's Express
King Rat
Operation Crossbow
Hell Raiders
Morituri
Up from the Beach
Once Before I Die
To The Shores of Hell
In Harm's Way
None But the Brave

DOCUMENTARY

Letters from Vietnam—Two months in the life of an Army lieutenant stationed in Vietnam as he dictates letters to his wife into a tape recorder.

Why Vietnam—Department of Defense film explains U.S. policies in Vietnam using World War II newsreel footage of the Nazi invasion of Austria and Italian takeover of Ethiopia.

OTHER GLOBAL EVENTS

South Koreans riot against Park government, mass arrests ensue; mine workers revolt in Bolivia; U.S.S.R. warns U.S. to halt Vietnam bombings; new government formed in Dominican Republic; Castro permits Cuban exodus; demonstrations in Tokyo, Rome, and London against U.S. policies in Vietnam; Indonesian army crushes communist coup; Marcos becomes president of Philippines.

1966 / HISTORICAL EVENTS

UNITED STATES

Domestic
U.S. clergymen call for an end to the Vietnam War; anti-war protests spread; 38 state governors issue statement supporting war; Johnson urges housewives to boycott high-priced consumer goods in anti-inflation effort; renewed rioting in Watts; White House sponsors civil rights conference; Medicare goes into effect; Johnson denounces violence in urban race riots; number of military draftees increases; civil rights march in Ciro, Illinois; riots in Atlantic City, New Jersey; whites attack black students and parents trying to enter school in Mississippi; Democratic state governors criticize Vietnam policies; National Organization for Women (NOW) is founded.

Foreign
U.S. sends tanks and planes to Israel; U.S. begins shelling of Cambodian targets; Robert Kennedy denounces apartheid during South African visit.

VIETNAM

U.S.S.R. increases aid to North Vietnam; Ky promises South Vietnamese elections as anti-government demonstrations grow; ground war intensifies; reacting to Buddhist demonstrations, Ky's troops occupy Da Nang and Hue; U.S. troops increased to over 330,000 by end of year.

OTHER GLOBAL EVENTS

Coup in Syria; army topples government in Ghana; Rhodesia proclaims independence; new government installed in Argentina, followed by student protests; "Cultural Revolution" begins in China.

Other Documentary Films:

The Battle of Ia Drang Valley
The Battle
Marines-65
Christmas in Vietnam
Vietnam Perspective, the CBS series, begins

AMERICAN FILM / 1966

FICTION

Ambush Bay—Group of U.S. marines join guerrilla forces on Japanese-held island during World War II.

Other Fiction Films:

What Did You Do in the War, Daddy?
The Heroes of Telemark
Lt. Robin Crusoe, U.S.N.
Cast a Giant Shadow
The Longest Hundred Miles
Is Paris Burning?
The Sand Pebbles
The Russians Are Coming, the Russians Are Coming

DOCUMENTARY

Know Your Enemy: The Viet Cong—Department of Defense film using captured NLF footage as an example of 'communist propaganda.'

Other Documentary Films:

Asia Perspective: Election Day in Vietnam
Battle for Asia: Thailand, the New Front
Campaign '66: Vietnam and the Elections
Vietnam: The Other War
Fulbright: Advice and Dissent
Survival and Evasion in Southeast Asia
Vietnam: Eric Sevareid's Personal Report
Westmoreland on Vietnam
The President in Asia, Parts 1 through 6
The Councils of War
While Brave Men Die
Vietnam: The Home Front
ABC Scope: The Vietnam War series begins
Vietnam Perspective series continues

1967 / HISTORICAL EVENTS

UNITED STATES

Domestic
Johnson calls for increased taxes to pay for war and anti-poverty programs, sends bill to congress to end housing discrimination; anti-war demonstrations continue, Martin Luther King, Jr. urges resistance to draft; Executive Order 11375 prohibits employment discrimination by federal contractors and sub-contractors; American Medical Association favors easing of abortion restrictions; race riots in Newark and Detroit; war protesters march on Pentagon, draft resistance grows.

Foreign
Controversy mounts over North Vietnamese civilian deaths due to bombing; U.S.-U.S.S.R. summit meeting takes place; U.S. Green Berets aid major counterinsurgency campaign in Guatemala.

VIETNAM

Hanoi demands U.S. halt bombing before peace talks can begin; Ky announces election date, but forced to step down by General Nguyen Van Thieu; Thieu is elected president of South Vietnam, opposition charges fraud; number of U.S. troops reaches 500,000.

OTHER GLOBAL EVENTS

Sukarno yields power to Indonesian military; following two military coups, Biafra moves to secede from Nigeria, civil war begins; Thailand agrees to U.S. use of air bases for North Vietnamese air raids; army junta seizes power in Greece; the Six-Day War in the Middle East; Che Guevera killed in Bolivia.

1968 / HISTORICAL EVENTS

UNITED STATES

Domestic
Key anti-war activists indicted for aiding draft violators; investigating urban riots, Civil Disorders Commission cites white racism as underlying factor in black unemployment, inadequate housing, discriminatory police practices, and urges increased federal spending in areas of housing, job creation, income supplementation; Senator Fulbright accuses Defense Secretary McNamara of distorting facts in 1964 Gulf of Tonkin incident; draft deferments curtailed for graduate students, occupational deferments eliminated, ACLU announces it will defend draft evaders; Johnson announces he will not seek reelection; Martin Luther King, Jr. assassinated;

AMERICAN FILM / 1967

FICTION

The Born Losers—Ex-Green Beret takes on motorcycle gang terrorizing community.

Other Fiction Films:

Beach Red
The Dirty Dozen
The Young Warriors
Tobruk

DOCUMENTARY

The Anderson Platoon—Film follows a U.S. Army combat platoon during six weeks' duty in Vietnam's central highlands.
Sighet, Sighet—Elie Wiesel returns to his Austrian home town, from which thousands of Jews were taken to Auschwitz by the Nazis.

Other Documentary Films:

A Face of War
Morley Safer's Vietnam: A Personal Report
Sons and Daughters
The United States Air Force in Vietnam
The United States Navy in Vietnam
The People of Vietnam: How They Feel About the War
Vietnam: The Bombings
March on the Pentagon
Saigon
The Four Navy Deserters
Another Day of War
Where We Stand in Vietnam, Parts 1 & 2
Battle for Asia: Laos, the Forgotten War
ABC Scope: The Vietnam War series continues
Vietnam Perspective series continues

AMERICAN FILM / 1968

FICTION

Angels from Hell—Vietnam vet leads a motorcycle gang terrorizing community.
The Green Berets—U.S. Special Forces fight the Vietcong and infiltrate enemy territory to kidnap North Vietnamese general.

Other Fiction Films:

Anzio
Counterpoint

antiwar demonstrations on college campuses across the U.S., "Poor People's March" in Washington; Robert Kennedy assassinated; demonstrators beaten by police at Democratic National Convention in Chicago; Nixon defeats Humphrey in presidential election.

Foreign
Johnson visits Central America.

VIETNAM

Tet offensive begins: Saigon, Hue, and Khe Sahn become key areas of battle; heavy ground fighting throughout the south; bombing raids on North Vietnam targets continue; North Vietnamese officials meet with U.S. delegation in Paris; Saigon boycotts Paris talks because of NLF participation; number of U.S. troops reaches 540,000.

OTHER GLOBAL EVENTS

U.S.S. *Pueblo* seized by North Korea; students and labor organizations strike in France; Mexican students protest government economic policies, several hundred killed when military attacks peaceful demonstration; Western-backed mercenaries leave Zaire; U.S.S.R. invades Czechoslovakia in response to liberal reforms; Egypt begins "war of attrition" against Israel in Sinai; Nationalist military coup in Panama led by Torrijos; North Korea releases *Pueblo*.

1969 / HISTORICAL EVENTS

UNITED STATES

Domestic
Campus demonstrations grow, SDS chapter occupies Harvard administration offices, black and Puerto Rican students demand admission and curriculum reforms at City College of New York; thousands attend antiwar protests in Washington, D.C., and San Francisco; probe of My Lai massacre begins; Native Americans occupy Alcatraz prison; black students occupy administrative offices at Vassar; Black Panther leader Fred Hampton killed in shoot-out with Chicago police; National Commission on the Causes and Prevention of Violence issues a call for increased government spending in the areas of social programs, urban renewal, and education;

The Devil's Brigade
In Enemy Country
The Sergeant
Greetings
The Secret War of Harry Frigg
Hell in the Pacific
Ice Station Zebra
Sergeant Ryker
Mission Batangas
The Private War of Sergeant O'Farrell
Attack on the Iron Coast

DOCUMENTARY

No Vietnamese Ever Called Me Nigger—Interviews with black veterans focus on the relationship between racism in the U.S. and the war in Vietnam.

Other Documentary Films:

Inside North Vietnam
Chomsky-Resist
Four Americans
Mill-In
Time of the Locust
The Viet Cong
Last Reflections on a War
Boston Draft Resistance Group
Chicago Convention Challenge
The Jeanette Rankin Brigade
No Game
Yippie
The Resistance
Hill 943
America Against Itself
USAF Combat Photography: Southeast Asia
ABC Scope: The Vietnam War series continues

AMERICAN FILM / 1969

FICTION

The Angry Breed—Vietnam veteran joins motorcycle gang in Hollywood.
Medium Cool—Reporter is caught up in antiwar demonstrations at the 1968 Democratic Convention in Chicago.

Other Fiction Films:

Alice's Restaurant
The Ballad of Andy Crocker

Harvard suspends 75 black students for occupation of administration; first draft lottery since World War II begins in December.

Foreign
Nixon orders bombing of Cambodia, later announces "Vietnamization" policy; Vice-President Rockefeller's tour of Latin America sparks riots, Nixon promises to loosen political restrictions on economic aid.

VIETNAM

Ho Chi Minh dies in Hanoi; NLF representatives join peace talks in Paris, talks deadlock over MIA issue; heavy ground fighting continues; by year's end, number of U.S. troops is reduced to 480,000.

OTHER GLOBAL EVENTS

New pro-Soviet Czech regime takes power; Peru seizes U.S. oil company; coup in Libya brings Kaddafi to power; violent clashes between Lebanese army and Palestinians; coup in Dahomey, sixth since independence in 1960.

1970 / HISTORICAL EVENTS

UNITED STATES

Domestic
Demonstrations continue on many college campuses; four students killed by National Guard troops at Kent State University anti-war demonstration; two students killed at Jackson State civil rights demonstration; Labor Department lays out requirements for affirmative action programs; construction workers clash with antiwar demonstrators in New York City; civil rights march in Georgia; FBI brands Black Panthers the "most dangerous and violence-prone of extremist groups"; New England Free Press begins distribution of *Our Bodies, Our Selves* in unbound, photocopied format, later published in book form by Simon and Schuster; Chicano antiwar protest in Los Angeles leads to police riot, and noted Chicano journalist Rubin Salazar is subsequently killed under suspicious circumstances; United Farm Workers win first contract; Angela Davis arrested on charge of killing a California judge; FBI seizes Reverend Daniel Berrigan; William Calley goes on trial for My Lai massacre; Nguyen Cao Ky visits U.S.

Foreign
Kissinger begins secret talks with North Vietnamese; partial withdrawal of U.S. troops from Thailand; U.S. planes downed over Laos; U.S. closes bases in Libya.

The Big Bounce
Castle Keep
Hail, Hero!
The Battle of Britain
The Bridge at Remagen
Where Eagles Dare
Carter's Army
Operation Cross Eagles

DOCUMENTARY

Good Bye and Good Luck—Discussions between a black Vietnam veteran and black militants
   in his community.

Other Documentary Films:

Army
In the Year of the Pig
America
The People's War
Summer '68
The Battle of Khe Sanh
Men with Green Faces
R.O.T.C.
Pig Power
A Timetable for Vietnam

AMERICAN FILM / 1970

FICTION

M*A*S*H—American doctors save lives and undermine military authority during the Korean
   War.

Other Fiction Films:

Kelly's Heroes
Captain Milkshake
Catch-22
Cowards
Darling Lili
Getting Straight
Hi, Mom!
Homer
Joe
Patton
The Revolutionary

VIETNAM

Sweden begins sending aid to North Vietnam; American and South Vietnamese troops attack bases in Cambodia; North Vietnam launches spring offensive; heavy bombing in Hanoi area; fighting increases along DMZ; Paris talks enter fourth year; Cambodian troops fight North and South Vietnamese forces; U.S. troops reduced to 280,000.

OTHER GLOBAL EVENTS

Nassar dies in Egypt; Prince Sihanouk is deposed in Cambodia, Lon Nol requests aid to fight Hanoi; Nigerian civil war ends; PLO driven out of Jordan and into Lebanon; Socialist Allende wins Chilean election.

1971 / HISTORICAL EVENTS

UNITED STATES

Domestic
Army drops charges against other officers involved in My Lai massacre, court-martial of Captain Ernest Medina ordered, Calley found guilty of premeditated murder; thirteen Black Panthers acquitted in N.Y. bomb-conspiracy trial; Berrigan brothers and 11 others indicted for destroying draft records and conspiracy; Daniel Ellsberg gives the Pentagon Papers to the *New York Times*, and is later indicted by the government; Supreme Court sanctions busing to achieve desegregation; riots in Wilmington, North Carolina; antiwar demonstration in Washington results in mass arrests; 2,000 Vietnam veterans stage antiwar rally in Washington, D.C.; Calley sentence reduced, Medina acquitted; Congress votes to raise military pay and drop undergraduate deferments; inmates revolt at Attica prison, 49 prisoners and hostages are killed when state police storm prison; antiwar veterans occupy the Statue of Liberty, 80 more are arrested in demonstration at the Lincoln Memorial in Washington, D.C.

Foreign
Shipment of arms to Pakistan ends.

VIETNAM

South Vietnamese troops cross into Laos; North Vietnam and NLF boycott Paris peace talks; Australian and New Zealand forces pull out of South Vietnam; Thieu runs unopposed in presidential election; number of U.S. troops is reduced to 140,000.

OTHER GLOBAL EVENTS

Antileftist military coup in Turkey; separatist students demonstrate against U.S. in Puerto Rico; Chilean government establishes diplomatic ties with China, Cuba, and Russia; India-Pakistan war; Bangladesh established.

Too Late the Hero
Tora! Tora! Tora!
The Strawberry Statement

DOCUMENTARY

Sad Song of Yellow Skin—The effects of the war on the lives of residents in Saigon's urban neighborhoods.
Hiroshima-Nagasaki, August 1945— Originally suppressed by the U.S. government, film documents the effects of the atomic bomb on two Japanese cities.

Other Documentary Films:

Street Scenes-1970
Eagle Eye Bravo
Vietnam: Voices in Opposition
Where We Stand in Indochina
The World of Charlie Company

AMERICAN FILM / 1971

FICTION

The Losers—Five members of a motorcycle gang are brought to Vietnam on a secret mission to rescue a U.S. diplomat held by communists.

Other Fiction Films:

The Hard Ride
Billy Jack
Raid on Rommel
Summertree
Clay Pigeon
Johnny Got His Gun
My Old Man's Place
Von Richthofen and Brown
If Tomorrow Comes
Chrome and Hot Leather
Welcome Home, Johnny Bristol

DOCUMENTARY

Another Part of the Family—A look at three families who lost sons, one in Vietnam, one at Kent State, and one at Jackson State.
Only the Beginning—Film documents the 1971 antiwar demonstration by Vietnam Veterans in Washington, D.C.

Other Documentary Films:

Basic Training
Bright College Years

1972 / HISTORICAL EVENTS

UNITED STATES

Domestic

Angela Davis released on bail; Berrigan case ends in mistrial; J. Edgar Hoover dies; Congress passes Equal Rights Amendment; presidential candidate George Wallace shot and paralyzed; burglars arrested in break-in at Watergate offices; Nixon defeats McGovern in presidential election; commission finds widespread corruption in New York City police department.

Foreign

Nixon announces reduction of U.S. forces in Vietnam; House committee investigates unauthorized air strikes on North Vietnam; Kissinger resumes secret talks with North Vietnamese; Nixon visits China.

VIETNAM

Eleven newspapers in Saigon closed by South Vietnamese police; U.S. suspends Paris peace talks; North Vietnamese and NLF troops launch major offensive; U.S. ground forces leave Vietnam; U.S. mines Haiphong harbor; peace talks resume in Paris; U.S. resumes bombing of Hanoi.

OTHER GLOBAL EVENTS

Blacks riot in Rhodesia; U.S.S.R. and Iraq sign friendship pact; South Africa bans student rallies; Marcos declares martial law in the Philippines; truck owner and factory lockout paralyzes Chilean economy, military brought in to regain control; Park consolidates power in South Korea, declares martial law, and is re-elected.

1973 / HISTORICAL EVENTS

UNITED STATES

Domestic

Watergate burglars found guilty; Supreme Court hands down *Roe v. Wade* decision, legalizing abortion; FBI agents clash with Native Americans at Wounded Knee, South Dakota; special

The Selling of the Pentagon
Requiem 29: Racism and Police Oppression against Chicanos
Heroes and Heroin
When Johnny Comes Marching Home
The Court Martial of William Calley
The POW's: Pawns of War

AMERICAN FILM / 1972

FICTION

The Trial of the Catonsville Nine—Dramatization of legal proceedings against group who set fire to draft board files.
Limbo—American wives of MIA/POWs become friends while awaiting news of their husbands.

Other Fiction Films:

Black Gunn
Georgia, Georgia
Outside In
Parades
Slaughter
Slaughterhouse Five
The Visitors
Welcome Home, Soldier Boys
To Kill a Clown

DOCUMENTARY

Interviews with My Lai Veterans—Five soldiers describe their experiences during the My Lai massacre.
Winter Soldier—Film documents testimony of Vietnam veterans about atrocities committed by U.S. forces in Vietnam.

Other Documentary Films:

So the People Should Know
F.T.A.
Escalation in Vietnam: The Rogers Testimony
Vietnam: A Plan for Peace

AMERICAN FILM / 1973

FICTION

The Stone Killer— Mob boss employs Vietnam veterans to assassinate rivals.
Gordon's War—Black Vietnam veteran takes on drug syndicate operating in his neighborhood.

Senate committee investigates Watergate break-in; top Nixon aides and appointees resign; Ellsberg and Russo acquitted in Pentagon Papers case; battle over audiotapes of Nixon staff meetings relating to Watergate triggers more resignations and firings; Vice-President Agnew does not contest corruption charges, later resigns; Gerald Ford appointed Vice-President.

Foreign
Pentagon admits U.S. bombs hit Hanoi hospitals and killed Americans in Da Nang; U.S. establishes informal relations with China; Congress overrides Nixon's War Powers Bill veto, thus limiting presidential power to commit U.S. forces to hostilities abroad without congressional approval; U.S. renews official ties with Egypt.

VIETNAM

Peace agreements signed in Paris; POWs released by North Vietnam.

OTHER GLOBAL EVENTS

Peronists return to power in Argentina as economic crisis and dissent grow; Libya nationalizes 51% of all foreign oil companies; Allende is assassinated in CIA-backed Chilean military coup, thousands arrested and shot as Pinochet takes power; October War between Israel and Egypt-Syria; OPEC oil embargo begins.

1974 / HISTORICAL EVENTS

UNITED STATES

Domestic
House Judiciary committee begins hearings on Watergate cover-up, later votes to impeach Nixon; Alberta Williams King (Martin Luther King's mother) is assassinated; Nixon resigns; Gerald Ford becomes President, grants Nixon an "absolute" pardon, offers conditional amnesty to Vietnam era draft evaders and military deserters; Cally conviction overturned and he is released; Senate begins probe of CIA activities; Watergate cover-up trials begin.

VIETNAM

Thieu declares war has begun again between North and South; China seizes Paracels Islands from Vietnam.

OTHER GLOBAL EVENTS

OPEC oil embargo ends; Portuguese military seizes power; Peron dies, wife Isabel takes over in Argentina; United Nations and World Court demand self-determination for Polisarios in Western Sahara; junta seizure of Greek government leads to Turkish invasion of Cyprus, Greek junta falls; civilian government returns to power in Greece; Ethiopian Emperor Haile Selassie is deposed.

Magnum Force—Police detective goes after a group of Vietnam veterans, now policemen, who employ vigilante tactics in dealing with criminals.

Two People —Army deserter on his way to turn himself in falls in love with fashion model.

Other Fiction Films

Death Race
Trained to Kill
The Last Detail
Electra Glide in Blue
Massacre in Rome

DOCUMENTARY

I. F. Stone's Weekly—A look at the life of an American journalist who dedicated his career to uncovering governmental deception.

The Sins of the Fathers—NBC documentary examines the lives of Amerasian children in Vietnam.

AMERICAN FILM / 1974

FICTION

The Crazy World of Julius Vrooder—Vietnam veteran feigns insanity in order to cope with those around him.

The Execution of Private Slovik—TV-film about the execution of an American soldier for desertion during World War II.

Other Fiction Films:

The Bears and I
The Trial of Billy Jack
Two
Manhunter

DOCUMENTARY

Hearts and Minds—Peter Davis's documentary about the Vietnam War and American society.

Other Documentary Films:

Year of the Tiger
Peace and the Pentagon

1975 / HISTORICAL EVENTS

UNITED STATES

Domestic
Senate issues CIA investigation report, giving details about assassination plots in Chile, Cuba, and other countries.

Foreign
Ford declares U.S. involvement in Vietnam is over; 38 U.S. marines die rescuing 39 U.S. sailors captured in Cambodian waters aboard the U.S.S. *Mayaguez*; U.S. bans aid to Angola.

VIETNAM

NLF-NVA offensive routs ARVN forces; Americans evacuate embassy in Saigon; South Vietnamese leaders surrender to North Vietnam.

OTHER GLOBAL EVENTS

Morocco fights the Polisario rebels in Spanish Sahara; Portugal leaves Angola in a state of civil war; Mozambique wins independence; Argentinian military suppresses dissidents, thousands disappear; Madrid agreement transfers jurisdiction of Western Sahara from Morocco and Mauritania to Spain; civil war begins in Lebanon; People's Democratic Republic of Laos is established; Indira Gandhi declares state of emergency and dissolves parliament in India; Spanish dictator Franco dies; Socialists establish new government in Portugal.

1976 / HISTORICAL EVENTS

UNITED STATES

Domestic
House Intelligence Committee report of CIA and FBI funding stirs debate; Senate urges new laws sharply limiting covert actions abroad; Carter defeats Ford in presidential election.

Foreign
U.S. vetoes Vietnam's admission to the U.N., citing MIA issue; U.S. signs new accord with Turkey to maintain military bases; U.S. signs $10 billion arms deal with Iran.

VIETNAM

Vietnam is reunified, Hanoi is named capital, Saigon is renamed Ho Chi Minh City; First Worker's Party Congress is held in Hanoi.

OTHER GLOBAL EVENTS

Syrian troops move into Lebanon; Syria signs agreement with PLO, then launches offensive against PLO; anti-Israeli riots in the West Bank; U.S. ambassador slain in Beirut; Egypt ends treaty with U.S.S.R., Sadat seeks western support; Spanish Army withdraws from Western

AMERICAN FILM / 1975

FICTION

The Man in the Glass Booth—German industrialist goes on trial for Nazi war crimes.

Collision Course—TV-movie dramatizes the clash between Truman and MacArthur over Korean War policies.

The Desperate Miles—Based on a true story, TV-film version of disabled Vietnam veteran's 130-mile odyssey in a wheelchair.

Returning Home—Updated TV-movie remake of the post-World War II film *The Best Years of Our Lives*, focusing on the readjustment of three Vietnam veterans.

DOCUMENTARY

G.I. Jose—Documentary traces the effects of military training and service in Vietnam on a young Hispanic soldier.

Other Documentary Films:

Introduction to the Enemy
Vietnam: An Historical Document
Cambodia: An American Dilemma
Indochina 1975: The End of the Road?

AMERICAN FILM / 1976

FICTION

Green Eyes—TV-film in which black U.S. soldier returns to Vietnam to find the child he fathered.

Tracks—Brooding Vietnam veteran escorts the body of fallen comrade home for burial.

Farewell to Manzanar—TV-movie about the lives of Japanese Americans forced into a U.S. internment camp during World War II.

Other Fiction Films

Baby Blue Marine
The Enforcer
Midway
Special Delivery
Mean Johnny Barrows
Voyage of the Damned
The Eagle Has Landed
Taxi Driver

Sahara; Cuban troops aid Angolan government against invading South African troops; Isabel Peron ousted from Argentina by military coup; antiapartheid riots in South African townships; military seizes power in Thailand.

1977 / HISTORICAL EVENTS

UNITED STATES

Domestic
Carter grants unconditional amnesty to Vietnam draft evaders; 194 students arrested in Kent State memorial demonstration; Carter increases Indochina refugee quota.

Foreign
U.S. starts normalizing relations with Vietnam, despite disagreements about postwar recovery aid; U.S. and Cuba exchange diplomats; U.S. and Panama sign Canal Zone treaties.

VIETNAM

Vietnam admitted to the United Nations.

OTHER GLOBAL EVENTS

Border clashes between Angola and Zaire, Egypt and Libya, Somalia and Ethiopia; coup in Ethiopia is suppressed; Spain holds first free election in 41 years; United Nations increases sanctions against Rhodesia, assisting the subsequent independence of Zimbabwe; Bhutto overthrown, Zia-ul-Haq seizes power in Pakistan; demonstrators fired on by Salvadoran military; Indira Gandhi loses Indian elections; Begin becomes Israeli prime minister; Steven Biko dies in prison of brain damage, South African government represses black activists.

1978 / HISTORICAL EVENTS

UNITED STATES

Domestic
Supreme Court rules against reverse discrimination in the Bakke case; Equal Rights Amendment march in Washington.

Foreign
U.S. signs agreement with Panamanian government to gradually end U.S. control of Panama Canal.

DOCUMENTARY

All This and World War II—News footage of World War II set to music of the Beatles.

Other Documentary Films:

Southeast Asia: Lands and Peoples
Underground

AMERICAN FILM / 1977

FICTION

Twilight's Last Gleaming—Air Force officer seizes missile silo in an attempt to force governmental admission of deception regarding its policies in Vietnam.

Other Fiction Films

Heroes
Black Sunday
A Bridge Too Far
Just a Little Inconvenience
MacArthur
Star Wars
Rolling Thunder
Fighting Mad

DOCUMENTARY

The Class That Went to War—ABC film looks at the effects of the Vietnam War on a New Jersey High School's 1964 graduating class.
Vietnam: Picking Up the Pieces—Documentary about life in Vietnam after the war.
Men of Bronze—Story of the 369th regiment, black U.S. soldiers who fought in the trenches in France during World War I.

AMERICAN FILM / 1978

FICTION

The Big Fix—War protestor-turned-private detective takes a case involving leaders of the anti-war movement.

Other Fiction Films

The Boys from Brazil
Big Wednesday
The Boys in Company C
Coming Home

VIETNAM

Tensions between Vietnam and Cambodia increase as relations between Vietnam and China deteriorate; thousands of boat people begin to flee Vietnam; Vietnam signs treaty with Russia.

OTHER GLOBAL EVENTS

Anti-Shah demonstrations in Iran; Camp David Accord signed by Begin and Sadat; anti-Samosa revolt led by Sandinistas breaks out in Nicaragua; Communist coup in Afghanistan; Ethiopia and Russia sign treaty; Bolivian president deposed.

1979 / HISTORICAL EVENTS

UNITED STATES

Domestic
Three Mile Island accident, antinuclear power rallies are held throughout the U.S.; 200 CIA workers retire or resign; Klu Klux Klan marches from Selma to Montgomery; first meeting of National Women's Studies Association in Kansas City; General Accounting Office reports thousands of U.S. troops were exposed to Agent Orange in Vietnam; Carter raises Indochina refugee quota to 14,000 a month.

Foreign
China and U.S. establish diplomatic relations, formal ties with Taiwan are severed; Iranians seize hostages in U.S. embassy.

VIETNAM

Government makes first attempt to liberalize economy; China invades Vietnam.

OTHER GLOBAL EVENTS

Revolution in Iran: Shah leaves, Ayatollah Khomeini returns; Cambodia government of Pol Pot is overthrown, famine in countryside; Bhutto is hanged in Pakistan; Idi Amin overthrown in Uganda; Margaret Thatcher elected prime minister of Britain; first black government elected in Rhodesia; in Nicaragua, Samosa defeated by Sandinistas with aid from Venezuela, Panama, and Costa Rica; El Salvadoran military president deposed by reform minded military-civilian junta, dissident military factions continue actions against grass-roots Salvadoran organizations, death squads assassinate Archbishop Romero and other opponents at the rate of 500 a month, ranks of guerilla movement expand; U.S.S.R. enters Afghanistan to prop up Communist regime; Guatemalan military government begins three-year scorched-earth policy against dissidents; U.N conference takes up question of Indochina refugees.

The Deer Hunter
Force 10 from Navarone
Go Tell the Spartans
Our Winning Season
Who'll Stop the Rain?
Youngblood

DOCUMENTARY

Charlie Company at Home: The Veterans of Vietnam—CBS documentary interviews with eight soldiers who originally appeared in *The World of Charlie Company* about their lives since returning from Vietnam.

AMERICAN FILM / 1979

FICTION

More American Graffiti—Episodic film follows the experiences of high school friends during the sixties, including military service in Vietnam.
Night-Flowers—Story of developing friendship between two veterans, one of Hispanic and one of Irish descent.
When You Comin' Back, Red Ryder?—Psychotic Vietnam veteran terrorizes group of people at a roadside diner.

Other Fiction Films

Apocalypse Now
The Great Santini
Hair
1941
Good Guys Wear Black
Friendly Fire

DOCUMENTARY

The Phans of New Jersey—Members of a South Vietnamese family discuss their final days in Saigon and their adjustment to living in America.
The War at Home— A look at the effects of the antiwar movement on the lives of students at the University of Wisconsin.

Other Documentary Films:
American Dream, American Nightmare . . . the Seventies, Parts 1 & 2
The Boat People
War Shadows

1980 / HISTORICAL EVENTS

UNITED STATES

Domestic
FBI coverups of Klu Klux Klan activities revealed; new law requiring draft registration goes into effect; Reagan defeats Carter in presidential election.

Foreign
U.S. breaks diplomatic relations with Iran, military plan to rescue hostages fails.

VIETNAM

Vietnam invades Cambodia.

OTHER GLOBAL EVENTS

Indira Gandhi wins landslide election in India; Zimbabwe wins independence; military coup in Turkey; Yugoslav president Tito dies; Samosa assassinated in Paraguay; Iraq invades Iran and begins the Gulf war.

1981 / HISTORICAL EVENTS

UNITED STATES

Domestic
Reagan increases authority of CIA.

Foreign
U.S. hostages released in Iran; U.S. agrees to arms deal with Saudi Arabia; new military command assigned to protect U.S.interests in the Persian Gulf; U.S. downs Libyan jets in the Gulf of Sidra.

OTHER GLOBAL EVENTS

Miltary clash between Libya and Chad; civil war continues in El Salvador, death squads assassinate more civilians; Israeli planes bomb Iraqi nuclear plant; Botha confirms South African forces are fighting in Angola; U.S. sponsored Contra war against Nicaraguan government begins; Egypt's President Sadat is assassinated, Mubarak is successor; Panamanian leader Torri-

AMERICAN FILM / 1980

FICTION

The Stunt Man—A Vietnam veteran on the run from the law becomes involved with a movie company making a war film.

Other Fiction Films

The Big Red One
Dogs of War
The Children of An Lac
The Exterminator
A Small Circle of Friends
A Rumor of War
Return of the Secaucus 7
Fighting Back
Enola Gay: The Men, The Mission, The Atomic Bomb

DOCUMENTARY

Vietnam: An American Journey—A look at the lingering effects of the war on the people and the culture of Vietnam.

Other Documentary Films:

Abran la Puerta
The Day After Trinity
Vietnam: The 10,000 Day War
Vietnam: Five Years After the War

AMERICAN FILM / 1981

FICTION

Raiders of the Lost Ark—American anthropologist battles Nazis for possession of religious artifact.

Other Fiction Films

Americana
Four Friends
Southern Comfort
Cutter's Way
Stripes
The Bunker
Fly Away Home
Victory
Search and Destroy

jos killed in plane crash, Noriega begins to assume power; Greece votes in a socialist government, headed by Papandreou; liberal party elected in Honduras, ending 17 years of military rule; Polish government declares martial law; Israel annexes Golan Heights.

1982 / HISTORICAL EVENTS

UNITED STATES

Domestic
Reagan continues draft registration; first conviction on failure to register is decided by courts; Pentagon announces rising weapons costs; ERA fails to be ratified; Vietnam Memorial dedicated in Washington, D.C.

Foreign
U.S. increases aid to government of El Salvador; U.S. begins long series of military exercises in Honduras along Nicaraguan border; 800 U.S. marines land in Beirut.

OTHER GLOBAL EVENTS

Fighting continues in El Salvador, Human Rights Commission reports 35,000 dead in 33 month-old revolution; antimilitary coup in Guatemala; unrest in Nicaragua; Argentina seizes the Falkland Islands, with U.S. support, Britain defeats Argentina in war, leading to downfall of Argentine military government; state of emergency declared in Peru; repression escalates in the Philippines; 1,000 civilians in Hama, Syria reported dead in civil war; Israel invades Lebanon; Iran-Iraq war continues; Solidarity banned in Poland; Socialists win elections in Spain; Portugal has new constitution, ending eight years of military rule; South African forces raid Lesotho and Maseru.

DOCUMENTARY

Smothering Dreams—Veteran Dan Reeves's film juxtaposes images of children at play with those of men at war.

Other Documentary Films:

Agent Orange: A Story of Dignity and Doubt
Ben Da, U.S.A.
Bittersweet Survival
Ecocide: A Strategy of War
Front Line
Frank: A Vietnam Veteran
Are You Listening: Indochina Refugees
Warriors' Women
El Salvador: Another Vietnam?
Vietnam—Chronicle of a War
The Problems of Peace
Bittersweet Memories—A Vietnam Reunion

AMERICAN FILM / 1982

FICTION

Ashes and Embers—Black Vietnam veteran confronts racism and poverty at home.
Some Kind of Hero—Black Vietnam veteran returns home after six years as a POW.

Other Fiction Films

An Officer and a Gentleman
Inchon
Don't Cry, It's Only Thunder
Firefox
First Blood
Missing
World War III

DOCUMENTARY

Going Back: A Return to Vietnam—The first group of American combat veterans return t Vietnam.
Vietnam Requiem: Vets in Prison—Film explores reasons why a large number of Vietnam ve erans are in U.S. prisons.

Other Documentary Films:

The Atomic Cafe
Blood and Sand: War in the Sahara
Monterey's Boat People

1983 / HISTORICAL EVENTS

UNITED STATES

Domestic
Chicago elects its first black mayor; civil rights commemorative march in Washington; federal holiday honors Martin Luther King, Jr.; Jesse Jackson enters presidential race.

Foreign
U.S.-Nicaraguan relations deteriorate; Congress debates U.S. involvement in Central America; U.S. plans military manuevers near Nicaragua; U.S. invades Grenada; car-bomb attack on U.S. embassy in Beirut; U.S. Marine headquarters in Beirut bombed; U.S. warplanes attack Syrian positions near Beirut; U.S. aids Chad against Libyan-backed rebels.

VIETNAM

Increased governmental debate over pace and direction of economic reforms.

OTHER GLOBAL EVENTS

Poland ends martial law, sanctions unions; antigovernment demonstrations grow in Chile as Pinochet celebrates tenth anniversary in power; democratic regime takes over in Argentina under Raul Alfonsin; Syria rejects Schultz plan for Israeli withdrawal from Lebanon; Arafat shifts PLO offices to Tunis; Polisario war flares up in Western Sahara; French troops enter Chad; opposition leader Benigno Aquino assassinated in the Philippines, demonstrations against Marcos continue; Begin steps down, Shamir takes over in Israel.

1984 / HISTORICAL EVENTS

UNITED STATES

Domestic
Agent Orange class action suit against chemical companies settled out of court, victims' fund established; Geraldine Ferraro nominated by Democrats as vice-presidential candidate, Reagan defeats Mondale/Ferraro in presidential election.

Fire on the Water
Becoming American
The Uncounted Enemy: A Vietnam Deception
Vietnam: The Ten Thousand Day War series

AMERICAN FILM / 1983

FICTION

Testament—Film examines the effects of nuclear war on an American family.
Uncommon Valor—Retired Army officer recruits Vietnam veterans for a secret mission to free
   POWs in Laos.

Other Fiction Films

The Big Chill
Return of the Jedi
Streamers
Daniel
Under Fire
Twilight Zone-The Movie
The Keep
Brady's Escape
The Day After
Memorial Day

DOCUMENTARY

How Far Home: Veterans After Vietnam—Recorded at the dedication of the Vietnam Memorial
   in Washington, D.C., film focuses on the adjustment of Vietnam veterans since the war.

Other Documentary Films:

The Secret Agent
Vietnam Memorial
Vietnam: This Was the Vietnam War
Inside Story: Uncounted Enemy/Unproven Conspiracy
Marching Along Together Again
Vietnam: A Television History series

AMERICAN FILM / 1984

FICTION

Birdy—Childhood friends are reunited in an Army hospital after service in Vietnam.
Missing in Action—Veteran returns to Vietnam to find and free American POWS.
Fatal Vision—TV-film based on true story of ex-Green Beret captain convicted of murdering
   his family.

Foreign

Withdrawal of U.S. marines from Beirut; CIA role in mining Nicaraguan harbors revealed; Congress debates military aid for Central America; U.S. embassy in Beirut is bombed; World Court rules that the U.S. should halt blockading and mining Nicaraguan ports, U.S. claims court lacks jurisdiction.

OTHER GLOBAL EVENTS

Iraq uses chemical weapons against Iran; Duarte elected in El Salvador; pro-U.S. candidate supported by Noriega wins fraudulent election in Panama; Daniel Ortega wins Nicaraguan elections; agreement signed for simultaneous withdrawal of French and Lybian troops from Chad; Iran and Iraq attack ships in the Persian Gulf; Filipinos opposing Marcos gain in elections; Indira Ghandi assassinated, violence sweeps India; Bopal chemical accident in India; famine in Ethiopia.

1985 / HISTORICAL EVENTS

UNITED STATES

Domestic

Westmoreland-CBS case settled; Pentagon loses ground in budget fight.

Foreign

Reagan asks for more aid for Contra "freedom fighters"; Congress rejects military aid to Contras; U.S. ends trade to Nicaragua; CIA linked to Beirut bombing; Congress approves humanitarian aid for Contras.

VIETNAM

Vietnamese forces overrun Cambodian resistance bases.

OTHER GLOBAL EVENTS

Brazil gets civilian government after 21 years of military rule; Israel begins partial pull-out from Lebanon; death toll increases in South Africa, many more injured and arrested, South Africa declares state of emergency; Israelis bomb PLO headquarters in Tunis.

Other Fiction Films

The Killing Fields
Limousine
Exterminator II
Lassiter
Purple Hearts

DOCUMENTARY

Aspects of a Certain History—Filmmaker and veteran John Knecht uses Hollywood film clips and animated sequences to explore the roots of U.S. involvement in Vietnam.

Other Documentary Films:

Jesse Trevino: A Spirit Against All Odds
Kim Phuc
Requiem for the Vietnam Unknown
Soldiers in Hiding
Television's Vietnam, Parts 1 & 2

AMERICAN FILM / 1985

FICTION

Alamo Bay—Americans and Vietnamese refugees clash in Texas fishing port.
Cease Fire—Years after returning from Vietnam, veteran finds he is still troubled by his memories of wartime experiences.
The Annihilators—Group of Vietnam veterans take on street gang terrorizing the community.

Other Fiction Films

American Commandos
Hitler's SS: Portrait in Evil
Latino
Missing in Action II: The Beginning
Invasion U.S.A.
Rambo: First Blood Part II
White Nights
Year of the Dragon
Volunteers

DOCUMENTARY

The Haunted Heroes—Film looks at Vietnam veterans who have chosen to live in reclusion since returning to the U.S.

1986 / HISTORICAL EVENTS

UNITED STATES

Domestic
Government "disinformation" practices angers U.S. press; Ivan Boesky pleads guilty to "insider trading" practices.

Foreign
U.S. and Libyan forces clash in the Gulf of Sidra, U.S. launches air strike against Libyan targets; $100,000,000 Contra military aid bill backed by Senate, first voted down by House of Representatives, later approved by both houses; $20,000,000 in military aid to Honduras approved by Congress; U.S. aid to El Salvadoran government reaches half a billion dollars annually; Nicaraguans down U.S. plane containing arms for Contras, capture pilot Hasenfus, who is later convicted of violating Nicaraguan laws and immediately pardoned; Reagan announces resignation of security advisor Poindexter and relieves Oliver North of National Security Council duties; Senate opens Iran-Contra investigations, McFarland, Poindexter and North refuse to testify.

VIETNAM

6th Party Congress debates changes in economic policies.

OTHER GLOBAL EVENTS

Civil war in South Yemen, 13,000 killed; Duvalier flees Haiti; Portugal elects first civilian president in 60 years; Marcos flees Philippines, Corazon Aquino becomes president; nuclear power plant accident at Chernobyl; South African air and ground forces attack suspected guerilla bases in Botswana, Zambia, and Zimbabwe, mass strikes and violence in South Africa; Panama leader Noriega linked to arms and drug crimes; strikes in Chile, Pinochet escapes assassination attempt.

1987 / HISTORICAL EVENTS

UNITED STATES

Domestic
March against racism in Forsyth County, Georgia, is disrupted by the Klu Klux Klan; ex-Reagan aide Deaver indicted for illegal lobbying practices, later convicted; Reagan asks for mandatory AIDS testing of prisoners, new immigrants, and those seeking treatment for drug

Other Documentary Films:

Inside Story: Vietnam: Op. Ed., Parts 1 & 2
Vietnam Perspective
Vietnam-Talking to the People
Witness to War

AMERICAN FILM / 1986

FICTION

P.O.W.: The Escape—In the waning days of the Vietnam war, captured American G.I.'s attempt to escape from a prisoner-of-war camp.
Heartbreak Ridge— Tough Marine sergeant trains unruly recruits for invasion of Grenada.
Iron Eagle—Son of air force pilot held captive in the Middle East undertakes rescue mission.
House—Vietnam veteran who now writes horror stories is plagued by nightmares of his war experience.

Other Fiction Films
Back to School
The Delta Force
Platoon
Salvador
Top Gun
Whatever It Takes

DOCUMENTARY

The Bloods of Nam—Interviews with Black veterans focus on their struggles against racial discrimination.
The Invisible Force: Women in the Military— A look at the impact of military service on the lives of women from World War II to the present.

Other Documentary Films:

Vietnam Reconsidered: A Veteran's Perspective
A Program for Vietnam Veterans and Everyone Else Who Should Care

AMERICAN FILM / 1987

FICTION

Steele Justice—Vietnam veteran goes after former ARVN officer, now leader of drug ring in the U.S.
Suspect—Disabled Vietnam veteran goes on trial for murder in Washington, D.C.
Full Metal Jacket—Film follows young Marine recruit from basic training to the Tet offensive in Hue, Vietnam.

abuse; Goetz acquitted in New York City subway shootings; stock market plunges; three New York teenagers convicted in the death of a black man at Howard Beach.

Foreign

Secretary of State Shultz meets with African National Congress leadership for the first time; *New York Times* reports that administration provided false information to both sides in Iran/Iraq conflict; CIA chief Casey resigns; former National Security Advisor McFarlane hospitalized after apparent suicide attempt; Tower Commission Report on Iran-Contra affair issued, depicting Reagan as confused and uninformed about National Security Council activities and placing responsibility on chief of staff Donald Regan, who later resigns; House and Senate hold joint Iran-Contra hearings, North admits destroying documents; U.S. Congress blocks portion of Contra aid; Reagan endorses Arias peace plan for Central America, later presents additional demands; Shultz asks Congress for more Contra aid; U.S. clashes with Iranian forces in the Persian Gulf.

VIETNAM

Government announces intention to pull out of Cambodia by 1990.

OTHER GLOBAL EVENTS

Civil wars continue in El Salvador and Sudan; striking railway workers clash with police in South Africa; first U.S. citizen, Benjamin Linder, killed by Contras in Nicaragua; Iraqi missile kills 37 on U.S.S. *Stark* in the Persian Gulf; Noriega suspends civil and political rights in Panama; antigovernment riots in South Korea; "glasnost" reforms endorsed by Soviet politboro; 200 die in Haitian clash over land reforms, government later cancels elections; Aquino puts down fifth military revolt in the Philippines; Tibetans protest Chinese rule; Ortega proposes cease-fire in Nicaragua; Palestinian uprising begins in West Bank and Gaza Strip; corruption charged in South Korean presidential elections; peace plan signed by Central American leaders.

1988 / HISTORICAL EVENTS

UNITED STATES

Domestic

Federal grand jury hands down indictments in Iran-Contra affair; Bush defeats Dukakis in presidential elections.

Foreign

Federal grand jury indicts Panamanian General Noriega on drug trafficking charges, Noriega refuses to cooperate with U.S. anti-Sandinista policies; U.S. sends more troops to Panama; U.S. and Iran continue to clash in Gulf; Iranian airliner shot down by U.S. missile in Persian Gulf; Nicaragua expels U.S. diplomats; Ferdinand and Imelda Marcos indicted by U.S..

VIETNAM

Government announces new foreign investment policies.

Gardens of Stone—Tough sergeant stationed at Arlington National Cemetery tries to prepare young soldier for duty in Vietnam.

Good Morning, Vietnam—Brash U.S. Armed Forces Radio disc jockey provokes the anger of his superiors in Saigon.

Escape from Sobibor—TV-film depicts true story of plot by inmates to escape Nazi death camp during World War II.

The Hanoi Hilton—American POWs are tortured and tormented by their Vietnamese captors.

Hamburger Hill—Film depicts ten-day assault by U.S. troops on heavily defended position in Vietnam's Ashau Valley.

Death Before Dishonor—Marines attempt to rescue kidnapped American officer from terrorist group in the Middle East.

Empire of the Sun—British youth becomes separated from his family as the Japanese invade China in the early days of World War II.

In Love and War—TV-film based on true story of U.S. POW during the Vietnam war.

DOCUMENTARY

Dear America: Letters Home from Vietnam—Letters from GIs are coupled with news footage and popular music from the Vietnam era.

Why Vietnam?, Parts 1 & 2—Documentary based on a conference held at the University of Southern California, in which scholars, journalists, veterans, and Vietnamese refugees discuss the history of the Vietnam War.

AMERICAN FILM / 1988

FICTION

Distant Thunder—One of a group of reclusive Vietnam veterans attempts first meeting with his son, now eighteen years old.

Fear—Escaped convicts lead by psychotic Vietnam veteran abduct family on camping trip.

Above the Law—Chicago policeman finds the leader of a drug ring is a former CIA agent with whom he once worked in Vietnam.

Other Fiction Films

The Presidio
Bat 21
Rambo III
Hanna's War
Gleaming the Cube

OTHER GLOBAL EVENTS

Palestinian uprising continues; Iran-Iraq war intensifies; Nicaragua and Contras agree to cease fire; right-wing ARENA party gains control of El Salvadoran assembly in elections; continuing wars in Nicaragua and El Salvador devastate economies, refugees flood into U.S.; students demonstrate in South Korea, bombing U.S. embassy and calling for reunification; Soviets begin Afghan withdrawal; Pakistani President Zia-ul-Haq assassinated; two million South African blacks go on strike; Iran-Iraq implement cease-fire; Gorbachev named Soviet president.

Iron Eagle II
The Iron Triangle
Platoon Leader
Off Limits
Running on Empty

DOCUMENTARY

The War in El Cedro—A group of U.S. veterans helps rebuild a medical clinic destroyed by Contras in a small Nicaraguan village.

Other Documentary Films:

Vietnam Vets: Dissidents for Peace
Waiting for Cambodia

APPENDIX B
Selected Filmography:
The Vietnam War on Film

The following list contains pertinent information about films dealing with some aspects of the Vietnam War, including films produced outside the United States. Films about wars during other historical periods are not included here, although they have been included in the chronology. The films are divided into two categories—fiction and documentary—and within each category films are listed chronologically according to their year of release and then alphabetically within each year. For each film, we have listed the title, country of origin, year of release, releasing organization, approximate running time, and the name of the current distribution agency. For fiction films, we have also included the director(s), screenwriter(s), and cast members; for documentaries, the director(s) and/or producer(s). Since items like dates of release and running times often vary depending on the source of information, these elements of each film's citation are approximations based on a general consensus usually derived from a number of sources. Consistent with the general status of information pertaining to the Vietnam era, data on films produced by the mainstream American motion picture industry are readily available; information about independent productions in both the fiction and documentary categories is often difficult to locate. Consequently, some of the citations here are less detailed than others. Nonetheless, we have included as much information as we could find on as many films as possible, in the hope of encouraging further interest in representations of the war and expanding the discourse surrounding the canon of Vietnam War films.

Though all films have subtexts and resonances that confound attempts at classification, the letters in parentheses following each film's citation correspond to a schema designed to help identify a few of its salient features:

> AVW = Films that contain images of the American war in Vietnam.
> FVW = Films that contain images of the French war in Vietnam.
> S = Films that contain images of Southeast Asia other than Vietnam.
> VV = Films in which at least one major character is purposefully identified as a Vietnam veteran.
> H = Films of the American homefront that make specific allusions to the Vietnam War.
> A = Films that contain images of the antiwar movement.
> P = Films that contain images of American prisoners of war.
> R = Films that contain images of Southeast Asian refugees.
> V = Films that contain images of Vietnam after American military involvement.

FICTION FILMS

Rogues' Regiment (USA:1948) Released by Universal-International. Director: Robert Florey. Screenplay: Robert Buckner. Cast: Dick Powell, Marta Toren, Vincent Price. 86 mins. (FVW)

Saigon (USA:1948) Released by Paramount Pictures. Director: Leslie Fenton. Screenplay: P. J. Wolfson, Arthur Sheekman. Cast: Alan Ladd, Veronica Lake, Douglas Dick. Distribution: Swank Motion Pictures. 94 mins. (FVW)

A Yank in Indochina (USA:1952) Released by Columbia Pictures. Director: Wallace Grisell. Screenplay: Samuel Newman. Cast: John Archer, Douglas Dick, Jean Willes. 67 mins. (FVW)

Jump into Hell (USA:1955) Released by Warner Brothers. Director: David Butler. Screenplay: Irving Wallace. Cast: Jacques Sernas, Kurt Kaszner, Peter Van Eyck. 93 mins. (FVW)

China Gate (USA:1957) Released by 20th Century Fox. Director: Samuel Fuller. Screenplay: Samuel Fuller. Cast: Gene Barry, Angie Dickinson, Nat "King" Cole. Distribution: Ivy Films. 97 mins. (FVW)

Fraudulent Death (France:1957) Released by J. Arthur Rank. Director: Marcel Camus. Screenplay: Michel Audiard, Marcel Camus, Jean Hougran. 105 mins. (FVW)

The Quiet American (USA:1958) Released by United Artists. Director: Joseph L. Mankiewicz. Screenplay: Joseph L. Mankiewicz. Cast: Audie Murphy, Michael Redgrave, Claude Dauphin. Distribution: Films, Inc. 120 mins. (AVW)

Five Gates to Hell (USA:1959) Released by 20th Century Fox. Director: James Clavell. Screenplay: James Clavell. Cast: Delores Michaels, Patricia Owens, Neville Brand. 98 mins. (FVW)

Brushfire (USA:1961) Released by Paramount Pictures. Director: Jack Warner, Jr. Screenplay: Irwin Blacker. Cast: John Ireland, Jo Morrow, Everett Sloane. Distribution: Films, Inc. 80 mins. (AVW)

The Ugly American (USA:1963) Released by Universal-International. Director: George Englund. Screenplay: Stewart Stern. Cast: Marlon Brando, Sandra Church, Pat Hingle. Distribution: Swank Motion Pictures. 120 mins. (S)

The Young Woman of Bai-Sao (North Vietnam:1963) Released by Hanoi Film Studios. Director: Phan Ky Nam. Screenplay: Bui Duc Ai. 120 mins. (FVW)

The 7th Dawn (USA/UK:1964) Released by United Artists. Director: Lewis Gilbert. Cast: William Holden, Susannah York, Capucine. Distribution: MGM/UA. 123 mins. (S)

A Yank in Viet-Nam (USA:1964) Released by Allied Artists. Director: Marshall Thompson. Screenplay: Jane Wardell, Jack Lewis. Cast: Marshall Thompson, Enrique Magalona, Mario Bari. Distribution: Hurlock Cine. 80 mins. (AVW)

The Young Soldier (North Vietnam:1964) Released by Hanoi Film Studios. Directors: Hai Ninh. Screenplay: Hai Ho. 90 mins. (FVW)

Operation C.I.A. (USA:1965) Released by Allied Artists. Director: Christian Nyby. Screenplay: W. Ballinger, Peer Oppenheimer. Cast: Burt Reynolds, Danielle Aubrey, Kieu Chinh. Distribution: Hurlock Cine. 90 mins. (AVW)

Platoon 317 (France:1965) Released by J. Arthur Rank. Director: Pierre Schoendoerffer. Screenplay: Pierre Schoendoerffer. 94 mins. (FVW)

To the Shores of Hell (USA:1965) Released by Parade Pictures. Director: Will Zens. Screenplay: Will Zens, Robert McFadden. Cast: Marshall Thompson, Kiva Lawrence, Richard Arlen. 81 mins. (AVW)

Rising Storm (North Vietnam:1966) Released by Hanoi Film Studios. Directors: Huy Thanh, Le Huyen. Screenplay: Dao Hong Cam, Huy Thanh, Le Huyen. 100 mins. (AVW)

The Born Losers (USA:1967) Released by American International Pictures. Director: T. C. Frank (Tom Laughlin). Screenplay: E. James Lloyd (Elizabeth James). Cast: Tom Laughlin, Elizabeth James, Jeremy Slate. Distribution: Films Inc. 110 mins. (VV, H)

Angels from Hell (USA:1968) Released by American International Pictures. Director: Bruce Kessler. Screenplay: Jerome Wish. Cast: Tom Stern, Arlene Martel, Ted Markland. 86 mins. (VV)

The Green Berets (USA:1968) Released by Warner Brothers. Directors: John Wayne, Ray Kellogg. Screenplay: James Lee Barrett. Cast: John Wayne, David Janssen, Jim Hutton. Distribution: Swank Motion Pictures. 141 mins. (AVW)

Greetings (USA:1968) Released by West End Films. Director: Brian DePalma. Screenplay: Charles Hirsch, Brian DePalma. Cast: Jonathan Warden, Robert DeNiro, Gerrit Graham. 88 mins. (H)

Alice's Restaurant (USA:1969) Released by United Artists. Director: Arthur Penn. Screenplay: Venable Herndon, Arthur Penn. Cast: Arlo Guthrie, Pat Quinn, James Broderick. Distribution: MGM/United Artists. 111 mins. (H)

The Angry Breed (USA:1969) Director: David Commons. Screenplay: David Commons. Cast: Jan Sterling, James McArthur, William Windom. 89 mins. (VV)

The Big Bounce (USA:1969) Released by Warner Brothers. Director: Alex March. Screenplay: Robert Dozier. Cast: Ryan O'Neal, Leigh Taylor-Young, Van Heflin. 102 mins. (VV)

Explosion (Canada:1969) Released by American International Films. Director: Jules Bricken. Screenplay: Alene and Jules Bricken. Cast: Gordon Thomson, Don Stroud. Distribution: Swank Motion Pictures. 96 mins. (H, A)

Fire (North Vietnam:1969) Released by Hanoi Film. Director: Pham Van Khoe. Screenplay: Pham Van Khoe. 70 mins. (AVW)

Hail, Hero! (USA:1969) Released by National General Pictures. Director: David Miller. Screenplay: David Manber. Cast: Michael Douglas, Arthur Kennedy, Teresa Wright. Distribution: Swank Motion Pictures. 97 mins. (A, H)

Medium Cool (USA:1969) Released by Paramount Pictures. Director: Haskell Wexler. Screenplay: Haskell Wexler. Cast: Robert Forster, Verna Bloom, Peter Bonerz. Distribution: Films Inc. 110 mins. (A, H)

The American Soldier (West Germany:1970) Director: Rainer Werner Fassbinder. Screenplay: Rainer Werner Fassbinder. Distribution: New Yorker Films. 80 mins. (VV)

Captain Milkshake (USA:1970) Director: Richard Crawford. Screenplay: Richard Crawford, Barry Lichtling. 89 mins. (H)

Cowards (USA:1970) Released by Jaylo International Films. Director: Simon Nuchtern. Screenplay: Simon Nuchtern. Cast: John Rose, Susan Sparling, Thomas Murphy. 88 mins. (H)

Getting Straight (USA:1970) Released by Columbia Pictures. Director: Richard Rush. Screenplay: Robert Kaufman. Cast: Elliott Gould, Candice Bergen, Jeff Corey. Distribution: Ivy Films. 126 mins. (H, A)

Hi, Mom! (USA:1970) Released by West End Films. Director: Brian DePalma. Screenplay: Brian DePalma. Cast: Robert DeNiro, Lara Parker, Allen Garfield. 87 mins. (VV)

Homer (USA:1970) Released by National General. Director: John Trent. Screenplay: Claude Harz. Cast: Don Scardino, Tisa Farrow, Alex Nicol. 90 mins. (H)

Joe (USA:1970) Released by Cannon Films. Director: John Avildson. Writer: Norman Wexler. Cast: Peter Boyle, Dennis Patrick, K. Callen. 107 mins. (H)

O.K. (West Germany:1970) Released by Alpha Films. Director: Michael Verhoeven. Screenplay: Michael Verhoeven. 80 mins. (AVW)

Peace (France:1970) Released by Warner Brothers. Director: Raoul Coutard. Screenplay: Raoul Coutard. Cast: Phi San. 90 mins. (AVW)

The Revolutionary (USA:1970) Released by United Artists. Director: Paul Williams. Screenplay: Hans Konigsberger. Cast: Jon Voight, Jennifer Salt, Seymour Cassel. 100 mins. (H)

The Strawberry Statement (USA:1970) Released by MGM. Director: Stuart Hagmann. Screenplay: Israel Horovitz. Cast: Bruce Davison, Kim Darby, Bob Balaban. 103 mins. (A, H)

Billy Jack (USA:1971) Released by Warner Brothers. Director: T. C. Frank (Tom Laughlin). Screenplay: T. C. Frank, Teresa Cristina (Dolores Taylor). Cast: Tom Laughlin, Dolores Taylor, Ken Tobey. 114 mins. (VV, H, A)

Chrome and Hot Leather (USA:1971) Released by American International Pictures. Director: Lee Frost. Screenplay: Michael Haynes, David Neibel, Don Tait. Cast: William Smith, Tony Young, Michael Haynes. 91 mins. (VV)

Clay Pigeon (USA:1971) Released by MGM. Directors: Tom Stern, Lane Slate. Screenplay: Ronald Buck, Buddy Ruskin, Jack Gross, Jr. Cast: Tom Stern, Telly Savalas, Robert Vaughn. 97 mins. (VV)

The Hard Ride (USA:1971) Released by American International Pictures. Director: Burt Topper. Screenplay: Burt Topper. Cast: Robert Fuller, Sherry Bain, Marshall Reed. Distribution: Swank Motion Pictures. 95 mins. (VV, H)

The Losers (USA:1971) Released by Fanfare Films. Director: Jack Starrett. Screenplay: Alan Caillou. Cast: William Smith, Bernie Hamilton, Adam Rourke. Distribution: Budget Films. 95 mins. (AVW, VV)

My Old Man's Place (Glory Boy) (USA:1971) Released by Cinerama Releasing Corp. Director: Edwin Sherin. Screenplay: Stanford Whitmore. Cast: Arthur Kennedy, Mitchell Ryan, William Devane. Distribution: Swank Motion Pictures. 93 mins. (VV, H)

Summertree (USA:1971) Released by Columbia Pictures. Director: Anthony Newley. Screenplay: Edward Hume, Stephen Yafa. Cast: Michael Douglas, Brenda Vaccaro, Jack Warden. Distribution: Budget Films. 89 mins. (H, A)

Welcome Home, Johnny Bristol (USA:1971) Released by CBS-TV. Director: George Mc-Cowan. Screenplay: Stanley Greenberg. Cast: Martin Landau, Jane Alexander, Brock Peters. 100 mins. (VV)

AWOL (USA-Sweden:1972) Released by BFB Productions. Director: Herb Freed. Screenplay: Richard Z. Chesnoff, Herb Freed. Cast: Russ Thacker, Isabella Kaliff. 82 mins. (VV, A)

Deathdream (Canada:1972) Director: Bob Clark. Cast: John Marley, Richard Backus, Lynn Carlin. 90 mins. (VV)

Georgia, Georgia (USA:1972) Released by Cinerama Releasing Corp. Director: Stig Bjorkman. Screenplay: Maya Angelou. Cast: Diana Sands, Dirk Benedict, Minnie Gentry. Distribution: Swank Motion Pictures. 91 mins. (VV, A)

Limbo (USA:1972) Released by Universal Pictures. Director: Mark Robson. Screenplay: James Bridges, Joan Silver. Cast: Kathleen Nolan, Kate Jackson, Katherine Justice. Distribution: Swank Motion Pictures. 112 mins. (H, P)

Outside In (USA:1972) Released by Harold Robbins International. Director: Allen Baron. Screenplay: Robert Hutchinson. Cast: Darrel Larson, John Bill, Dennis Olivieri. 90 mins. (H, VV)

Parades (USA:1972) Released by Confron Productions. Director: Robert J. Siegel. Screenplay: George Tabori. Cast: David Doyle. Distribution: Swank Motion Pictures. 95 mins. (A, H)

Slaughter (USA:1972) Released by American International Pictures. Director: Jack Starrett. Screenplay: Mark Hanna, Don Williams. Cast: Jim Brown, Stella Stevens, Rip Torn. 92 mins. (VV)

To Kill a Clown (USA:1972) Released by 20th Century Fox. Director: George Bloomfield. Cast: Alan Alda, Blythe Danner, Heath Lamberts. Distribution: Films, Inc. 104 mins. (VV)

The Trial of the Catonsville Nine (USA:1972) Released by Melville Productions. Director: Gordon Davidson. Screenplay: Daniel Berrigan, Saul Levitt. Cast: Ed Flanders, Richard Jordan, Nancy Malone. Distribution: Almi Cinema 5. 85 mins. (A, H)

The Visitors (USA:1972) Released by Associated Artists. Director: Elia Kazan. Screenplay: Chris Kazan. Cast: Patrick McVey, Patricia Joyce, James Woods. 88 mins. (VV)

Welcome Home, Soldier Boys (USA:1972) Released by 20th Century Fox. Director: Richard Compton. Screenplay: Guerdon Trueblood. Cast: Joe Don Baker, Paul Koslo, Alan Vint. Distribution: Films Inc. 90 mins. (VV, H)

Electra Glide in Blue (USA:1973) Released by United Artists. Director: James William Guercio. Screenplay: Robert Boris. Cast: Robert Blake, Mitchell Ryan. Distribution: MGM/United Artists. 106 mins. (VV, H)

Gordon's War (USA:1973) Released by 20th Century Fox. Director: Ossie Davis. Screenplay: Howard Friedlander, Ed Spielman. Cast: Paul Winfield, Carl Lee, David Downing. 90 mins. (VV)

Magnum Force (USA:1973) Released by Warner Brothers. Director: Ted Post. Screenplay: John Milius. Cast: Clint Eastwood, Hal Holbrook, Mitchell Ryan. Distribution: Films, Inc. 124 mins. (VV)

The Stone Killer (USA:1973) Released by Columbia. Director: Michael Winner. Cast: Charles Bronson, Martin Balsam, Ralph Waite. Distribution: Budget Films. 95 mins. (VV)

Trained to Kill (The No Mercy Man) (USA:1973) Director: Daniel J. Vance. Cast: Steve Sandor, Rockne Tarkington, Heidi Vaughn. 91 mins. (VV)

Two People (USA:1973) Released by Universal Pictures. Director: Robert Wise. Screenplay: Richard DeRoy. Cast: Peter Fonda, Lindsay Wagner. Distribution: Swank Motion Pictures. 100 mins. (VV, A)

The Bears and I (USA:1974) Released by Buena Vista. Director: Bernard McEveety. Screenplay: John Whedon. Cast: Patrick Wayne, Chief Dan George, Andrew Duggan. Distribution: Swank Motion Pictures. 89 mins. (VV)

The Crazy World of Julius Vrooder (USA:1974) Released by 20th Century Fox. Director: Arthur Hiller. Screenplay: Daryl Henry. Cast: Timothy Bottoms, Barbara Hershey, George Marshall. Distribution: Films, Inc. 98 mins. (VV)

The Trial of Billy Jack (USA:1974) Released by Warner Brothers. Director: T. C. Frank (Tom Laughlin). Screenplay: T. C. Frank, Teresa Cristina (Dolores Taylor). Cast: Tom Laughlin, Dolores Taylor, Victor Izay. 175 mins. (VV)

Two (USA:1974) Released by Colmar Ltd. Director: Charles Trieschmann. Screenplay: Charles Trieschmann. 93 mins. (VV, H)

The Desperate Miles (USA:1975) Director: Daniel Haller. Cast: Tony Musante, Joanna Pettet, Jeanette Nolan. 78 mins. (VV)

The Girl from Hanoi (North Vietnam:1975) Director: Hai Ninh. Screenplay: Hoang Tigh Hy, Hai Ninh, Tiah Ankh. 98 mins. (AVW)

Returning Home (USA:1975) Director: Daniel Petrie. Cast: Dabney Coleman, Tom Selleck, James R. Miller. 78 mins. (VV)

The Enforcer (USA:1976) Released by Warner Brothers. Director: James Fargo. Cast: Clint Eastwood, Tyne Daly, Harry Guardino. Distribution: Swank Motion Pictures. 96 mins. (VV)

Green Eyes (USA:1976) Released by ABC-TV Films. Director: John Erman. Screenplay: David Seltzer. Cast: Paul Winfield, Rita Tushingham, Victoria Racimo. 100 mins. (VV, AVW)

Mean Johnny Barrows (USA:1976) Released by Atlas Films. Director: Fred Williamson. Cast: Fred Williamson, Jenny Sherman, Aaron Banks. Distribution: Films, Inc. 85 mins. (VV)

Special Delivery (USA:1976) Released by American International Pictures. Director: Paul Wendkos. Screenplay: Don Gazzaniga. Cast: Bo Svenson, Cybill Shepherd. 98 mins. (VV)

Taxi Driver (USA:1976) Released by Columbia. Director: Martin Scorsese. Screenplay: Paul Schrader. Cast: Robert DeNiro, Cybill Shepherd, Jodie Foster. Distribution: Swank Motion Pictures. 113 mins. (VV)

Tracks (USA:1976) Released by Rainbow Pictures. Director: Henry Jaglom. Screenplay: Henry Jaglom. Cast: Dennis Hopper, Taryn Power, Dean Stockwell. Distribution: Rainbow Pictures. 90 mins. (VV, H)

Billy Jack Goes to Washington (USA:1977) Released by Taylor-Laughlin Distribution. Director: T. C. Frank (Tom Laughlin). Screenplay: T. C. Frank, Teresa Cristina (Dolores Taylor). Cast: Tom Laughlin, Dolores Taylor, E. G. Marshall. 155 mins. (VV)

Black Sunday (USA:1977) Released by Paramount Pictures. Director: John Frankenheimer. Screenplay: Ernest Lehman, Kenneth Ross, Ivan Moffat. Cast: Robert Shaw, Marthe Keller, Bruce Dern. 143 mins. (VV)

Fighting Mad (USA/Philippines:1977) Director: Cirio H. Santiago. Cast: James M. Iglehart, Jayne Kennedy, Leon Isaac Kennedy. 96 mins. (AVW, VV)

Heroes (USA:1977) Released by Universal Pictures. Director: Jeremy Paul Kagan. Screenplay: James Carabatsos. Cast: Henry Winkler, Sally Field, Harrison Ford. Distribution: Swank Motion Pictures. 113 mins. (VV)

Just a Little Inconvenience (USA:1977) Released by Universal TV. Director: Theodore J. Flicker. Screenplay: Theodore J. Flicker, Allan Balter. Cast: Lee Majors, James Stacy, Barbara Hershey. 100 mins. (VV)

Rolling Thunder (USA:1977) Released by American International Pictures. Director: John Flynn. Screenplay: Paul Schrader, Heywood Gould. Cast: William Devane, Tommy Lee Jones, Linda Haynes. Distribution: Swank Motion Pictures. 100 mins. (VV, P)

Twilight's Last Gleaming (USA:1977) Released by Allied Artists. Director: Robert Aldrich. Screenplay: Ronald Cohen, Edward Huebsch. Cast: Burt Lancaster, Richard Widmark, Charles Durning. Distribution: Hurlock Cine. 146 mins. (VV)

The Big Fix (USA:1978) Released by Universal Pictures. Director: Jeremy Paul Kagan. Screenplay: Roger L. Simon. Cast: Richard Dreyfuss, Susan Anspach, John Lithgow. Distribution: Ivy Films. 108 mins. (A)

Big Wednesday (USA:1978) Released by Warner Brothers. Director: John Milius. Screenplay: John Milius, Dennis Aaberg. Cast: Jan-Michael Vincent, William Katt, Gary Busey. 120 mins. (H)

The Boys in Company C (USA:1978) Released by Columbia Pictures. Director: Sidney J. Furie. Screenplay: Rick Natkin, Sidney J. Furie. Cast: Stan Shaw, Michael Lembeck, Andrew Stevens. Distribution: Swank Motion Pictures. 127 mins. (AVW)

Coming Home (USA:1978) Released by United Artists. Director: Hal Ashby. Screenplay: Nancy Dowd, Waldo Salt, Robert Jones. Cast: Jane Fonda, Jon Voight, Bruce Dern. Distribution: Films Inc. 127 mins. (VV, H)

The Deer Hunter (USA:1978) Released by Universal. Director: Michael Cimino. Screenplay: Deric Washburn. Cast: Robert DeNiro, John Savage, Christopher Walken. Distribution: Swank Motion Pictures. 183 mins. (AVW, VV, H, P)

Go Tell the Spartans (USA:1978) Released by Avco Embassy. Director: Ted Post. Screenplay: Wendell Mayes. Cast: Burt Lancaster, Craig Wasson, Marc Singer. Distribution: Clem Williams Films. 114 mins. (AVW)

Our Winning Season (USA:1978) Released by American International Pictures. Director: Joseph Ruben. Screenplay: Nick Niciphor. Cast: Scott Jacoby, Deborah Benson, Joe Penny. Distribution: Swank Motion Pictures. 92 mins. (H)

Who'll Stop The Rain? (USA:1978) Released by United Artists. Director: Karel Reisz. Screenplay: Judith Rascoe; based on the novel *Dog Soldiers* by Robert Stone. Cast: Nick Nolte, Tuesday Weld, Michael Moriarty. Distribution: Films Inc. 126 mins. (VV, H)

Youngblood (USA:1978) Released by American International Pictures. Director: Noel Nosseck. Screenplay: Paul Carter Harrison. Cast: Lawrence Hilton-Jacobs. 90 mins. (VV)

The Abandoned Field (Vietnam:1979) Released by Vietnam Feature Film Studios. Director: Nguyen Hong Sen. Screenplay: Nguyen Quang Sang. Cast: Lam Toi, Thuy An. 90 mins. (AVW)

Apocalypse Now (USA:1979) Released by United Artists. Director: Francis Ford Coppola. Screenplay: John Milius, Francis Ford Coppola. Cast: Marlon Brando, Robert Duvall, Martin Sheen. Distribution: Films Inc. 150 mins. (AVW)

The Call of the Front (Vietnam:1979) Released by Vietnam Feature Film Studios. Director: Long Van. Screenplay: Phu Thang. 82 mins. (AVW)

Friendly Fire (USA:1979) Released by ABC-TV. Director: David Greene. Screenplay: Fay Kanin. Cast: Carol Burnett, Ned Beatty, Sam Waterston. 145 mins. (H)

Good Guys Wear Black (USA:1979) Released by American Cinema Releasing. Director: Ted Post. Screenplay: Bruce Cohn, Mark Medoff. Cast: Chuck Norris, Anne Archer, James Franciscus. 96 mins. (AVW, VV)

Hair (USA:1979) Released by United Artists. Director: Milos Forman. Screenplay: Michael Weller. Cast: John Savage, Treat Williams, Beverly D'Angelo. Distribution: MGM/United Artists. 121 mins. (H, A)

More American Grafitti (USA:1979) Released by Universal Pictures. Director: B. W. L. Norton. Screenplay: B. W. L. Norton. Cast: Ron Howard, Cindy Williams. Distribution: Swank Motion Pictures. 111 mins. (AVW, A, H)

Night-Flowers (USA:1979) Released by Leonard Franklin Associates. Director: Luis San Andres. Screenplay: Gabriel Walsh. Cast: Jose Perez, Gabriel Walsh. 92 mins. (VV)

The Odd Angry Shot (Australia:1979) Released by Roadshow Productions. Director: Tom Jeffrey. Cast: John Hargreaves, Graham Kennedy, Bryan Brown. (AVW)

When You Comin' Back, Red Ryder? (USA:1979) Released by Columbia Pictures. Director: Milton Katsela. Screenplay: Mark Medoff. Cast: Marjoe Gortner, Lee Grant, Hal Linden. 118 mins. (VV)

Charlie Bravo (France:1980) Released by Gaumont. Director: Claude Bernard-Aubert. Screenplay: Claude Bernard-Aubert, Pascal Jardin. 104 mins. (FVW)

The Children of An Lac (USA:1980) Director: John Llewellyn Moxey. Screenplay: Blanche Hanalis. Cast: Shirley Jones, Ina Balin, Beulah Quo. 100 mins. (AVW)

The Exterminator (USA:1980) Released by Avco Embassy Films. Director: James Glickenhaus. Screenplay: James Glickenhaus. Cast: Christopher George, Samantha Eggar, Robert Ginty. Distribution: Films, Inc. 101 mins. (VV)

Fighting Back (USA:1980) Director: Robert Lieberman. Cast: Robert Urich, Art Carney, Bonnie Bedelia. 100 mins. (VV)

Return of the Secaucus 7 (USA:1980) Released by Specialty Films. Director: John Sayles. Cast: Mark Arnott, Maggie Renzi. Distribution: Cinema Five. 100 mins. (A)

A Rumor of War (USA:1980) Director: Richard T. Heffron. Screenplay: John Sacret Young. Cast: Brad Davis, Keith Carradine, Michael O'Keefe. 200 mins. (AVW, VV)

A Small Circle of Friends (USA:1980) Released by United Artists. Director: Rob Cohen. Screenplay: Ezra Sacks. Cast: Brad Davis, Karen Allen, Jamison Parker. Distribution: MGM/United Artists. 112 mins. (H)

The Stunt Man (USA:1980) Released by 20th Century Fox. Director: Richard Rush. Screenplay: Lawrence B. Marcus. Cast: Peter O'Toole, Barbara Hershey, Steve Railsback. Distribution: Films, Inc. 129 mins. (VV)

When Mother Is Out (Vietnam:1980) Released by Vietnam Feature Film Studios. Director: Khanh Du. Screenplay: Khanh Du. 80 mins. (AVW)

Americana (USA:1981) Director: David Carradine. Screenplay. David Carradine. Cast: David Carradine, Barbara Hershey, Michael Greene. 91 mins. (VV)

Cutter's Way (USA:1981) Released by United Artists. Director: Ivan Passer. Screenplay: Jeffrey Alan Fiskin. Cast: Jeff Bridges, John Heard, Lisa Eichhorn. Distribution: Films Inc. 105 mins. (VV)

Fly Away Home (USA:1981) Director: Paul Krasny. Screenplay: Stirling Silliphant. Cast: Bruce Boxlietner, Tiana Alexandra, Michael Beck. 100 mins. (AVW)

Four Friends (USA:1981) Released by Filmways. Director: Arthur Penn. Screenplay: Steve Tesich. Cast: Craig Wasson, Jodi Thelen, Jim Metzler. 115 mins. (H)

Search and Destroy (USA:1981) Director: William Fruet. Cast: Perry King, Tisa Farrow, Don Stroud. 93 mins. (VV, R)

Ashes and Embers (USA:1982) Released by Mypheduh Films. Director: Haile Gerima. Screenplay: Haile Gerima. Cast: John Anderson, Evelyn A. Blackwell, Norman Blalock. Distribution: Mypheduh Films. 120 mins. (VV)

Don't Cry, It's Only Thunder (USA:1982) Director: Peter Werner. Cast: Dennis Christopher, Susan Saint James, Lisa Lu. 108 mins. (AVW)

Firefox (USA:1982) Released by Warner Brothers. Director: Clint Eastwood. Screenplay: Alex Lasker, Wendell Wellman. Cast: Clint Eastwood, Freddie Jones, David Huffman. Distribution: Swank Motion Pictures. 124 mins. (VV)

First Blood (USA:1982) Released by Orion Pictures. Director: Ted Kotcheff. Screenplay: Michael Kozoll, William Sackheim, Sylvester Stallone. Cast: Sylvester Stallone, Richard Crenna, Brian Dennehy. Distribution: Swank Motion Pictures. 97 mins. (VV, P)

Some Kind of Hero (USA:1982) Released by Paramount Pictures. Director: Michael Pressman. Screenplay: James Kirkwood, Robert Boris. Cast: Richard Pryor, Margot Kidder. Distribution: Films, Inc. 95 mins. (VV, P)

The Big Chill (USA:1983) Released by Columbia Pictures. Director: Lawrence Kasdan. Screenplay: Lawrence Kasdan, Barbara Benedek. Cast: Tom Berenger, Glenn Close, Jeff Goldblum. Distribution: Films, Inc. 105 mins. (A)

Memorial Day (USA:1983) Director: Joseph Sargent. Screenplay: Michael Bortman. Cast: Mike Farrell, Shelley Fabares, Keith Mitchell. 100 mins. (VV)

Streamers (USA:1983) Released by United Artists. Director: Robert Altman. Screenplay: David Rabe. Cast: Matthew Modine, Michael Wright, Mitchell Lichtenstein. Distribution: Films, Inc. 118 mins. (H)

Twighlight Zone—The Movie (USA:1983) Released by Warner Brothers. Directors: Jon Landis, Steven Spielberg, Joe Dante, George Miller. Screenplay: John Landis, George Clayton Johnson, Richard Matheson, Josh Rogan, Rod Serling. Cast: Vic Morrow, Scatman Crothers, Kathleen Quinlan. 102 mins. (VV, AVW)

Uncommon Valor (USA:1983) Released by Paramount Pictures. Director: Ted Kotcheff. Screenplay: Joe Gayton. Cast: Gene Hackman, Robert Stack, Fred Ward. Distribution: Films Inc. 100 mins. (VV, S, P)

Birdy (USA:1984) Released by Tri-Star Pictures. Director: Alan Parker. Screenplay: Sandy Kroopf, Jack Behr. Cast: Matthew Modine, Nicholas Cage, John Harkins. Distribution: Films Inc. 120 mins. (VV)

Exterminator II (USA:1984) Director: Mark Buntzman. Cast: Robert Ginty. Deborah Geffner, Mario Van Peebles. 88 mins. (VV)

The Killing Fields (UK:1984) Director: Roland Joffe. Screenplay: Bruce Robinson. Cast: Sam Waterston, Haing S. Ngor, John Malkovich. Distribution: Swank Motion Pictures. 141 mins. (S)

The Last Hunter (Italy:1984) Released by World Northal. Director: Anthony Dawson (Antonio Margheriti). Screenplay: Dardano Sacchetti. 95 mins. (AVW)

Limosine (USA:1984) Director: Augustin B. Ramos. Distribution: A. B. Ramos Productions. 28 mins. (VV)

Missing in Action (USA:1984) Released by Cannon Films. Director: Joseph Zito. Screenplay: James Bruner. Cast: Chuck Norris, M. Emmett Walsh, Lenore Kasdorf. Distribution: Films Inc. 101 mins. (V, VV, P)

Purple Hearts (USA:1984) Released by the Ladd Company. Director: Sidney J. Furie. Screenplay: Rick Nathan, Sidney J. Furie. Cast: Cheryl Ladd, Ken Wahl, Stephen Lee. Distribution: Swank Motion Pictures. 115 mins. (AVW)

Alamo Bay (USA:1985) Released by Tri-Star Pictures. Director: Louis Malle. Screenplay: Alice Arlen. Cast: Amy Madigan, Ed Harris, Ho Nguyen. Distribution: Films Inc. 98 mins. (R)

American Commandos (USA:1985) Released by Panorama Films. Director: Bobby A. Suarez. Screenplay: Ken Metcalfe, Bobby A. Suarez. Cast: Christopher Mitchum. 88 mins. (VV)

The Annihilators (USA:1985) Released by New World Pictures. Director: Charles E. Sellier, Jr. Screenplay: Brian Russell. Cast: Christopher Stone, Andy Wood, Lawrence Hilton-Jacobs. 84 mins. (VV, AVW)

Cease Fire (USA:1985) Released by Cineworld Enterprises. Director: David Nutter. Screenplay: George Fernandez. Cast: Don Johnson, Lisa Blount, Robert F. Lyons. 97 mins. (VV)

Missing in Action 2—The Beginning (USA:1985) Released by Cannon Films. Director: Lance Hool. Screenplay: Arthur Silver, Larry Levinson, Steve Bing. Cast: Chuck Norris, Soon-Teck Oh, Steven Williams. Distribution: Films Inc. 96 mins. (AVW, P)

Rambo: First Blood Part II (USA:1985) Released by Tri-Star Pictures. Director: George Pan Cosmatos. Screenplay: Sylvester Stallone, James Cameron. Cast: Sylvester Stallone, Richard Crenna, Charles Napier. Distribution: Films Inc. 95 mins. (V, VV, P)

A Street to Die (Australia:1985) Director: Bill Bennett. Screenplay: Bill Bennett. 91 mins. (VV)

Volunteers (USA:1985) Released by Tri-Star Pictures. Director: Nicholas Meyer. Screenplay: Ken Levine, David Isaacs. Cast: Tom Hanks, Rita Wilson, John Candy. Distribution: Films Inc. 106 mins. (S)

White Nights (USA:1985) Released by Columbia Pictures. Director: Taylor Hackford. Screenplay: James Goldman, Eric Hughes. Cast: Mikhail Baryshnikov, Gregory Hines, Isabella Rossellini. 135 mins. (VV)

Year of the Dragon (USA:1985) Released by MGM/UA. Director: Michael Cimino. Screenplay: Oliver Stone, Michael Cimino. Cast: Mickey Rourke, John Lone. Distribution: Films Inc. 134 mins. (VV)

Back to School (USA:1986) Released by Orion Pictures. Director: Alan Metter. Screenplay: Steven Kampmann, Will Porter, Peter Totokvei, Harold Ramis. Cast: Rodney Dangerfield, Sally Kellerman, Burt Young. Distribution: Films Inc. 94 mins. (VV)

Heartbreak Ridge (USA:1986) Released by Warner Brothers. Director: Clint Eastwood. Cast: Clint Eastwood, Marsha Mason, Mario Van Peebles. Distribution: Swank Motion Pictures. 130 mins. (VV)

House (USA:1986) Director: Steve Milner. Cast: William Katt, George Wendt, Kay Lenz. 93 mins. (VV)

Karma (Vietnam/Switzerland:1986) Released by Vietnam Fiction Film Studios. Director: Ho Quang Minh. Screenplay: Ho Quang Minh, Nguy Ngu. Cast: Tran Quang, Phung Dung, Le Cung Bac. 100 mins. (AVW)

Platoon (USA:1986) Released by Hemdale. Director: Oliver Stone. Screenplay: Oliver Stone. Cast: Charlie Sheen, Willem Dafoe, Tom Berenger. Distribution: Swank Motion Pictures. 120 mins. (AVW)

P.O.W.: The Escape (USA:1986) Released by Cannon Films. Director: Gideon Amir. Screenplay: Jeremy Lipp, James Bruner, Malcolm Barbour, John Langley. Cast: David Carradine, Mako. 90 mins. (AVW, P)

Whatever It Takes (USA:1986) Released by Aquarius Films. Director: Bob Demchuk. Screenplay: Chris Weatherhead, Bob Demchuk. Cast: Tom Mason. 93 mins. (VV)

Full Metal Jacket (USA:1987) Released by Warner Brothers. Director: Stanley Kubrick. Screenplay: Stanley Kubrick, Michael Herr, Gustav Hansford. Cast: Matthew Modine, Lee Ermy. Distribution: Swank Motion Pictures. 118 mins. (AVW)

Gardens of Stone (USA:1987) Released by Tri-Star Pictures. Director: Francis Ford Coppola. Screenplay: Ronald Bass. Cast: James Caan, Anjelica Huston, James Earl Jones. Distribution. Films Inc. 112 mins. (H)

Good Morning, Vietnam (USA:1987) Released by Buena Vista. Director: Barry Levinson. Screenplay: Mitch Markowitz. Cast: Robin Williams, Forrest Whitaker. Distribution: Films, Inc. 120 mins. (AVW)

Hamburger Hill (USA:1987) Released by Paramount Pictures. Director: John Irvin. Screenplay: James Carabatsos. Cast: Anthony Barrile, Michael Patrick Boatman. Distribution: Films Inc. 110 mins. (AVW)

The Hanoi Hilton (USA:1987) Released by Cannon Films. Director: Lionel Chetwynd. Screenplay: Lionel Chetwynd. Cast: Michael Moriarty, Paul LeMat. Distribution: Swank Motion Pictures. 130 mins. (AVW, P)

In Love and War (USA:1987) Director: Paul Aaron. Cast: Jane Alexander, James Woods, Haing S. Ngor. 100 mins. (AVW, H, P)

Steele Justice (USA:1987) Released by Atlantic Releasing Corp. Director: Robert Boris. Screenplay: Robert Boris. Cast: Martin Kove, Sela Ward. 95 mins. (AVW, VV, R)

Suspect (USA:1987) Released by Tri-Star Pictures. Director: Peter Yates. Screenplay: Eric Roth. Cast: Cher, Dennis Quaid, Liam Neelson. Distribution: Films, Inc. 121 mins. (VV)

Above the Law (USA:1988) Released by Warner Brothers. Director: Andrew Davis. Cast: Steve Seagal, Pam Grier, Henry Silva. Distribution: Swank Motion Pictures. 97 mins. (AVW, VV)

Bat 21 (USA:1988) Released by Tri-Star Pictures. Director: Peter Markle. Screenplay: Willian C. Anderson, George Gordon. Cast: Gene Hackman, Danny Glover, Jerry Reed. Distribution: Films, Inc. 105 mins. (AVW)

Braddock: Missing in Action III (USA:1988) Released by Cannon Films. Director: Aaron Norris. Cast: Chuck Norris, Aki Aleong, Yehuda Efroni. Distribution: MGM/UA. 103 mins. (AVW, VV)

Distant Thunder (USA:1988) Released by Paramount Pictures. Director: Rick Rosenthal. Screenplay: Robert Stitzel. Cast: John Lithgow, Ralph Maccio. Distribution: Films, Inc. 114 mins. (VV, AVW)

Gleaming the Cube (USA:1988) Released by 20th Century Fox. Director: Graeme Clifford. Screenplay: Michael Tolkin. Cast: Christian Slater, Steven Bauer. Distribution: Films, Inc. 103 mins. (R)

Off Limits (USA:1988) Released by 20th Century Fox. Director: Christopher Crowe. Screenplay: Christopher Crowe, Jack Thibeau. Cast: Willem Dafoe, Gregory Hines, Amanda Pays. Distribution: Films Inc. 102 mins. (AVW)

Platoon Leader (USA:1988) Released by Cannon Films. Cast: Michael Dudikoff, Robert F. Lyons. Distribution: Swank Motion Pictures. 100 mins. (AVW)

The Presidio (USA:1988) Released by Paramount Pictures. Director: Peter Hyams. Screenplay: Larry Ferguson. Cast: Sean Connery, Mark Harmon, Meg Ryan. Distribution: Films Inc. 97 mins. (VV)

Rambo III (USA:1988) Released by Tri-Star Pictures. Director: Peter MacDonald. Screenplay: Sylvester Stallone, Sheldon Lettich. Cast: Sylvester Stallone, Richard Crenna. Distribution: Films Inc. 104 mins. (VV)

Running on Empty (USA:1988) Released by Warner Brothers. Director: Sidney Lumet. Cast: Judd Hirsch, Christine Lahti, River Phoenix. Distribution: Swank Motion Pictures. 116 mins. (A)

DOCUMENTARY FILMS

Eyewitness: Diem's War—or Ours? (USA:1961) Director: Bob Quinn. Distribution: CBS News. 30 mins. (AVW)

End of an Empire (USA:1962) Producer: Isaak Kleinerman. Distribution: CBS News. 30 mins. (FVW)

Eyewitness: Our War in Vietnam (USA:1962) Distribution: CBS News. 30 mins. (AVW)

Eyewitness: Yanks in Vietnam (USA:1962) Director: Vern Diamond. Distribution: CBS News. 30 mins. (AVW)

The Village That Wouldn't Die (USA:1962) Producer: Stan Atkinson. Distribution: International Historic Films. 56 mins. (AVW)

Vietnam: The Deadly Decision (USA:1964) Producer: Leslie Midgley. Distribution: CBS News. 60 mins. (AVW)

The Battle (USA:1965) Produced by the U.S. Naval Photographic Center. Distribution: International Historic Films. 14 mins. (AVW)

The Battle of Ia Drang Valley (USA:1965) Producer: Sam Zelman. Distribution: CBS News. 30 mins. (AVW)

Christmas in Vietnam (USA:1965) Director: Joe Gorsuch. Producer: Bernard Birnbaum. Distribution: CBS News. 28 mins. (AVW)

Marines—65 (USA:1965) Produced by the U.S. Marine Corps. Distribution: International Historic Films. 25 mins. (AVW)

Letters from Vietnam (USA:1965) Director: Robert Drew. Distribution: Direct Cinema Ltd. 56 mins. (AVW)

Why Vietnam? (USA:1965) Released by the U.S. Directorate for Armed Forces Information and Education. Distribution: International Historic Films. 32 mins. (AVW)

Asia Perspective: Election Day in Vietnam (USA:1966) Distribution: CBS News. 30 mins. (AVW)

Battle for Asia: Thailand, the New Front (USA:1966) Produced and directed by Ted Yates. Distribution: NBC News. 50 mins. (AVW, S)

Campaign '66: Vietnam and the Elections (USA:1966) Producer: Av Westin. Distribution: CBS News. 60 mins. (H, AVW)

The Councils of War (USA:1966) Distribution: CBS News. 60 mins. (H, AVW)

Eyewitness—North Vietnam (UK:1966) Released by Rogosin Films. Director: James Cameron (AVW)

Fulbright: Advice and Dissent (USA:1966) Producer: William Small. Distribution: CBS News. 60 mins. (H, AVW)

Know Your Enemy—The Viet Cong (USA:1966) Produced by the U.S. Armed Forces Information Service. Distribution: International Historic Films. 22 mins. (AVW)

The President in Asia: Parts 1 through 6 (USA:1966) Distribution: CBS News. 180 mins. (AVW)

Survival and Evasion in Southeast Asia (USA:1966) Produced by the U.S. Air Force. Distribution: International Historic Films. 21 mins. (AVW)

Vietnam: Eric Sevareid's Personal Report (USA:1966) Producer: Leslie Midgley. Distribution: CBS News. 30 mins. (AVW)

Vietnam: The Home Front (USA:1966) Director: Robert Priaulx. Producer: Chet Hagan. Distribution: NBC News. 60 mins. (H, AVW)

Vietnam: The Other War (USA:1966) Director: Joe Gorsuch. Producer: Bernard Birnbaum. Distribution: CBS News. 60 mins. (AVW)

Westmoreland on Vietnam (USA:1966) Distribution: CBS News. 30 mins. (AVW)

While Brave Men Die (USA:1966) Directors: Donald C. Bruce, Fulton Lewis III. Distribution: Newscope. 30 mins. (H, A)

The Anderson Platoon (France/USA:1967) Director: Pierre Schoendoerffer. Distribution: Films, Inc. 65 mins. (AVW)

Another Day of War (USA:1967) Produced by the U.S. Air Force. Distribution: International Historic Films. 14 mins. (AVW)

Battle for Asia: Laos, the Forgotten War (USA:1967) Produced and directed by Ted Yates. Distribution: NBC News. 50 mins. (AVW, S)

The Benefit of the Doubt (UK:1967) Released by Lorrimer-Saga. Director: Peter Whitehead. 70 mins. (A)

A Face of War (USA:1967) Produced and directed by Eugene S. Jones. Distribution: International Historic Films. 72 mins. (AVW)

Far from Vietnam (France:1967) Directors: Jean-Luc Godard, Joris Ivens, William Klein, Claude Lelouch, Chris Marker, Alain Renais, Agnes Varda. Distribution: Contemporary Films (London). 115 mins. (FVW, AVW)

The Four Navy Deserters (USA:1967) Producer: Don Hewitt. Distribution: CBS News. 30 mins. (H, AVW, A)

Hanoi, Tuesday the 13th (Cuba:1967) Director: Santiago Alvarez. Distribution: Third World Newsreel. 40 mins. (AVW)

Laos: The Forgotten War (Cuba:1967) Director: Santiago Alvarez. Distribution: Third World Newsreel. 20 mins. (S)

March on the Pentagon (USA:1967) Director: David Ringo. Distribution: Filmmaker's Cooperative. 20 mins. (A)

Morley Safer's Vietnam: A Personal Report (USA:1967) Producer: Morley Safer. Distribution: CBS News. 60 mins. (AVW)

The People of Vietnam: How They Feel About the War (USA:1967) Distribution: CBS News. 60 mins. (AVW)

Saigon (USA:1967) Director: Beryl Fox. Distribution: CBS News. 60 mins. (AVW)

Sons and Daughters (USA:1967) Released by American Documentary Films. Director: Jerry Stoll. 98 mins. (A)

The United States Air Force in Vietnam (USA:1967) Produced by the U.S. Air Force. Distribution: International Historic Films. 28 mins. (AVW)

The United States Navy in Vietnam (USA:1967) Produced by the U.S. Naval Photographic Center. Distribution: International Historic Films. 29 mins. (AVW)

Vietnam: The Bombings (USA:1967) Produced by the U.S. Air Force. Distribution: International Historic Films. 59 mins. (AVW)

Where We Stand in Vietnam. Parts 1 & 2 (USA:1967) Distribution: CBS News. 120 mins. (AVW)

America Against Itself (USA:1968) Producers: Documentary-Interlock. Distribution: Catticus Corperation. 45 mins. (A)

The American Dreadnought (USA:1968) Produced by the U.S. Naval Photographic Center. Distribution: International Historic Films. 29 mins. (H, AVW)

Boston Draft Resistance Group (USA:1968) Producers: The Newsreel. Distribution: Third World Newsreel. 18 mins. (A)

Chicago Convention Challenge (USA:1968) Producers: The Newsreel. Distribution: Third World Newsreel. 17 mins. (A)

A Day of Plane Hunting (North Vietnam:1968) Distribution: Third World Newsreel. 20 mins. (AVW)

First Cavalry Airmobile: The First Team (USA:1968) Produced by the U.S. Department of Defense. Distribution: International Historic Films. 29 mins. (AVW)

Four Americans (USA:1968) Producers: The Newsreel. Distribution: Third World Newsreel. 17 mins. (A)

Hill 943 (USA:1968) Executive Producer: Burton Benjamin. Distribution: CBS News. 60 mins. (AVW)

Inside North Vietnam (USA/UK:1968) Producer: Felix Greene. Distribution: California Newsreel. 85 mins. (AVW)

The Jeanette Rankin Brigade (USA:1968) Producers: The Newsreel. Distribution: Third World Newsreel. 8 mins. (A)

Last Reflections on a War (USA:1968) Producers: NET. Distribution: Indiana Audio-Visual Center. 44 mins. (AVW)

Mill-In (USA:1968) Producers: The Newsreel. Distribution: Third World Newsreel. 12 mins. (A)

No Game (USA:1968) Producers: The Newsreel. Distribution: Third World Newsreel. 17 mins. (A)

No Vietnamese Ever Called Me Nigger (USA:1968) Released by Paradigm Films. Director: David Loeb Weiss. Distribution: Cinema Guild. 68 mins. (AVW)

Paris: The Peace Game (USA:1968) Distribution: CBS News. 60 mins. (AVW)

The Resistance (USA:1968) Producer: Leonard Henny. Distribution: Canyon Cinema. 18 mins. (A)

The 17th Parallel (France:1968) Released by Argos Films. Director: Joris Ivens. Distribution: Argos Films (Paris). 113 mins. (AVW)

Struggle for Life (NLF-South Vietnam:1968) Distribution: Third World Newsreel. 20 mins. (AVW)

Tell Me Lies (UK:1968) Released by Continental Films. Director: Peter Brooks. Distribution: Budget Films. 118 mins. (A)

Time of the Locust (USA:1968) Director: Peter Gessner. Distribution: Third World Newsreel. 19 mins. (AVW)

USAF Combat Photography: Southeast Asia (USA:1968) Produced by the U.S. Air Force. Distribution: International Historic Films. 27 mins. (AVW)

U.S. Techniques and Genocide in Vietnam (North Vietnam:1968) Distribution: Third World Newsreel. 35 mins. (AVW)

The Viet Cong (USA:1968) Executive Producer: Charles Collingwood. Producer: James B. Faichney. Distribution: CBS News. 60 mins. (AVW)

Vietnam Assignment (USA:1968) Produced by the American National Red Cross. Distribution: The American National Red Cross. 8 mins. (AVW)

Vietnam: Journal of a War (UK:1968) Distribution: Time-Life Multimedia. 52 mins. (AVW)

Yippie (USA:1968) Producers: The Newsreel. Distribution: Third World Newsreel. 10 mins. (A)

America (USA:1969) Producers: The Newsreel. Distribution: Third World Newsreel. 30 mins. (A)

Army (USA:1969) Producers: The Newsreel. Distribution: Third World Newsreel. 25 mins. (H)

The Battle of Khe Sanh (USA:1969) Produced by the U.S. Department of Defense. Distribution: International Historic Films. 30 mins. (AVW)

Good Bye and Good Luck (USA:1969) Produced by WNET. Distribution: PBS Films. 30 mins. (VV, A)

In The Year of the Pig (USA:1969) Released by Cinetree. Director: Emile de Antonio. Distribution: New Yorker Films. 103 mins. (FVW, AVW)

Men with Green Faces (USA:1969) Produced by the U.S. Naval Photographic Center. Distribution: International Historic Films. 29 mins. (H, AVW)

The People's War (USA:1969) Producers: The Newsreel. Distribution: Third World Newsreel. 40 mins. (AVW)

Pig Power (USA:1969) Producers: The Newsreel. Distribution: Third World Newsreel. 6 mins. (A)

R.O.T.C. (USA:1969) Producers: The Newsreel. Distribution: Third World Newsreel. 20 mins. (H)

The Seventy-nine Springtimes of Ho Chi Minh (Cuba:1969) Director: Santiago Alverez. Distribution: Third World Newsreel. 25 mins. (AVW)

Summer '68 (USA:1969) Directors: Norman Fruchter, John Douglas. Distribution: Third World Newsreel. 60 mins. (A)

Terry Whitmore, For Example (UK/Sweden:1969) Released by Grove Press. Director: Bill Brodie. 98 mins. (AVW, A)

A Timetable for Vietnam (USA:1969) Executive Producer: Ernest Leiser. Producer: Bernard Birnbaum. Distribution: CBS News. 60 mins. (AVW)

Women of Telecommunications Station #6 (North Vietnam:1969) Director: Nguyen Chi Phuc. Distribution: Third World Newsreel. 20 mins. (AVW)

Young Puppeteers of Vietnam (NLF-South Vietnam:1968) Distribution: Third World Newsreel. 25 mins. (AVW)

Eagle Eye Bravo (USA:1970) Produced by the U.S. Department of Defense. Distribution: International Historic Films. 14 mins. (AVW)

The Sad Song of Yellow Skin (Canada:1970) Released by the Film Board of Canada. Director: Michael Rubbo. Distribution: Films Inc. 58 mins. (AVW)

Street Scenes—1970 (USA:1970) Released by New York Cinetracts Collective. Postproduction Director: Martin Scorsese. Distribution: Images Film Archive. 75 mins. (A)

Vietnam (Japan:1970) Directors: Kentaro Musada. Takashi Koizumi. 135 mins. (AVW)

Vietnam: Voices in Opposition (USA:1970) Distribution: CBS News. 60 mins. (A, H, AVW)

Where We Stand in Indochina (USA:1970) Director: Norman Gorin. Producers: Philip Scheffler, Bernard Birnbaum. Distribution: CBS News. 60 mins. (AVW, S)

The World of Charlie Company (USA:1970) Director: James Clevenger. Producer: Russ Bensley. Distribution: CBS News. 60 mins. (AVW)

Another Part of the Family (USA:1971) Released by Summer Morning Films. Director: Paul Ronder. Distribution: Museum of Modern Art. 75 mins. (H)

Basic Training (USA:1971) Director: Fred Wiseman. Distribution: Zipporah Films. 89 mins. (H)

Bright College Years (USA:1971) Released by Avco Embassy. Director: Peter Rosen. Distribution: Films, Inc. 52 mins. (A)

The Court Martial of William Calley (USA: 1971) Executive Producer: Ernest Leiser. Distribution: CBS News. 30 mins. (AVW)

Heroes and Heroin (USA:1971) Producer: Av Westin. Distribution: ABC News. 60 mins. (VV, AVW)

Lyndon Johnson Talks Politics (USA:1971) Producer: John Sharnik. Distribution: CBS News. 60 mins. (H, AVW)

Only the Beginning (USA:1971) Producers: The Newsreel. Distribution: Third World Newsreel. 20 mins. (A, VV)

The POW's: Pawns of War (USA:1971) Director: James Clevenger. Producer: Ernest Leiser. Distribution: CBS News. 60 mins. (H, AVW)

Requiem 29: Racism and Police Oppression against Chicanos (USA:1971) Producer: Moctesuma Esparza. Director: David Garcia. Distribution: UCLA Film Library. 30 mins. (A)

The Selling of the Pentagon (USA:1971) Executive Producer: Perry Wolff. Producer: Peter Davis. Distribution: CBS News. 60 mins. (H, AVW)

When Johnny Comes Marching Home (USA:1971) Producer: Ernest Pendrell. Distribution: ABC News. 60 mins. (VV)

Escalation in Vietnam: The Rogers Testimony (USA:1972) Producer: Ernest Leiser. Distribution: CBS News. 30 mins. (H, AVW)

F.T.A. (USA:1972) Released by American International Pictures. Director: Francine Parker. Distribution: Films, Inc. 96 mins. (A, H)

Interviews with My Lai Veterans (USA:1972) Director: Joseph Strick. Distribution: Films Inc. 27 mins. (AVW)

Letter to Jane (France:1972) Directors: Jean-Luc Godard, Jean-Pierre Gorin. Distribution: New Yorker Films. 55 mins. (A)

So the People Should Know (USA:1972) Released by Resolution Films. Distribution: Third World Newsreel. 30 mins. (A, H)

Vietnam: A Plan for Peace (USA:1972) Executive Producer: Ernest Leiser. Distribution: CBS News. 60 mins. (AVW)

Winter Soldier (1972) No director or producer credited. Distribution: Third World Newsreel. 95 mins. (AVW, A, VV)

The Sins of the Fathers (1973) Producer: Robert Northshield. Distribution: NBC News. 60 mins. (VV, AVW)

Hearts and Minds (USA:1974) Released by Warner Brothers/Columbia. Director: Peter Davis. Distribution: Nelson Entertaiment. 112 mins. (AVW, A, H)

Cambodia: An American Dilemma (USA:1975) Producers: Hal Haley, Bernard Birnbaum. Distribution: CBS News. 30 mins. (S)

G.I. Jose (USA:1975) Director: Norberto Lopez. Distribution: Third World Newsreel. 20 mins. (H, AVW)

Indochina 1975: The End of the Road? (USA:1975) Producers: Hal Haley, Bernard Birnbaum. Distribution: CBS News. 60 mins. (AVW, S, R)

Introduction to the Enemy (USA:1975) Released by IPC Films. Director: Christine Burill. 60 mins. (AVW, A)

Spooks and Cowboys, Gooks and Grunts (Canada:1975) Producer: Don North. Distribution: Canadian Broadcasting Corporation. 50 mins. (AVW, VV)

Vietnam: An Historical Document (USA:1975) Distribution: CBS News. 56 mins. (AVW)

Year of the Tiger (USA:1975) Directors: David Davis, Deirdre English, Steve Talbot. Distribution: Odeon Films. 62 mins. (AVW)

Devil's Island (East Germany:1976) Released by Studio Heynowski. Directors: Walter Heynowski, Gerhard Schuemann. Distribution: Unifilm. 61 mins. (AVW)

Southeast Asia: Lands and Peoples (USA:1976) Distribution: Coronet Instructional Media. 16 mins. (V, S)

Underground (USA:1976) Directors: Mary Lampon, Emile de Antonio. Distribution: First Run Films. 88 mins. (A)

The Class That Went to War (USA:1977) Produced and directed by Richard Gerdau. Distribution: ABC News. 60 mins. (H, AVW, VV)

Vietnam: Picking Up the Pieces (USA:1977) Released by Downtown Community TV. Directors: Jon Alpert, Keiko Tsuno, Karen Ranucci. Distribution: Electronic Arts Intermix. 60 mins. (V)

Charlie Company at Home: The Veterans of Vietnam (USA:1978) Directors: Joe Gorsuch, H. Richard Mutscheler. Producer: Bernard Birnbaum. Distribution: CBS News. 60 mins. (AVW, VV)

American Dream, American Nightmare . . . the Seventies, Parts 1 & 2 (USA:1979) Executive Producer: Perry Wolff. Producer: Shareen Blair Brysac. Distribution: CBS News. 120 mins. (H, AVW, VV, A)

The Boat People (USA:1979) Produced and directed by Andrew Lack. Distribution: CBS News. 60 mins. (AVW, R)

No More Vietnams . . . But (USA:1979) Produced by NBC News. Distribution: Films, Inc. 103 mins. (AVW)

The Phans of New Jersey (USA:1979) Directors: Stephen L. Forman, Dennis Lanson. Distribution: Films Inc. 49 mins. (R)

The War at Home (USA:1979) Released by Wisconsin Educational Television Network. Directors: Glenn Silber, Barry Alexander Brown. Distribution: First Run Films. 100 mins. (A)

War Shadows (USA:1979) Produced and directed by Jody Eisemann. 25 mins. (AVW, VV)

Abran la Puerta (Open The Door) (USA:1980) Producer: Gabriel Garcia. Distribution: Boston Broadcasting Inc. 60 mins. (VV)

Vietnam: an American Journey (USA:1980) Released by First Run Films. Director: Robert Richter. Distribution: First Run Films. 85 mins. (V)

Agent Orange: A Story of Dignity and Doubt (USA:1981) Producer: Jim Gambone. Distribution: New Day Films. 28 mins. (VV)

Are You Listening: Indochina Refugees (USA:1981) Director: Martha Stuart. Distribution: Martha Stuart Communications. 60 mins. (R)

Bittersweet Memories—A Vietnam Reunion (USA:1981) Distribution: CBS News. 60 mins. (VV)

Bittersweet Survival (USA:1981) Directors: Christine Choy, Orinne Takagi. Distribution: Third World Newsreel. 30 mins. (R)

Ecocide: A Strategy of War (USA:1981) Director: Dr. E. W. Pfeiffer. Distribution: Green Mountain Post Films. 23 mins. (AVW)

Frank: A Vietnam Veteran (USA:1981) Director: Fred Simon. Distribution: Fanlight Productions. 52 mins. (VV)

Front Line (USA:1981) Director: David Bradbury. Distribution: Filmakers Library. 55 mins. (AVW)

The Problems of Peace (USA:1981) Director: Steve Besner. Producer: Mark Kramer. Distribution: CBS News. 60 mins. (V, AVW, R, S)

Smothering Dreams (USA:1981) Director: Daniel Reeves. Distribution: Electronic Arts Intermix. 23 mins. (AVW, A)

Vietnam—Chronicle of a War (USA:1981) Distribution: CBS News. 89 mins. (H, AVW, VV, A)

Warriors' Women (USA:1981) Director: Dorothy Tod. Distribution: Dorothy Tod Films. 27 mins. (VV)

Becoming American (USA:1982) Produced and directed by Kenneth Mark Levine. Distribution: Iris Film and Video. 58 mins. (R)

Fire on the Water (USA:1982) Produced and directed by Robert Hillmann. Distribution: Cinergy Films. 57 mins. (R)

Going Back: A Return to Vietnam (USA:1982) Director: David Munro. Distribution: Bullfrog Films. 55 mins. (VV, V)

Monterey's Boat People (USA:1982) Director: Vincent DiGirolamo. Distribution: Yakuza Productions. 28 mins. (R)

The Uncounted Enemy: A Vietnam Deception (USA:1982) Produced and directed by George Crile. Distribution: CBS News. 90 mins. (AVW)

Vietnam Requiem: Vets in Prison (USA:1982) Directors: Jonas McCord, Bill Couturie. Distribution: Direct Cinema Ltd. 52 mins. (VV)

How Far Home: Veterans After Vietnam (USA:1983) Director: Bestor Cram. Distribution: Northern Lights Productions. 29 mins. (VV)

Inside Story: Uncounted Enemy/Unproven Conspiracy (USA:1983) Director: Chet Lishawa. Producer: Rose Economou. Distribution: Panavideo Productions. 26 mins. (AVW)

Marching Along Together Again (USA:1983) Produced and distributed by the American Legion. 30 mins. (VV)

The Secret Agent (USA:1983) Directors: Jacki Ochs, Daniel Keller. Distribution: Green Mountain Post Films. 56 mins. (VV)

Vietnam Memorial (USA:1983) Directors: Steven York, Foster Wiley. Distribution: York/Wiley Productions. 51 mins. (VV)

Vietnam: This Was the Vietnam War (USA:1983) Producer: Michael A. Kukler. Distribution: Kukler Film Productions. 60 mins. (AVW)

Aspects of a Certain History (USA:1984) Director: John Knecht. 55 mins. (VV, H)

Jesse Trevino: A Spirit Against All Odds (USA:1984) Director: Skip Cilley. Distribution: Busch Creative Services. 20 mins. (VV)

Kim Phuc (USA:1984) Director: Manus van de Kamp. Distribution: Icarus Films. 25 mins. (AVW, V)

Requiem for the Vietnam Unknown (USA:1984) Distribution: CBS News. 74 mins. (VV).

Soldiers in Hiding (USA:1984) Director: Malcolm Clarke. Producer: Japhet Asher. Distribution: Filmworks, Inc. 58 mins. (VV)

Television's Vietnam, Parts 1 & 2 (USA:1984) Directors: Douglas Pike, W. E. Crane. Producers: W. E. Crane, Ron Nickell. Distribution: Accuracy in Media. 116 mins. (AVW)

The Haunted Heroes (1985) Producer: Tony Salmon. Distribution: Films, Inc. 50 mins. (VV)

Inside Story: Vietnam: Op. Ed., Parts 1 & 2 (USA:1985) Produced and distributed by Panavideo Productions. 85 mins. (AVW)

Vietnam Perspective (USA:1985) Produced and directed by Dennis S. Johnson. Distribution: Encyclopedia Britannica Educational Corporation. 32 mins. (FVW, AVW)

Vietnam—Talking to the People (USA:1985) Director: Jon Alpert. Producers: Jon Alpert, Steve Friedman. Distribution: Downtown Community Television Center. 120 mins. (V)

Witness to War (USA:1985) Producers: Deborah Shaffer, David Goodman. Distribution: First Run Films. (AVW, VV)

The Bloods of Nam (USA:1986) Director: Wallace Terry. Distribution: PBS Video. 60 mins. (AVW)

The Invisible Force: Women in the Military (1986) Producer: Julia Perez. Distribution: William Joiner Center. 61 mins. (VV)

A Program for Vietnam Veterans and Everyone Else Who Should Care (USA:1986) Director: Michael Lorentz. Producer: Michael Hirsh. Distribution: PBS Video. 88 mins. (VV)

Vietnam Reconsidered: A Veteran's Perspective (USA:1986) Director: Bestor Cram. Distribution: Northern Lights Productions. 15 mins. (VV)

Dear America: Letters Home from Vietnam (USA:1987) Director: Bill Couturie. Distribution: HBO Films. 100 mins. (AVW, VV)

Why Vietnam? Parts 1 & 2 (USA:1987) Director: Joe Domanick. Distribution: Churchill Films. 95 mins. (AVW, VV, R, A)

Vietnam Vets: Dissidents for Peace (USA:1988) Director: Ying Ying Wu. Distribution: Filmmakers Library. 29 mins. (VV)

Waiting for Cambodia (USA:1988) Producers: David Feingold, Sherri Robertson. Distribution: PBS Video. 57 mins. (S)

The War in El Cedro (USA:1988) Producer: Don North. Distribution: Northstar Productions. 50 mins. (VV)

Disobeying Orders: GI Resistance to the Vietnam War (USA:1989) Producer: Pamela Sporn. Distribution: Filmmakers Library. 29 mins. (AVW, A, VV)

TELEVISION DOCUMENTARY SERIES

ABC Scope: The Vietnam War (USA:1966–1968) 68 episodes. Various producers and directors. Distribution: ABC News. Each episode: 30 mins.

CBS News Special Report: Vietnam Perspective (USA:1965–67) 10 episodes. Various producers and directors. Distribution: CBS News. Episodes run either 30 or 60 mins.

Vietnam: The 10,000 Day War (Canada: 1980; syndicated and telecast in the U.S. in 1982) 26 episodes. Producer: Ian McLeod. Distribution: Nelson Entertainment. Each episode: 30 mins.

Vietnam: A Television History (USA:1983) 13 episodes. Executive producer: Richard Ellison. Distribution: Films Inc. Each episode: 60 mins.

The Motion Picture, Broadcasting and Recorded Sound Division of the Library of Congress in Washington, D.C., has an extensive collection of documentary films about the Vietnam War. In addition to many of the ABC, CBS, NBC, and PBS documentaries listed above, the collection also includes episodes of NBC's *Vietnam Weekly Report* (1966–1967), NBC's *Meet the Press*, and CBS's *60 Minutes* that relate specifically to aspects of the war and its consequences. The collection also contains over five hundred documentary films produced by the South Vietnamese government during the war. For further information, contact: Reference Librarian, Motion Picture, Broadcasting and Recorded Sound Division; Library of Congress; Washington, D.C. 20540.

FILM DISTRIBUTORS

Almi Cinema 5
1585 Broadway
New York, NY 10036
(212) 975–0555

Budget Films
4590 Santa Monica Boulevard
Los Angeles, CA 90029
(213) 660-0187

Bullfrog Films
Oley, PA 19547
(215) 779–8226

Busch Creative Services
5240 Oakland Avenue
St. Louis, MO 63110
(314) 289-7737

California Newsreel
630 Natoma Street
San Francisco, CA 94103
(415) 621-6196

Canadian Broadcasting Corperation
Box 500, Terminal A
Toronto, Ontario
M5W 1E6 Canada

The Catticus Corperation
2600 Tenth Street
Berkeley, CA 94710
(415) 548-0854

CBS, Inc.
51 West 52nd Street
New York, NY 10019
(212) 765-4321

The Cinema Guild
1697 Broadway, #802
New York, NY 10019
(212) 246-5522

Direct Cinema, Ltd.
P.O. Box 69589
Los Angeles, CA 90069
(213) 891-8240

Electronic Arts Intermix
10 Waverly Place
New York, NY 10003
(212) 473-6822

Fanlight Productions
47 Halifax Street
Boston, MA 02130
(617) 524-0890

Filmmakers Library
133 East 58th Street
Suite 703A
New York, NY 10022
(212) 355-6545

Films Inc. (Northeast)
440 Park Avenue South
New York, NY 10016
800-223-6246

Films Inc. (Central)
5547 North Ravenswood Avenue
Chicago, IL 60646
800-323-4222

Films Inc. (Southeast)
476 Plasamour Drive, N.E.
Atlanta, GA 30324
800-241-5530

Films Inc. (West)
5625 Hollywood Boulevard
Hollywood, CA 90028
800-421-0612

First Run Features
153 Waverly Place
New York, NY 10014
(212) 243-0600

Green Mountain Post Films
P.O. Box 229
37 Ferry Road
Turners Falls, MA 01376
(413) 863-4754

Hurlock Cine
13 Arcadia Road
P.O. Box W.
Old Greenwich, CT 06870
(203) 637-4319

Icarus Films
200 Park Avenue South, #1319
New York, NY 10003
(212) 674-3375

Indiana University Audio-Visual Center
Bloomington, IN 47405
(812) 335-8087

Ivy Films
165 West 46th Street
New York, NY 10036
(212) 765-3940

William Joiner Center
University of Massachusetts
Harbor Campus
Boston, MA 02125
(617) 929-7864

Mypheduh Films
48 Q Street, N.E.
Washington, DC 20002
(202) 529-0220

National Film Board of Canada
1251 Avenue of the Americas
New York, NY 10020
(212) 586-5131

Nelson Entertainment
1901 Avenue of the Stars
Los Angeles, CA 90067
(213) 553-3600

New Day Films
22 Riverview Drive
Wayne, NJ 07470
(201) 633-0212

New Yorker Films
16 West 61st Street
New York, NY 10023
(212) 247-6110

Northern Light Productions
165 Newbury Street
Boston, MA 02116
(617) 267-0391

PBS Video
1320 Braddock Place
Alexandria, VA 22314
(703) 739-5380

Phoenix Films
468 Park Avenue South
New York, NY 10016
(212) 684-5910

Martha Stuart Communications
P.O. Box 246
Hillsdale, NY 12529
(518) 325-3900

Swank Motion Pictures
201 South Jefferson Avenue
St. Louis, MO 63166
(314) 534-6300

Third World Newsreel
335 West 38th Street
5th Floor
New York, NY 10018
(212) 947-9277

Dorothy Tod Films
20 Bailey Avenue
Montpelier, VT 05602
(802) 223-3181

Warner Brothers
4000 Warner Boulevard
Burbank, CA 91505
(213) 954-6000

Clem Williams Films
2240 Nobleston Road
Pittsburgh, PA 15205
(412) 921-5810

Yakuza Productions
3101 Ellis Street
Berkeley, CA 94703
(415) 845-4730

York/Wiley Productions
1065 31 Street, N.W.
Washington, DC 20007
(202) 333-7300

Index